THE REMINISCENCES OF
Vice Admiral Samuel L. Gravely, Jr.
U.S. Navy (Retired)

INTERVIEWED BY
Paul Stillwell

U.S. Naval Institute • Annapolis, Maryland

Copyright © 2003

Thoughts for the Foreword for Vice Admiral Samuel Gravely's
Oral History

It is my honor to play a role in documenting our nation's naval history. Vice Admiral Sam Gravely, Jr. was the first black officer to command a Navy warship and to reach the rank of Rear Admiral and Vice Admiral. His unusual opportunity to enter the V-12 Program during World War II, launched his path to serve in patrol craft, in Iowa and Toledo, working his way up to cruisers and destroyers. He commanded the Taussig (DD-746), Jouett (DLG-29), and Falgout (DER-324), and was Commander Third Fleet.

When he was in command of Taussig, I was a new Ensign assigned to the USS Buck (DD-761). I had heard about this "only black Commanding Officer in the Navy." My opportunity to meet Captain Gravely came when his ship, USS Taussig was tied up outboard the Buck for two days. I had to see him that first morning, so I went up to the Buck's bridge quite early and waited. Then the magic moment happened.... Captain Gravely came to the bridge of the Taussig and I sounded off in a loud voice across Buck's bridge to the Taussig's bridge. I said, "Good morning Captain Gravely!" I am Ensign Gaston!" The Captain replied back to me, " Morning, Ensign Gaston!" "What is your first name?" "Mack, Sir!" At that moment, he reached across to me and shook my hand. He was a tall man with incredible stature and presence. His handshake was firm but friendly and somehow I knew in meeting him that he would have a profound impact on me as a naval officer, role model and long-time friend.

Admiral Gravely's Oral History is a book for leaders and others who seek inspiration from successful leaders. It is a book for enlisted and officers of the military, government civilians, business leaders, and all who seek to grow and learn through the experience of an accomplished leader. This book goes beyond age, race or gender. It exemplifies the living history of a naval pioneer who achieved the best through opportunity, hard work, and dedication.

Rear Admiral Mack C. Gaston, U.S. Navy (Retired)

Preface

Without question, Vice Admiral Sam Gravely is a pioneer in the U.S. Navy. He was the first African American officer to command a warship in the 20th Century. He was the first black officer in the U.S. Navy to become an admiral, and he was the first to command a numbered fleet.

As Admiral Gravely points out in this history, part of the reason for his success was timing. He was in the right place when opportunities opened up. But there was much more to the story than that. He succeeded on the Navy's terms; he repeatedly performed well in the fundamentals of naval service: sea duty and particularly command at sea. It is no accident that the sections of this memoir that deal with shipboard duty are longer and detailed than the accounts of shore duty. He relished going to sea.

The career of Admiral Gravely coincided with a period of dramatic changes in American society. In his youth he faced the hurts and discrimination that were commonplace in the segregated South of that era. His early months in the Navy came at a time when opportunities for black sailors opened in unprecedented fashion—first the general service ratings for enlisted personnel and then officer training. Before 1944 the Navy had no commissioned line officers. By the end of that year Gravely was an ensign, the first step in his pioneering career as a naval officer.

In 1948 President Harry S. Truman issued an executive order that ordered the U.S. military services to integrate. That provided both an opportunity and a challenge for Sam Gravely. He had left the Navy after World War II; now he was called back to active duty to recruit officers and enlisted personnel for a service that was opening up but far from colorblind. The recruiting stint led him to the Navy that was fighting at sea in the Korean War. He liked what he found there and resumed his climb up the promotion ladder.

As he tells the story in this volume, Gravely was assigned to communications. That specialty, along with recruiting, was a pigeonhole in which black officers of the era often found themselves. It was necessary work but kept individuals from accumulating the fully rounded backgrounds they needed for command. Gravely did his job and kept pushing to do more. He describes the process step by step, first into an amphibious warfare ship, then into a destroyer, and then command of a destroyer escort. Because of the firsts he achieved, he became the focus of media attention. It was not attention he courted, for he is an innately modest man. He just wanted to be left able to do his job for the service.

In the early 1970s Admiral Elmo Zumwalt became the Chief of Naval Operations. He, more than any of his predecessors, pushed aggressively for still further opening of opportunities for African Americans. In 1971, during Zumwalt's watch as CNO, a selection board picked Captain Sam Gravely, then the commanding officer of the guided missile frigate Jouett, for flag rank. Vice Admiral Ray Peet was a member of that board and voted for Gravely's promotion. After the results were announced, Peet received a letter from, as he put it, "an obviously elderly and disturbed retired officer in Coronado chastising me for the selection and threatening my life." Admiral Peet, who was then Commander First Fleet, had the pleasure of frocking Gravely when he became the first black American to wear the two-star shoulder boards of a rear admiral.

In subsequent years, Admiral Gravely continued to break new ground as he headed naval communications, became the first black admiral to fly his flag at sea, commanded the Third Fleet, and finally served as Director of the Defense Communications Agency. Through it all, while serving as an inspiration and a role model for many who followed, he has said he was just doing his job.

Rear Admiral Mack Gaston and his wife Nancy were vital to the completion of this memoir. Mack put together a package of donors to provide financial support for the project. Nancy went through the transcript page by page with Admiral Gravely to ensure that it truly expresses his recollections. During that process she reviewed with him the editing I had done in the interests of accuracy, smoothness, and clarity and got answers to some follow-up questions I had posed. In addition, I have inserted footnotes to provide further information for readers who use the volume.

Ms. Ann Hassinger of the Naval Institute's history division has made a significant contribution through her diligence in the overall process of printing, proofreading, and overseeing the binding of the completed volumes.

Finally, the Naval Institute expresses its gratitude to the Tawani Foundations and the Pritzker Military Library for their generous financial support of the oral history program that produced this memoir.

Paul Stillwell
Paul Stillwell
Director, History Division
U.S. Naval Institute
October 2003

VICE ADMIRAL SAMUEL LEE GRAVELY, JR.
UNITED STATES NAVY (RETIRED)

Samuel L. Gravely, Jr., was born in Richmond, Virginia, on 4 June 1922, the son of Samuel L. and Mary George (Simon) Gravely. He attended Armstrong High School and Virginia Union University in Richmond, from which he later graduated with a degree of bachelor of arts in history. After enlisting in the U.S. Naval Reserve on 15 September 1942, he reported for recruit training at the Naval Training Center, Great Lakes, Illinois. He reported in January 1943 as a student at the Service School, Hampton (Virginia) Institute, and in May of that year was assigned to the Section Base, San Diego, California. During the period from November 1943 to June 1944 he was a member of the V-12 officer training unit at the University of California at Los Angeles, and then attended the Pre-Midshipmen School, Asbury Park, New Jersey.

Appointed midshipman in the U.S. Naval Reserve in August 1944, he attended the Midshipmen School, Columbia University, New York City, and was graduated in December of that year. Commissioned as an ensign in the Naval Reserve, to date from 14 December 1944, he subsequently advanced to the rank of vice admiral, having transferred to the U.S. Navy on 16 August 1955.

Following his commissioning, Ensign Gravely reported in December 1944 as assistant battalion commander at the Naval Training Center, Great Lakes, where he remained until February 1945. For two months thereafter, he had instruction at the Subchaser Training Center, Miami, Florida, and in May 1945 he joined the USS PC-1264. He served during the latter months of World War II, and until February 1946, as communications officer, electronics officer, and later as executive officer and personnel officer of this submarine chaser. After brief duty as communications watch officer with the Fleet Training Group, Norfolk, Virginia, he was released from active duty, effective 16 April 1946. Prior to returning to active duty, he was employed as a railway postal clerk based in Richmond, Virginia.

Called again into active naval service, Lieutenant (junior grade) Gravely reported on 30 August 1949 as assistant to the officer in charge for recruiting at the Naval Recruiting Station and Officer Procurement, Washington, D.C. From October 1951 to January 1952, he had instruction in the Communications Officers Short Course at the Naval Postgraduate School, Monterey, California, after which he served duty afloat as radio officer on board the USS Iowa (BB-61). In June 1953, he transferred to the USS Toledo (CA-133), in which he served as communications officer and in various other capacities, including assistant operations officer. In both vessels he participated in action against North Korean and Chinese Communist forces in the Korean area.

Detached from the Toledo in July 1955, Lieutenant Gravely was assigned to Headquarters, Third Naval District, New York, where he served two years as assistant security officer. Between September and November 1957 he had instruction in amphibious warfare, attached to the Amphibious Training Command, Pacific Fleet, headquartered at Coronado, California, and then joined the USS Seminole (AKA-104) as operations officer. Lieutenant Commander Gravely had temporary duty under training for executive officer of a destroyer on the staffs of Commander Destroyer Squadrons Seven and Five during the period August 1959 to January 1960, when he became executive officer of the USS Theodore E. Chandler (DD-717). On 15 January 1961 he became commanding officer and remained in command of that destroyer until 21 November 1961, when he again became her executive officer.

On 31 January 1962 he assumed command of the radar picket destroyer escort USS Falgout (DER-324) at Pearl Harbor, Hawaii. Under command of then Lieutenant Commander Gravely, the Falgout patrolled the Pacific Early Warning Barrier. From August 1963 to June 1964 he attended the senior course in naval warfare at the Naval War College, Newport, Rhode Island, after which he served as program manager for the National Military Command Center and the National Emergency Airborne Command Post at the Defense Communications Agency, Arlington, Virginia. In January 1966 Commander Gravely became commanding officer of the USS Taussig (DD-746). On 6 June 1968 Captain Gravely was detached from the Taussig to report as coordinator, Navy Satellite Communications Program in the Office of the Chief of Naval Operations (Communications and Cryptology) with additional duty in the Navy Space Program Division.

On 22 May 1970 Captain Gravely assumed command of the guided missile frigate USS Jouett (DLG-29), home-ported in San Diego. He was subsequently relieved from that command on 2 June 1971 and donned the two stars of a rear admiral that day. On 16 July 1971 he assumed duty as Commander, Naval Communications Command, and Director, Naval Communications Division under the Chief of Naval Operations. After serving in that job for two years, he moved to duty as Commander Cruiser-Destroyer Group Two, assuming command on 1 August 1973. He then served as Commandant of the Eleventh Naval District from 29 August 1975 until 28 July 1976, when he was relieved and donned three stars on board the USS Jouett. He commanded the U.S. Third Fleet, based in Pearl Harbor, Hawaii, from September 1976 until September 1978. His final Navy assignment was as Director, Defense Communications Agency from September 1978 to July 1980. He retired from active duty on 1 August 1980.

Vice Admiral Gravely has been awarded the Navy Distinguished Service Medal, Legion of Merit with gold star, Bronze Star medal, the Joint Services Commendation Medal and the Navy Commendation Medal with gold star and combat V. He is also authorized to wear the World War II Victory Medal, the Naval Reserve Medal, the American Campaign Medal, the Korean Presidential Unit Citation, the National Defense Medal with one bronze star, the China Service Medal (extended), the Korean Service Medal with two bronze stars, the United Nations Service Medal, the Armed Forces Expeditionary Medal, the Vietnam Service Medal with six bronze stars, the Vietnamese Campaign Medal, the Antarctic Service Medal, and the Venezuelan Order of Merit Second Class.

His civic awards include the following: The Scottish Rite Prince Hall Masonic Bodies of Maryland, Prince Hall Founding Fathers Military Commanders Award; Savannah State College Major Richard R. Wright Award of Excellence; Alpha Phi Alpha Fraternity Alpha Award of Merit; Los Angeles Chapter, National Association of Media Women, Inc., Communications Award; San Diego Press Club Military Headliner of the Year; Golden Hills United Presbyterian Church Military Service Award; San Diego Optimists Club Good Guy Award; and Distinguished Virginian by Governor Linwood Holton.

Vice Admiral Gravely is married to the former Alma Bernice Clark of Christianburg, Virginia. They are the parents of three children: Robert (deceased), David, and Tracey Gravely.

Deed of Gift

The U.S. Naval Institute is hereby authorized to make available to individuals, libraries, and other repositories of its choosing the tapes and/or transcripts of seven oral history interviews concerning the life and naval career of the undersigned. The Naval Institute may also, at its discretion, use the material in electronic/digital format, including posting on the Internet. The interviews were recorded on 25 June 1986, 7 July 1986, 7 August 1986, 12 August 1986, 19 August 1986, 17 October 1986, and 21 January 2003 in collaboration with Paul Stillwell for the U.S. Naval Institute.

The undersigned does hereby release and assign to the U.S. Naval Institute the rights and title to these interviews, with the exception that the undersigned retains the right to use the material for his own purposes, as he sees fit. The copyright in both the oral and transcribed versions shall be the sole property of the U.S. Naval Institute. The tape recordings of the interviews are and will remain the property of the U.S. Naval Institute.

Signed and sealed this 21st day of Jan. 2003.

Samuel L. Gravely, Jr.
Vice Admiral, U.S. Navy (Retired)

The U.S. Naval Institute

gratefully acknowledges

Captain Jerome D. Davis, USNR

Rear Admiral Mack C. Gaston, USN (Ret.)

Captain Gilbert H. McKelvey, USN (Ret.)

Commander Ernest N. Taylor, Jr., USN (Ret.)

National Naval Officers Association, Inc.

Surface Navy Association

for underwriting the oral history of

Vice Admiral Samuel L. Gravely,

U.S. Navy (Retired)

ACKNOWLEDGEMENTS

I with to thank those who personally helped me with this document and assisted in getting it to publication.

Mrs. Alma Gravely, my wife and partner for over 50 years

RADM Mack C. Gaston, USN (Ret) and his wife Nancy Gaston

CAPT Desiree Linson, USN (Ret)

LCDR Tina Caston, USN (Ret)

Paul Stillwell, author

Mrs. Anne B. Fuller, USA (Ret) for her writings and inspiration,

And many others who have influenced my life.

Interview Number 1 with Vice Admiral Samuel L. Gravely, Jr., U.S. Navy (Retired)

Place: Admiral Gravely's office in Burke, Virginia

Date: Wednesday, 25 June 1986

Interviewer: Paul Stillwell

Paul Stillwell: Admiral, to begin at the very beginning, what do you remember about your early years growing up, something on your parents, and other aspects of your background?

Admiral Gravely: Well, I was born on 4 June 1922 in Richmond, Virginia. My father and my mother were native Virginians. My father had come from a small area near Danville. My mother had come from a little place called Clover, Virginia. My father served in World War I in the Army as a draftee, then extended his enlistment until about 1921, when he came out. Then he married my mother. I was the first of five children. I have two brothers and two sisters, who are all younger than me: Ed, Robert, Christie, and Betsey. Obviously, that's why I am junior, versus one of the others being junior.

Paul Stillwell: Did your father get overseas during the war?

Admiral Gravely: My father did not get overseas. He spent most of his time out at Fort Huachuca.* I heard a lot about Fort Huachuca as a young lad who had not at that point in time decided what I wanted to do—obviously.

Neither my father nor my mother had a high school education, really. They had considerably less. My mother was an orphan. My father was one of two children, and frankly I've only met one grandparent. That was my grandmother on my father's side. So I don't have much past that. My father was a Pullman porter.† He worked for the Southern Railroad, as I recall, and that's what I remember about the early part of his life.

---

* Fort Huachuca is an Army post in southeast Arizona, a few miles north of the border with Mexico.
† Pullmans were railroad cars that could be converted from day to night use by folding down berths and separating them by curtains. The porters, who were black men, were essentially servants who took care of the railroad passengers.

He used to run roughly from Richmond, Virginia, to Chase City, Virginia, and I got a lot of free rides on trains until I got to be six years old, when school came.

Despite the fact that my parents didn't have any advanced education or anything like that, I can remember that I knew by the time I was five years old, really, that one of these days I'd go to college. They had planned for me to go to college someplace. In fact, it was probably Hampton Institute.* I can remember that my mother specifically said that, "If you go to Hampton Institute you can learn a trade, and you can probably get into the Army ROTC program down there and come out as a second lieutenant. Then you can make up your mind which way you want to go at that point in time."†

Paul Stillwell: What do you think spurred this interest on the part of your parents in having you get a college education?

Admiral Gravely: Well, I think it was more that civil service was a sort of a way of life. My father always hoped that at some point in time he would get into civil service. Now, as you well know, the Depression came along about 1929-30, those years.‡ Frankly, my father was laid off, and so he did a lot of other things during that period. But he seemed to have always worked towards something in civil service for the security aspect of it. As luck would have it, he went into the post office in 1932 or '33 as a laborer and worked in the post office the rest of his life until he retired.

I went to the local elementary schools around there, starting at six. Frankly, elementary school was just a breeze for me, despite the fact that I didn't have any kindergarten or any of the other pre-school things that they have in this day and age. But it was just simply a breeze. I don't think I was that smart, but somehow I mastered most of the things that went on. The other thing that was a little significant was that my mother felt that I should go to school year round. I'm not sure what happened to the

---

* Brigadier General Samuel Chapman Armstrong (1839-1893) was colonel of a black regiment in the Civil War. That led to his interest in vocational education for black students. In 1868 he founded the Hampton Normal and Agricultural Institute at Hampton, Virginia. The school has since broadened in scope and is now known as Hampton University.
† ROTC—reserve officers' training corps.
‡ Following the crash of the New York Stock Exchange in late October 1929, the United States was plunged into the Great Depression, from which it did not recover until the nation geared up for World War II at the beginning of the 1940s. The Depression was marked by high unemployment and business failures.

other kids, but I went every summer as well, which meant that each fall I started out with a new bunch of kids, because I was a half a grade ahead of them.

Paul Stillwell: Did they run a year-round program?

Admiral Gravely: Well, there was always a summer school, which was designed primarily for those kids who had not done well. But somehow I got forced into summer school, and I went for about four years to summer school, which put me really about two years ahead of my class.

Paul Stillwell: What subject areas were you best in?

Admiral Gravely: Well, frankly, I was probably best in math and English, those subjects. I wasn't much on the public speaking aspect of English, but probably math was one of my better subjects.

In 1937 my mother died, which was rather traumatic. I was 15 years old at the time when she died. The youngest child was a baby girl who was about two and a half. At the same time, my brother Ed lost his right leg in an accident one week later right in front of the house. In fact, it was in my front yard as the result of a streetcar jumping the track. So things were kind of traumatic about then. The next year I graduated from high school, just a young 16-year-old boy, with no idea as to what he really wanted to do.

Paul Stillwell: Was this all in the Richmond public school system?

Admiral Gravely: Yes, it was all in Richmond public school system.

Paul Stillwell: How would you describe your family's economic condition during those growing-up years?

Admiral Gravely: Well, my father was a laborer, so basically he was earning an hourly wage. If he made $600 a year, that was a lot of money. I doubt very seriously if he made that much. Despite that, my mother was just a tremendous cook and saver and partner, and as a result we saved money. I can remember as an ensign I told my dad that I was making more money than he'd ever made in his life. And that was about right. What was I making, about $1,800 a year?* So he made even less than that, really.

Paul Stillwell: Did you have a sense of being disadvantaged, or did you just accept it as it was?

Admiral Gravely: I had no sense of being disadvantaged. We were as well off, or better, than most of the other people in our neighborhood, particularly after my father went to the post office. When I was born, my father was buying the house in which he lived. Of course, we moved to a larger house when the other children came along, and he was buying that one too. So we were right along with the norm of the people in that particular area.

As you well know, the sort of social pecking order in those days was the preacher, who probably made more than my father; the doctor or dentist, who I know made more, and we had those in the neighborhood. And probably the civil servant, the mail carrier or the mail clerk, who were doing well. My father's job was mail handler in the post office, so he was sort of right in that pecking order.

Paul Stillwell: How big a part did religion play in the family's life?

Admiral Gravely: From day one when I was born, I was taken to church. It was a small church by the name of Rising Mount Zion Baptist Church. I don't recall my father going very much, because most of the Sundays he was away. He spent his weekends down in Chase City for the longest kind of time. He did ultimately, when he got into the post office, go to Rising Mount Zion. I did the normal things, like Sunday school. I was expected to be there every Sunday for Sunday school, which I did, and went to church. So about two services a Sunday, and possibly sometimes in another church I went in the

---

* In 1944 base pay for a newly commissioned ensign with less than three years of service was $1,800 plus an allowance of $255.50 for subsistence.

afternoon to what they call BYPU.* But we were a regular church-going family, and, of course, I was a Baptist. I was baptized at age 12. I don't think I ever thought about being a preacher, if that's what you're asking.

Paul Stillwell: No, I was wondering if that church implanted values that have stayed with you?

Admiral Gravely: Well, that's part of it. It implanted some values that have stayed with me for a long time, and we are regular churchgoers today as a result of that. I think the biggest thing, or at least one of the big things, was that it gave me some contact that I needed later in life, particularly at a time when I was trying to make a decision as to what I wanted to do. I was able to go to my minister, who I looked up to, and talk to him. There were a couple of other preachers in the neighborhood that were friends of mine, and I could talk to them. Ultimately it made the difference in the decision, frankly, to join the Navy.

In any event, in 1938, I graduated from high school with practically no real decision other than the fact that my mother wanted me to go to Hampton, and I had thought in terms of going to Hampton. My father made a decision that he really did not want me at 16 years old to leave the family nest. So instead I enrolled at Virginia Union University. Virginia Union is also in Richmond, which meant that I commuted back and forth each night.

Virginia Union was a very, very good school, and it was basically a religious school, one of the predominantly black colleges. In fact, it was all black except for the senior people and some instructors. The president was white, and there were some instructors there who were white. I didn't quite fit in, unfortunately, and the biggest reason, of course, was my age. I was 16 years old, and most of the other freshmen were 17, 18. Those who lived on the campus were not exactly at loose ends, but at the same time, they could make their own decisions about this or that, and my father wanted me home every afternoon as soon as school was out. And for good reason, because somebody had to take care of the kids. I learned to cook and those kinds of things,

---

* Baptist Young People's Union.

because I did a lot with helping to raise those younger brothers and sisters. My baby sister was, as I said, two and a half years old when my mother died.

Paul Stillwell: I'm sure he needed extra help, because he no longer had her around.

Admiral Gravely: That's right. He no longer had her around. We tried what you might call maids or cooks, and that didn't work very well, to be honest with you. Some of them were much poorer than we were. Whereas anything that was left over from dinner my mother would fix the next day for soup or something else, then we had the problem of these people who felt that my dad was well enough off so they could take it home to feed to their families. Christ, he was spending more money than he wanted to. The whole thing was just a big mess.

Paul Stillwell: How much were you involved in extracurricular activities and sports as you were coming up through school?

Admiral Gravely: I was not involved in sports in high school, although I played on the local playground all the time. I played football on the local playground. I played tennis on the local playground, and, frankly, was very, very sports oriented and minded.

At some point I had decided that what I really wanted to do was to become a high school football coach. The problem, of course, was my father was deathly afraid of me getting injured. I can remember that I went out for the high school football team, and at that time they did not have a gymnasium where you could change your clothes. So you had to come home from school with your football uniform. So when I came home, I had mine packed and hid it behind the refrigerator. When my father found that thing, he just made me take it back. So that was the end of the football career. When I went to Virginia Union, they did have a gym where you could change clothes, and I didn't have to let him know, so I did play there for my sophomore and junior years.

Despite the fact that I breezed through high school and the other schools, I found it a little tougher in college. You had to study then, and I didn't do very well. So in 1940 I dropped out of college and thought in terms of possibly joining the Army. And I read at that point in time about a special program that the Army had in its transportation corps. What they said was, "Enlist in the Army as a sergeant, and you will be taught to drive all this heavy equipment, and trucks, and those kinds of things."

So I went up one day. I took the examination, and I failed the physical. The doctor said that I had a heart murmur. Of course, that frightened me a little, so I immediately went home and talked to my father about it, and we went to see a civilian doctor. The civilian doctor declared that I did not have a heart murmur at all. So, of course, this was the Army's way of getting rid of me, I guess. In any event, I went home and forgot that one.

Well, I worked around home, first in a tobacco factory, and, frankly, my father was just deathly afraid of me being in the tobacco industry. He just simply did not want me in there. He felt that there was no incentive to go anyplace else, that ultimately you'd get into the tobacco factory; you'd then marry some broad. That would be the end of you. You'd be in the tobacco factory the rest of your life. But I worked there for about a year until a friend of mine, who worked at a clothing manufacturer, got me a job there where I pressed coat linings. I was doing that when I joined the Navy.

Well, on 7 December 1941 I guess I was at home, just about like everybody else who was around at that point in time, when Pearl Harbor was attacked.* Frankly, my question was, like many other people, "Where is Pearl Harbor, and what effect is that going to have on me?" But very shortly thereafter you knew what effect it was going to have on you, because they stepped up the draft and those kinds of things.

I began to look around as to, okay, I can sit here and wait until I'm drafted, or I can volunteer for some branch of service and pick what I want to do. Well, I guess about May or so of 1942 I read that the Navy had opened the various branches of service enlisted ratings to Negroes.† So I began to investigate that. I talked to my father about it. My father had been in the Army, as I said before, and he really didn't necessarily try to

---

* In late November 1941, the Imperial Japanese Navy dispatched from the Kurile Islands in the North Pacific a task force built around six aircraft carriers. A force of some 350 fighters, dive-bombers, and torpedo planes attacked U.S. military installations on the island of Oahu, Hawaii, on Sunday, 7 December 1941. The principal focus of attack was the collection of American warships at the naval base at Pearl Harbor. The U.S. Congress declared war on Japan the following day.

† On 7 April 1942 the Navy agreed to accept black sailors into general service ratings as of 1 June of that year. That change meant an opportunity to go into a range of different occupational specialties, rather than being confined largely to duties as cooks, stewards, and messmen.

talk me into the Army. He wanted me to make my own decision about it. Finally it came down to maybe what you ought to do was join the Navy and learn a trade, and, frankly, we thought it would be a short war. Then when you got out of the Navy you'd have something that you could fall back on, providing you didn't go back to college and finish your education.

And, as I said earlier, I had talked to several of my ministers around there, because I went to a couple of churches. There were about three or four in the neighborhood, as I recall, and I knew them all. Finally, I guess, I reached the decision based on the fact that, number one, I could continue my education basically in the Navy, and I would learn some kind of trade. Number two, this was something brand new, and I kind wanted to be a part of it, just like Alan Shepard and his crowd wanted to go to the moon—the astronauts.[*]

Paul Stillwell: Was it a new thing that other ratings besides steward's mate were opening up?[†]

Admiral Gravely: It was that, just that. That I could join the Navy, and I could be a regular sailor just like everybody else. This was completely new to blacks, because there'd been a lot of hue and cry from the black press, from the NAACP about, "Why? Now we've got a war on, and we need all these men, and you're not taking people into the Navy."[‡]

Paul Stillwell: Had you been thwarted in any sense in civilian life because of racial discrimination?

---

[*] On 5 May 1961 Commander Alan B. Shepard, USN, became the first American astronaut to fly into space. He completed a 15-minute sub-orbital flight in a Mercury spacecraft. After splashdown he was recovered by a helicopter and landed on the deck of the aircraft carrier Lake Champlain (CVS-39). He was later commander of the Apollo 14 mission, which reached the moon in 1971.

[†] For Navy enlisted personnel a rating denotes a job specialty such a boatswain's mate, while a rate, such as petty officer second class, represents a pay grade within that rating. A petty officer is a rated man or woman, while an individual in a lower grade is classified as non-rated.

[‡] NAACP—National Association for the Advancement of Colored People.

Admiral Gravely: Not really before, by any stretch of the imagination, because it was a way of life. Every school that I'd ever been to before my Navy career was predominantly—was all black. There's no sense in my wasting my time saying predominantly. It was all black. I worked in a drugstore, for example, as a part-time job and couldn't drink a Coke in the store. I couldn't buy one at the fountain. You automatically went to the back of the streetcar or the back of the bus. And you knew if you sat in the front of a train, that was the first place the coal hit. So it was a completely segregated society, and I knew no other. So that I would not say that I was frustrated as much as concerned. It was a way of life, it was the law of the land, and that was the way I had to live.

Well, after making this decision on joining the Navy, I went up and I enlisted. I enlisted 15 September 1942, and we were going to leave the next day. Now that you're talking in terms of segregation, there were ten people from my hometown, all black, who were in this group. We were put on a train in Richmond, Virginia, went up to Great Lakes.* There was a black older guy who was sort of the senior man that was in charge of this group.

We got on the train in Richmond, and in very short order a Pullman porter came through picking up the tickets, etc. He noticed that there was one kid there that was just so much fairer than all the rest of us, although he had registered there as a black. He objected; he said, "Hey, you're in the wrong car." My petty officer in charge objected to him doing anything about it. But this porter moved that guy to the back of the train, and, to be honest with you, I never saw him again. All I know is that nine of us were admitted to the company when we got to Great Lakes.

Well, we arrived, and, frankly, Great Lakes was almost a breeze for me as well. The regimentation was no problem. I'd been regimented at home all my life. Reveille at 6:00 o'clock was just more than a breeze. One of the things I did as a youngster was to carry newspapers. I had to get up every morning at 5:00, so I could sleep an hour later

---

* Great Lakes, Illinois, a town on the shore of Lake Michigan, about 30 miles north of downtown Chicago, was the site of a large naval training station that included recruit training and a number of specialized schools. It is now known as Great Lakes Naval Training Center.

when I joined the Navy. The drilling and marching—I'd been a boy scout, and so it was no problem falling into line there.

Paul Stillwell: Was boot camp segregated?*

Admiral Gravely: Boot camp was segregated. We went to a special camp called Camp Robert Smalls. Camp Robert Smalls was named after a light guy, who, during the Civil War, and I believe he was a slave, stole a southern or Confederate barge and turned it over to the Union Navy.† From then on throughout the war, I believe, he was left in charge of that thing. Robert Smalls ultimately became a congressman from South Carolina. But, anyway, that's who the camp was named after.

Paul Stillwell: Were there some predecessors in this camp before, or were you among the first blacks there?

Admiral Gravely: I can't give you a really good answer on that, but I think that Camp Robert Smalls was a sort of new adjunct which was added to the camp when the decision was reached that there would be blacks in boot camp. I think the decision was made something like April or May that blacks could enlist in any other rating, and the first groups went there in June. So figuring that there were 100 men in a company, and probably four or five companies there at a time, you had about 8,000 to 10,000 people who had gone to Great Lakes or were still there when I arrived in September.

My company was number 10-43 at Camp Robert Smalls. You went consecutively, I guess, throughout the Navy, whether it was there or Hampton or whatever. Again, boot camp was a breeze. I easily passed the tests that would send me on to service school. I chose motor machinist; it just sounded sort of interesting, diesel engineering and the whole bit. And, of course, also thinking of terms of what could you

---

* "Boot" is a slang term for a newly enlisted sailor or Marine. Recruit training is known as boot camp.
† Within the Great Lakes Naval Training Station, Camp Robert Smalls was the site of training for black recruits. It was named for an escaped slave who captured the Confederate steamer Planter during the Civil War and turned her over to the U.S. Navy. He served as pilot of the Planter and later of the gunboat Keokuk. After the war, Smalls (1839-1915) served in the U.S. Congress as a representative from South Carolina from 1875 to 1879 and from 1884 to 1887.

do next when you got out. You could run your own gas station—repair cars and those kinds of things. So I chose diesel engineering.

Well, it so happened also that the motor machinist school was placed at Hampton Institute. As you well know, Hampton Institute has been a black engineering school for many, many years—in fact, right after it was set up as one of the land-grant colleges. So it was quite convenient, I guess, for the Navy to set it up at that place, where they had already the instructors, and they had certain amounts of machinery. Thus most of the artificer rates went to Hampton to service school. The seaman rates stayed at Great Lakes, and service schools were set up there.

Paul Stillwell: Had you been given any guarantee when you enlisted that you would get some kind of school?

Admiral Gravely: No, no.

Paul Stillwell: What was the recruiting setup that you recall going through?

Admiral Gravely: Well, the recruiting setup was one wherein you had a desk here with a white chief petty officer behind it who basically handled the black people who would come into the recruiting station. I assume we all took the same test. I don't think they modified the test for blacks or anything like that. Despite discrimination and those kinds of things, there were no overt attempts to either discourage me or cause me to want to do anything differently. No insults, no nothing. I just was another recruit who made a good score on the examination, incidentally.

Paul Stillwell: They didn't try any games on the physical at that point, I take it?

Admiral Gravely: No, there were no games played on the physical. I sort of breezed through that. And, of course, you've got to remember that by this time the war was raging. We needed people now much worse than we did in 1940, when I had the game played on me on the physical. I didn't have any problem.

Paul Stillwell: Were you compelled by a sense of patriotism in addition to the desire to learn a trade?

Admiral Gravely: There was a certain amount of patriotism, yes. I knew that this is a great country, and I've got to do my part to support it, just like anybody else. I probably was not as patriotic as some, but I certainly had a sense of patriotism and felt that it was my duty. If not, I would have waited, I think, until the draft came and said, "Take me," and I would have probably shortened my time in.

Paul Stillwell: What happened at Hampton?

Admiral Gravely: Now, I should mention this. I came home on the normal nine-day leave. That's the only thing that was ever promised. You know, you went to boot camp, and you got nine days' leave after that. Richmond, Virginia, was kind of warm that November. Then, because of rules and regulations, I had to go back to Great Lakes, where it was colder than hell. But, anyway, I caught pneumonia.

The companies came down to Hampton once a month, and usually the first of the month. So I missed my company, which meant that I was held over in Great Lakes for a month. Then on New Year's Day of 1943 I arrived in Hampton with a different group of guys, and I didn't know any of them. We were assigned rooms at Hampton by alphabetical order, and I just had three really fantastic roommates—Foster, Green, and Gibbons—just great guys.

At Hampton Institute I discovered that I just was not as technically minded as I thought I was, so I didn't do very well at service school. There were people who came out of those classes as motor machinist's mate second class. I came out as a fireman second, so I didn't do very well. At the same time, we were offered choices of duty when we graduated from service school. There were six places. You could go to New York, Boston, Philadelphia, San Diego, Seattle, or San Francisco.

I guess, having been on the East Coast, my normal inclination would have been to say New York or Philadelphia. Not only that they were close to home, I still had a lot of home in me. I still had the younger brothers and sisters at home. I saw them during my boot leave, but I didn't see as much as I normally used to. But I had a guy in my room by the name of Gibbons. Gibbons had been a schoolteacher. He'd been one of the great football players of Prairie View Institute down there.* And, of course, I idolized him, because he was a football player. He hit a baseball a country mile. And he was sort of a man's man. Gibbons and I were sitting around discussing this one day, and he said, "Hey, do you know what Horace Greeley said? Horace Greeley said, 'Go West young man.'"† He said, "We ought to go to San Diego."

So I said, "All right. How do we assure that we go to San Diego?" Obviously there was no way to do that, and we agreed on that. So we said, "Well, everybody in this class wants to go to New York, so what we're going to do is put down New York as our first choice and San Diego as our second." That's exactly what we did, and we went to San Diego. [Laughter]

Paul Stillwell: You've described how closely your father kept you under his wing. Did you have any sense of wanting to get out on your own at this point?

Admiral Gravely: Not exactly at this point. It happened later when I realized that, "Hey, you've got to be your own man." I was still quite a father's boy, and my father directed my entire life growing up. I probably had never been to a dance with a date. For example, I went alone to my own high school ball. Can you imagine this guy going to a high school dance all by himself? And those kinds of things. Well, I wanted to go to a couple of fraternity affairs after I got into Virginia Union. These would have kept me out after 10:00 o'clock, and my father just said no. You know, "Go, fine, if you're going to be home by 10:00 o'clock." But who in the hell is going to go to something that lasts till 12:00 and have to be in at 10:00? My father was a very strict man, but at the same time he was a very fine man.

---

* Prairie View A&M in Prairie View, Texas, is a traditionally black college.
† Horace Greeley (1811-1872) was a prominent 19th century newspaper publisher and a leader in the antislavery movement. He was the founder and editor of the New York Tribune.

Paul Stillwell: So you weren't ready to break that tie yet.

Admiral Gravely: Not quite ready to break the tie.

Well, we arrived in San Diego, and we were mustered in, the whole bit, as you might anticipate. Frankly, when I arrived in San Diego, I thought I had reached the most beautiful place in the world. I made a decision at that point in time, that ultimately I would come back to San Diego, and I would stay the remainder of my life. And, of course, all during my Navy career I felt that that's where I would end up—in San Diego. I planned to retire there, and I'll tell you more about that later.

In any event, I guess there were about 15 of us, and the first thing that happened to us was that the first class petty officer who was the master-at-arms came around and said, "All right, I need one mess cook and I need one compartment cleaner. Who's going to volunteer for those two?"* Knowing that I was probably one of two or three fireman second in the group, I knew that I'd get one of those chores. So I said, "I will volunteer for the compartment cleaning job." I simply didn't want to go mess cooking. Mess cooking reminded me of being a steward. In any event, I was compartment cleaner.

The other guys, except for one who was picked for the mess-cooking job, all were assigned to various machine shops on the base. At that point there were very few blacks on ships, and certainly when you reported to the naval base the base commander didn't have any authority to transfer you to an oceangoing tug or a seagoing ship anyway. But they did have some, I guess you'd call them gate vessels or harbor craft that guarded the entrances to the harbor. Some of the men went there in their rates.

I did this compartment-cleaning job for about two months. And I should tell you a little bit about the place. San Diego, despite the fact that I really loved it, was to some degree more segregated than my own hometown.

Paul Stillwell: That's surprising.

---

* A mess cook does the extra chores involved with feeding the crew but not the cooking itself. Mess cooks serve the food, wash mess trays, and clean up the mess deck.

Admiral Gravely: It was surprising to me. The Navy still was as segregated as could be. Blacks were separate. They had this big base, blacks on one end of it, whites on the other end. In fact, the Navy didn't permit the blacks to live in the barracks. There was a group of huts that were on sort of the western end of the base. This was where all the blacks were assigned. These huts would hold eight people. They had four double-decker bunks. And for a guy 6-foot-3, I could not stand in my hut. The only time I was ever in my hut was when I was asleep, or we could go in there and sit and play cards at a little table.

Now, my job as compartment cleaner was basically to go around each morning and pick up the cigarette butts and make sure that all of the cigarette receptacles had water in them, because they had little coffee cans and that kind of thing. To sweep this area, to go up and pick up the mail, and deliver the mail and put it around on each guy's bunk. And I guess I had to go in and make sure the bunks were clean and all made up. But at the same time they did have a chief master-at-arms, for whom I worked.

Well, one day I was down there doing my job. The chief master-at-arms had gone off someplace, and he said, "Look out for my phone." So the phone rang, and it was the welfare and recreation officer, Lieutenant Stubbs. He was looking for the chief master-at-arms, but since I had answered the phone, he would talk to me. He said, "We have decided that the Negroes aren't really taking advantages of the welfare and recreation things that we have on this base. They are spending most of their time either going to Tijuana or some of the undesirable locations in San Diego. So we've decided that we'd like to have two people to work in welfare and recreation department. Specifically, we're going to run a pool hall, and I want you to put the word out that I'm looking for two people."

So I just simply said, "Mr. Stubbs, I'll volunteer for one of these positions, and I'll see if I can find you someone else." Now, at that point in time I'd never been in a pool hall in my life. But, anyway, I found another guy, and we went up there that day to work for Mr. Stubbs in running a pool hall. Well, frankly, to some degree, I think, that turned things around a little bit, because obviously where you've got two blacks working, others are going to come. Well, we worked this job of the pool hall for two or three months. It was simply cleaning the table, charging a nickel fee, making sure the place was cleaned, orderly, and the whole bit.

I'd been there, I guess, about two months when Lieutenant Stubbs came up one morning, and I was in there cleaning, and he said, "Why aren't you taking the V-12 test?"

I said, "Mr. Stubbs, I'm not sure I know what the V-12 test is."

He said, "Well," he said, "you should have read it in the plan of the day." Well, welfare and recreation, despite the fact it had a division, never mustered people at quarters or anything. They just sort of assumed you were there. You also kept your own liberty card, etc. You did your work, and that was about the end of it. I had not read this, so I said, "Well, what is it about?"

He said, "Well, the V-12 program is a program wherein a grown person will get an opportunity to go to college and ultimately become an officer in the Navy."[*] He said, "You finished high school, didn't you?"

I said, "Yes, sir." I didn't volunteer that I had a couple of years of college. And I said, "Mr. Stubbs, I'm not sure that there's any reason for me to go down there and take this test. To the best of my knowledge, the Navy has no Negro officers, and I don't know of anything about them anticipating any."

He just simply said, "Get your ass down and take the test."

"Yes, sir." And I went down and took the test. I was one of three people on the base to be selected. I don't know what the passing score was, or whether there was such a thing. I was selected along with two white boys.

Paul Stillwell: Had you felt stagnated up to that point? You weren't really getting into one of these trades that you had sought when you enlisted.

Admiral Gravely: Well, it was sort of frustrating from that aspect of it, but, frankly, I knew more people on that base, and I probably had better relations with everybody as a result of running that pool hall than anybody up there, so I was quite happy with what I was doing. Frustrated only that the thing that I started out to do in the Navy just had not

---

[*] V-12 was a Naval Reserve officer training program in which individuals received naval instruction at the same time they worked toward bachelor's degrees. The program, which was held at civilian colleges and universities, took about two years. See James G. Schneider, The Navy V-12 Program: Leadership for a Lifetime (Boston: Houghton Mifflin, 1987). For specific information on Gravely and other black sailors in the V-12 program see Schneider's article, "'Negroes Will Be Tested!'—FDR," Naval History, Spring 1993, pages 11-15.

come to fruition. Because I expected that I would have finished motor machinist school, and, frankly, I was disappointed that I didn't become a motor machinist second class when I got out of Hampton.

Paul Stillwell: So it really took that kind of motivation that he supplied.

Admiral Gravely: That's right, that's right. Well, in any event, shortly after taking the test and everything else, the Navy came out with a new policy on service school graduates. That policy was that service school graduates could only work in their rates. So I was quickly transferred from the pool hall down to one of the machine shops. And, frankly, that was even more frustrating than before. By now I'd been away from the machinist's mate business for about four or five months, which is no long time. But the guys in the shop were all white, didn't particularly want to help me learn, or any of that kind of stuff. I was just an odd guy in the shop. "What the hell did they send this guy down here for?" and those kinds of things.

But I was saved, obviously, by the fact that I had been selected, and I was on my way to the V-12 school. Now, I should tell you this. The Navy gave me a choice of V-12 units to go to. They just said in my sort of application to put down a choice of schools. And they had V-12 units in practically every school in the country. I recognized that there was no such thing as trying to come to the University of Richmond, which is where I probably would have liked to come, since that was my hometown. So I just simply wrote, "No choice." When my orders came, I was sent to the University of Southern Cal in Los Angeles. I reported to the University of Southern Cal. I think it was about the 31st of October 1943. I was accepted. I began registration, and, of course, was assigned five roommates who were there in the V-12 program—all white. I was one of the first five or six blacks to get into this program.

But the next morning I was quite surprised when I was called down to the administration office, and I was told that I had been transferred to UCLA. Now, I didn't know any more about UCLA than I did about USC. I was a little concerned about this, but said, "I'll go to UCLA." So they put my gear in a truck and drove me to University of California at Los Angeles, which was just right across town. Now, I've had a lot of time to think about that since that time, and the only thing that I can equate it to is the fact that in those days blacks predominantly went to UCLA, not to USC. If you remember, just a couple of years before that Kenny Washington and Jackie Robinson were there.[*] And I got the impression from talking to a few of my friends that UCLA was the school that mostly black students went to, although there were a few at USC. So, for that reason, I guess, I was sent there.

Well, I got to UCLA, and I think a couple of things began to really hit me. One was that here I had an opportunity, and I had to take advantage of it. Number two, there was to be no failure; failure couldn't enter my mind. I couldn't get out, I thought, if I wanted to, because I felt that, "Hey, I've been given a rare opportunity here, and I can't screw it up for these other people who may come along." So I watched my decorum, I watched everything. I made sure I was going to do everything right, and I guess I did. I got out successfully.

Now, I was quite taken aback by a couple of things. One was that I was put into a company with a group of kids from Stanford. They were all pre-med students, and most of them were going to be doctors. For example, Dr. Bobby Brown, who was a Yankee, was in that class, and two or three other guys.[†] A couple of them are doctors now. But one of the significant things was that, for no reason that I can think of, with rooms all over that building, I was assigned to the basement. It was a good room, no complaint about that. There was one other guy in the basement with a good room. But the guy who was my next-door neighbor was a foul-up, and they put him down there for that reason. [Laughter] I was a little concerned that I was put down there for that reason.

There were no major incidents or even minor incidents. I was treated just like another V-12 student. Of course, there was no social contact for me or any of my classmates, except for the black girls, and there was one black guy who I really socialized with. V-12 was regimented much more so than the ROTC is now. Today's midshipmen wear civilian clothes, but we wore our uniforms all the time. So I marched with these

---

[*] The Los Angeles Rams became the first National Football League team to integrate when they hired black veterans Kenny Washington and Woody Strode in 1946. In 1947 Jackie Robinson became the first black major league baseball player.
[†] Bobby Brown played baseball for the New York Yankees in the 1940s and 1950s. He subsequently became a cardiologist and in 1984 became president of baseball's American League.

guys, I played with these guys. We did everything together, but there was no social interchange over weekends. They all went their way, and I found my way through Los Angeles.

Paul Stillwell: Did you raise any objections to these slights that you perceived?

Admiral Gravely: I asked the question about why was I consigned to the basement, but I really didn't get a good answer to that one. So far as slights, when I talked in terms of the social activity, I don't think I expected any real social activity. That just was not the norm in that day and time. As a V-12er, and during the war, you were kind of restricted to that campus anyway, so there was no opportunity to go downtown to have a beer at the local beer garden and those kinds of things. It was basically a policy of separation of races then. Despite the fact that Los Angeles was a little more open on those kinds of things, we didn't do it at all. I've thought about it since, but not to waste a lot of time thinking about it.

Paul Stillwell: How did you do academically?

Admiral Gravely: Academically I did about as well as the majority of them that went there. I think the pre-med students were sort of biding their time, really. In fact, I can remember that while I was there, a whole batch of them were hauled down to San Diego and put into recruit training. I'm not sure why. It may be they were also medically inclined and the Navy couldn't use all those doctors, and they weren't going to commission all those doctors after that. I can't answer your question. But as a student I kept my grades up well enough to pass. I didn't work too hard at it, but I wasn't going to fail. I wasn't going to fail.

Paul Stillwell: Was this a concentrated, speeded-up program?

Admiral Gravely: It was a concentrated, speeded-up program. You basically took college courses, except every Saturday morning we had about three hours of Navy orientation. The program was basically designed so that the guy who had only finished high school would be able to pick up about 70 hours in two and a half years, and from there go to a midshipman school and be commissioned. In fact, I had maybe 40 or 50 hours when I entered the program, so I only stayed two semesters, and I left UCLA in June of 1944.

Paul Stillwell: Did you have a major during this program?

Admiral Gravely: No, I did not have a major. I just sort of took courses. Now, I had been a pre-med student to some degree, because I wanted to be an undertaker. Can you imagine that? I guess I was kind of mixed up in my younger life. I first wanted to be a football coach. And then when I went to college I decided that I'd take courses in order to get into embalming and that kind of thing. And then, of course, when I got to UCLA I just let it swing. Nobody really asked me about a major, and I think I probably put down pre-med, and so my courses were along that nature. There were only two semesters of it anyway, and, of course, the other thing I should say was that a lot of the credits that I had at Virginia Union were not acceptable out there. Certainly they could care less about six hours of Bible, which you had to take at Virginia Union.

Well, anyway, I got out in good stead and left there en route to what they called pre-midshipman school. Now, they had something like about four midshipman schools: Columbia, Notre Dame, Fort Schuyler, and Northwestern near Chicago. There were about four midshipman schools, but they must have had 60, 70, 80 V-12 places. So a new class went into midshipman school every two months, with the duration being four months. They had so many that they had to funnel some through what they called the pre-midshipman school, so I went through Asbury Park, New Jersey, where I stayed for two months.

Now, I was the only black in that unit down at Asbury Park. I went through all the normal wickets that everybody else went through. There was no problem. I had five white roommates. Nobody said anything, slurred, or any of that kind of crap. I did take a turn at mess cooking. I wasn't a very good swimmer, so I couldn't life-save on the beach. But it was just another training camp where nothing untoward happened.

Paul Stillwell: Was there any attrition rate built into this V-12 program?

Admiral Gravely: I can't answer that question. I do know that people did attrite. You generally went to the fleet. I would assume that the guy who left there and had been a straight civilian went to boot camp, but they took a lot of fleet people in. So, for example, there was a signalman first class there, in my class at UCLA, who couldn't hack the academics, so he went back to the Navy as a first class signalman. I had a successor at UCLA, from all I hear, although I never met him. And when I say successor, I'm thinking about a black guy who failed the program. I don't know why. But I was told ultimately that the guy who came in after me failed.

Paul Stillwell: Was there a sense of competition instilled in you?

Admiral Gravely: I think it was more significant than that. I think that for the first time I was in a world where I had to compete with the people that I'd be competing with the rest of my life. I knew then it was a little different from what I'd been going through all the time. And I knew that if I were to compete successfully, then I had to do it just like everybody else did it. I think I discovered for the first time that all men put their pants on one leg at a time. No matter what his complexion is, that you all do it the same way.

I think the most interesting thing for me and the thing that amounted the most was the fact that I could do it successfully. That was when I began to think a little bit seriously, "When I get out of the Navy, I'm going back to college and get that degree, and I'm going to do some of these other things that I have been thinking about." Well, I was 21 years old, approaching 22 at this point, and so I really cut the strings. I knew that I was on my own at that point, and that I would do it, and do it successfully.

Paul Stillwell: In officer training the Navy imposes irritants and pressures and stresses, the inspections and so forth.

Admiral Gravely: Yes.

Paul Stillwell: How did you react to those?

Admiral Gravely: I have never had any problem with inspections or those kinds of things. I have never been unready in one. Some nitpicker might find something wrong, but I took a lot of pride in shining my shoes, and I got a haircut every two weeks, whether I needed one or not, and those kinds of things. I kept my uniforms up to snuff, so I didn't have any problem. And I didn't have any problem going through them. A little nervous, yes; everybody's nervous going through inspection, but I knew that I was in good shape with all those things. So, whereas you call it an irritant, I learned that it was a necessary evil and had no real problem. [Laughter]

Paul Stillwell: How long was that period at Asbury Park?

Admiral Gravely: Asbury Park was roughly two months. As I recall, it was about mid-August or something. I must have gotten there about mid-June. About mid-August we were then transferred up to Columbia University, to the midshipman school.[*] Midshipman school was tough. There were some subjects that they taught that I hadn't taken. For example, I'd never been through any navigation. I didn't know very much about ordnance, although you got a sort of a general thing that the Navy's got 16-inch guns and that kind of crap. But we got into some fairly specifics on the 5-inch guns, the 16-inch guns, got fairly specific in engineering courses.

But I'd already told myself I wasn't going to fail the thing. Normally, if you didn't pass a subject, you had to stay there some extra time on a Saturday. The course was 16 weeks, and I think I got caught one Saturday. But it was a sort of a minor thing. I just talked to a guy who was in my class just recently, and he reminded me that during one of the drills that our company was the lowest in drilling for that week. It brought back memories, because I was the guy that did it. In this particular instance I was on the inboard side in marching.

---

[*] Herman Wouk's classic naval novel of World War II, The Caine Mutiny, was published by Doubleday & Company in 1951. Though fiction, it presents a good idea of midshipman school at Columbia University in World War II because a portion of the story is based on Wouk's own experiences there.

As I think back, when you go past the reviewing stand and you go eyes-right, it was the three ranks outside immediately turn their heads right and look, but the inboard side continues to march, facing straight ahead. And that's what I did. Commodore Richards, who headed the place, marked this down as a result of that and told my company commander that if I ever passed a reviewing stand again, that I was to do eyes-right like everybody else.[*] And, of course, I said, "Sir."

He said, "Don't tell me about that. Do it."

"Yes, sir." From then on I was on the eyes-right, big smile, the whole bit. The next week we were the outstanding company. [Laughter] But it was quite interesting—well, it was easy to notice me. We had 1,600 people, I think, drilling—well, I guess we had twice that number. But, anyway, I was the one guy he saw out there.

Paul Stillwell: It sounds as if it was very much a fleet-oriented training program you went through.

Admiral Gravely: It was a fleet-oriented training program. It was basically designed to make an officer out of you. It was just like any other pre-midshipman school. I would think the thing you would equate it to was Officer Candidate School in Newport.[†]

Paul Stillwell: Were you getting a dose of customs and traditions of the Navy along with it?

Admiral Gravely: Oh, yes. You got all of that. It was strictly officer training in those things that you needed. Now, you didn't get a period of "Right full rudder" and those kinds of things. It wasn't a destroyer school or anything like that. But tradition, customs, touched base with navigation. You were not a navigator when you left there. You obviously went as assistant to somebody, but you knew a couple of instruments you were going to use. Had a recognition course; you had to recognize ships: flash them on for a

---

[*] Commodore John K. Richards, Jr., USN (Ret.).
[†] At the time of this interview the Navy's Officer Candidate School was held at Newport, Rhode Island. It has since moved to Pensacola, Florida.

Samuel L. Gravely, Jr., Interview #1 (6/25/86) – Page 24

second, and you had to call out what it was, ships, aircraft, and those kinds of things.

Very, very, very good course, fairly intensive, highly competitive, because guys were dropping out of there every week. Now, as I recall, my company was originally at about 1,600, and when we graduated we were at about 1,030 or something like that. So roughly a third of the class left, and I was in the top remaining third. So I thought I'd done fairly well.

Paul Stillwell: Were you aware of other black officer midshipmen at that point?

Admiral Gravely: At that point the only thing that I was really aware of was the Navy had commissioned 12 black officers and one warrant in March.[*] I saw the Life magazine story on that.[†] That was the only thing that I knew at that point in time.

Paul Stillwell: The Golden 13.

Admiral Gravely: The Golden 13, yes. I think I'd heard of my successor at UCLA writing correspondence with the people back there. I'm sure there must have been something in the paper at that point in time about Lieutenant Commander Hope, who was a civil engineer at Howard University, who was selected and commissioned as a lieutenant and then finally made lieutenant commander.[‡]

Paul Stillwell: I'm interested in whether you had role models, or were you pretty much on your own?

Admiral Gravely: I was on my own. I knew a couple of the Golden 13. Johnny Reagan, for example, was in the class ahead of me at Hampton, but I knew him there.[§] Also he

---

[*] These men were commissioned on 17 March 1944 through a special training program at Camp Robert Smalls at Great Lakes, Illinois. For details see Paul Stillwell, The Golden Thirteen: Recollections of the First Black Naval Officers (Annapolis: Naval Institute Press, 1993).
[†] A one-page photo feature, titled "Negro Ensigns," appeared in the 24 April 1944 issue of Life.
[‡] Lieutenant Edward Hope, CEC, USNR.
[§] Ensign John Walter Reagan, USNR, was a member of the Golden Thirteen. His oral history is in the Naval Institute collection.

and I were in San Diego together, played on the same softball team together. There were a couple of the other guys that I had touched base with, didn't know very well. Johnny Reagan was probably the guy I knew best. In fact, I know him today. He married a girl named Dede that I recommended to him.* [Laughter]

Paul Stillwell: But mostly it was an abstraction, as far as you were concerned.

Admiral Gravely: Yes, right. They were out in left field somewhere. In fact, the first time I saw one was when I went back to Great Lakes, and I'll tell you about that.

Midshipman school kept us so busy until you didn't have time to think about race. As I remember, Johnson Hall had about 17 floors in there, and you were timed. I ran from the first floor of Johnson Hall all the way to the 17th floor for 16 weeks. I had leg muscles like that. [Laughter] And, of course, you ran down to formation. You had to be down there.

We were kind of happy to get away from there on a Saturday, and I spent a lot of time in Harlem, which is right where it is.† Again, there was very little mixing of social activity. There was no such thing as a club for these guys to go in, or any of that. We did some studying together. I always had at least one white roommate. I roomed with about four, five guys, and I didn't think of it very much at that point in time, but I moved around a lot. And I'm not sure why, but maybe this was part of somebody's idea of a social experiment, because I moved several times. I had about ten roommates during my four months there, moving to a two-man room with one guy, a two-man room with another guy, and a four-man room. But that didn't bother me, because usually some guy had flunked out and left. That was the reason probably why that room was available again, and I moved into that room.

Paul Stillwell: Were you of any sort of celebrity when you went on liberty in Harlem, let's say?

---

* Willita T. "Dede" Reagan was married to John Reagan up to the time of his death in 1994.
† Columbia University is in the Harlem section of the upper portion of New York's Manhattan Island.

Admiral Gravely: No, nobody knew what this uniform was. [Laughter] At that time there was a black captain who commanded a merchant ship, and there were a lot of blacks who got into the merchant marine, so you'd see a lot more merchant marine uniforms out there in Harlem than you would see Navy types.* There were no midshipmen out there. So people just wondered, "What the hell is he? Who is this guy?"

Paul Stillwell: Well, I think patriotism in general, that anyone in uniform was pretty well treated, wasn't he?

Admiral Gravely: Yes. Everybody in uniform was treated very, very well. In fact, when you would go into any number of bars some guy would look at you and say, "Well, I don't know exactly what service you're in, but you must be in some. Come on up and have a drink." [Laughter] And you'd go get a drink.

Paul Stillwell: You talked about going to your school dance stag. Had you developed a social life by this time with girls?

Admiral Gravely: Well, I had a social life. I knew girls, and I'd been on a lot of dates, and I met some girls that I went out with at UCLA. I met a couple of girls in the Harlem area. In fact, one girl from my hometown was a nurse there, and she took me around a couple places. I met girls and this kind of thing. And, interesting that you ask, but I had met the girl who is my wife before that time.† She went to school with my sister over in Petersburg, Virginia. As I said, I played football at Virginia Union but my father didn't know I was doing it. But, anyway, I went over there with a bunch of football players, and my sister introduced me to one of her roommates. I corresponded with a lot of girls. She was one of those, and ultimately we got married, but that's another story.

When you started out in midshipman school, you were treated like a boot. That was the first month. Then finally you got your midshipman uniform, and you were

---

* The black merchant ship master was Captain Hugh Mulzac, whose memoir, done in collaboration with Louis Burnham, is A Star to Steer By (New York: International Publishers, 1972).
† Her maiden name was Alma Bernice Clark.

someplace between an officer and a boot. But, anyway, treatment got a little better, the requirements weren't quite as stiff, those kinds of things. I had some really, really good friends there, because we were all struggling trying to survive.

But, in any event, after the period was over, I got my set of orders, and I was very, very disappointed. Now, you talk about patriotism and those kinds of things. You've got, well, in this case, 1,000 guys ready to go out and fight the war, fight the Japanese, the whole bit. Most people had orders that either took them to sea or took them to some school wherein they would then go to sea. They would get a short course in communications, or a short course in math, then orders for further transfer to such-and-such. My orders read to proceed to Great Lakes, Illinois, to train Negro recruits, and I was let down. I really felt that that was a blow. What do you call a line of guys, all in the same company?

Paul Stillwell: Platoon.

Admiral Gravely: Platoon, yes. My platoon decided that we would go out one night and just have a ball. We had one week in which you could go back to anyplace you wanted to and got measured for uniforms and the whole bit, but in the afternoon you could go out and stay until about 10:00 o'clock.

Paul Stillwell: Was this before you were commissioned?

Admiral Gravely: Before I was commissioned, yes. So we were all out, and some guy from the Pennsylvania Dutch country said, "How many of you belong to the 50-beer club?" I didn't even know what the 50-beer club was. Well, in any event, apparently the 50-beer club is you drink 50 mugs of beer without moving. And so everybody at that point in time wanted to join the 50-beer club, I in particular. Well, I'm not sure I got past about 20. [Laughter] But I didn't join. At the same time I got pretty well loaded.

So we all went back to the barracks. Here I was, in the passageway on the top floor of my building, yelling and screaming, "Goddamn it, if all of my friends are going to sea, I ought to go to sea too. I cannot understand why I got to go train recruits." The

OOD heard this down on the first floor and came up, and he put me to bed, obviously.* But I have always been convinced that something good came out of that, because I finished midshipman school on the 14th of December 1944, and very shortly went to Great Lakes. Six weeks later I was on my way to sea. So I think it all came as the result of raising a stink after the beer.

Paul Stillwell: Do you remember that individual's name?

Admiral Gravely: I don't remember right off, but he was the ensign or jaygee, or something like that.† He was the duty officer.

Well, anyway, we all graduated, big ceremony the 14th December, and, of course, I then came home for my 15 days' leave or something like that and proceeded to go to Great Lakes the next day. I arrived in Great Lakes and was shocked again to tears. Despite the fact that I recognized—and I did then—that it was a segregated world, I had been treated differently, and now I had to drop back down to this old state again.

As a midshipman, I ate in the mess with everybody else who was on the same level. There were quarters available for everybody else. When I got to Great Lakes, first of all, there were no quarters left. There was a BOQ there, but it wasn't for me.‡ The second thing was that the officers' club was not available to me, which meant that I had to find a place in town. I was 22 years old, and I probably should have had some experience at doing that, but I'd never had to find a hotel room or anything in my whole life. So I had to look around to see if I could find a room, number one. And I always ate over in the enlisted mess with the other black men. No major problems because I had never been to an officers' club anyway. BOQ, I was disappointed about that.

Now, what made disappointment even worse was the fact that you stood duties for the entire camp. I was a duty officer not just for Camp Robert Smalls but also Camp Moffett, etc. At Great Lakes there was a bunk wherein the duty officer slept. But the black duty officer went over there in the morning at about 8:00 o'clock. He relieved as

---

* OOD—officer of the day.
† Jaygee—lieutenant (junior grade).
‡ BOQ—bachelor officers' quarters.

the officer of the deck, went back to Camp Robert Smalls, where he spent the day, then went back over there again sometime in the afternoon, and he stayed in the thing until it was time to go to bed. Then he quickly went back over to Robert Smalls, where he went to bed, and then stayed there until the next morning when he'd go over there. And obviously by 8:00 o'clock he was relieved.

That was one of the hardest things for me to take of anything that happened to me during my Navy career. The chore there was just exactly what was implied, training black recruits. So basically as an assistant battalion commander, we reviewed the drills, we helped the companies. I guess I used to get a little charge out of going over there and taking the kids away from whoever the company commander was, drilling them, putting them through their paces and the whole bit, which I enjoyed giving orders. In any event, that went on for six weeks.

Six weeks later, I was transferred to the Naval Training Center at Miami for an eight-week course in antisubmarine warfare. Now, I'm trying to think what the base called that specifically. It wasn't called antisubmarine warfare.

Paul Stillwell: Well, there was a subchaser school at Miami.

Admiral Gravely: Subchaser—submarine chaser training school, that's what it was.[*] And that's where I was at Miami. Okay. I got down there, and I was quite concerned with going to Miami. But then not quite as concerned as I found out later that my father was. Because my father wrote a letter to the President of the United States saying, "Hey, you're going to send that boy down there to be killed or something like that." Well, in any event, I think he got an answer back said, "Don't worry about your son; he'll be okay."

I went down to Miami, and here again I was shocked a little bit. I wasn't shocked because all the kids who lived in the Biscayne Bay Boulevard Hotel, and that I had to go someplace else. I was shocked because they put me there. But I moved into the same hotel with everybody else, right on Biscayne Bay Boulevard. They must have had an officers' club, but I never went to the officers' club. Social activity was a little bit better,

---

[*] The official name was Submarine Chaser Training Center.

because the guys down there and the guys from my midshipman company who'd gone directly down there were still there for another two or three weeks. So I saw a lot of them. We went out to drink on Biscayne Bay Boulevard and those kinds of things.

Now, the program down there was one of a sort of a stepped-up midshipman school, because you knew that you were going someplace, to sea on a ship, and they were trying to teach you to be at least a junior division or maybe a division officer, as the case may be. It was a good course.

One of the things that I'll always remember—in fact, I was talking about it to someone this morning—was that you had to take a message by semaphore, blinking light, and also by the dot and dash thing. You had to take at least one message, about 20 words, I guess. And you had to read the light, and those kinds of things, 15 words a minute. You had an opportunity to go over there every morning in one of the three training rooms to take one of these messages. The minute you took one message you were exempted from the course. If you didn't take one message during the first four weeks, then it was mandatory that you went there from then on until you passed. I really don't know what would happen if you never passed it.

Paul Stillwell: How did you learn the code?

Admiral Gravely: Well, okay, okay. You learned the code by that set of cards. You remember the little deck of cards? Well, I used to play with those cards, and you did that to some degree in midshipman school. But when I got down there, it was just a concentrated thing of sitting down there, looking at the signal flags, looking at dots and dashes and those things.

Paul Stillwell: Did you practice with flashlights?

Admiral Gravely: You'd practice with flashlights, and you had a little device that you used. And it was just simply a matter of concentrating and learning how to do it. Well, the signalman gets up to that in four weeks; I didn't see why I couldn't. But, anyway, I was fortunate enough so that I passed it during my first four weeks down there, and I didn't have to go mandatory during the rest of the time.

Paul Stillwell: Did you get your first taste of ship handling there?

Admiral Gravely: I got my first taste of going to sea there. They had a DE that was attached to the school.* I'm not really sure, but I think we just went out for day cruise. I don't remember spending the night on there. And it was quite interesting. I really enjoyed it. Not ship handling as much, but you did get a chance to be a JOOD and those kinds of things, and it all went well.† I think that I might have got a few stares. But, what the hell, stares didn't bother me at all. No snide remarks.

Paul Stillwell: Did you get tactical training in ASW?‡

Admiral Gravely: Not from the degree that you'd think in terms of tactical training at this point in time. You got a little bit of it, but certainly you didn't have a trainer like you've got a tac trainer and that kind bit. You did it mostly by eyeball. Carl Rowan, incidentally, came four weeks after I did.§ He was in the class right behind me. And there was another black officer. You were asking me something about role models, etc., and I should tell you that the first time that I saw a second naval officer, other than myself, was I met Dennis Nelson when I went to Great Lakes.** At that point in time we were about five or six black officers at Great Lakes. All of them were ensigns except for

---

* DE—destroyer escort.
† JOOD—junior officer of the deck.
‡ ASW—antisubmarine warfare.
§ Ensign Carl T. Rowan, USNR, was commissioned through the V-12 program in early 1945. In later years he became a nationally syndicated newspaper columnist, television commentator, and in 1963-64 served as U.S. ambassador to Finland. For details see Carl T. Rowan, Breaking Barriers: a Memoir (Boston: Little, Brown, 1991).
** Ensign Dennis Denmark Nelson II, USNR, was a member of the Golden 13. He eventually retired from the Navy as a lieutenant commander. He died in 1979 before he could be interviewed as part of the Naval Institute's oral history program. Nelson's master's thesis was published by the Navy Department in 1948 and later came out as a book, The Integration of the Negro into the U.S. Navy (New York: Farrar, Strauss and Young, 1951).

two chaplains who were there. They were jaygees, of course. And I guess there were a doctor and a dentist there too. They were jaygees. All the line officers were ensigns.

Paul Stillwell: When you would get together with these other individuals, did you talk about the hypocrisy of the situation—that you had had to prove yourself by Navy standards, but the Navy wasn't treating you the way it treated others?

Admiral Gravely: No. I'm not sure we got together that much, because we were all in different aspects of it. For example, Dennis Nelson ran a remedial school for a group of sailors who could not read or write. He was pretty proud of that job that he was doing there. He lived probably in North Chicago, and I found a room someplace in North Chicago. So we really didn't have that much of an opportunity to get together. There were no big social events. Nobody could go to a club, for example, wherein you might have set up something.

My social activity was basically I met a couple of girls there, and I used to go into Chicago. I knew a girl who lived in North Chicago and those kinds of things. But there wasn't that much with the other black naval officers. In retrospect, most of them are older than I anyway. In fact, there was a lot of complaint about the fact that Dennis Nelson probably should have been commissioned as a lieutenant, based on an age-rank structure, but here he was an ensign.[*] In fact, most of that Golden 13 would have been either jaygee or lieutenant, and probably one or two of them as lieutenant commanders, but the Navy didn't do that.

Paul Stillwell: Did you have any sense that if you complained you would jeopardize what you had already achieved?

Admiral Gravely: Well, no, I didn't have that sense. You sort of wondered, though, who you would complain to. [Laughter]

Paul Stillwell: Exactly.

---

[*] Nelson was born 3 November 1907, so he was 36 years old when he was commissioned.

Admiral Gravely: There just wasn't that kind of an atmosphere. Now you read that every commanding officer has an open-door policy. Well, I never heard of there being an open-door policy until here late in the '60s, early '70s.

Paul Stillwell: Indeed, the Navy was very autocratic back then.

Admiral Gravely: That's right. Frankly, except for the reserves who came on, everybody in the Navy was obviously an old Naval Academy guy, and they'd been raised in the Southern tradition for years and years and years. It was a closed-door thing. In fact, I think that the Naval Academy guys resented the reserves more than anything else. In fact, they probably resented the reservists more than they resented me, except I was reserve too. They resented that too.

Paul Stillwell: Did you get to know Carl Rowan at all in Miami?

Admiral Gravely: I knew Carl fairly well. Carl and I socialized a couple of times. In fact, we knew two girls who were cousins, so we went on double dates and that kind of thing. And, of course, I see Carl around here periodically.* He and I know a mutual friend, and we sometimes get together at their homes. I'm just always really pleased to see the extent to which Carl Rowan went from his V-12 and went on up. He's just really a truly outstanding guy. I wish I were that sharp. He's smart, really.

Okay, Miami was not as open as you might expect, but at the same time, I had a normal time down there. When I went out in town by myself, I lived by the set of rules that they had down there. They had a black district outside of town, and that's where I went to socialize more than I did with the group of guys. Now, when the guys who I had known at Columbia left, and they left ahead of me, well then it was just strictly my classmates. My classmates were not cold to me by any stretch of the imagination. But I didn't have the openness with them that I'd had with the guys that fought through the battle of Columbia University.

---

* Rowan was based in Washington, D.C, during his career as a journalist.

Samuel L. Gravely, Jr., Interview #1 (6/25/86) – Page 34

Paul Stillwell: And that's understandable too.

Admiral Gravely: And in the meantime, Carl Rowan was there, and this other guy, and I can't think of his name right now. But he was there, and so we went out several times together. And, of course, the big thing was studying and getting through that course successfully.

Paul Stillwell: How much did you keep up with the war at large during this period?

Admiral Gravely: You didn't really keep up with it except from what newspaper reports you got. You know, when I became a communicator, I read every message that came into that ship. Except for the big battles that were going on, you heard about those, but, in fact, I'm not sure you really felt much a part of the Navy, other than the fact that you wore a uniform. If you recall, except for that period in San Diego, which was about six or seven months, up until this time all of my time has been spent in schools anyway. And despite the fact that I probably kept up fairly well in the stages at Columbia, it just all a waste of time when I got sent first to Great Lakes there.

Well, my orders sent me via the sub chaser school to the PC-1264, which was home-ported out of New York City.* It was a 170-foot subchaser. It was commanded by a lieutenant who had four white officers in his wardroom, and I reported aboard to relieve one of those officers.†

Paul Stillwell: This was Eric Purdon?

Admiral Gravely: Eric Purdon.‡ There were 60 enlisted men aboard when I arrived; all of them were black. Now, I didn't know much about the PC-1264, and I'm not sure what

---

* USS PC-1264 was commissioned 25 April 1944. She was 170 feet long, 23 feet in the beam, had a maximum draft of 7½ feet, and displaced 280 tons. She had two diesel engines that gave her a top speed of 20 knots. She was armed with one 3-inch gun and one 40-millimeter gun.
† Ensign Gravely reported to the ship on 2 May 1945.
‡ For a detailed history of this ship, written by the skipper, see Eric Purdon, Black Company: The Story of Subchaser 1264 (Washington-New York: Robert B. Luce, Inc., 1972).

I expected of the PC-1264. But I did know that the PC-1264 plus a destroyer escort, the Mason, were commissioned around that time.* The idea was to find out if blacks could really sail, if they could take orders from one another, and if they could do it successfully at sea. In the case of the PC-1264, it started, I believe with nine senior white petty officers and five white officers. But by the time I got there, Captain Purdon had successfully moved the black senior petty officers up into those positions of leadership, and there were none of the white petty officers there. I reported aboard, I think, in May, and my first job was as engineer.

Paul Stillwell: Was that in any sense based on your enlisted experience?

Admiral Gravely: I think it was based on the fact that I did have some enlisted experience, and, secondly, the engineer officer was fleeting up to be executive officer. And, of course, in that case then the junior guy would take that empty billet there. About two or three days, or maybe a week, or even less, a guy named Don Morman came on.† He was from the University of Michigan, as I recall, had an engineering degree, etc., and he relieved me. In the meantime, we were losing a second officer, and I had fleeted up to be communications officer, which was probably closer to my line of work, despite the fact that I had this diesel engineering background.

Paul Stillwell: Why do you say closer to your line of work?

Admiral Gravely: Well, I discovered that I was not as engineering oriented as I had originally thought when I first picked diesel engineering as a place to go. And that's always been kind of strange to me, because I took a course in automobile mechanics in high school, and I kind of felt that maybe that that might be something I might be interested in later on. But I have a feeling that I really didn't care to get my hands as dirty [laughter] as to be an engineer.

---

* USS Mason (DE-529), an Evarts-class destroyer escort, was commissioned 20 March 1944. The ship's officers were white; nearly all the enlisted men were black.
† Ensign Donald G. Morman, USNR.

Well, I was truly welcome aboard that ship. I was welcome from both aspects. I was welcomed from Captain Purdon, who had tried to get a black officer aboard. The first officer I met on there was a guy by the name of Ben Shanker.[*] Ben Shanker was the gunnery officer. And Ben welcomed me aboard, made me comfortable, the whole bit. If there were any problems, it was simply that the ship was only designed for four officers, and the fifth guy had to sleep in the wardroom. [Laughter]

In fact, when Don Morman came aboard, it meant that two of us slept in the wardroom. They had to set up double bunks right above the wardroom table. So, no matter what time you got up in the morning, or what time you went to bed at night, you had to be up in time when breakfast was served in the morning. But that was the only thing. But then, if you had had the 4:00 to 8:00 watch, either Ben Shanker or one of the other guys would say, "Hey, go on down to my bunk and rest."

Paul Stillwell: Was this the first time in your Navy experience you'd really been made to feel to welcome?

Admiral Gravely: The first real time, yes, right. Certainly, I guess, in the case of most of the other places people were glad to see you, but then to really make you feel at home was what they did. I think that all the black personnel were happy to see me and welcome me aboard. It just made me feel very, very comfortable and the whole bit. But ultimately that changed a little bit, and it changed simply because of the fact that as an officer I had certain responsibilities, and when guys were wrong, hey, I'd take note of it. They said, "Hell, this guy's just another member of the establishment." [Laughter] Which was right. But at the same time, I had to do my job.

Paul Stillwell: Well, I think they'd have to expect you to do that.

Admiral Gravely: Yes, right, right.

Paul Stillwell: How was Purdon as a leader?

---

[*] Ensign Benjamin Shanker, USNR.

Admiral Gravely: Purdon was a top-notch leader. He was easy to get along with. I think he was a great ship handler, and I guess he'd had some sea experience, small boat handling. So he was a good ship handler, he knew when to chew, when not to chew. You couldn't help but respect and admire him, because he was just a tremendous guy. That's all I can say about him. And, of course, we see each other now periodically.

Paul Stillwell: Was he pushing you to learn and grow?

Admiral Gravely: I don't think it was an obvious push, but at the same time it was a sort of compelling thing, with you, because he had trained such guys as Ben Shanker, and trained Hardman and those guys, and you knew you had to learn your job.[*] And you weren't going to let Purdon down. He was the kind of guy that, no matter what you did, you didn't want to let him down. The crew had tremendous respect for him and liked him. He was kind of easygoing, but at the same time you knew that if you didn't do it right, he could have gotten as hard as nails.

In fact, I can remember one time specifically, and I know he would have forgotten it now, but he wanted a message, and I just happened to be the guy available. He said, "Sam, go get me such-and-such a message." I was kind of lackadaisical, you know, "What the hell does he need the message for, and blah, blah, blah?" And the next time he saw me, he said, "You didn't bring me that message."

I said, "Well, Captain—"

He said, "Goddamn it, the next time I tell you I want a message, I want that message."

I said, "Yes, sir." You respected him, and you knew that he knew what he wanted and those kinds of things, how he wanted it done.

I was immediately put on, of course, as a JOOD. I stood junior officer watches at sea. But I spent about a month with the guy that I was to relieve. He stayed on there about a month. We escorted convoys. We went down to Norfolk, as I recall, and we did a couple other things, but I was a fairly quick learner. I just loved being on that bridge,

---

[*] Lieutenant (junior grade) Ernest V. Hardman, USNR.

not only that bridge, but every bridge I've ever been on. I love to go up there. I got a sense of "I can do it, and I know I can do it," and I was a quick learner.

Paul Stillwell: Was that where you began to learn ship handling?

Admiral Gravely: No it really wasn't. A PC, of course, was a small ship, went out on a mission, had diesel engines, of course. You could stay out there forever almost, and you didn't do any refueling. You had a couple of dummy drills, and you could play around picking up Oscar and those kinds of things.[*] But you didn't really get a chance to handle it that much in port. You came into port so infrequently that generally the skipper handled the ship, although Captain Purdon was the kind of guy who let somebody else handle it. He sort of stood over your shoulder and watched. But you didn't really get that many chances to handle the ship. You got a feel for turns and those kinds of things, for how quickly you could get the speed up.

My real ship-handling experience didn't really come until I had to do it myself. That's when I had the DER.[†] But I learned enough that I knew that I wasn't the type who was going to get seasick all the time. In fact, I was quite surprised I got seasick once in my whole Navy career, and it was on that PC, but the reason was my own fault. It was down in the Miami area, Key West area. I went up on the forecastle to lay in the sun and get a little salt spray over my face, and a big wave came over. I just swallowed some salt water, and I got to tell you it came out in a hurry. But I think that's where I got my start, my love of the sea, and my desire to be on ships and those kinds of things, working with Captain Purdon.

Paul Stillwell: How much of a threat was there that late in the war? How much of a need for convoying?

Admiral Gravely: Well, previous to that they had developed some sonar contacts,

---
[*] "Oscar" is the traditional name for the dummy a Navy ship throws into the water for recovery during man-overboard drills.
[†] In 1962-63 Gravely commanded the USS Falgout (DE-324).

worked them over, and those kinds of things. We did not have any during my stint. I got aboard in May of 1945, and I know that the war ended, I think we just about licked the Germans by that time.[*] The war really ended September, as I recall.[†]

Paul Stillwell: The war in Europe ended in May, in that same month.

Admiral Gravely: Right, okay. And the war with the Japanese ended in September. So whereas you were ready for it, and you constantly had GQs and those kinds of things, there were no real opportunities to mix with the enemy during the last days of war.[‡]

We had another chore, which I thought was kind of dull, although it quit very shortly after I got aboard. That was a patrol off of New York wherein it was called the buzz bomb patrol, basically.[§] I guess they put four DEs out there, and some patrolled around the area, if the B-bomb came to hit New York, we were going to shoot it down. We only did that once, as I recall. The rest of the time we escorted convoys.

We came down to Norfolk, got some refresher training, and my last chore on board there was we were going down to Miami for some more refresher training prior to proceeding to the Pacific. We were scheduled to go, and then the war ended, so we didn't go. We came back and went on up to New London. Now, Miami was the place that I got in trouble. What happened was that we were proceeding into Miami, and I guess I had the deck. One of the youngsters said, "Mr. Gravely, are you going ashore?"

I said, "I'll tell you what. I've been to Miami, I know the town, I know the people. In fact, I know a bunch of girls, and I know some clubs there." I gave them an address, and I said, "Why don't you guys meet me over there about noon, and I will be there, and I will have three or four girls that I know." So that's when we started designing, basically, a party. Well, the ship got in, and, of course, I went on in, made the

---

[*] V-E Day—Victory in Europe Day, 8 May 1945, when the German surrender was ratified in Berlin.
[†] V-J Day—Victory-over-Japan Day, 15 August 1945, marking the end of hostilities in the war in the Pacific. The formal Japanese surrender was on 2 September on board the battleship Missouri (BB-63) in Tokyo Bay
[‡] GQ—general quarters, in which the ship's crew is at battle stations.
[§] The German V-1 was a pulse-jet flying bomb, also known as a "doodlebug" and "buzz bomb." It was 25 feet long and had a 16-foot wingspan. It carried a one-ton warhead some 150 miles (later increased to 250) at a speed of about 400 miles per hour. It was first successfully flown in December 1943. The Germans fired more than 13,000 V-1s during the course of World War II.

arrangements, and I met them there. And it was, oh, 3:00 or 4:00 o'clock in the afternoon or some time like that, and I must admit I'd had a couple more than I was used to drinking as a young boy. Then an MP came over—the military police; it was an Army guy. And he said, "You're out of uniform."

I said, "Well, I don't know what you mean."

He said, "Well, you're not an officer. I've never seen a Negro Navy officer."

I said, "I am." I was getting ready to pull out my ID card. And he said something else, but, in any event, I was pulled off my stool, etc., and they decided to lock me up for impersonating an officer. Well, whenever you find an MP or SP or anything, you're going to find a patrol wagon very close behind that, so I was put in the patrol car.* And the fellows off the ship just weren't going to let that happen. So they began to riot. I quelled the riot, but in any event, I went down to the shore patrol headquarters down in Miami. I went through the routine of being drunk and physical examination, everything else. Nothing untoward happened to me, because my commanding officer came down very shortly after that, when he discovered it, and took me back to the ship. But, unfortunately, the charges were brought up to the commandant down there, and the charges were much more than impersonating an officer. Drunk and disorderly in public, and I really hadn't done any of that. Using foul language, and I hadn't done that either. Associating with enlisted men, yes, I was doing that.

Paul Stillwell: That was to cover themselves for their mistake.

Admiral Gravely: Yes. But, in any event, two or three days later I heard from the commanding officer, Captain Purdon, who had had lunch with somebody off of that admiral's staff every day that week practically—with me sweating tears as to when my general court-martial would be. He said that they finally had basically agreed that he would write me a bad fitness report. Captain Purdon was not that kind of guy, and secondly I hadn't done that much anyway. In fact, it had all started because some guy just had never seen a black naval officer.

---

* SP—shore patrol, the Navy equivalent of the military police.

But, anyway, I got out of that one. We ultimately went to New London, where we operated with the sub people up there as a submarine target vessel. Very shortly after that, it was roughly about February of 1946, the PC-1264 was decommissioned.*

Now, just before that I'd gone home on New Year's leave, and that's when I revisited with my wife-to-be. She was talking about marrying some guy sometime in June. She and her intended were going to the University of Wisconsin. He was working on his PhD, and she was going to work on her master's. And in about five weeks I convinced her that that wasn't really the right thing to do. [Laughter] I told Alma that she should marry me, and I was coming home on 30 days' leave, so we got married on the 12th of February.

Paul Stillwell: That was quick.

Admiral Gravely: Well, I'm pretty convincing when I want to be.

Paul Stillwell: On the matter of fraternizing with the enlisted men, had there been sort of a tacit understanding that you could do that since there were no black officers?

Admiral Gravely: No, no, no, but that was one of the points that Captain Purdon raised in the discussion with the admiral's staff—that there were no black officers for me to associate with. That helped me beat that charge, I guess. But no, there was no tacit understanding that I could do anything contrary to Navy regs. And, frankly, I'd never thought of that.

Paul Stillwell: Well then, apparently the captain hadn't made a point of it.

Admiral Gravely: No, no. There'd been no points made that I wasn't supposed to associate with the enlisted men. I guess nobody really thought of that, you know. Certainly there's a fine line between an officer and an enlisted man, but I've been to social affairs with enlisted men after that, and even before that. This was just another one

---

* The ship was decommissioned 7 February 1946.

of those stacking of charges, I think, more than anything else. But it all came out for the best, I guess.

Paul Stillwell: You mentioned that Life magazine had publicized the Golden 13. Was there any publicity for your ship's crew?

Admiral Gravely: Not while I was aboard that I can think of. There might have been a couple of small mentions of it. Certainly I would think that there was something when the PC-1264 and the Mason were originally commissioned. A lot of photographs, but I don't remember that specifically. There was some publicity with the review of ships by President Truman right after the war, because we were in New York harbor. And, despite the fact we were the smallest ship up there, we led the line. In fact, we were the first ship that he was to see, which included the Missouri.[*] So there was some publicity about that. We got all kinds of ship's visitors and those kinds of things but nothing much that talked about any specific person or even me or anybody else.

Paul Stillwell: Did you have any sense then of movement toward integrating the service?

Admiral Gravely: No, I didn't, and I'll talk about that one in just a minute, because I'll cover that point.

After transferring off the 1264, of course, we came down to Virginia, where I spent roughly 30 days, which I had for leave time. Then I went to Norfolk, to the fleet training group. Fleet training group was up at Little Creek. At that point there was no place for me to live. So it meant going out and finding a place to live again and those kinds of things, because I did not have officers' club or BOQ privileges. Finally one day my commanding officer, who was a captain, said, "Sam, why don't you live in the BOQ?"

---

[*] On 27 October 1945 President Harry S. Truman went to New York City to celebrate Navy Day the month after the end of World War II. He visited the battleship Missouri (BB-63), which his daughter Margaret had christened the year before. After lunch on board the battleship he boarded the destroyer Renshaw (DD-499), which made a trip up and down a stretch of the Hudson River where dozens of U.S. warships were moored.

I said, "Sir, I'm not permitted to. I'm married"

He said, "Where do you live?" I had rented a room that, frankly, was pretty bad. When my wife came down to see me once, I wasn't there, so she called one of my friends to find me. He took her by there, and he said, "He's not here, and I'm not going to let you stay over here." So that's that kind of place it was.

But, in any event, the CO went and saw that, and he said, "What a dump." He went back and wrote a message to BuPers, and the next day I was told I could move to the BOQ.[*] Now, I think there must have been some rules set up that you could go to the BOQ, and probably the officers' club, by that time. But, frankly, the word just hadn't filtered down to me, and it hadn't filtered down to the yeoman in the office who stamped my orders "No quarters available," those kinds of things. But I moved into the BOQ, and I lived there for about two months, and then I was discharged.

Okay, now, getting back to what we were talking about a little bit earlier, there were a couple of reasons why I left the Navy at that point. Well, I guess the uppermost one in my mind was that I'd heard about the school business under the GI Bill of Rights.[†] So I had made up my mind that I was going back to college and finish. My father had tried awfully hard before that time. I didn't know what school cost really, but he paid it, and I knew he couldn't spare it, particularly while he was trying to raise four other people. So I was going to do it, and I was going to do it on my own.

Okay, that was the first reason that I was leaving the Navy. The second reason that I think I really left at that point in time was that nobody really asked me to stay. Now, I know of an awful lot of people who had not really made up their minds, and I was in that category. When you get down to a discharge station they'd ask, "Hey, have you ever thought about staying." And they'd stay longer. Nobody really asked me to stay. So I just said, "Well, I'll just go on out, and I will go back to school." Of course, that was my first choice. Shortly after I'd gotten out, I heard about a couple of college programs that the Navy offered.

---

[*] BuPers—Bureau of Naval Personnel.
[†] The GI Bill, officially the Servicemen's Readjustment Act of 1944, provided educational assistance and other benefits to all veterans honorably discharged with six or more months of active service after 16 September 1940.

I've often wondered if my career would have changed or if it'd been any other things that might have happened, if I had stayed in and tried to get into one of those college programs. In fact, I worked for a guy subsequently who went to Miami University in Ohio. That's where he got his degree from, based on the fact that he only had a high school degree, and he'd been elevated to officer status and did that. So all I can say is that I had basically made up my mind, because I did want to go back to college, and secondarily nobody asked me to stay. So I took my discharge and went home.

Now, one of the things that most of the concerns or businesses outside had said was that, "We will rehire you in your old job." So I went back to Friedman Marks as a clothes presser, because I got out in May, and school didn't really start until mid-June. So I might as well work for six weeks or so, right? In addition to that, this concern that made clothing had publicly announced that they would give each returning veteran a new suit of clothes. So I had to go back to earn my suit of clothes. But somehow word got out that, well, I was going back to school, so nobody ever asked me to come down for a fitting [laughter], so I never got my new suit. But I went back to Virginia Union with a determination to finish it as quickly as I could. I now had a wife and hopefully was going to have more family.

Paul Stillwell: And you were a lot more mature than when you'd been there before.

Admiral Gravely: A lot more mature. I had continued playing a little football. I'd played on a semi-pro team down in Norfolk, while the PC-1264 was down there, and had played against Virginia Union in one of our games down there. In fact, we beat Virginia Union 14 to nothing. And I talked to the coach, Sam Taylor, a guy I had liked. He had also been coach for Roger Gibbons, whom I mentioned earlier. So I'd heard about him. Gibbons was the guy who was from Prairie View who was my roommate. And so I kind of looked forward a little bit to playing football for Sam Taylor.

I worked at Friedman Marks, as I said, for six weeks; then I enrolled in Virginia Union for the summer. I had also decided I was going to live on the campus. My wife was teaching in a little place called Blackstone, Virginia, as a home economics teacher.

We had basically decided that she would work until I finished school, and then we would move someplace together, and either work together, and work certainly in the same city. But until that time we would just remain apart. Now, Blackstone is only about 60 miles away, so I got down there quite frequently. And, of course, she came to Richmond quite frequently.

Paul Stillwell: Did you have career goals in mind at that point?

Admiral Gravely: My career goal was that I would major in history, and I would be a football coach. Basically, football. I was not a basketball player. I wasn't very good at baseball either. But football was going to be my future, and most of the black high schools, which is where I expected to go, required a degree in something that you could teach, because they didn't just have people who were only football coaches. So that was the career goal. Living on a campus was different from living in town, but it was easy to get adjusted to it. I'd lived on the campus of UCLA. I'd lived on the campus basically at Columbia, no big problem.

I was not a big man on campus by any stretch of the imagination, despite the fact that I was about the only ensign they'd ever had there. [Laughter] But not really a big man on campus. I enjoyed it. As I said, I'd made up my mind I was going to concentrate on my studies, and I did. In fact, I probably had close to a B average when I finally graduated, because I made some good grades. I played football down there for two years, '46 and '47.

Each year, however, my father still being in the post office, would always remind me that the post office hires extra people during the Christmas holidays. As a matter of fact, I did it before I went into the service, and I started again after the service. I went down there and worked as a mail handler. I worked 12 hours a day as long as the Christmas holiday ran. I made a chunk of money.

In the year of 1947, my wife, who, as I said, had been teaching, decided that our commuting was just out of this world. So she felt that we should do something about settling in Richmond someplace, and obviously on the campus. Now, the main reason was that the campus had a group of trailers that they used for married couples. And so we took one of those trailers, and we lived there for that year, '47. Ninety dollars a month wasn't that hard to live off of either, because $90.00 a month was quite a bit in those days.

Paul Stillwell: Did she get a job in Richmond then?

Admiral Gravely: She worked a couple of times, not steadily. Being a home economics major, she worked as a helper for the guy who prepared the food for the students on campus. So she worked there for a while. She'd get winter jobs like at Christmas helping with one of the big stores when most of the kids weren't on campus. So she did quite a bit. Meantime, I had an athletic scholarship as well as this GI Bill, so we were fairly comfortable at that point in time.

Well, Christmas of 1947 rolled around, and, of course, my father got me my same old job again, and I went down there. During the holiday period someone said that the examinations for postal clerk and for railway mail clerk were open, and they were giving the tests such and such a day. So I said, "I'll go down and take them." So I took those tests, and, of course, then continued to work.

Well, for some reason, and I'm not sure what it was, at the beginning of 1948 I just continued to work 12 hours, and nobody told me Christmas was over. Then I looked very carefully at what I was doing, so as far as school was concerned, and I realized that I had to give up one or the other. I had enough credits to graduate that February, so I just said, "Well, I'll continue to work, and I won't go back to school from February to June." Which is what I did. Of course, I had earned my degree, so there was no problem there.

Well, I continued to work as a Christmas helper until March. Then they sent me a letter saying that, "We've had you on as a Christmas helper for so long; in short, Christmas is over. [Laughter] And there's nothing else we can find." So my wife and I moved down to her folks down in Roanoke, Virginia. I did some odd jobs, those kinds of things.

Then one day I got a letter from the post office saying that they wanted me in Richmond for some interviews, and I had been selected as a potential railway postal clerk. So I came up, faced the interviews, and started to work there in less than a month after I quit the post office. In about five months' time I was notified that I was a regular railway postal clerk. They were short of people after the war, so they took on a few temporary guys. It was a very, very enjoyable job. I enjoyed it. Here again, to some degree, you were breaking some barriers, but the people on the railway car just made me as comfortable as anything. They tried to teach me the various things about it. There was no problem whatsoever, and I became a member of a regular crew. I just enjoyed the hell out of it.

Paul Stillwell: Again, more separation from your wife, though.

Admiral Gravely: No, we moved to Richmond then. You see, she was in Roanoke, but when you said more separation, I should say this. The way they worked it, you had about an 80-hour period in two weeks. I'd go to work in Richmond at 4:00 o'clock in the afternoon on, say, Monday evening. The train left about 6:30 that afternoon, got to Washington here about 9:00 o'clock, and you worked about an hour. Then you went out in town, got your lunch, etc., came back, slept on the car until about 1:00, when you started again. Then a train got here about 6:00 o'clock in the morning. So you worked enough time in three days that you had the next three days off. It was sort of a split thing. So despite the fact that she didn't see much of me, say, Monday to Wednesday, I was home the rest of the week. So we had plenty of time together, no problem.

Paul Stillwell: Well, that's really an occupation that is outmoded today, so maybe you could describe more about what was involved in that.

Admiral Gravely: Okay. Of course, there was only one railway postal car on the train. You picked up loose mail from the post office, which for the most part was sorted and shipped on, and put it off the train at the next stop, say, Washington, D.C., which is where it came to the post office. But while you were coming up, you worked the mail, and we had three guys who worked the states. For example, just break it down by states—three guys doing that. Then you had like Washington City, and a couple of guys would break it down right to the post office. So you had that much of a head start.

The other thing, of course, was that as you came along the road, you got all of these little stops, towns and everything else, that had a mail pouch hung out there, and so you'd use the arm on the train to pick up that mail pouch, which was quite interesting when we would go by and do that. Those were the kinds of things we did. We handled the registered mail and everything else. For example, the registered mail clerk carried a little gun, and you had to get your signatures and those kinds of things. But working the mail, just like you did on regular city post office, on a much smaller scale. That's what we did. Each rail car that carried the mail was a small post office. We did everything that the other post offices did except to deliver the mail to individuals and sell stamps.

Paul Stillwell: In those days before zip codes you learned a lot of geography, I'm sure.

Admiral Gravely: You learned a lot of geography. I knew that there were about 1,900 post offices in Virginia, and I knew where every one of them was and how to route mail to them. So quite an interesting job.

Paul Stillwell: Was it unusual to have you as a college graduate in that kind of work?

Admiral Gravely: No. You've got to remember that in those days things were limited so far as employment of blacks were concerned, particularly on businesses. If you taught school, you taught school in a strictly black school, and there were few of those. If you were a lawyer, if you were fortunate enough to go into business with somebody, you probably had a job, but just as a lawyer you didn't expect to go into, say, some white firm as a lawyer or even as a law clerk. So getting into the post office—and as I said before, my father thought in terms of security and government service and those kinds of things—that was a fairly good job for me. There were debates, believe it or not, between my father and my father-in-law. My father-in-law said, "Hey, here's a young man who has prepared himself to teach and coach, and he ought to do that. He owes it not only to himself, but to a lot of people who have helped him."

My father would always say, "Yes, but whether he wears dungarees or a blue suit, the guy is making a hell of a lot more money and has got more security, and can take care of your daughter better as a regular postal clerk." [Laughter] And I think my father won the argument.

Well, I did that for about a year, and one day I got this letter from the Navy Department saying, "We plan to select 25 young Negro officers to bring them on active duty for one year, and place each of them in a recruiting station. Would you like to come back on active duty? If so, write a letter requesting it."

I thought about that for a while, and I said, "It'll be almost a year's vacation, and so why not? Why not do that?"

I still had a certain amount of love for the Navy. I missed the Navy atmosphere. Despite the fact that I really hadn't gotten a real flavor of Navy life, I did miss what little I'd seen. I should have told you this, that when I was discharged it was basically released to inactive duty, and, of course, I had a reserve commission. I had applied for a reserve two weeks' active duty program on two occasions. On one I was accepted, and was at the point wherein I was awaiting orders. But there were no funds available, so I had missed on it. In the meantime, I'd kept up enough so that I went over and got my reserve jaygee promotion and those kinds of things.

Paul Stillwell: Did you drill at all?

Admiral Gravely: I did not drill. I guess they had the paid drillers, etc., but I did not. I'm not sure, frankly, in Richmond that I would have been very well accepted as a driller, unless there was a set of orders which said, "You will do this." But, in any event, I applied so that I would come on active duty. And I think that here again funds probably shortchanged the program, but there were at least five young black officers who came back on active duty. In this program all of us were jaygees, I believe. I was, of course, living in Richmond, so I guess that's the reason they sent me to Washington, D.C. So I came to the recruiting station here as assistant to the officer in charge for recruiting. It didn't specifically say minorities or blacks or anything like that, but I knew that's what my forte was, and that's where I was to work.

Now, coming back into the Navy, really, it surprised me what I found. This was in 1949, when I reported for active duty, and I was very pleased with what happened in that the commanding officer said to me, "Have you found a place to stay yet?"

I said, "No, sir, I have not." I said, "I expect to try to find a room tonight, sir."

He said, "Well, what do you mean?" He said, "Are you going to have your wife?"

I said, "No. My wife is working, and she's going to stay down there, and I'm going to sort of bach it until we decide whether or not she wants to come here, and whether or not I'm going to stay more than a year."

He said, "Well, wait a minute. Chief, take Lieutenant (j.g.) Gravely over to the officers' BOQ and get him squared away." I was really flabbergasted that here I was going to live in the BOQ. I'd never been able to do that except, as I said, I got into one in Norfolk. But I didn't expect that the Navy had really advanced to the point wherein that was sort of routine. And I wasn't ready to try at that point in time. But welcomed aboard in a big way, introduced around the office, etc.

Now, everything went fine except for one minor thing, and I'm glad it came up. We had weekly staff meetings, just like they do every place else. I'd been around there for about two weeks, and the senior enlisted recruiter, who was a white guy, said at the meeting one day, "Captain, you know, Lieutenant (j.g.) Gravely is here, and I assume that he is supposed to enlist Negro recruits. Basically that's his job. But now can he enlist white recruits? And can he swear in white as well as Negro recruits?"

The commanding officer stuttered for about a couple minutes, and he said, "Lieutenant (j.g.) Gravely is assistant officer in charge of this recruiting station, and he can enlist anybody you guys get." And, frankly, I really think that that made—in fact, I know—that made my day, but it certainly made the difference in a successful tour versus one that wasn't.

There began to be a little bit more of a move toward social activity, but not from the officers, because there were about three of us there, and we had some social affairs in maybe a hotel or something like that. But there were a couple of chiefs around here, and I must tell you, I never thought of us officers associating with enlisted men, even after the thing that happened down there in Florida. But a couple of them invited me into their homes. And I met a couple of them. Frankly, I know where both of them are today, and we still hear from each other.

But, in general, recruiting is recruiting. I'm not sure I got any more people than anybody else, but I got my share. The quota around here was very small at that point in time. It actually was eight men a month, and six of them had to be high school graduates. Of course, it didn't say about the other two, but certainly if they could pass the test, the other two were accepted.

Now, the one significant thing that happened during that tour was that the Korean War broke out.* As a result, I was extended another year. A second significant thing was that the quota just ballooned, and we were told to get as many men as we could. So we were kicking that one around one day when the commanding officer just basically asked a question, "How do you sell the Navy?"

I'm not sure who said it, but some guy said, "Well, we've got to put more guys on the street." And that's right. We've got to get more people to ask more people. The way to ask them is to see them, and walk around all day.

So the commanding officer made the decision and said, "Okay, I want everybody out on the street that's not assigned to a regular sub recruiting station." And he said, "Sam, that means you too."

I said, "Sir, I don't think you really want me to do that, because, as you well know, there are no officers out doing this thing. You mean the chiefs?"

He said, "No, no, no, I mean you too."

I said, "Okay. Yes, sir." And then I said, "You know what? Now, it seems to me that with conditions being what they are, that probably I would be more successful if I went into a predominantly Negro area and set up a small recruiting station in that area, where they would all be coming by, and I don't really have to walk the streets."

He said, "Okay, do what you can."

"Thank you, sir."

---

* The Korean War began on 25 June 1950, when six North Korean infantry division and three border constabulary brigades invaded the South Korea. The troops were supported by approximately 100 Russian-made T-34 tanks. In New York that same day the United Nations Security Council adopted a resolution condemning the invasion.

So I went up to the area of about 14th and U, which is in northwest there, and I found a government building. I went into that government building, and I talked to the guy in charge there. In the meantime, I was a lieutenant then, so I had a big two bars on. He said, "You know, that might be a good idea. You can set up down the corridor."

So I said, "Fine." I went back and I told the commanding officer, and he agreed with it. There was a black chief petty officer, a reserve who had been recalled for the Korean War, and he and I went up there and set up our station. Well, we'd been in there for about two or three days, I guess, when in walked a guy that I knew really didn't want to enlist in the Navy. But at the same time, he said he did, so we began to process him. We went through all the papers and everything else to where he was supposed to come up for his physical in the next couple of days. And he didn't show. We didn't pay any attention to that, but one day I got this frantic call from the commanding officer: "Come back to the recruiting station right away."

"Yes, sir." So I went back there.

He said, "I'm taking you out of there."

I said, "Oh?"

He said, "Well, look at this." Well, the Chicago Defender is a predominantly black paper out of Chicago, and they had an article in there. "Navy sets up segregated recruiting station." [Laughter] And obviously this guy was a reporter who did that. Well, the station remained open for a while, but the solution obviously was that two blacks couldn't be in there running a recruiting station, so we sent a young white yeoman up there, and I then came back to the station.

The other part of this job was that very shortly after the Korean War started the naval officer recruiting stations and the naval officer procurement stations, which were separate activities at that time, became combined. So we had a staff of about three additional officers. So about six or seven were there, and we handled the ROTC program. We handled the various other procurement programs, and so I got kind of familiar with those, as well as did a lot of work in processing people for that—not concentrating on blacks or anything else. I helped with the interview of the ROTC types who were in that program. Helped with all the other programs. Just, just really a great experience for me.

We had one officer who was much older than I. He was a temporary officer who was recalled to active duty. He and I had a ball, we did really. I really socialized with the guy, because we both lived at the BOQ, and we could ride back and forth together. We could have our dinner together, and then sit around a bar together. So it was a good tour.

I decided, though, close to the end of that tour, which was my second year there, that I wasn't really being truthful with myself. Here I was, a Navy recruiter who really hasn't seen very much Navy. So rather than just sit around that recruiting station and constantly go to these high schools and other places, talking to these kids about things, the Navy ROTC program and the enlisted programs, maybe I ought to go out and see some of these things, and see if I really thought they are as good as I was telling these kids they were. So I volunteered for sea duty, and in a very short order I received a set of orders sending me to the USS Iowa via comm school out in Monterey.*

Paul Stillwell: There's one thing I'd like to ask you before that.

Admiral Gravely: Yes.

Paul Stillwell: In trying to sell Navy to potential black recruits, were you able to make the point that it was now a better, more appealing Navy to join than the one that you had gotten into eight or ten years earlier?

Admiral Gravely: Well, you did that sort of indirectly by giving a little history of the Navy. You could talk in terms of what the Navy was like in 1941, after Pearl Harbor, when thousands of people went to various recruiting stations. Unfortunately, blacks were all turned away, etc. Then I could bring them through my experience at Great Lakes and at Hampton, and ultimately I got commissioned and those kinds of things. What you really tried to tell them was that, "Hey, there's an opportunity out here, and there's more opportunities opening up all the time. This is really not necessarily the thing that you've got to do, but you ought to look at it as a viable alternative when you get out of high

---

* Comm—communications.

school." That was the approach that I took most of the time. Then I told them that, yes, it was a little difficult years ago, it is much brighter today than it was then. And, of course, it was.

Paul Stillwell: Did you also sell them the idea of learning a trade, which had appealed to you?

Admiral Gravely: You sold the idea of learning a trade, travel, security, and those kinds of things, because those were what we were advertising in those days. And, of course, I could tell them about my experience and some of my travels. In those days particularly, when you talked to the young black high school guy, he'd never left his hometown. I didn't leave my hometown, really, except for a little rural place where my mother had been born, until I traveled with the college football team. That was the first time I really went someplace. So you could talk in terms of travel, despite the fact that I hadn't been on any ships except the PC-1264. But San Diego, Key West, those kinds of things, and some of the great things that had happened to me. And how many people we got as a result of that, I couldn't give you an answer on that. But Jerry Thomas was a '51 graduate from the ROTC program, so he might have been somebody who was talked to by, say, the New York recruiter.*

Paul Stillwell: Did you sell it as an attractive alternative to being drafted during wartime?

Admiral Gravely: No, didn't sell it as that. Sold it as an alternative to something else in life, and really an opportunity. Early responsibility was also one of the things we sold. You've got to remember that most of these people weren't looking forward to some responsibility other than teach another bunch of kids. I know that when I went to high

---

* Ensign Gerald E. Thomas, USN, was commissioned in June 1951 upon graduation from Harvard University. He was the first black officer to be commissioned through the NROTC program of an Ivy League university. In early 1974, three years after Gravely, he was selected as the U.S. Navy's second black admiral. He retired from active duty as a rear admiral in 1981 and subsequently became a member of the faculty at Yale University.

school, you couldn't look much past being a preacher, a doctor, or a teacher. That was about it, really. The lawyer you didn't look at. I can't think of a single one in my high school classmates who became a lawyer. I can think of many, many schoolteachers and certainly some doctors. There are a lot probably doing different things, but it's because they changed their careers later in life. Well, obviously, the good old government service was a big one, post office. You didn't think of terms of say the Department of Education or the Department of Environmental Sciences, or some of that crap, but the post office was a big thing.

Paul Stillwell: The very fact that you were recalled to active duty suggests that the Navy was making more of an effort to get black recruits than it had been.

Admiral Gravely: It was. You've got to remember now it was 1948, wasn't it, that Truman signed the bill that integrated the services as a presidential directive.[*] Well, as a result of that presidential directive, the Navy, which had very, very few blacks other than stewards, had to change. And it was losing its stewards at about that time, because blacks just weren't enlisting to be stewards. Some few did. It wasn't too long after that, if not about that time, that we began to have the tie with the Philippine government, wherein we brought in a lot of Filipino stewards. To some degree, blacks were being pushed out of that sphere of employment, as well as they wanted to go anyway.

So with that integration of the services, the Navy had to do something, and so it did. As I said, they tried to recall 25, but I guess funds got hit, so they recalled these five, and then we made trips all over the county. We went down south to those high schools, etc., and tried to talk blacks into enlisting, as well as those who we thought could make good officer candidates into ROTC programs, and advised them of the possibilities there, etc.

---

[*] On 26 July 1948, President Harry S. Truman issued Executive Order 9981, which said, "It is hereby declared that there shall be equality of treatment and opportunity for all persons in the armed services without regard to race, color, religion, or national origin."

Samuel L. Gravely, Jr., Interview #1 (6/25/86) – Page 56

Paul Stillwell: Did you have any later contact with the people that you had influenced to go into the service?

Admiral Gravely: I've seen a couple, and I can't remember any specific names or anything like that. But it's just impossible to have done that for two years and not run across a couple guys. I've seen my name in guys' service jackets when I would be reenlisting them or for some other reason. I'll be darned, here's a guy I enlisted. You know, pass a few words and gone again.

Paul Stillwell: You mentioned that you had gone to this comm course on the way to the Iowa.

Admiral Gravely: Yes, right. It was about a 16-week course in communications, en route to the Iowa. I got to Monterey, and Monterey was a very, very interesting place to me.* I enjoyed the tour out there. One of my classmates ultimately became an admiral there. In fact, he got selected a year before I did, and so we talk all the time about our experiences out there.

Paul Stillwell: Who was that?

Admiral Gravely: A guy by the name of Spence Matthews.†
 Things, again, were not that hard for me. I enjoyed that course. We did socialize and a lot of things like that. In the meantime, my wife stayed back on the East Coast here. Once I can remember being at the club with a group of guys. We'd had a little party going. We had been shooting the breeze, and they had their wives there. For some reason I decided to call my wife. So I searched around and found enough change to call her. I was just outside of the bar, making this phone call. Suddenly the telephone booth was upside down. Well, these guys were just playing a prank, turning the telephone booth. I was talking to my wife, and she said, "I can't hear you."

---
* Monterey, California, was the site of a General Line School course for naval officers.
† Lieutenant Herbert Spencer Matthews, Jr., USN, who, like Gravely, was a former enlisted man.

I said, "You'd probably hear me better if this telephone booth was right side up." [Laughter] Of course, they'd all disappeared, because they expected me to come charging out of there like a bull, which I probably did. But it was just all in good fun. We had a great group of guys, about 15 of us, I guess, in that course. We all enjoyed it very much. It was strictly Monterey. You were almost a college student again, except that you did wear uniforms all day. I went to San Francisco a couple of times with a couple of my classmates. We would spend the weekend and chase around bars and those kinds of things. I can't think of anything else that might be of importance there.

Paul Stillwell: You were telling me earlier that you had the perception that blacks were relegated to communication as a less desirable specialty than some of the others.

Admiral Gravely: Yes. Obviously one of the reasons that I was sent to Monterey in communications was because I'd been a communicator on the PC. Now, I had fleeted up to executive officer before I left there. But I still had that feeling—particularly after I got aboard a couple of ships, and I watched what happened to people who were sent down as assistant comm officer, or who were sent as a cryptographer, and those kinds of things—that the Navy really didn't pick its best people for that. Probably that also was why I went to communications rather than going, say, to one of the operational-type schools, or a short course in engineering or something like that and going to the Iowa in something else other than the communications department. But if that's the way it was, so be it.

I left the area. School was interrupted by the Christmas holidays or something, so I had a couple of weeks to kick around. Went down to Los Angeles a couple of times. But, in any event, I left there in January, as I recall, to report aboard the Iowa. Most of the transportation was done by train. So I discovered that I would never make Long Beach in time with my luggage. So I dragged my feet a little bit, and as I got into the Long Beach Harbor, there was the Iowa sailing out of the harbor.

So I missed it, and then went in to report to ComNavBase, who gave me a very interesting week.* That week was as an assistant to one of the pilots. I worked with this pilot, and we'd go out on board the ship, give them the port directories and all the rest of

---

* ComNavBase—Commander Naval Base.

that stuff. Then I could watch this guy handle that ship. It was the greatest thing in the world. I really enjoyed it.

Plus the fact that there was a Navy small boat, and I guess it was about an 80-footer, or something like that, that made the trip from Long Beach to San Clemente, and I was put in charge of that one day. And, boy, I really felt great about it. Here I was, already commanding officer of this small vessel to make this cruise. [Laughter] Of course, they had about a first class who was really in charge of the boat. And before it was over with, he knew that I was also in charge at that point in time, because we did have a couple of discussions of when I thought at one point that he wasn't handling it as safely as I thought he should. So I had to bring him up short a couple of times, but we made it.

Well, when I got in that weekend, the Iowa had just come back in, so I was transferred over and I went aboard the Iowa.*

Paul Stillwell: She was just newly in commission at that point, wasn't she?

Admiral Gravely: She'd been in commission for about five months. As I recall, she was commissioned something like about September of 1951. They'd had a chance to go down through their shakedown cruise down in San Diego, and she was just making some routine operations at that point in time. In fact, we were about two months away from the deployment when I went aboard.

I went aboard her, and Captain Smedberg was the skipper at that point in time.† And, of course, the first thing you do on ships that size is go in to see the exec, and he was great. He took me up, and I talked to the captain. They all welcomed me aboard, etc. I began to meet the officers in the wardroom, and no problems. They all welcomed me aboard.

---

* USS Iowa (BB-61), the lead ship of her class of battleships, was originally commissioned 22 February 1943. She had a standard displacement of 45,000 tons and full-load displacement of 57,600 tons. She was 887 feet long and 108 feet in the beam. Her top speed was 33 knots. She was decommissioned in 1948 and put into the reserve fleet.
† Captain William R. Smedberg III, USN, commanded the battleship Iowa (BB-61) from the time of her recommissioning on 25 August 1951 to 29 July 1952. The oral history of Smedberg, who retired as a vice admiral, is in the Naval Institute collection.

The little thing that I found out subsequently, was that there had been a letter sent from the Chief of Naval Personnel advising them that I was coming aboard. And apparently there'd been a meeting in the wardroom to prepare these officers for this young Negro officer who was coming aboard. I think that worked well, except for the one thing that I learned later. I saw the letter which had been written by BuPers, and I was discussing it with my roommate, Herb Yarbrough.[*] And he said that he was the only guy who would agree to room with me. Now, he was not a Naval Academy guy. Maybe a Naval Academy guy would not have done that. He was an ex-enlisted man who had gotten a regular Navy commission. And, of course, I think we talked a little bit about the old Navy versus what happened when the reservists came in, etc.

Paul Stillwell: Did you have a feeling that you were under a great degree of scrutiny in that job?

Admiral Gravely: Some scrutiny, but I don't think anybody really watched my every move or any of those kinds of things. I went on liberty by myself. That was no change.

When I arrived there, they didn't have a radio officer. In fact, I came on, and I reported as the assistant radio officer. Now, a ship of that size had a communication officer, who was a lieutenant commander; they had a radio officer who was normally a lieutenant; they normally had a signal officer who was a lieutenant. They had at least one warrant radio electrician attached to the group, and they had an electronics department with two or three radio electronics types in that. We normally got two or three other JOs as communication watch officers basically.[†] So you had a CR division with about 40 people and with really about four or five officers in that group. But we never before had a guy with the title of assistant radio officer. Well, the radio officer at that time was acting as comm officer, and so I became his assistant.

Now, within about a week of my arrival, in came a lieutenant commander who was to be the communications officer. I happened to be talking to him one day, and I guess I was making a little complaint. Basically, having just gotten out of comm school,

---

[*] Lieutenant Herbert A. Yarbrough, USN.
[†] JOs—junior officers.

I felt that the guy who was the radio officer—and I guess I'd told him initially—but I didn't think he knew how to write a comm plan. Now, he had not been to this great school at Monterey like I had been, and he did write something that passed as a comm plan, but I was telling my boss that I felt that way, so he said, "Well, you do it then, obviously." And, of course, I did from then on.

But somehow in the discussion we got to talking about race. And I never will forget it, because Gene Horrall said, "Sam, I might as well tell you now. I don't give a goddamn whether you're red, green, black or what color you are. All I want is a radio officer, and you are it."[*]

"Yes, sir." He and I had relations that were very close until just recently when I haven't heard from him in, say, a year. But I know if I went to Gene Horrall's house today, Gene Horrall would welcome me in there. In fact, he was the godfather to one of my sons.

Paul Stillwell: Did that ease the other guy out?

Admiral Gravely: Well, I guess I'm getting a little ahead of myself, because what happened was that very shortly after I got there, and I think it might have happened before Gene and I had the discussion, the guy who was radio officer got orders to another ship. When his orders came, for some reason he did not want to leave. Now, I can't tell you why. He must have had some personal reasons for not wanting to leave. But somehow a message was sent off the ship, saying that they could not afford to lose this officer, because we were just getting ready to go on deployment, and we needed an experienced radio officer to work with the Com7thFlt people while we were out there.[†]

The ship requested non-detachment of this guy, and a message came back from BuPers which said, "Your so-and-so, negative, recommend Lieutenant Gravely as a relief." The message then went back from the Iowa which said that whereas I was a recent graduate of comm school, that I had postal service and those kinds of things.

---

[*] Lieutenant Commander Eugene F. Horrall, USN, was the new communication officer.
[†] Com7thFlt—Commander Seventh Fleet. The Iowa was due to serve as the fleet commander's flagship once she deployed to the Western Pacific.

Despite the fact that I felt I was a good officer, they didn't feel that I had the experience.

A message came back from BuPers the third time said, "In view of the fact that you have three radio electricians aboard, Lieutenant Gravely having finished comm school at Monterey, your signal officer has also finished comm school at Monterey, that your so-and-so declined. Lieutenant Gravely will be his relief." Fine. So I got to be his relief. I think that that was about the time Gene Horrall and I talked about me, and he made the statement he really didn't care what color I was; all he wanted was a radio officer.

Paul Stillwell: Well, it makes you wonder, though, who was sending those messages trying to keep the other guy.

Admiral Gravely: Well, I don't think that it was really Gene who was trying to keep him. I think it was someplace between the ops officer and the guy himself, who really didn't want to leave. I don't know how long he came before commissioning, but actually he'd only operated with the ship for about five months, and he was pretty comfortable where he was. Herb Yarbrough was a very, very fine gentleman, and I relieved him a second time later on. So I liked him. I just think that he didn't want to move.

Paul Stillwell: So it was more to help him than anything else.

Admiral Gravely: Yes, I think it was more to help him than for anybody to say that I wasn't qualified to do something. But, anyway, BuPers made the decision, and, of course, I think I worked as close with Lieutenant Commander Horrall as I've ever worked with anyone in my life. I think he respected me, and I certainly respected him, and we got to be big friends. Our families are friends today. He was godparent to one of my children.

Iowa deployed. Of course, I was the radio officer, so I didn't get a chance to really spend much time on the bridge. Certainly not as a routine watch officer. But what happened was that the general quarters spot for the communicator was the bridge, and our communicator preferred, or maybe he felt that with his experience he could run the radio shack better than I could, so he preferred that he go to the radio shack, and I swapped with him, and I went to the bridge during general quarters.

Well, here again was just a great learning experience for me, because I could watch those guys handling that big 45,000-ton battleship, and I really got a kick out of watching them. I really also got fairly familiar with the signal book, which really helped me in my next job, because my next job was as communication officer. And that was my GQ station. There was no way for me to send some junior officer up there to do it. So I got a real feel for the sea. I knew that I loved it, and I knew that if there was ever an opportunity for me to apply for the regular Navy, that I would. And so I sort of awaited my chance. Well, we went on the deployment. There was nothing really significant about that deployment against what the other battleships were doing.

Paul Stillwell: It was pretty much shore bombardment and Task Force 77.[*]

Admiral Gravely: Task Force 77 ops, shore bombardment. Of course, we had Com7thFlt aboard. And I got a chance to work a little bit with the admiral, and it was—

Paul Stillwell: Jocko Clark.[†]

Admiral Gravely: Jocko Clark, that's right.

Paul Stillwell: What do you recall about him?

Admiral Gravely: Well, I remember once there was a discussion between his CIC people and his radio officer, and I got invited up for some reason while I was radio officer on the Iowa.[‡] We were talking about air controlling of the various destroyers that we were assigned. And for some reason I felt that one of those destroyers should have been able to handle the air control assignments for the group. There weren't that many. And when

---

[*] Task Force 77 is the fast carrier striking force of the U.S. Seventh Fleet.
[†] Vice Admiral Joseph J. Clark, USN, served as Commander Seventh Fleet from 10 May 1952 to 1 December 1953.
[‡] CIC—combat information center.

we were talking about them, Admiral Clark said something, and I said, "Well, why can't destroyer so-and-so handle it?"

I was told that, "Hey, I'll make the decision on who handles it. All I want to know from you is, does the guy have equipment enough to do it?"

"Yes, sir. Fine." But I respected the man, certainly, because he was a great admiral.

The other significant thing that I can remember happened was missing a movement report. I made all of the movement reports on board the ship. And, of course, if you missed one, you immediately got a growl, and if it was any way screwed up, somebody would say plots over land, or you couldn't possibly make your ETA based on your speed, etc., do it again.[*] It was kind of embarrassing, and ships didn't like to receive those kinds of reactions. But, in any event, I watched them very carefully. But on this particular day the flag radio officer cornered me, and we were discussing the assignment of one of my men. Then, with the movement report in my pocket, getting ready to go to the bridge, somehow I got turned around, and I didn't go to the bridge. But the next day I discovered that I hadn't done it.

Paul Stillwell: You'd put it in your pocket.

Admiral Gravely: I found it in my pocket. It was the next morning when I was getting up, showering, etc., changing. So I quickly went down, upped the precedence to op immediate, sent it out, and then decided that I'd better tell somebody about it. Of course, I told my boss, who then said go tell Commander Rock, who was ops officer, and then we went to see the captain.[†] The captain gave me a little lecture on the importance of getting these out, and never doing that again. Fine.

Unfortunately, that movement report didn't get there in time, and so we were reported, along with our destroyer escort, as two Russian cruisers going through the Tsugaru Straits.[‡] The Air Force came out en masse, and, of course, we went to GQ, the

---
[*] ETA—estimated time of arrival.
[†] Commander Herman K. Rock, USN.
[‡] Tsugaru Strait is between the Japanese islands of Honshu and Hokkaido.

whole bit. But finally it was all sorted out, and, of course, Admiral Clark wanted to know what had happened. And, of course, it was my delay of that movement report.

Paul Stillwell: Didn't you also miss getting mail at the next port?

Admiral Gravely: That's right. We didn't get our mail at the next port, and I guess that's what brought it really to Admiral Clark's attention more than anything else. I survived it. I always felt that a couple of people either wanted me reprimanded or certainly chewed out, but Captain Smedberg felt, I believe, that he had already done that, so there was no sense in doing anything else, despite the fact that we didn't get that mail.

Paul Stillwell: What are your recollections of Smedberg? He's a really enthusiastic individual.

Admiral Gravely: Yes. Smedberg was very enthusiastic. And this is only hearsay, but I guess in his recommissioning speech he made a statement something like, "All of you guys now have at least one chance. Everybody starts out equal here." As a result, he had a lot of masts, because everybody took their one chance.* And when I came aboard, he certainly was not a hard man by any stretch of the imagination, but sailors knew that he was serious. He was just a tremendous ship handler, had all kinds of leadership abilities, and I liked him. He was just a great skipper, really. A really good man.

We had a fairly good team of people on board there. The ops officer was a big man who was also a good man. Gene Horrall, my boss, was tremendous. Most people tried to help me. I got into one little minor scrape in the wardroom with a Marine who said something that I didn't think he should have said, and we got into it. He wanted to meet me down on some corner, but I knew I should stay out of that kind of trouble. One of my best friends was a guy who was the medical service officer aboard. In fact, one thing I remember him doing for me was that he made me drink my coffee black, with no

---

* Captain's mast is a sort of court in which the commanding officer of a unit listens to requests, awards non-judicial punishment, or issues commendations. Most often captain's mast is used for punishment of lesser offenses than those that merit courts-martial

Samuel L. Gravely, Jr., Interview #1 (6/25/86) – Page 65

sugar, because I was putting on the weight with high blood pressure and those kinds of things, how to do that. It was a great group. I don't have any feeling other than goodness at having met and been associated with those guys.

Paul Stillwell: What kind of liberty experiences did you have overseas?

Admiral Gravely: Well, Yokosuka and Sasebo were basically the liberty ports.* I certainly went to the local clubs and those kinds of things. Went most of the time alone, although probably I was coming back with somebody, because I generally had to carry somebody. I wasn't a big drinker or anything like that. I really didn't get out into the towns other than to do some shopping. I didn't have any bad experiences. I was an American sailor.

I can remember going ashore from the Toledo, my next ship. I'd be sitting around bars talking to some girls with a big snickering going on, and I couldn't figure out what was going on. My roommate, who was with me at that time, said that they were trying to find out if Negroes really had tails, because that was one of the stories. The Iowa was a great ship. I ultimately got a new skipper, just like anybody else does. Captain Joshua Cooper, who, frankly, was more friendly—if that could be possible—and greater to me, really, than Admiral Smedberg.† He was particularly pleased in that that movement report thing was well handled. Because, and maybe you'd better get that little article out of that thing that you sent me.‡

Paul Stillwell: Well, he spoke very warmly of you, and it sounded almost as if you were the protocol officer too.

Admiral Gravely: No, I wasn't the protocol officer, but he knew that he could count on me if something came up. Joshua Cooper ultimately did me a couple of favors, too, and

---

* Yokosuka and Sasebo were the two principal Japanese ports that the U.S. Navy used as Far East support bases during the Korean War.
† Captain Joshua W. Cooper, USN, commanded the Iowa from 29 July 1952 to 8 July 1953. The oral history of Cooper, who retired as a rear admiral, is in the Naval Institute collection.
‡ Joshua Cooper, "As I Recall . . . Commanding the Iowa," U.S. Naval Institute Proceedings, May 1984, pages 310, 313-314, 316.

I'll talk about that a little later. But he was just a tremendous leader. He had the proper carriage, straight like a ramrod, the whole bit, and I really did like him. I can remember that when we got back to Long Beach, we had the ship's party, and Joshua Cooper made sure that I was well taken care of. I don't know, he thought he had to mother me, I guess. But he did, and so I had a great tour.

Paul Stillwell: How would you compare the communications demands operating as a single ship, as opposed to when you were the flagship for the fleet?

Admiral Gravely: Well, when you are the flagship for the fleet, the communications requirements are trebled compared to operating alone. Operating alone you're copying the fleet broadcast. You don't have anybody in company, so you don't have to worry about UHF that much, and copying 500 and those kinds of things.* But as a flagship, you're copying broadcasts for yourself, you're guarding for also the fleet commander. He's got a half a dozen titles and those kinds of things, so you're getting three, four times as much traffic, which you've got to be alert to make sure you get.

In addition to that, usually the flagship is going to have a couple other ships dragging around with it. So you had to have instantaneous communication to those things, as well as instantaneous communications for everything. It's a much more demanding job than just driving around independently. You've normally got enough equipment. Part of your problem is keeping it up and keeping it operating. We had a couple of good radio electronics technicians aboard, as well as some good radiomen who could shift those frequencies at the snap of your finger, who worked together to do a good job. So except for at times not having enough of the proper equipment on board, you didn't have any major problems with broadcasts.

HF broadcast was quite unreliable, so you missed a message every once in a while, but somehow, using hook or crook, you'd get it in fairly short time.† We would hate to miss a message that said move, because you were to move instantaneously. Sometimes you might miss one of those, but you go through hell and high water, and you

---

* UHF—ultra-high frequency. The international distress frequency was 500 kilocycles.
† HF—high frequency.

ask somebody to send it again, if you think you've missed something. Certainly the communications requirements of working for any admiral or any commander are much greater than just working on a single ship.

Paul Stillwell: Could you talk about the crypto requirements of the job?

Admiral Gravely: Well, normally when Seventh Fleet came aboard, instead of having a crypto watch officer, as we normally did, whose basic job was to break a few messages, you were breaking messages 24 hours a day.[*] A couple of the admirals I worked for, and I think Jocko Clark was one, not only wanted to look at all of their own traffic, but he wanted to see everything that was on that fox file.[†] It meant that we, the ship, had to supply six CWOs, or crypto watch officers, not communications watch officers—it was a little different. But six people in crypto during any one specific day, which meant that we had at least two people on watch all the time.

    Frankly, I contended, and you've seen me with glasses on, that I really lost my eyesight as a result of being in that little dark hole down there, sitting down breaking messages. Seventh Fleet not only had his own people on board with special communications circuits and crypto people, but we in our place supplied six additional to augment that staff.

Paul Stillwell: And crypto involved a tedious system back then.

Admiral Gravely: It was a tedious system. You broke them all by hand. You didn't have anything that would automatically do it like we do it today. So you sat there. And the easy messages to break, I guess to some degree, were those that came in on a fox file, because you got a considerable number of those by teletype. And you could really read the smooth teletype, which was fairly smooth. But then when you got them CW—and a

---

[*] In this context, "break" means to decrypt a coded message.
[†] "Fox" was the word for the letter F in the phonetic alphabet of the day. The fox schedule referred to the messages sent on the fleet broadcast.

guy thinks he's got an E and it's an A, and those kinds of things.* It got to be a mess. But we had some good people who did the job, and that's all you could ask for.

Paul Stillwell: Did you become fairly proficient technically from your exposure to the radio equipment?

Admiral Gravely: It was that and that alone, because I didn't have a technical background in communications. We have a course now that is about a year and a half or two years, where we get our PG in communications management, which goes into the technical aspects of it.† Mine came from, basically, working with the equipment, and watching the radio electrician, the electronics technicians, as well as the radiomen do the job. I got to the point wherein I could really set up a frequency on a transmitter, and I got to tell you, I could patch them as fast as anybody else could. So I knew my equipment fairly well, and I knew all of the requirements and the limitations and those kinds of things.

Paul Stillwell: Well, Admiral, we're right at the end of the tape. Maybe we could resume the tale of the Iowa the next time.

Admiral Gravely: Okay, okay. That sounds pretty good.

---

* CW, or continuous wave, referred to a type of radio wave interrupted into the dots and dashes of the Morse code for the purpose of communication.
† PG—postgraduate.

Interview Number 2 with Vice Admiral Samuel L. Gravely, Jr., U.S. Navy (Retired)
Place: Admiral Gravely's office in Burke, Virginia
Date: Monday, 7 July 1986
Interviewer: Paul Stillwell

Paul Stillwell: Admiral, to resume our discussion of the Iowa from last time, you faced a situation there that any Navy man would on a deployment, and that was coping with the separation period from your family. How did you deal with that?

Admiral Gravely: Well, when I came back in the Navy in 1949, my wife went down to southwest Virginia to take a job as an agricultural extension agent for Southampton County. She lived in Franklin, Virginia. When I got the orders two years later to go to the Iowa, we sat and discussed it. She wasn't quite ready to leave the job, and I faced a rather uncertain future so far as going to the Iowa was concerned. So we basically decided that we would leave things at the status quo. I knew a little bit about the Iowa's schedule. For example, I knew that shortly after I got aboard she would deploy, and I would be gone for roughly seven or eight months. But I felt when I got back that we would then reconsider and decide what we really wanted to do.

Of course, as I said earlier, going aboard the Iowa was my choice. Because of having been in recruiting for two years, and trying to tell people about the Navy, I really wanted to see something about the Navy and see if I liked it as much as I was trying to tell people that I liked it. The Iowa did a normal deployment to Korea. We went to the line about three times, which was about normal. You'd go up to the line, operate with CTF 77.[*] Did an awful lot of shore bombardment and those kinds of things.

I can remember specifically one incident, and that involved a destroyer—I think it was the Tucker—that had been fired on at Wonsan Harbor.[†] We went alongside this destroyer to take off the wounded, etc. I was really flabbergasted, because this was the

---

[*] CTF 77—Commander Task Force 77, the fast carrier task force.
[†] On 28 June 1951, when the Iowa and the destroyer Henry W. Tucker (DDR-875) were firing shore bombardment from inside Wonsan Harbor, North Korea, the destroyer was hit by six enemy shells. Two crewmen were wounded, and the destroyer's radar equipment was heavily damaged.

first time I really saw men bleeding. I was looking over the port side, because she was alongside our port. As I looked, I saw the legs of a man hanging on a life raft, and I didn't see the rest of him. It almost made you sick to see something like that. But there was nothing unusual about the deployment. It was normal, as I said, CTF 77 ops, and certainly the shore bombardment.

Paul Stillwell: Did you have any children yet by that point?

Admiral Gravely: No, that happened later. We'd been married about three years. We sort of wondered why we didn't have children, but didn't really concern ourselves with it.

Paul Stillwell: I imagine you were keeping up with the correspondence.

Admiral Gravely: Yes, we wrote regularly, which was certainly a source of enjoyment to hear that everything was fine back home. My wife is quite independent. She's not a dependent, nagging, crying wife. And I guess about this time we really made some decisions about life, and that is that no matter what I did, so long as I liked it and it was honorable, that I would do my thing and she would do her thing, until it interfered with what we were doing, and then we'd make some more decisions about it.

Paul Stillwell: It's a blessing to have that kind of support back home.

Admiral Gravely: That's right. That was a real blessing to have her back there, and know that she was well and she was going to take care of herself. Then there was no problem—no problem whatsoever.

Paul Stillwell: Do you have any recollections of being fired upon there at Wonsan. Battleships typically were.

Admiral Gravely: I don't think the _Iowa_ was fired on during the whole time we were out there. If the enemy doesn't have much of a navy, there's not much of a naval battle. We exchanged shore bombardment, but I don't remember anything of us being fired on. When you've got nine 16-inch barrels to poke fire at the enemy, he's got to be fairly close or way back to shoot something, and they didn't have that much capability, as I recall.

They did fire at a couple of the battleships, but they were north of the DMZ.* We went up there once, as I recall. In fact, I remember a real foggy morning we went up north to shoot, and it was a big, hairy decision as to whether we wanted to shoot, because you couldn't see a darn thing visually, but certainly we had radar. We let go with a nine-gun salvo, and it seems to me the whole island blew up. I remember that.

Paul Stillwell: What do you recall about the tactical voice communications? That would have fallen under your domain.

Admiral Gravely: Well, yes, tactical voice communications did, but, of course, CTF 77 ran most of the ops up there. Now, it was my responsibility basically just to set it up and to make sure that the machinery and equipment were operating. Certainly I was directly responsible for the communications being on our bridge. We had fairly good communications in those days, the TED-RED series and TBS.† TBS was sort of the secondary tac, as I recall. CIC basically guarded that.

I got to be quite a tactical communicator, because at GQ I had a team of three people. I had a talker, and a guy who basically would open the signal book for me, and I had to break all the tactical signals. I got to be fairly good with that, and frankly it stood me in good stead later when I went to the Toledo, when it was my prime responsibility.

Paul Stillwell: Well, then you also had to run the radio net between the ship and the spotters, which were either in a plane or on shore.

Admiral Gravely: Yes. I was responsible for that shore bombardment net, and also I was responsible for fixing the code. See, the code would come in, and you had to go through

---

* DMZ—demilitarized zone.
† These letters designated specific types of radio equipment that were used for short-range communications.

it. I've forgotten exactly how we did it, but we had to duplicate it basically, and give a copy to the gunnery officer and his people. I was responsible for making sure that that was correct. I had no problem with that, but crypto came kind of easy for me.

Paul Stillwell: Did you get involved with the registered publications at all?

Admiral Gravely: Yes I was the RPS custodian, and I guess I should tell you the story about that.* When I reported aboard, the registered publications officer was the administrator. Normally there was someone in the communications department, but I guess the communications department was so small at that time they didn't have the men. So immediately I was assigned that chore. But I was to take over after the next inventory. As you recall, they used to inventory these pubs quarterly, and you sent your inventory in to the Naval Security Group.

    I took over at the end of March, I guess, and I was quite flabbergasted because my first inventory came back uncleared. Normally you get a letter saying that you've been cleared, you've got all the stuff. But apparently we had failed to report about four pubs or something like that. In investigating that, we found that the Iowa had never received a cleared inventory since going into commission the August before. Well, I went up and talked to Captain Smedberg, the commanding officer. I told him, "Sir, I verified everything that the former custodian turned over to me, so it really wasn't my fault."

    He agreed there, but he said, "Hey, the next time I want a cleared inventory on that." And, sure enough, the next time we got a cleared inventory, because I found everything that we were supposed to have and had them in my RPS-10. I kept fairly close tab on them.

Paul Stillwell: What was the discrepancy, some that hadn't been put on the inventory?

Admiral Gravely: The custodian had drawn some pubs that he didn't put on his RPS-10, and so he was remiss there. As a result, we really didn't look for them. In fact, I didn't

---

* RPS—registered publications system, which required strict accountability in the storage, transfer, and destruction of specific publications, particularly those that involved communication codes.

concern myself with anything that was not on the RPS-10, and that was basically what it was. But we got that all squared away and no major problems from then on.

Paul Stillwell: Could you cover a little of what was involved in drawing publications, then accounting, and then destroying them?

Admiral Gravely: Yes. First of all, you have what you call an RPS-10. That RPS-10 is a complete compilation of all of the registered pubs that that ship receives and that that ship has custody of. Periodically notices would come out which would tell you to destroy certain pubs. So you would take your RPS-10, you would go down to your vault, and we had a fairly good-sized vault at that point in time. I would then mark off the pubs that I would destroy, inventory those pubs against the list that I'd gotten, plus make sure they were on the RPS-10.

Then two of us did the destruction.[*] I'd find some other subordinate, an officer, and the two of us would go to the fantail, and we would burn those pubs one at a time in a small incinerator. Then, whenever I got into port, the first thing I would do would be to take my RPS-10—which had a list of all the pubs that I had—show what I had burned, the whole bit, carry that over there. Then the people at the RPS issuing office would issue me the latest pubs. And, of course, they'd give me a little inventory. I'd sign for the inventory, put the pubs in a pouch, big gun on my side, come back to the ship, and then I would make sure that they were put on his RPS-10. So it was continuous control of this pouch.

If anyone came down to draw out one of these pubs, then I'd have a little card I kept in my card file, and I'd get his signature on it. And there were a couple of times when I had problems. These were not with our people, because I could fairly well keep track of the naval officers on board the ship, but once in a while I loaned a pub out to the Seventh Fleet people. The Seventh Fleet people also had RPS-10 and went through the same procedure. I can remember distinctly when one captain had one of my pubs, but he swore it belonged to Seventh Fleet, and frankly he had lost one of the pubs. It turned out

---

[*] To guard against malfeasance by a single individual serving as custodian, there had to be an additional witness who signed the destruction report

that he had lost the Seventh Fleet pub and not my pub. He swore for the longest kind of time, but I had a registered number on it, the whole bit, so I could prove which one was missing. So the other guy had to do the explaining. RPS wasn't a tough job, but it was a tedious job.

Paul Stillwell: Very precise.

Admiral Gravely: Yes, very precise, very demanding, and you constantly had to be on your toes about it. Particularly true of the crypto pubs. You'd take the crypto pubs down to the large, walk-in crypto vault, and a half a dozen people might use them. We had a daily inventory to make sure that they were down in the vault, and everybody who used them signed for them. But it wasn't the hardest job in the world, really.

Paul Stillwell: Your professional development had been specializing along these communication lines. Were you actively working in some of the other areas, such as CIC and tactics and gunnery?

Admiral Gravely: Well, no, because I was not assigned those duties. Communications was my duty, and I was assigned as a communications division officer. Communications was divided into two branches: signals and radio. I was assigned as a radio division officer, which involved radio transmissions.

However, remember that I went to the Iowa to learn some specifics about the Navy for any future jobs. Therefore, I took correspondence courses and also ship's courses. I was exempted from most of them, because I was a mid-grade lieutenant, and usually junior officers took them. But I felt that I just had to do some of those courses to learn something about the ship. So I did those courses. In fact, I almost got us in trouble once, because I took a classified course that was run by Com7thFlt. Basically it described the communications equipment on board the ship and everything else. I sent the thing off to be graded, and I forgot to classify it. [Laughter] So we got a nasty little letter, but there weren't very many people taking courses, so they were very happy that I was taking courses. But, at the same time, I learned that you obviously have to classify things correctly, and I did from then on.

Paul Stillwell: Did anybody specifically take you under his wing and point out steps you could take to bring yourself along?

Admiral Gravely: No, not directly. I learned by observation. I had a very fine communicator, who was my boss, but I think he was more interested in making sure that the communications job was done well. He was particularly interested in CW radio and loved being in the radio shack. He was also a ham radio operator.

I guess when you talk about professional development, one of the things that was done for me was that I was put on different inspection parties, and so I was constantly getting around to all the spaces on the ship. Of course, I made my own damage control inspection each week, which meant I had to go through those 14 radio spaces every week. But I got around through the engineering department, through the weapons department, etc. But communicators generally stood watches down in the radio shack, and not so much on the bridge or in CIC. CIC was almost a mystery to me for the longest time.

One other thing that happened that you might be interested in was that about that time a letter came from the Chief of Naval Personnel, talking about regular Navy. They wanted a certain number of reservists to apply. I guess the notice said they were going to select about 25. I applied for the regular Navy at that point in time, but I have never, to this day, found out what really happened to my application. I am positive it left the ship. I don't know what happened to it when it got to BuPers, but I was not selected. Of course, with a limitation of about 25, I imagine they got thousands of applications, and I just was not one of those.

Getting back to the family situation again, I knew that the ship would return to the West Coast in October of '52, and also very shortly after that we would change homeport. Now, the four battleships that were in commission belonged to BatDiv 2, which was home-ported out of Norfolk.* So shortly after returning to the States, we then

---

* BatDiv 2—Battleship Division Two.

went to Norfolk, which frankly was only about 50 miles from where my wife was living, so we had our great reunions and those kinds of things.

Socially, ship's parties and things like that, I went to with no problem. I didn't really have a problem with either the young officers or the enlisted men taking orders from me. One night here recently I was invited to a party given by a young black group who call themselves "Young Navy Retireds" or something like that. I've forgotten what the name of the group is. Interestingly enough, the president of that group was a young man who came on the Iowa as a seaman second class.

I really had forgotten the story, but supposedly when he came on board I asked him to come up to my stateroom, and he came up there. I talked to him a little bit about where he'd been, the rate, and everything else. He said that he was a seaman second, he'd been through radio school, and he was striking for radioman.* And he said that I told him that I wanted him to be a radioman seaman first within three months, or I was going to kick his tail out of my division. Eventually, he retired as a warrant officer, which I thought was pretty good. At least I led him along the right path.

At that point in time there was a shortage of radiomen throughout the fleet. The policy set up by Captain Cooper, the next skipper I served under, was that I got in my division two new men every month. But if I had anybody who wasn't learning, or who I didn't think was cutting the mustard in the radio gang, then I booted them out, and I got two more. So I had a real flourishing gang. Of course, I had a lot of other people who were a little angry that there I was, getting the best people in the fleet, and I was getting a really good group of people. So that also attributed to the fact that there were no real problems with them, because I basically handpicked them. I had some really good guys.

Paul Stillwell: Did you have division officer responsibilities?

---

* A striker is a non-rated enlisted man officially designated as being in training for a specific petty officer rating.

Admiral Gravely: Yes, as radio officer I was a CR division officer, and that accounted for the radiomen and telemen.* We had four divisions: a CIC group, which was a K division; the ETs; the radiomen; and the signalmen.† These divisions all worked for Commander Rock, who was the operations officer. A tremendous guy. He went from there to command of a destroyer, as I recall.‡ I remember that subsequently when I was aboard the Toledo, I believe it was, that he invited me over to his wardroom for lunch with him.

The Iowa came to the East Coast, came through the Panama Canal, which was quite an interesting trip for me, because I'd never been through the Panama Canal. We arrived in Norfolk some time in November. And, of course, the grand reunion with the wife. There's an interesting story about that. I seemed to have been doing quite well, and the wives were really interested in seeing that my wife did well, and that she was comfortable and enjoyed the wardroom, etc. So the first wives' luncheon that she was invited to, they practically babied her. I think that she felt that she really didn't need the babying, but at the same time they did. They took care of her, made sure that she was invited to everything, that I was invited to those things that I should have been invited to, and she just really became a real dedicated Navy wife after that.

We made one operation out of Norfolk—Springboard, I guess, was the annual exercise down there. After Springboard, came back to Norfolk and went into the Norfolk Naval Shipyard for repair. Stayed in the yards for about four months, wherein we had just a routine yard overhaul. Of course, they were much shorter in those days. You got about four months in the yard instead of a year like you do now.

Paul Stillwell: Well, and she had just been reactivated, too, so probably she was in pretty good shape.

Admiral Gravely: Yes, she was about 18 months away from reactivation and everything else. So they changed some equipment and those kinds of things. I still was the radio

---

* Teleman was the title of a Navy rating established in 1948 as a combination of mailman, some radioman ratings, and some specialist Q (communications) ratings. In 1956 the telemen were merged into the yeomen and radiomen ratings.
† ETs—electronics technicians.
‡ Commander Rock served as commanding officer of the destroyer Willard Keith (DD-775) in 1953-54.

officer, still had basically the same people. We lost a few people just prior to transiting to the East Coast. They were transferred to CruDesPac ships and those kinds of things but had basically the same crew.[*]

Paul Stillwell: Do you have any stories about being the division officer, that is, signing the special request chits, going to mast with people, helping them with their personal problems and that sort of thing?

Admiral Gravely: Well, not very many, because I had a fairly good, intelligent group of people, who for the most part didn't really commit any offenses. The one thing that I realized you had to work with, and that was the special group of people who had special watches. For example, I was amazed initially, because the ship was on a regular four-hour watch, but the radiomen stood watch from something like noon till the evening meal, from the evening meal to midnight, and from midnight till breakfast.

Paul Stillwell: Chow to chow.

Admiral Gravely: Yes, chow-to-chow watches. And I had a little problem with that, because what do you do with these guys who've been up all night and you've got to inspect the ship that day? Every time we had an inspection I had to explain why these four or five guys were still in the bag. But most people seem to have understood it, although it was very easy to wake them up, and then have a guy practically dead on you during the next watch, but for the most part I'd let them sleep through.

I guess the most interesting one that I had, so far as people were concerned, was a seaman I picked up out of the weapons department. When we got to Norfolk, he went on his normal leave and didn't return. So one day I got a call to come to the quarterdeck, and I went up there and I met the mother and father of this young man, and they had him with them. The mother said, "Our son has been home for about 30 days, and I know darn well that he doesn't have that much leave. So we felt that we would bring him back."

---

[*] CruDesPac—Cruiser-Destroyer Force Pacific Fleet.

I said, "Yes, Ma'am. He really had 15 days' leave, and he's been over the hill for 15 days. I'll take care of it." So he came aboard, went on down to the radio gang with me, and I told the chief to put him on report obviously, muster him, etc., and take him to his bunk and get him squared away. At the next morning's muster he wasn't there again. Then one day about a week later I got a call from his mama, who apologized and said that, believe it or not, when they got to New Jersey, he was in the trunk of their car. [Laughter] They wondered what had happened to him.

But this kid just wasn't about to stay in the Navy, and, of course, the weapons people were a little angry at me, because I immediately transferred him to the weapons department, because I didn't have any troublemakers or anything else. I could get another man for him, and here I transferred a guy who was AWOL to the weapons department.[*] So they were a little unhappy with me, too, but that's about it so far as stories and divisional type things.

Paul Stillwell: Did you sit on any court-martials?

Admiral Gravely: No, but I was a member of the special court-martial board.

Paul Stillwell: Do you have any comments on the severity of discipline then, compared with when you were a skipper later?

Admiral Gravely: No, I really don't, and maybe I'll inadvertently stumble across something in answer to you. At the moment I don't have anything.

Paul Stillwell: Did you have any other collateral duties besides the RPS job?

Admiral Gravely: Well, I was the RPS custodian, I was the postal officer; I was a member, as I said, of special court-martials. We only had about four or five, but I didn't sit on any of those. It took a whole day to do some of those duties.

---

[*] AWOL—absent without leave.

Paul Stillwell: Between RPS and postal you had a lot of accountability there.

Admiral Gravely: Right. Right. Postal was sort of up my line, because I'd been a railway mail clerk, as well as I had worked in a post office all my young life. So that was no problem for me.

Paul Stillwell: Did the relations in the wardroom ease after you'd been there a while and had proved yourself?

Admiral Gravely: The relations eased, and you just hit on another story.

The relations weren't really bad from the start. I had two or three guys that I sat beside for every meal, and these guys were my friends. But for some reason the weapons officer—I don't know whether it was the weapons officer or the exec—decided to change the officers' stateroom assignments, and they wanted to go to a more permanent-type assignment. So if a guy came aboard as the first division officer, he knew exactly where his bunk was going to be, or if he came aboard as a radio officer he knew where his bunk was going to be.

Paul Stillwell: So it would be based on billets?

Admiral Gravely: Yes, based on billets. But, frankly, I had a good room, and I liked it there. But unfortunately I was one of the guys who was told to move. And I tried to figure out why I was moving. I was being assigned my own room, which normally was just for lieutenant commanders and above. I could find no reason for it other than the fact that it was a room the weapons department decided they wanted. So I went up to see the exec one day about it.

Paul Stillwell: Was this Commander Stephan?

Admiral Gravely: It was Commander Gardner at that time, and he said, "Well, Sam, if you like your room, you just stay there, and they can put whoever they want in there when the next guy comes aboard."* It turned out that my relief was already on board, so he's the guy who stayed in his room rather than moving up there, and that solved the problem.

But we were talking about personnel problems, and I did have one that set me to thinking for a long time. We had an officer on board, and I'm not sure exactly what his problem was, but he was an oddball. He did something—and I really don't know what it was—but they decided to get rid of him. So one day I was called to the operations officer's stateroom, and the operations officer said, "Sam, here's a message. It's classified confidential, and it has to be sent out, and I want you personally to handle it."

I said, "Sir, as you well know, any messages that go off classified have to have a check decrypter."

He said, "I don't want anybody else to see the message. Do you hear what I say?"

I said, "Yes, sir." So I took the message down, and I wasn't even supposed to read it [laughter]. But how do you encrypt one without reading it? Of course, I did read it, and I encrypted it. I did not have a check decrypter. I sent it out.

It obviously went out on the right system, because we got an answer shortly thereafter, and the guy was detached immediately, and I've never seen anybody leave a ship so fast. In fact, he didn't even have time to pack. He was told to get off the ship, had a boat alongside, and sent him on over to Yokosuka. The ship sent his gear about four hours later after an inventory. He was a sick sister, and I'm not sure what the problem was. But I remember that, and it set me to thinking, "Please don't make these people angry, because they know how to take care of those situations." [Laughter]

Paul Stillwell: What do you recall about the BatDiv 2 staff?

Admiral Gravely: Well, the BatDiv 2 staff rode with us, and they rode us during Exercise Springboard. The most interesting part about it was that the BatDiv 2 staff, contrary to the Seventh Fleet staff, made all movement reports. I never will forget that very shortly after we departed, maybe about the first day or something like that, I got this call to come up to Captain Cooper's stateroom. I went up there, and he was practically in hysterics

---

* Commander Earle G. Gardner, Jr., USN. His predecessor was Commander Edward C. Stephan, USN.

laughing. I wondered what this was all about. Then finally he said "Sam, you're a real jewel. I've been on here now for about six months, and you've never missed a movement report, and the first time we turn it over to the staff, they miss it."

What had happened, of course, was they had failed to send the movement report, and we got a big blast back: "Your movement report not received." Captain Cooper was, in my mind, a great man. I liked him, worked well with him, no problems. As you well know, a lieutenant doesn't get up to a captain's stateroom or talk to him, other than informally on the bridge or something like that. But we just got along just really great, and he wrote me some good fitness reports, and he did me some favors later on that I'll tell you about.

Paul Stillwell: What do you remember about the administrative part of dealing with the staff, the inspections and so forth?

Admiral Gravely: We got along fairly well with them. No major problems with the staff. One of them, in fact my counterpart on that staff, was a personal friend. In fact, he lives out in Haymarket with me, and I see him every once in a while. It was Donald Poe, who subsequently made admiral—a very, very fine gent.[*] I worked with him in naval communications subsequent to that and have worked with him in this living community, where he and I are great friends. We visit each other periodically. I just didn't have any problem working with the staff. And maybe it was the other way around. I don't think they had too many problems working with me.

Paul Stillwell: A number of black Navy men from that period had difficulties in Norfolk trying to go on liberty, and I would suspect that you were spared some of that by being married, because you had a place to go.

Admiral Gravely: Well, yes. Okay, maybe I should talk about that a little bit, because I was spared in more than just that one way. In 1945, when I was on the PC-1264, the PC-1264 went to Norfolk and stayed there for about two or three months. I was walking

---

[*] Lieutenant Donald T. Poe, USN.

through the Navy shipyard one day, and a guy spoke to me. His name was Clyde Hassle. We struck up a conversation, and Clyde said, "Well, hey, why don't you come around my house with me?" And I went to Clyde's house with him when I was in town in Norfolk. I didn't have a car; Clyde had a car. Clyde worked in the shipyard as a stevedore. Clyde also was a very, very energetic young man who was constantly striving to go places and to do things, etc. He had not completed high school, but had a lot of drive, a lot of energy. So I went to his house, and he said, "Come on, go with me. I play with a little football team down here, and we're going out to practice." The team was called the Brown Bombers.

So I said, "Well, my God, why don't I play with the Brown Bombers?" So okay, fine. So Clyde played one end, and I played the other. And that's the way we'd always refer to each other, as "the other end." Clyde and I became great friends, and, of course, I had Clyde as an asset in Norfolk when I got there. In addition to that, as you're saying, being married, I spent a lot of time in Franklin, where my wife lived, but at the same time my wife and Clyde also became friends.

Clyde subsequently married. He'd been married before, but he's married again, and our whole family's still close. Today if I go to Clyde's house, his kids call me Uncle Sam. [Laughter] Just like my kids called him Uncle Clyde. So I had those things going for me when I went to Norfolk, and so I had no real problem.

Well, anyway, after the yard period on Iowa we then started ops again. But in the meantime, I had a set of orders, and, frankly, I was going as communications officer of the Toledo to relieve Herb Yarbrough again. And whereas I had no problem with relieving Herb Yarbrough, I really wanted to stay in Norfolk, so I got on the phone and called BuPers, and I talked to the detailer there. I said that our signal officer, for example, had gone to the Wisconsin, and someone else had gone to another one of the battleships and cruisers around there. So I talked to him in terms of maybe swapping me with somebody else and letting me stay in Norfolk. But he said, "No, you've been specifically picked to go the Toledo, so here you go." Well, there was no problem. We happened to be down in Gitmo when I got off the ship, and I got off with orders to report to the Toledo about a month later.*

---

* "Gitmo" is the nickname for Guantanamo Bay, Cuba.

Paul Stillwell: She was based in Long Beach, wasn't she?

Admiral Gravely: The Toledo was based in Long Beach, but at that point in time she was in a shipyard in San Francisco, so that's where I was to meet her. I got off the Iowa and, of course, went over to transportation. I'm not sure what our problem with the Cubans at that time was, but we were not taking anything out of Cuba but dependents. So there I was, "tail-end Charlie," and I promised my wife that I would be there the next day. So the young lady in transportation said, "You might as well go over to the BOQ, because we don't think we're going to get you out of here for another five or six days." So I was signing into the BOQ when a young lieutenant, a naval officer, just happened to be there, and he said, "You look like you're going someplace."

I said, "Well, I thought I was. I wanted to go to Norfolk. I promised my wife that I'd be there tomorrow, but it looks like I'm going to be around here for five or six days."

He said, "Well, you know, I'm going to Patuxent River. I fly right over Norfolk. Tomorrow, in fact. If you'd like to ride with me, I'd be happy to take you." He said, "But I'll tell you what, we are going to operate with the Iowa this afternoon." And it was a specifically radar-configured B-25 which was to operate for the Fleet Training Group with the Iowa. Then he went to San Juan, and then the next morning we got up and flew to Patuxent River.*

Well, we went out into San Juan, had a fairly good time. I enjoyed San Juan—first time I'd ever been there. And he said, "I'm crossing over Elizabeth City, North Carolina, now, and the next time you see us we'll be passing over Norfolk, and we will then be going into Patuxent River."

I said, "My god, you really could do me a favor if there was some way to let me off in Norfolk."

He said, "Do you want to go to Norfolk?"

I said, "Sure." And damn if he didn't drop the plane down and let me off in the middle of the runway—my bags and everything else. [Laughter]

---

* Patuxent River Naval Air Station is in southern Maryland.

I called my wife, and she came and picked me up. Christ, we were off for about a month. But I never will forget that guy. I don't think he violated any rules. I'm sure he did it all right and everything else, but he could have very easily said no and just kept on to Patuxent River. But he didn't. He dropped me off.

I'd only been gone maybe about ten days, so it wasn't quite a reunion or anything else like, but we then began to plan about going to San Francisco. My wife had never been to the West Coast, and at that point in time I had a new car, so we decided that we would drive to San Francisco. The plan was that she would probably come on back, and we still weren't going to set up a home on the West Coast yet.

In any event, we took off from there with probably about 25 to 30 days to drive across country. We enjoyed the trip, but in those days it was always a problem as to where do you spend the night. We obviously drove basically the southern way—Route 66. There just weren't places to find good motels that would take us, because we were black. So we learned how to find a town, and you knew where the railroad tracks were, and you went across the railroad tracks, and you either got a room, which was hotter than hell, or you slept in the car at night. And that's basically the way we got across country.

Things really didn't change a hell of a lot even in California. We drove into Los Angeles. My wife had cousins there, so we stopped there for a while. Then we went to San Francisco, where there was a Navy-Marine Corps Hotel. I guess we visited some friends there for a while, and then she caught a train coming back East.

I reported to the Toledo—I never will forget this—the fourth of July 1953.[*] Frankly, I was amazed at the difference in the size of ships. I'd spent 18 months on the Iowa, huge beam, etc. God, I walked on the quarterdeck, and I started through a little passageway, and, Christ, I was getting ready to jump over the other side, it was so small in comparison. So that was kind of amazing to me, but they took care of me in good shape, the normal routine. No one was surprised about my coming aboard, because I had relieved Lieutenant Yarbrough 18 months earlier on the Iowa.

---

[*] USS Toledo (CA-133), a Baltimore-class heavy cruiser, was commissioned 27 October 1946. She had a standard displacement of 14,472 tons, full-load displacement of 17,031 tons, was 673 feet long, 71 feet in the beam, and had a draft of 21 feet. Her top speed was 33 knots. She was armed with nine 8-inch main battery guns and twelve 5-inch dual-purpose guns. She served almost entirely in the Pacific Fleet until eventually being decommissioned on 21 May 1960.

The next day I went up to see the captain. This was Captain F. B. C. Martin, who was a fine gent.[*] He reminded me of a North Carolina tobacco man or something. I guess the reason he did was because he welcomed me aboard, shook my hand, and he said, "You know, I'm really happy to meet you." He said, "You took care of a friend of mine once."

I said, "Oh?"

He said, "Yes, a friend of mine from North Carolina came up to see me about getting his son into the ROTC program. I really didn't have all of the specifics at hand, but I called the Washington office, and you were the guy that met this gentleman when he came in there and gave him all the information. The guy called me back and thanked me profusely, because he thought you had done a good job in explaining the program, etc." So F. B. C. Martin had heard of me, and in some way he knew me.

There were no problems on getting aboard. I got introduced to the wardroom at breakfast the next morning, and those kinds of things. Of course, my good friend Herb Yarbrough didn't particularly want to leave, because he'd taken the ship through the yard period, and he wanted to see it operate with all the new equipment aboard. But we got along famously, most of the crew.

I soon got a roommate by the name of Norman Algiers.[†] Norman Algiers was the damage control officer. Both of us were lieutenants, of course, and Norman was just a tremendous guy. He was ex-enlisted; I think he was a temporary officer. Norman is a hard guy to describe. He's very interesting and a very good conversationalist. We got along famously. I guess I got the bottom bunk, and I'm not sure why I got the bottom bunk, and he got the top bunk. But one of the things that was really unique about Algiers was that he wore his hat with it cocked to one side. It was about 30 degrees off course. And he always drank his coffee from his cup without ever touching the cup. He always used a saucer for his coffee. [Laughter] But besides being a character, he was also an artist, and those flimsies you see in the Toledo cruise book were all drawn by Norman Algiers.

---

[*] Captain Farar Benjamin Conner Martin, USN, commanded the Toledo from December 1952 to December 1953.
[†] Lieutenant Norman A. Algiers, Jr., USN, a former machinist's mate.

The yard period went along fairly routinely. I got to know a few shipyard workers up there who really helped me subsequently, because I went back there in another ship.

One of the most interesting things I remember is that we got a brand-new chief radioman. This guy unfortunately had been in Seattle, Washington, as I recall, at the commsta for something like six years.* But he really had been the chief master-at-arms. And what he needed to know about radio procedures, and what he had known six years ago, just were not the same. He had lost his proficiency as a result of that. So whereas he tried to lead the guys, I really relied on a second class petty officer down there. The main reason I found out that this chief didn't have it was that he was unable to give the Morse code part of the test to a second class radioman. So you can imagine a chief like that. He just didn't have it anymore. And he'd lost an awful lot of other things too. Well, one of my hardest jobs was trying to figure out how to get rid of this guy and get me a chief radioman. I thought I was pretty well set in the signal gang and everything else, but I had to get rid of this chief radioman.

Paul Stillwell: I think that would create an awkwardness in the chain of command, when you had to work around him.

Admiral Gravely: It did. I had to work around him all the time. He had another thing which was unfortunate, and I'm not speaking about his character at all, but he had an effeminate-type voice. So when he'd get on a squawk box, God, everybody was on the bridge laughing, etc.

Well, anyway, <u>Toledo</u> finished the yard period, and we went down to San Diego for refresher training. And when we got to San Diego, I discovered that Captain Cooper was the chief of staff to ComCruDesPac. So Captain Martin said he was going over to the flagship, and I just happened to mention to him, "Captain, do you mind me riding over with you, because I'd like to see Captain Cooper."

He said, "Oh, jump in, jump in. Yeah, we'll take you." So I went over, and the

---

* Commsta—communications station.

next thing I know, there were the bongs, and he was leaving.*

I rushed up to the quarterdeck and said, "Well, I haven't seen Captain Cooper yet, and I'll stay over here. I'll get back somehow."

So he said, "Fine."

Well, Captain Cooper took the time, and he saw me, and he said, "Sam, how are you getting along?"

I said, "Fine."

He said, "Is there anything I can do for you?"

I said, "Captain, yes there is. I need a chief radioman." Immediately he got on the squawk box and called a personnel officer up. The personnel officer said, "Well, they have a chief radioman. They're only allowed one. Chief radiomen are hard to find."

Captain Cooper said, "Get him a chief radioman." [Laughter] So the personnel officer and I went and sat down. He said, "Well, let me tell you. I got just one guy that's possibly available. He has just finished the teletype repair school [I believe it was]. And he's sitting around here now, and getting ready to go to crypto repair school. When are you guys sailing?"

I said, "We're sailing Monday." This was a Saturday.

He said, "Well, I can't get a message to him for certainty to get him aboard."

I said, "Give me the orders. I'll find him." So they gave me his address. I went to his house, and he, like most chief radiomen about noon on a Saturday, wasn't home.

His wife said, "He's at such-and-such a beer garden."

So I went down to this beer garden, and I said, "I'm looking for Chief Gause."†

Some guy said, "He's over there." Sure enough, there he was over there with a crowd of sailors. They were sitting around swapping lies and everything else. I went over there, introduced myself to him. I said, "Chief, I'm the communication officer on the Toledo, and I've got a set of orders in my hand for you, and I need you aboard tomorrow morning." Jesus, he almost upchucked.

---

* When a senior officer is going aboard or leaving a ship, his movement is accompanied by an announcement on the public address system, accompanied by a number of bell rings—"bongs"—commensurate with his rank.
† Chief Radioman D. C. Gause, USN.

In any event, Monday morning that guy was aboard. He made my life so much easier on board that ship that it wasn't funny. And, of course, on this ship also I made all the movement reports. I got to be the guy who wrote the logreqs too.* I also decided that, "Hey, somehow I got to get on this bridge." Of course, I was a tactical communicator on the bridge all the time, and they had plenty of watch officers, but finally I talked to the senior watch officer, and he agreed that I could go up there. So I began to stand watches on the Toledo. And I just loved the bridge on ships. I think they all knew it, and so I qualified for independent steaming.

Paul Stillwell: How did the ships of that class handle?

Admiral Gravely: We were a little sluggish at times, certainly not as easy as the good old DD or the Taussig, as I remember.

Paul Stillwell: A lot of momentum there.

Admiral Gravely: A lot of momentum there, not the smallest turning circle in the world and those kinds of things. But I got so I could handle her with no sweat, and I don't think there were any problems with my ship handling there. I made a couple of tactical errors, but who doesn't? I didn't collide with anybody, although one night I thought I was. But things went fairly well up there, and I continued to progress.

Now, I was the comm officer, and to some degree I ran the administrative office for the operations officer. However, when I first arrived the CIC officer, who was the assistant ops officer, was senior to me. But when this guy, Gibson his name was, was detached, then I became the assistant to the ops officer.

I remember one thing that happened to me at the first Monday morning muster at quarters that we had. I went to my divisions, and I then reported to the ops officer, "All men present and accounted for."

---

* Logreq—logistics requisition. When a ship is approaching a port, her captain sends a logreq message spelling out what the ships needs in the way of supplies and services.

About a half an hour later he came charging up to me. And I'll never forget this guy's name either. He said, "Where is Ralston?"

I said, "Ralston? Who in the hell's Ralston?"

"Well, Ralston is a lieutenant (j.g.) that you sent to school three weeks ago."

I said, "Sir, I didn't send Lieutenant (j.g.) Ralston to school, plus the fact that I've never met Lieutenant (j.g.) Ralston."

He said, "Well, he's not here. And you just made a false muster." We discussed that for a bit, and finally I just simply told him that I'd find out about Lieutenant (j.g.) Ralston, but I didn't know Lieutenant Ralston. "Lieutenant (j.g.) Ralston wasn't here when I reported, so I can't be responsible for his not being here today." But, anyway, I went down to talk to the admin people. I learned that Lieutenant (j.g.) Ralston had been sent to San Diego for about ten days of courses, and he had not returned. So nobody knew where he was down in San Diego.

So I went along with another officer and had the task of inventorying his gear. In inventorying his gear he had letters from BOQs and officer clubs all over. He'd been bouncing bad checks, doing this and doing that, and I'm not sure where he was, because I never heard any more about Lieutenant Ralston. But we finally got the fact that I didn't make a false muster all cleared up. I don't think that damaged me a bit. But the ops officer almost seemed a little wary. I don't think that was really my fault that Lieutenant (j.g.) Ralston had never been reported as being on board.

Well, with chief Gause on board, refresher training just became a dream. I had a real strong guy in the radio shack. Of course, I was on the bridge doing the tactical communicating. Had a good signal gang, and we went through with a fairly good set of colors. Frankly, I had the general signal book memorized; I really did. When somebody said tactical signal—well, the turns and corpens and those things were sort of understood, but most of the two-letter signals would come in, and I had them broken.*

The reason I had the signal book was just to double check to make sure. I usually told the captain right away what the meaning of the signal was, and then I'd double-check the signal book. Of course, I'd learned fairly well aboard the Iowa, and, of course, we'd

---

* A corpen signal orders the direction of movement by a number of ships in formation when they turn simultaneously to a new course.

had it at comm school going through frequently, so I was pretty well up on that. And I think a couple of times that people were impressed. In fact, as I recall during the refresher training, I was directed to read the book before giving the captain the explanation. [Laughter] But we went through it fairly well with flying colors.

We then left Long Beach and went on out to the Seventh Fleet. We were deployed out there for about seven months. Nothing untoward happened there, except I remember once that we were under way, and I was basically told that I had to paint the radio shack. I just told the exec, Commander Groner, "Sir, I would like to do that, but, frankly, that's unheard of during a operating period. The radio gang needs to sit down to do their job while the painting is going on at the same time. You just can't shut down your gear."[*]

He said, "I really don't give a damn whether it's unheard of or not, but it is filthy down there, and I want that place cleaned up."

I said, "Well, yes, sir."

We painted it and everything else, and when we were all through, he came again, he said, "Sam, it looks good down there."

I said, "Well, sir, normally, as I told you, people don't paint radio shacks while they're under way."

He said, "Hell, I know that. I just wanted to see if you could do it." [Laughter] Great. So we were great friends.

We had one other little incident that upset me to some degree. We were about ready to return from the deployment, and the welfare and recreation committee, which I was a member of that group, decided that they would have a contest. It was to be an article of so many pages describing an adventure by a sailor over in WestPac. And when the articles were done, I was put in charge of a committee which was told to read these articles and then declare a winner. There must have been 50 articles. So I took the other two guys on the committee and myself, and we went someplace and sat down and read the articles.

Everybody's not a fast reader, and we were running kind of late, so I said, "Well, what we ought to do maybe is to look at the articles and see if they meet the minimum

---

[*] Commander William T. Groner, USN.

criteria." They had to be so long, and describe a specific incident that happened in WestPac. You know, a couple of minor things. Unfortunately, in doing that we threw out about 20 of them. So which meant that we had about 30 to read, and we read those 30 and then came up with a winner.

Well, I went to Commander Groner to report to him that we had sat, and we'd met, and we'd declared a winner. Before he looked at the winner, he said, "What happened to the article on the cockfight?"

I said, "Cockfight? Sir, I really don't remember seeing an article on a cockfight."

He said, "Well, I know you've got that article, and it's a good article." He said, "Now, you take that committee and put them back together and review those articles again." So I went up there and got all the articles, got my guys together again, and I told them what had happened. We began to look, and, sure enough, there was the article on cockfighting. It had been written by the guy who was sort of a journalist on board, but really he was a ship's writer or something, and he described a cockfighting incident in the Philippines, as I recall. But he didn't meet the criteria. He had about four pages when it was supposed to be about eight or something like that, and so it just got thrown out.

So I told the gang what had happened, and we decided that we would re-read the articles, but we were not about to pick a different winner. And so shortly thereafter I went back to see the exec, and he accepted it but reluctantly. And the cockfight article didn't win.

Commander Groner was quite a guy. I probably shouldn't say this about him, but he had a love of birds. He had spent a lot of time in Japan. And when the ship got there, someone gave him a pair of lovebirds. The impression I got was that they specifically gave him two male birds, because if he'd gotten a female and a male they'd probably breed, and obviously the ship was no place for birds to breed. He kept them in his stateroom in a little cage. Periodically you could go in there, and the exec would be laying up there with his door locked. He was playing with his goddamn birds. Birds were fluttering about the room and everything else, and, of course, he'd put them back in the cage. Well, one day one of the birds died. So we had a wardroom meeting to determine who had killed the exec's bird.

Paul Stillwell: Who shot Cock Robin?

Admiral Gravely: Yes, who had killed the exec's bird. Obviously nobody volunteered that he had killed the bird, so the doctor was ordered to do an autopsy on the bird, to find out what happened. Well the ship's doctor was really upset, and obviously he told the commander that he was there to treat the humans, not any bird. The exec told him just to go do it. Lo and behold, the doctor did perform an autopsy on the bird, and he discovered that the bird was egg-bound. [Laughter] So he had a female, and so all the officers got off scot-free. We didn't have to pay the supreme price because the exec's bird died.

Paul Stillwell: What do you remember about the operations during that cruise? Did you work with carriers?

Admiral Gravely: The big thing that I remember more than anything else was the Tachens. Do you remember those two little islands off of China, the Tachens? We were involved in the evacuation of the Tachens.[*]

Paul Stillwell: Admiral Pride, whom I've talked to, was the Seventh Fleet Commander.[†] He relieved Jocko Clark, and that's one of the things he was involved in.

Admiral Gravely: Okay. The biggest thing I remember about that operation was that we went to general quarters at dawn every morning, for some 10 or 12 days, and then we stayed at general quarters until about 10:00 o'clock at night. Now, what we were doing was lying off the Tachen Islands with a hook down, really, and watching the evacuation, etc. Then at dusk we'd steam out and operate with the task force all night. And, of course, at dawn we were right back in there to start the same procedure.

---

[*] The small Tachen Islands, north of Formosa (as Taiwan was then called) were subject to attack from mainland China in the early 1950s. On 7 February 1955, on the advice of the U.S. Government and with the assistance of the U.S. Seventh Fleet, the Nationalist Chinese evacuated the Tachens.
[†] Vice Admiral Alfred M. Pride, USN, served as Commander Seventh Fleet from 1 December 1953 to 19 December 1955. The oral history of Pride, who retired as a four-star admiral, is in the Naval Institute collection.

The biggest thing I remember about it was one night about 12:00 o'clock or something, GQ went for some strange reason. I got up and, Christ, I thought I was just going to my normal dawn launch or something. But it was kind of tiring and everything else. But I stayed on the bridge from dawn every morning till about 10:00 o'clock every night, which was a long haul up on that bridge, eating the sandwiches, etc. We went straight GQ, I think.

I enjoyed the Toledo. She was a good ship. Captain Cockell came aboard and relieved F. B. C. Martin. Captain Cockell came aboard, I think, in December of '53.[*] We were down at Hong Kong when he relieved. Captain Cockell, another real fine gent. He had been a dirigible pilot, I believe. He wasn't a straight line officer, but everybody got their destroyer if you didn't get your carrier, and he was one who got a cruiser vice that. Captain Cockell was a fairly good ship handler, kind of meticulous, an easy man to work for. Treated me no differently from anybody else, and I had a lot of respect for him.

He was fairly well satisfied, I think, with his communications. I can remember specifically one time, and this was a Seattle Seafair, when we had Admiral Maurice Curts aboard, who was CruDesPac, and he was to make a radio broadcast to the city of Seattle.[†] We had to pipe him into a radio station and pipe him out. And we were all set for it, and, lo and behold, I looked, and, as you know, on each of these handsets there were boxes or red lights that tells you the transmitter is on. I looked, and no light. And Maurice Curts was coming to the bridge. I started calling radio frantically, and as he stepped up to pick up that handset, the light came on. I'm not sure what happened, but, boy, I was sweating blood. But he made that successfully, so there was no problem after that.

Paul Stillwell: Did you have a flag officer embarked during that first cruise to the WestPac?

---

[*] Captain William A. Cockell, USN, served as commanding officer of the Toledo from 11 December 1953 to 6 May 1955.
[†] Rear Admiral Maurice E. Curts, USN, Commander Cruiser-Destroyer Force, Pacific Fleet.

Admiral Gravely: Yes, we had Admiral R. E. Wilson.* I remember more about Ralph Wilson than I do about any other flag officer. I can't remember whether he was there for two deployments with me or not, but I went on two deployments on the Toledo. Ralph Wilson is the guy I worked with more than anybody else.

Paul Stillwell: What do you recall about him?

Admiral Gravely: Basically a dedicated sailor. I remember he was the guy who insisted that all officers had to wear hats ashore, and I didn't wear a hat. So I was in Hong Kong, and I purchased a thing I could fold and put in my pocket as soon as I got to end of the gangway. [Laughter] I guess my dealings with him were not many. After all, he had his own comm officer, whom I admired, and we worked very, very well together. So I didn't have any major problems.

Part of the problem with communications for the flag was that—or at least I think so—they had a band. The job of the band players when they were in port was to stand the watches of the CIC, and they did most of the talking. Well, they were pretty good with the band instruments, but they were lousy communicators. You know, if you printed it out the, guy knew what to say, but otherwise they were kind of at a loss. Sometimes they created more problems than they solved. But you've got to put those guys to work doing something, so that's what their task was. There were no major problems.

Paul Stillwell: After the war ended was there more of an emphasis on training than there had been?

Admiral Gravely: No, we had a fairly big emphasis on training on each deployment, and that didn't let down a bit. Concentrating on GQs, man overboards, and those kinds of things. We did that just religiously.

---

* Rear Admiral Ralph E. Wilson, USN, became Commander Cruiser Division Three on 1 May 1954.

Paul Stillwell: Did you get the opportunity to handle the ship in things like man overboard and going alongside a replenishment ship?

Admiral Gravely: No, I did not. No, I did not. We had a special sea detail group who did most of the conning in close quarters and those kinds of things. I normally did just plain old independent steaming and handling the ship. I wasn't able to get up there mostly during task force ops. Task force ops you usually get into a much stricter watch condition than at any other time.

Paul Stillwell: Did they have a smaller number of OODs who did that?

Admiral Gravely: Yes, right, right, right. You had about eight or ten people independent steaming. You had about four people who did task force ops, and generally, if a guy died or something like that, you'd move somebody else up, but that was the only way you were going to get up there, if somebody got transferred or if something happened to him.

Paul Stillwell: Well, it's understandable. The captain wants a small group of people . . .

Admiral Gravely: He wants a small group of people that he knows well, and he trusts that he's checked out under varying conditions and has watched them operate. And when I was a skipper, I was no different, I got to tell you. I probably had more independent steamers, and I guess I got to the point wherein I was watching who was going to be on watch all night, and so I knew how sound I could sleep. [Laughter] But these skippers were no different from that.

Paul Stillwell: You were now on a smaller ship than the Iowa, and you had a more important job. Did you get a corresponding increase in status?

Admiral Gravely: No, a lieutenant is a lieutenant is a lieutenant, and so far as an increase in status, I don't think so. I think it was about the same. I sat in the same position at the wardroom table along with the lieutenants. And contrary to the Iowa mess, you know, you sat at the second mess, because they had so many senior officers where they always served two messes. But Toledo was the same. I sat with the same guys, and I knew them very well and very close to them.

My good friend, of course, was Norman Algiers, who was just a tremendous guy to know. I never met anybody in his family. I think once in Long Beach I might have met his wife, but I don't think I've met anybody else from that family. Social life then wasn't that much. Of course, I was out on the West Coast by myself, and so I didn't go to any ship's parties.

I guess I should have told you one other thing. I remember specifically that after we moved down to Long Beach a couple of the young officers asked me why I didn't have my wife with me. I told them that she was on the East Coast, and I said, "There's probably a little bit of a problem trying to find housing out here."

And, oh no, they pooh-poohed that. A guy said, "Well we live someplace," and I've forgotten where that was. It was sort of a group of apartments in Long Beach. And he said, "I know that you can get a place where we live." So I investigated that, and, believe it or not, they would not let me in because we were black. They just weren't quite ready. So, in fact, we'd already made up our minds that we would wait until the tour was completed to rejoin. Well, at the end of the first deployment my time in San Francisco plus this deployment equaled about 11 months. And I, of course, took some leave, came back home, and saw my wife. And as I've said, at that point in time we made a decision that my two-year tour would be up fairly shortly, at least within the next year, and at the end of that tour, no matter where I went, we'd set up a home.

Well, much to the chagrin of most of us, the Toledo only stayed in Long Beach for about three months, and then we were turned around back out again. And I stayed on board for the next deployment. We changed execs, we changed ops officers, but the bulk of the other people were still there. Captain Cockell was there. We did another deployment, which was fairly routine. I don't think anything special went on during that deployment.

Paul Stillwell: This was in the show-the-flag era primarily.

Admiral Gravely: Basically we did a lot of showing of the flag, went to Hong Kong and all the rest of the places.

Paul Stillwell: Any recollections of individual liberty ports?

Admiral Gravely: None specifically. I went most places alone. I got to like Yokosuka quite a bit. I liked Sasebo quite a bit. Hong Kong we visited, and, of course, Subic Bay, although I never really got to Manila.* A lot of guys went in groups and went up to Manila. Guys I just sort of hung around with didn't get to Manila.

Paul Stillwell: Were you continuing to work on your correspondence courses in this period?

Admiral Gravely: Yes, I continued to work on correspondence courses, and I'll tell you one about that a little later. But that stood me in fairly good stead a little later on. But there were so many things that I felt that somehow I needed: courses in military justice, courses in navigation, damage control, the whole bit, and I took all kinds of courses, and this continued on into my next tour.

Paul Stillwell: Did you feel a need to overcome the fact of your broken service—that you didn't have all the experience your contemporaries did?

Admiral Gravely: That was the big thing, and I'm firmly convinced today that if there are any mistakes we make with young officers, it is that we let a certain bunch of them come ashore before about six to eight years at sea. Because that's where the tools of the trade are. That's where you learn those tools and how to use them. So I'm a firm believer that the first about six years in a naval officer's career ought to be spent in ships. Obviously you go aboard as a junior officer for a couple of years, then you go as assistant department head for a couple years, and then you ought to be ready for a department head job. Particularly in the destroyers or something like that, obviously department head on

---

* Subic Bay is a protected anchorage on the island of Luzon in the Philippines.

the cruisers and things like that are commanders or lieutenant commanders, and you don't make that rank by that time, but you've got the experience, and all you do is play on that same experience and you're doing a little larger job; that's all it amounts to. So I felt that I had missed an awful lot, and that I had to catch up somehow.

One of the significant things that happened during that cruise was that I began to really just love the Navy, and I knew that I wanted to make it a career. So far as black officers were concerned in the Navy, there were Dennis Nelson, of course, who was a regular Navy officer; John Lee, whom I'd met, and who was also a regular Navy officer; and I didn't know too many other regular Navy officers.[*] I think Parham, who was a chaplain, might have gone USN by that time.[†] Wes Brown had graduated from the Naval Academy, and there were a few others.[‡]

Paul Stillwell: A pretty exclusive group.

Admiral Gravely: Yes, 25 or 30 people, roughly. So I began to think in terms of how do I go about this naval career thing. And about that time a couple of programs opened up that would at least extend my active duty time, whether I became regular Navy or not. One was the TAR program. So I looked into that. Of course, it was training and administration of reserves. And generally you spent some time at a reserve training center, and then, of course, whatever your sub-specialty may be, you would do a tour in that sub-specialty. That seemed like a good program, so I applied for it.

Lo and behold, very shortly before I got an answer, there was a program called the contract program, wherein a reservist could get a contract which assured him a maximum of five years on active duty. I said, "That looks pretty good, and so I'll try that." So then the next thing that came out was a regular Navy program. And, lo and behold, I wasn't eligible, simply because of seniority. The program stated that you had to be a lieutenant with a date of rank of something like '52, as I recall, as a lieutenant. My

---

[*] On 15 March 1947 Lieutenant (junior grade) John W. Lee, Jr., USNR, became the first black officer with a commission in the regular Navy. He served on active duty until his retirement as a lieutenant commander in 1 July 1966. His oral history is in the Naval Institute collection.
[†] Lieutenant Thomas D. Parham, Jr., CHC, USN.
[‡] Ensign Wesley A. Brown, USN, became the first black graduate of the Naval Academy in 1949, then entered the Civil Engineer Corps. He retired as a lieutenant commander in 1969. His oral history is in the Naval Institute collection.

date of rank was '51, so I was about a year senior for the program. But I kept reading everything about it, and, lo and behold, one day there was a change to the program.

They had not received enough applications, so anybody could apply to the program if he met the eligibility requirements, including date of rank, no matter what it was, if you would agree that if you were selected and that your date of rank could not be senior to a lieutenant of 6-1-52 or something like that. So I applied for that too. And shortly thereafter I got a change in designator to 1107. I was a TAR. The next thing that happened I got a four-year contract. And then, lo and behold, the last thing that happened I got selected for regular Navy. So that was my good year. No matter what I touched, it turned out gold that year.

Paul Stillwell: Did you have to sacrifice some seniority to get in the regular Navy?

Admiral Gravely: I sacrificed the seniority of about a year's drop in date of rank. I was being transferred at this time from the Toledo to go to the Commandant of the Third Naval district for duty. And I was going as an 1107, but the appointment to regular Navy was transferred up there, so when I got to New York that's when the appointment came.

Paul Stillwell: That made you an 1100.*

Admiral Gravely: That made me an 1100, right. Well, the Toledo came back into Long Beach, stayed in Long Beach for about a month. I had my orders. The ship then went to Bremerton for another overhaul.† And on July the fourth of 1955, two years to the day, I left the Toledo. I rode a train down to Long Beach. I had a car in Long Beach, so I picked that up, and drove across country to meet my wife. My wife and I had decided that no matter where I went next time, we would go together. The best time for her to end her contract—she had a contract year to year—was, I think, about December or so of the previous year, so she informed her employer that she was going to leave. Then she

---

* The designator 1100 applied to general unrestricted line officers—for the most part, those in surface ships—from the 1950s to the 1970s, at which time a separate surface warfare designator was created.
† Puget Sound Naval Shipyard, Bremerton, Washington.

went to live with her folks in Christianburg, Virginia. That's where I met her, and we then traveled up to New York together.

Paul Stillwell: Did you have an increasing feeling of confidence at that point? I mean, you'd been improved professionally and gotten the designator change. And you had a solider base of experience, too.

Admiral Gravely: Well, I did, but, frankly, I really didn't think at that time that I would go much past lieutenant commander. There'd been no black in the Navy who'd ever done that, so I felt that I would probably go to lieutenant commander. I didn't ever think in terms of passover or anything like that, but I felt that I'd have the 20 years in, and that I would retire as a lieutenant commander, and then go do something else.* I didn't have any idea what that would be, although I guess if I had really sat down to think about it, it would have been probably getting in the public school system—coaching and teaching were what I had always wanted to do. And so I kind of felt in terms of that.

Paul Stillwell: So were you planning a tour at a time at that time?

Admiral Gravely: Planning basically a tour at a time. I knew that as a regular Navy officer, why, if I ever made lieutenant commander I had to stay to 20 to retire, so it was that kind of a thing.

Well, anyway, we traveled up to New York to Com Three, and I reported. And I was quite surprised when I got to Com Three, because I thought in terms of only one of two ways I could go. I thought that they would probably send me to the reserve section, since I had been a TAR, and my designator was a TAR when I arrived there. And the second direction was possibly to the communications gang there.

But, much to my surprise, I was sent in to meet a little guy who was the district security officer. I became his assistant for ABC—atomic, biological, and chemical—warfare defense matters. I was really taken aback, but fine. I met a really gentle man.

---

* Being passed over means not being selected for the next higher rank.

Samuel L. Gravely, Jr., Interview #2 (7/7/86) – Page 102

His name was Kacharsky. Kacharsky had been a POW during World War II in Japan, and constantly we were talking about experiences there.

But I just happened to talk to him one day and said I was just curious as to how I got down here. He basically told me that he needed an assistant for the job, and he was very happy that I came there, because it didn't make any difference to him if I was black, blue, green, red or anything else. And I'd heard that once before too. But he was very happy to see me, and everything else, explained the job, and we hit it like two peas in a pod.

We did begin to socialize by that time. I met Kacharsky's wife, who worked over at Bayonne.* Now, when my wife and I first went to New York, my wife had a sister there. So we lived with her for a short while until we found our own apartment, and we moved into our own apartment over in Brooklyn. Brooklyn, not too far from the naval shipyard, was not my idea of the nicest community in the world, but at the same time it provided us our first real home, although we'd had rooms and those kinds of things before that, and we really enjoyed it.

We'd been there for about three months when I came home one day, and I noticed that there was a half a red brick in the living room. I couldn't figure out what that was. So then I looked, it had come in through the window, which was broken. Then I looked further, and somebody had been in the house, had been through the refrigerator, and somebody had drunk a Coke, and those kinds of things. But the most shocking part about it was that I had a piggy bank that I was saving to buy a fish aquarium. The guy had not only taken my piggy bank, but he'd laid on my bed and counted my money. [Laughter]

So I decided that I had to get out of that area, and whereas I tried to move over to Bayonne before, where the Navy had some housing over there, I was unable to do so. But my boss somehow made arrangements, he and his wife working over to Bayonne, and the next thing I knew I was offered an apartment over there. Eastern Sea Frontier, of course, was in that headquarters.

Paul Stillwell: Your office was at 90 Church Street in Manhattan?

---

* Bayonne, New Jersey, across New York Harbor from New York City, was then the site of an annex to the New York Naval Shipyard.

Admiral Gravely: This is at 90 Church Street, yes. And I got to know and work with the Eastern Sea Frontier staff as well as with the Com Three staff. Dennis Nelson was there also. So Dennis and I were old buddies, but whereas we certainly were friendly, and saw each other periodically, Dennis was 15 years older than I, so we weren't that kind of buddies. I had my wife there and he did not, so we saw each other frequently.

Admiral Miles was the commandant, and it was at his house that I went to the first set of flag officer quarters that I'd ever been to.[*] Miles was just a fantastic guy. My wife and I went there once, and he had a Sunday afternoon affair where we just thoroughly enjoyed ourselves. Obviously, in that day and time our social activity was mostly in the black community. New York had it all, you know, plus the fact my wife came from a rather large family. She had cousins galore, and they were all over the world. In fact, I kept running into them.

Well, her father had 15 brothers and sisters, and only two of them stayed down in Christianburg. The rest of them populated the country; I couldn't drive across country without running across them. But, in any event, most of the social activity was out there. But then we went to Admiral Miles's place. That was sort of a highlight. It was a beautiful set of quarters in Brooklyn Navy Yard. We thoroughly enjoyed it. In fact, I took a young nephew with us, and Admiral Miles seemed to have liked kids, sort of took to my nephew. We were quite pleased there, and I was quite pleased on the staff.

Things really proceeded fairly normally for me there. However, shortly after I'd been there, and since we were in the atomic, biological chemical warfare world, Kacharsky told me about—I guess we called him Ski—Ski said, "I'm going to send you down to Fort McClellan, Alabama, to go through a five-week course in ABC warfare." This was great, but I'd never been to Fort McClellan, Alabama, and really didn't have much of a desire to go to Fort McClellan, Alabama. And he said, "Hey, there'll be probably about 20 students in the class, and you're to be number one."

Paul Stillwell: That's an order.

---

[*] Rear Admiral Milton E. Miles, Commandant Third Naval District.

Admiral Gravely: That's an order, yes, sir. Well, I guess I should tell you a little bit about the job primarily. We were the district security office, and at that point in time we conducted security as well as a new term that was in fashion then called passive defense. Inspections of every naval activity in the Third Naval District. We inspected the large activities once a year and the minor activities—and there were a lot of minor activities—once every two years. Bayonne, for example, was a major activity, and so that got inspected every year. Niagara Falls, which was the airfield, got inspected every year. We went to the large activities, and I can't remember them all. So you were on the road quite a bit. We'd plan our trips where we'd hit eight or nine of these places. For example, when we went into Niagara Falls we also hit Scotia, obviously, and all of the places up in that area. Long Island Sound, you go out there and do a few of them, and go down and hit the bigger ones, etc. Ski took me along with him on the first couple, and then we sort of alternated. He let me go on my own, and I'd do a few.

Paul Stillwell: What sorts of things were you looking for?

Admiral Gravely: Well, the physical security things you can imagine what it was. Checking the size of the guard force, whether they had too many, too few. Looking at gates, seeing what should be locked, what shouldn't be locked. Passive defense—you sort of went into the opcon center to see if he had the proper radio communications down there, did he have water down there, and those kinds of things to make sure that in the event of a nuclear attack, then they would be fairly well set up.* Certain of the chemicals that you needed for defense against chemical warfare, certain things for biological warfare, and those kinds of things.

Paul Stillwell: This was during the Cold War era.

Admiral Gravely: This was during the Cold War era, and for some reason we were building our fortress America. We were talking in terms of shelters, deep underground

---

* Opcon—operational control.

shelters and those things, and we looked at their plans to see if they could properly take care of the people in case of an evacuation. We looked into all of those kinds of things.

Paul Stillwell: Stockpiles.

Admiral Gravely: Yes, the stockpiles and those things. And see if they had the gas masks and the suits for fighting chemical warfare as well as nuclear warfare.

Paul Stillwell: Did you tie in with civil defense authorities also?

Admiral Gravely: We did. In fact, there was normally an exercise at least once a year, and we used to go up to Scotia. That was sort of the alternate command center for Com Three. The Com Three staff would go up there and we would fight the battle from up in Scotia, New York.

Ski, as I said, said that he wanted me to go to Fort McClellan, and, of course, we got orders. As I recall, that January I went down to Fort McClellan, Alabama, and it was a very good school. We started with one week atomic, one week biological, and one week chemical, and then the last two weeks were passive defense—defense against those things. I didn't have any problems down there at all. I enjoyed Fort McClellan. I met a guy who was in the Army, who became a friend of mine for life.

I met another really interesting character down there who came from BuPers; he was in the BuPers training section. I can't think of his name either at the moment, but this young man and I were sitting around talking one day, and we were talking basically about the black officer in the Navy and what the future was and everything else. I gave him a rundown on my experience, etc., and that's when he told me, "You know, you probably are on the five-term list." It was a list wherein the Navy sent you to Monterey, as I recall. This was for ex-reserve officers, who had augmented, and then they were to go out for what we used to call five term. Anyway, it was a school program.

Basically this was to bring you up snuff with the regular Navy officer. And they had a short course in military justice and those kinds of things. Frankly, when I went through comm school at Monterey there was at least one student in my class who was there for this program. Now, I'm saying five term, but it seems to me that it was only about a six-month program. I've forgotten what it was. In fact, Spence Matthews was awaiting the school when he and I went through comm school together. Then we talked more, and he said, "You know, if you don't go to that program then, my God, you're ripe for a destroyer. What you need is ops officer on a destroyer."

So I said, "Well, both of those sound intriguing, but could I come by your office on my way back to New York to see about it?"

He said, "Please do, please stop by my office, and we'll talk about it." Well, I graduated out of the course number four, [laughter] not number one. Probably disappointed Ski, but in any event, I stopped in BuPers on my way up. This commander was a reserve. Now, what the reservists did was they'd go down for the first two weeks of the course one year, then the next year they'd take one week down there and one week someplace else for their two weeks' active duty. Then they'd take the last two weeks the third year. And this was what this guy was doing. When I got into BuPers at his office, he was not there. So I got to talking to this deputy, and we were looking through the school lists, and I can't figure out what you call it. He said, "Let's talk about your experience a little bit."

I went and gave him the same pitch, you know, "The PC-1264, went out of the Navy, came back into recruiting, spent a year and a half on the Iowa, spent two years on the Toledo, now I'm at Com Three. Yes, I'm now qualified OOD independent steaming, blah, blah, blah, went to Monterey, etc."

He said, "Well, your name's on this list here, but you don't need that." He struck my name right off the list. And he said, "Well, we got more people on there than we can possibly send to school, and we certainly don't want to send a guy there who doesn't need it." Well, I can understand that.

He said, "But I got to tell you, with your experience and background you really need to go as an ops officer on a destroyer. Now, you go down and see So-and-so," and he gave me the name.

I went down to see this guy, and I wish I knew his name. But he said, "Hey, what makes you think you're qualified to go on a destroyer? Hell, you don't have the background for destroyers. We like to send our ensigns out of the Naval Academy to the destroyer Navy. Grow them up in destroyers and everything else. You've never done that. Christ, you couldn't hack it as ops officer on a destroyer."

I said, "Yes, sir," and I walked out of his office and here I was—too fat for the thin work and too thin for fat work. [Laughter] I was very disappointed in that, but at the same time I went on back to Com Three and tried to do the job.

Paul Stillwell: Was that a case of bad luck, that that man you'd met just wasn't there that day, do you think?

Admiral Gravely: Now, in my case I drove straight from Fort McClellan, and I'd planned to take that Monday off and do my time really in BuPers with him. I assume that he took his time off in his backyard or something like that, forgetting that he'd promised to see me.

Paul Stillwell: I wonder if it would have gone better for you had he been there.

Admiral Gravely: I think it would have. I think it would have gone better for me. At least I don't think he would have deleted my name off of that school list right in front of me, which the other guy did. But, in any event, I went back to Com Three, and just determined to do the best possible job.

Now, one of the things that I have left out of this, and I've got to tell you about it, because it is fairly significant. When I reported to Com Three, and they gave me the appointment, obviously the first thing you need is a physical. I went down for my physical, and my eyes would not pass the test, and I got to tell you, I had one hell of a time with eyes. I really credit my becoming a naval officer today to a young warrant who was there. He insisted that, "Okay, so the poor guy can't read 20/20 on the chart, but that's really not what we're interested in. Is there anything really wrong with his eyeballs?" I took the test about six times, and I got to tell you, I don't give a damn what it is, if you keep reading it over and over again, you get so you can learn it. And that's basically what I did with those eye charts. But, anyway, I did manage to get through that and accepted my regular Navy appointment. But, frankly, if it hadn't been for a good warrant down there, this young lieutenant doctor would have just sent me on my way, saying, "Not physically qualified," and I probably would have killed him before the day was over.

Paul Stillwell: Do you have a problem with color blindness at all?

Admiral Gravely: No, I didn't have a problem with color blindness. I use glasses for driving, and I can't use glasses if I'm writing a letter. I've never worried about it, because I keep a pair of glasses in my pocket all the time. I put them on if I'm going to drive my car, although my driver's permit doesn't say that, but I do keep them along.

But, anyway, Com Three turned out to be a very, very interesting job as well as a good job for me, because I got to know some people who began to have a lot of faith in my ability. I can remember that when Ski left, a new officer came over to take over his job. Very, very competent officer, also ex-enlisted. In fact, I guess everybody you met as a lieutenant commander in those days was ex-enlisted just about.

He didn't quite understand the program and unfortunately made the decision to go to Scotia to run the operations for the ops officer, who was an old Navy captain—gruff, demanding, etc. The captain got on the phone, in the midst of the exercise, when he didn't believe my boss, and called me to give him answers. Then finally he said, "Get your ass up here." And, of course, I went up there, and my boss was flabbergasted. He didn't know that the ops officer had been calling on the phone asking for answers which he'd been giving them. I thought he'd been giving them fairly correctly. But the guy had more faith in me than he did in him.

One other thing that happened with being there was prior to Ski's leaving. We had the reserve ships at that point in time, the reserve DDs, DEs. Those ships were attached to the commandant's staff. The commandant was in the administrative chain of command. And each of those ships had to be inspected once every six months. Well, when my boss, Kacharsky, was there by himself, did it. And my predecessor in that job, who had been detached without relief, was a reserve officer who'd never been aboard ship, and Ski wouldn't let him. So Ski did them all.

So Ski said, "Sam, you've been aboard ship, and it's nothing but a damage control inspection. You do it." He said, "I got to warn you about Kowalzyk. Kowalzyk is a demanding guy, and I got to tell you, you will never pull any wool over his eyes, so don't try. But at the same time, just go down there, and do your normal good job, and everything will come out okay."* We inspected the ship, and then we had a critique in the wardroom. Well, I was still inspecting the ship when most people went to lunch. I had done certainly lots of inspections on board the Toledo and lots of inspections on board the Iowa as part of inspection parties, but I'd never really been on one on my own. So I was just walking around the ship, and I passed the ship's office. There was a yeoman in there banging away, so I said, "Hey, what are you typing?"

He said, "Oh, I got Captain Kowalzyk's inspection notes."

This may not have been kosher, but I said, "Let me see those notes." And I had practically all of the damage control discrepancies down, but there were a couple that Captain Kowalzyk highlighted in his report. So at the critique, then I remembered that these were the ones I better highlight too. So I highlighted those, and I gave the ship a satisfactory for the inspection or something like that. Of course, the exec, who became a great friend of mine, was a little upset that I didn't give him a good or something like that. But, in any event, Captain Kowalzyk said, "Boy, oh boy. That's what a call a good inspection."

Paul Stillwell: Really perceptive.

Admiral Gravely: [Laughter] Really. So I was welcome on all the inspection parties from then on. But learned a lot from that Captain Kowalzyk. You know, there are times when you've got to be demanding too, and you've got to call some spades a spade. You cannot sit around and say, "Hey, this guy is my friend, and he really ought to get a good grade." If it's wrong, it's wrong.

Paul Stillwell: People's lives could depend on that.

---

* Captain Alexander M. Kowalzyk, Jr., USN, was the Third Naval District chief of staff.

Admiral Gravely: People's lives could depend on it. There's an awful lot of other things at stake. In fact, unfortunately, my friend, the exec, got passed over for lieutenant commander.

Paul Stillwell: Were you involved with the mothball fleet ships at all in that job?

Admiral Gravely: Oh, no, no. Only that we went up and looked at the administrative chain of command, the physical security of the base, and those kinds of things. But not anything other than that. No planning or any of that. I did go down once to Com Four to do some joint planning in defense matters with them.[*] All the writing of emergency procedures. Went down to coordinate those things, and I was the guy who was sent down to do that.

Paul Stillwell: New York, of course, has much to offer in the way of entertainment with ball games and shows and movies and concerts. How much did you and your wife avail yourselves of that aspect?

Admiral Gravely: I guess most of the things that we got involved in were family affairs. We spent more time doing that than anything else. If there was some mutual agreement, we were going to go to a ball game, we went, but usually a firemen's ball or something the NAACP was hosting or something of that nature. We normally had to go to parties at either her quarters or my quarters or things like that. As I said, my wife was from a large family, so if you visit once a week you wouldn't run through the family in two years. We did a lot of that.

Paul Stillwell: Did she get involved in work up there too?

Admiral Gravely: No, she did not. She was not working at all.

---

[*] The Fourth Naval District (Com Four) was based at Philadelphia.

Oh, correspondence courses we were talking about. I know I completed more correspondences courses there than anywhere else. Scotia was near.* There was time to sit down and do these things, not only in the office, but in the afternoon. I probably completed about 50 correspondence courses from Scotia. You name it and I took it.

In addition to that, I finally decided I would tackle the Naval War College correspondence courses. They had one on operational tactics, as I recall. It was an eight-assignment course, but it was divided up into part one and part two, so I did the first four lessons. I never could have done it alone. What we used to do, I had two or three friends on the staff who were also taking it, because at that point in time you either had to take the exam, get the correspondence course completed on a subject, or go to a short course. If you didn't do the short course or somehow get exempted, you had to take this exam. And we were all painfully aware that we didn't particularly want to take the exam. So the four of us used to get together on a Saturday morning and sit down and discuss it. We discussed the problems, etc., and then we'd all go home and write out our individual answers to it, and there was no problem to that, I'm sure. But, anyway, I did complete an awful lot of correspondence courses there.

Now, on the personal side, you see, my wife had a back ailment, and we went through a series of doctors on that. Finally, they decided they would take her into the hospital, which was a merchant marine hospital, as I recall, on Staten Island, and they would do an exploratory operation. Ultimately, she ended up with a complete hysterectomy.

Paul Stillwell: Why did you not go to a Navy hospital?

Admiral Gravely: Well, Staten Island was much closer than going to the naval hospital out on Long Island. That was the main reason, plus the fact that they were supposed to have a good gynecologist over there. And I think maybe the doctor over there recommended it; I don't know. But it was a short hop from Staten Island over there on the ferry.

---

* Scotia, New York, was then the site of the distribution center for Navy correspondence courses.

But, anyway, here I'd just about spent my two years there, and so I began to think in terms of sea duty again. So it was roughly September of '57. I wrote my typical letter to the bureau, asking for sea duty, and I was really surprised when I got a letter back saying, "Yes, we've been looking at your jacket, and we have decided that you're going to an AKA out of San Diego as operations officer."[*] I really felt great, because now I was moving up in the world a little bit.

Unfortunately, my wife was still in the hospital at that time, and when she got out she was not able to travel for a while. So I took her down to her mother's home in Christiansburg, where she stayed there and convalesced until December of that year. In the meantime, I went on out to San Diego.

Well, I had an interesting set of orders there, which sent me to two courses out at PhibPac.[†] One was what they call P-1, and the other one was P-2; each of these courses was two weeks in length.

Paul Stillwell: This was in Coronado?

Admiral Gravely: This was in Coronado, yes, and the courses were basically designed to acquaint you with amphibious warfare. Well, my predecessor on the Seminole was also the training officer, and he felt I should go through a different set of courses than the bureau decided. So he wrote a letter over there and basically described the courses that I should take. One was three days in cold-weather communications. Another one was communicating with the amphibious ships of the task force and several things. When I got there, it was all confused because they'd have to keep me there for not just eight weeks, but 16. So we finally start talking, and I guess I went through P-1.

In the meantime, I knew the ship was there. So they had an interesting guy there by the name of Captain Bobo Thomson.[‡] There was another officer who was the first lieutenant, a lieutenant by the name of George Mau.[§] George had called over there, had located me in the BOQ, and had invited me over to his house for dinner on my first

---

[*] AKA was the designation used at that time for an attack cargo ship, one that was specialized for use in delivering cargo during an amphibious assault.
[†] PhibPac—Amphibious Force Pacific Fleet, based at Coronado, California.
[‡] Captain James W. Thomson, USN.
[§] Lieutenant George W. Mau, Jr., USNR.

Sunday there. I went over, met George and his family, and we were great. In fact, I just got a notice here about a month ago that his wife had died. You know, we saw them, because George and his wife came by to visit us earlier this year. She died of cancer. But we really became fast friends, talked about the ship, and everything else.

I said, "George, you know, I think somebody should tell the skipper that they're not going to keep me over here for 16 weeks. My curriculum is only for eight, and with this second letter from the ship there, I've got eight weeks to do nothing." So they were all concerned about it.

Well, in my third week there I got a call from Captain Thomson. He said, "Sam, you don't need all that crap. Get your tail over here. We're getting ready to go on an operation." [Laughter]

So instead of going for the full time, I went through that about three weeks of the course, I guess, and then reported to the AKA.[*]

Now, the Seminole was a little bit different from the kind of ship that I had been on. AKAs in those days, contrary to today, were not really fast movers. You know, we're talking about 16 knots, 17, 18 knots max. You're also talking about ships that have a lot of reservists on them.

Paul Stillwell: They didn't get the talent that a battleship or cruiser did.

Admiral Gravely: You didn't get the talent, good people. The exec was a fine guy, but he shocked me one day when I discovered that he felt that amphibious ships did dirty work, so they could be dirty. He said, "Not like that cruiser that you came off of, spit and polish." But I was determined to clean up my space. I didn't give a damn what the rest of it looked like, but I was going to clean mine up.

Also, what was quite interesting to me when I got aboard, instead of having one senior watch officer, they had two. One senior watch officer at sea, and one senior watch officer in port. The guy I relieved was the senior watch officer at sea, lieutenant

---

[*] USS Seminole (AKA-104), a Tolland-class attack cargo ship, was commissioned 8 March 1945. She displaced 14,160 tons, was 459 feet long, 63 feet in the beam, had a maximum draft of 26 feet, and a top speed of 16.5 knots. She performed long service, primarily in the Pacific Fleet, and was eventually decommissioned 23 December 1970.

commander, of course, senior to everybody else on board. And they had another guy who took it in port. I could never really figure that one out. But very shortly after I got there, I quickly told them that they had one senior watch officer, and that was me.

But then I was beginning to speak a little out of turn, because my relief had made up his mind that he was not going to leave that ship until Christmas, and I got there about the first week in November. So I had to live with him for about six to eight weeks, trying to not step in, because I thought I saw a lot of things that I could improve upon. Now, I do not mean to discredit the guy that I relieved, but he was an aviator, so this was his first shipboard duty. He got sent down, basically, because of ulcers, and so he probably should have gone to something to learn first, but anyway he got this job, and did the best he could. But I didn't think he really knew the job, particularly the communications of it. I didn't think he was that qualified a watch stander. But, you know, at some point in time everybody thinks a lieutenant commander can handle a ship, but that ain't so either.

Paul Stillwell: There are a lot of special requirements for amphibious warfare as well.

Admiral Gravely: That's right. He seemed to have done fairly well with some of the special requirements, but there were little things that bothered me. We were with this operation during the first two or three days, and the ship had a message to move in to unload, and they didn't receive the message. Everybody was moving in and beginning, and we got a message from the squadron commander saying, "Why haven't you carried out my so-and-so?"

The captain said, "Hey, hey I haven't seen anything."

And this guy said, "Well, we haven't gotten anything."

I said, "Hey, it's quite obvious to me you've missed a message. Now, go down there."

And this officer said, "Well, how am I going to get it?"

So I said, "Have that radioman get on the task group commander's net, and ask him for it." And, of course, we did, and we had been told to move about two hours before.

Well, Captain Thomson was just an outstanding guy, and he and I hit it off like two peas in a pod. When I got aboard, we were down in San Diego, and we were about ready to go the regular underway training. That was about five weeks, and then you go through another couple of weeks of amphibious training to make sure you get the boats to the point of departure, and the whole bit.

Paul Stillwell: And you had to be especially concerned about communicating with those boats.

Admiral Gravely: Yes. You got to be especially concerned about communicating with them. The ops officer's task was the duty of writing up a little op order and all the rest of this kind of stuff. Well, I dearly loved tactics. Captain Thomson knew where I had come from, and Captain Thomson had a hell of a lot more faith in me than I almost had in myself. But we would be on underway training, and we'd be the senior ship. So usually for an exercise of "tictacs," we were the number-one ship to perform the "tictacs."[*]

And I got to tell you, a couple of times I'd go up there to Captain Thomson and say, "Here's what I'd like for him to do today." I had it all plotted out with the signals I was going to give: the turns, the corpens, and all the rest of the stuff. Make one ship move from point A to point B, etc. And he liked that. So he'd just leave me up there, and he'd go off someplace else.

I enjoyed it, and I guess that's where I really got my really big feel that I could hack it, right there with Captain Thomson. I guess the thing that really built my confidence up came at the completion of refresher training, during which we made a decent grade on our operations portion. We were under way, coming out of San Diego, and then had to go over to off the Strand.[†] Captain Thomson said, "Sam, I'm going down to talk to a boat group. Now, take the ship over and drop the hook on it." [Laughter] And nobody'd ever told me that before.

Paul Stillwell: Had you ever anchored the ship before?

---

[*] "Tictacs," a play on the word "tactics," is a Navy slang term for multiship tactical maneuvers.
[†] The Strand is a section of beach near the Navy's amphibious base at Coronado, California.

Admiral Gravely: No. [Laughter] So I anchored this one. The navigator told me to drop, and I let her go. [Laughter] We might have been a little off, but we weren't that far off, so we didn't move. Captain Thomson had let me handle the ship one other time too. We were anchored in San Diego, getting ready to go out for the battle problem. The first exercise started when we were moored in San Diego; it was an emergency sortie, and you get the ship out without tugs or pilot. And it just so happened that this, being a single-screw ship, was hard to turn. It didn't make any difference if you were going this way or that way, backing, or going in the same direction. And I had to get the ship under way without it. So I got a great lesson and did it. And the only discrepancy was that I forgot to use the P-boats.* [Laughter] But I got it out without those things, and we did fairly well on the battle problem.

I had never made any calls on skippers before, and Captain Thomson was the first skipper who made it known that he expected me to call on him, and he was going to call on me. And, of course, he did. We did.

Now, on a personal note, my wife and I had discussed children, and, of course, we knew that there was no opportunity after the hysterectomy. So we thought we'd turn to adoption, and we basically decided that when we got into San Diego that we would do something about that. She had come out there in December, and we got a set of quarters, not much of a problem, but a guy who had been in recruiting with me as a chief petty officer had made LDO, and he was an ensign, was out in San Diego the same time.† I told him I was having a little problem getting on the list, and suddenly I was on the list, and there are quarters available. We had just one fine beautiful house out there. It was in Bayview Hills. I don't know if you're familiar with it.

Paul Stillwell: No, I don't know that area.

---

* P-boat or Papa boat is the nickname for the LCVP—landing craft, vehicle and personnel, a type of boat carried on board amphibious warfare ships of the era.
† LDO—limited duty officer, a former enlisted man whose duties are limited to the area of his enlisted rating specialty.

Admiral Gravely: If you would go out of the Eighth Avenue gate in the naval base, it comes right straight through National City, so you just keep going till you get to Bayview Hills. They had some really fine quarters up there. They were four to a unit, and we had a very good-sized one. So we started working with this adoption agency in San Diego. In the meantime, we were going through our little duties there in San Diego with the ship, etc. Social life had certainly improved, because I knew this guy Gene McGuire, who was a lieutenant, and he lived up in that area.* There were several other Navy up in that area. We visited each other, enjoyed each other, had great times.

We had a change of command, and a guy by the name of Captain Vern Allen came aboard.† And I had known Captain Vern Allen, because he was the staff operations officer on CruDiv 3 when I'd been aboard the cruiser. So I knew him. He knew me. And we just hit it off from day one. I guess I told you I changed that thing about the senior watch officer business, and I took it all over and did that.

Paul Stillwell: Did that carry with it the training function as well for upcoming OODs.

Admiral Gravely: Yes, it carried with it all of the functions of being a senior watch officer. It was my responsibility. In fact, Captain Bobo Thomson was just delighted to see that one guy was in charge. Hey, he knew which guy to call on now. But Captain Vern Allen insisted that I not only make out the watch bill, put the people on it he wanted on there, but when we were operating with task groups, Captain Allen would say, "Sam, I'm going to bed at midnight, and I want you on this bridge." And I'd stay there till dawn. So, in fact, I could even sit in his chair. [Laughter] So I got a real feel for operations, etc., with Vern Allen aboard.

Paul Stillwell: Where was the exec in all this?

Admiral Gravely: That was the problem. That was really a problem, because the exec was a reservist who really could not handle the ship. And it was too bad. He resented

---

* Lieutenant Eugene J. McGuire, USN.
† Captain Charles Vern Allen, USN.

my closeness with both skippers, and so whereas I think he might have tried on occasion to give me a hard time, I really didn't care about that. We were rather friendly from all outward appearances, but he made a couple of racial slurs at me a couple of times on the bridge. Christ, he accused me of not letting him see classified messages, because we'd get a message on an AKA that was classified. Generally we didn't get that much classified traffic, but sometimes I'd route the board around, particularly on messages which were of immediate concern to the captain. I took it to the captain, and I'd let somebody else take it to him, and he kind of resented that a little bit.

Well, before leaving Bobo Thomson, I've got to tell you one little thing that I thought was interesting from two aspects. I got selected that year, 1957, for lieutenant commander. Of course, the letter came in which appointed me, but basically it said, "We've got to make sure he's gotten all his correspondence courses, or he takes the exam, etc."

I went up to Captain Thomson with the letter from the administrative officer, and I said, "Captain Thomson, here in my hand is this little notebook which shows the list of correspondence courses I've completed. So I'm exempted from the exam."

He said, "Oh, Sam, give me that damn thing." Signed his name on it and everything else. But one day very shortly after that we had a new squadron commander to come aboard. He was crossing, and, of course, the bongs went, and I had duty that day, and I went there. I met him and escorted him across. About that time Captain Thomson came down, and I was a little ahead, and I could overhear them talking. This guy said, "Hey, Captain, I notice you have a colored lieutenant commander on board."

Bobo Thomson said, "I do?" He said, "What color is he?" All sincere and everything. And, of course, the commodore stuttered a little bit, but that was the end of that conversation. I've sometimes wondered if the guy didn't get to him on his fitness report, frankly, about that remark, but Captain Thomson was a strong supporter of mine, and, as I've said, so was Captain Allen.

Paul Stillwell: That was a time in the country when the civil rights movement was gaining momentum. The Brown versus Board of Education, the bus boycott in Alabama, and school integration in Little Rock.*

Admiral Gravely: Yeah, but that hadn't quite gotten there yet, I don't think. Martin Luther King, who really came on the scene about '55, didn't he?†

Paul Stillwell: Well, we're talking about later than that.

Admiral Gravely: Right, we're talking about '57.

Paul Stillwell: I'm wondering how much awareness you kept of these events on the national scene.

Admiral Gravely: It was a little bit difficult to really keep abreast of everything that was going on. Primarily because you were either going on a deployment, you were on it, or you were getting ready for it. And, whereas obviously in the radio shack we got the news in there—in fact, I was responsible, and I should have said this earlier, on the Toledo for putting out a four-page newspaper every day and also responsible on the Seminole for making sure that one was out, so the news was there. How alert I was to some of the incidents that were happening, I'm not sure. Now, Martin Luther King, let's see, that was '68 that he got killed, because I was on the Taussig, so we're still a long ways away from Martin Luther King and his big impact on the country.

Paul Stillwell: Well, he was starting the bus boycotts and so forth in Montgomery. And there was a big confrontation with Governor Faubus in Little Rock, in which the National Guard was called in.‡

---

* Brown v. Board of Education was a landmark civil rights case in which the U.S. Supreme Court voted 9-0 in 1954 to end segregation by law of public schools.
† Dr. Martin Luther King, Jr., a minister, came to national prominence in 1955 when he successfully led a boycott of buses in Montgomery, Alabama, to protest discrimination against black passengers.
‡ In the autumn of 1957 Governor Orval Faubus of Arkansas attempted to block integration of the high school in Little Rock. President Dwight D. Eisenhower called in National Guard troops to enforce the integration order.

Samuel L. Gravely, Jr., Interview #2 (7/7/86) – Page 120

Admiral Gravely: That's right. That was during Eisenhower's time, wasn't it? Yes. So you're right. Things had started.

Paul Stillwell: There were things to be aware of, but not much that you could do personally.

Admiral Gravely: Yes, right, right. Well, I'm not sure what I could have contributed from a personal standpoint, but when most of the things were happening, I just simply wasn't here. Or at least not in areas where there were hotbeds of activity.

Paul Stillwell: Did you have a membership in the NAACP or any part in its activities?

Admiral Gravely: I've been a member of the NAACP for practically all my life, really. But I've just carried a membership card around, paid my dues, and everything else like that. I've probably been more active in the last five or six years, since I've been retired since there is a Prince William County NAACP office, and I have been going to meetings. In fact, I was on the board of directors, but I haven't been to a meeting here lately. You can do just so many things I'm finding out, and there is a hell of a lot of things to do in retirement.

Well, in June of '58, I recall, the Seminole deployed to WestPac. When we arrived in Honolulu, I got a message that my home had been approved for adoption. However, they would wait until I got back from the deployment. Of course, there wasn't anything we could do about that. But it was approved, and we just sort of sat back and said, "Well, when I get back we'll contact them and see what the score is."

Went on a deployment, had two or three amphibious operations. None of any major import, because there wasn't that much going on, just training exercises basically. So we spent some time down at White Beach in Okinawa. Probably I felt more black at that time than any other time, primarily because Okinawa was not an integrated place. I can remember being in there with my good friend George Mau. We were sitting in the club, and somebody told him either take me out of there, or they were going to put me out. You know, that kind of stuff. The Marines were not our friends at that point in time. But nothing really untoward.

I was thinking about one incident. One night, and I think that we were in—I get it confused as to exactly where we were, but I know we were on the deployment, and I think it was probably Yokosuka. George said, "Sam, would you stand by and take my duty tonight? I'm the CDO."[*]

I said, "Well, I'm not going anyplace, so, sure, I'll take your duty." I lived on the 02 level, and most things happened on the main deck. But the next morning when I got up, the engineering officer, who was a department head and a friend of mine, said, "What are you going to do about it? What are you going to do about it?"

I said, "What the hell am I going to do about what?"

He said, "Well, didn't you know about the officers having a party on board last night?"

I said, "No, I didn't know about it. Let me investigate it." Well, I went on down to breakfast. I felt I had plenty of time to find out about it. There were two or three of the young officers talking about this terrible thing that went on during the night. Well, I still didn't know enough about it, and I began to get bits and pieces of it.

Well, there was a young officer on there who was ex-enlisted. He was an LDO ensign, I guess. He'd been an aviation boatswain's mate, I believe. Well, anyway, he and two other guys congregated in the engineering officer's stateroom, which was right across the hall from where George Mau lived. And they proceeded to have a party—liquor and the whole batch, and finally about 5:00 o'clock they were knocked out, basically. At least a couple of people came in there, and they were in this guy's stateroom. So I put them out, put them to their beds and everything else. But the incident was the drinking on board.[†]

Paul Stillwell: And they didn't inform you obviously.

---

[*] CDO—command duty officer.
[†] The U.S. Navy has prohibited drinking on board ship since 1914. In the 1980s the regulation was relaxed to permit the serving of wine and beer during command-sponsored receptions.

Admiral Gravely: No, nobody told me anything about it. Apparently they had loud music and everything else during the night. The OOD was normally on the starboard side, since the quarterdeck was there. The people having the party all moved over to the port side, so the quarterdeck watch couldn't hear anything. So nobody was going to do anything.

So, anyway, so here it was, Sunday morning. The captain was away, exec was away, nobody around. So I said, "Well, okay. I have to investigate a little bit and find out what was going on." I called a wardroom meeting on Sunday morning, must have been about 9:00 o'clock or whatever. I told them that I'd just been informed to what went on, and I was very sorry I didn't hear about it the night before, because I would have taken some action. I wanted to inform them all right here and now, that so far as I was concerned the <u>Seminole</u> bar was closed, and it would be as long I had the duty on here. So then I said, "Well, I've got to do a little bit more than that."

So I wrote a letter to Captain Allen, reporting all the facts. When the exec came on board, I was sorry that he came on board, because I really wanted to give it directly to the captain. But, anyway, the exec came on board so I gave it to him, but I had a copy made. I'm not sure what his plans were; I'm not sure he planned to give it to the captain. So I made sure the captain got the copy. The captain read it, and a couple of days later he decided to have mast on the three officers, and I had to be the witness against these three officers.

Of course, I went up there and described what had happened, and the officers knew and everything else. I think he said he was going to write it in the fitness report or something like that. But, anyway, it was a matter that it was taken care of. I think in the end that I gained an awful lot of respect from all those officers on board who knew that that was wrong, including the three guys who were involved. In fact, I still know the prime guy; we went by his house just last spring. So we all remained friends, despite the fact that I had an unpleasant chore to perform against some guys who were friends of mine. But that came off okay.

Paul Stillwell: You had these various responsibilities, the senior watch officer and CDO. You also for the first time had an entire department to run.

Admiral Gravely: That's right.

Paul Stillwell: What would you say about that responsibility?

Admiral Gravely: Well, the responsibility of running the department on the AKA, I think, was less trying, really, than being communications officer on one of those other ships. Certainly when we had an amphibious operation going on, it was kind of demanding, but the duties were just a little bit expanded on what I'd been doing all the time. Of course, the CIC guy worked for me, the communicator worked for me, the signal officer worked for me. I had the intelligence department, and I must tell you a story about intelligence, because these are the things I guess I keep remembering after the fact. When I relieved on the Seminole, I was told by my predecessor that I was the intelligence officer, so I simply asked him, "Well, what do I do as intelligence officer?"

He said, "Well, there's nothing to do." What the hell do you have the job for if there's nothing to do?

So, I said, "Well, are there any publications around here or anything?"

"Oh, there's something; it's someplace around here."

"Do I sign for anything?"

"No, you don't sign for anything."

Well, that guy got off, as I told you, just about the Christmas holidays, and shortly thereafter we get an inspection by Amphibious Group Three. They come on board with this team of people, and, of course, I had a communications inspection type, I had a CIC inspection type, I had a signal type, and I was running around. Suddenly a lieutenant came up and said, "I'm the intelligence officer, and I want to inspect your intelligence department."

I said, "Oh, come on, sit down. I'll answer your questions for you."

He said, "Well, as you know, there isn't much of an intelligence nature for an AKA to do. So what I really want to do is to go through and see if you've got this list of intelligence publications that you're supposed to have aboard, and that's about it."

I said, "Well, do you see that safe over there? Well, if you tell me what you want to see, I'll go over there and find it for you." So I unlocked the safe and went over there, and that guy started reading publications. You wouldn't believe this, but an AKA was supposed to have about 30 intelligence pubs, and there wasn't a one there. There was nothing in the damn safe. Well, we sat there and discussed it for a minute. I said, "Let me tell you something. My relief left here about three or four days ago, and he told me the pubs were here, so if the pubs are here, if they are on this ship, I'll find them. Now, when are you giving your critique?"

He said, "Well, I'm going to give my critique at 10:00 o'clock tomorrow morning, and I got to tell you, you got an unsat unless I can find those pubs."

I said, "Okay. I will have the pubs tomorrow morning."

He said, "Well, I'll be here about 9:00."

"Great." So I looked through that ship. I went through with the administrator, who I felt would be down in the ship's office someplace. The ship's office didn't have any. They weren't aboard. They just weren't there. So what the hell am I going to do about this?

Paul Stillwell: You found out then you should have queried your predecessor a little more thoroughly.

Admiral Gravely: Yes, I should have queried him. Well, I guess I was kind of thoughtless in this regard.

Paul Stillwell: Too trusting probably.

Admiral Gravely: Well, I thought if it was of an intelligence nature it probably would have been classified, but, no, they were all unclassified pubs, and he just didn't have them. So I started to think about it. Now, where could I do with something about that?

So were down at the foot of Broadway, and the only place that I could think about was Com 11.[*] I knew Com 11 had an intelligence officer. I went over to see the

---

[*] Com 11—Commandant of the 11th Naval District, which had its headquarters in San Diego.

intelligence officer at Com 11. I told him what my predicament was, and I said, "Do you have these pubs aboard?"

He said, "Yeah, I have them aboard." So we went down the list, and I checked out one of every one of those pubs.

I said, "Now, the first thing I want to do is to order me a set." And we made arrangements for a set to come. And I said, "But I got to have these tomorrow." [Laughter] Sure enough, I signed out for all of these pubs, and I took them over there, and I showed these to the guy the next day. He didn't look at them very carefully, or maybe he did. But at least he said, "I'm happy to see that you found your pubs."

I said, "Yes, sir."

Then had to take them back to Com 11, but I had a set coming, so I was in pretty good shape. But I got them. And I got to tell you, when my relief came aboard, I inventoried those damn things, and I kept an inventory of them, the whole thing and everything else. So just like you're saying, being too trusting. Maybe that wasn't quite kosher, but I was in an emergency situation, and the guy seemed to have been happy. In fact, his statement at the critique was that, "When I came over here yesterday and inspected this officer, I would have given him an unsat, but today he's much better."

Paul Stillwell: [Laughter] Very resourceful.

Admiral Gravely: "So I will give him a good," which I was very happy about.

Paul Stillwell: What do you recall about the competitive exercises and the competition with the other ships in your squadron?

Admiral Gravely: Well, we did the Zulu series, etc., but I don't remember very much about them.[*] It's not like a destroyer when you do things strictly in the squadron. In fact, the thing I remember more than anything else was that amphibious forces did a lot of

---

[*] Zulu is a word in the phonetic alphabet. Each ship was required to perform a number of training exercises designated by the letter Z and a series of numbers.

reorganizing. In fact, they went to what they called transdivs about the time I got there.* A transdiv was half a squadron. Captain Thomson was the senior skipper in the second division, so Captain Thomson hauled me over every Saturday morning to inspect somebody else's ship after having inspected ours on Friday. So I spent a hell of a lot of time in whites and swords, going back from ship to ship. Competitive exercises were things we did; certainly the communications group, I remember them more than anything else.

So far as the competitive year was concerned, we basically used our refresher training grade for part of that, and then there were just some individual exercises, bringing the boat groups over there; we did okay. I don't think we ever won the squadron E but got by them fairly satisfactory.†

The biggest one that I remember is that there was a security exercise, which people held on the various ships, as well as various ships were to hold them on various groups. So we happened to be up in San Francisco in the yards at the time, and I think it was a tacron group which in Alameda, and three of us were directed to go over there and break into their security.‡ And I must tell you, their security was good, because they caught us. When I tried to explain to them that this was just an exercise, and that my skipper had sent me over, they decided to call my skipper.

Captain Thomson said, "No, I don't know the guy." [Laughter] I thought I'd been had. But then shortly thereafter he admitted that I was part of the ship's company. [Laughter] Well, you can imagine, the other two guys—well, I was senior, so they treated me a little bit rougher than they treated the others. But they caught me hands down.

The deployment, as I said, was pretty routine, and, of course, Captain Vern Allen was aboard at this time. A very, very sharp guy. He had a good rapport with the entire wardroom. In fact, he had a better rapport with the wardroom than Captain Thomson had. Captain Thomson, though a very steady man, would do something once in a while that somebody would think wasn't quite kosher. You know, not necessarily wrong, but

---

* Transdiv—transport division.
† An "E," for excellence, is generally awarded to a ship or component of a ship as a result of top performance in competition with other ships during a given time period.
‡ Tacron—tactical air control squadron.

they thought it was strange. For example, on the last cruise he jumped off the wing of the bridge into the ocean. They had swim call, and he jumped off and almost broke his back.

Paul Stillwell: Sort of eccentric.

Admiral Gravely: Yes, yes, right, right. But still a tremendous guy, and I admired him as well as Vern Allen.

Well, we arrived back from WestPac roughly about December of '58. At that time we checked with the adoption agency, and we picked up our first son, and I named him Robert Michael. Robby was about eight months old, so he was born just about two or three months when we were approved. We probably would have gotten him even then, but he was about eight months old when we got him. Just a tremendous young lad.

Things were beginning to change a little bit for us too, because now that we were parents we began to think in terms of what do you do as parents, and those kinds of things. We felt, first of all, we probably needed a home with a backyard for him. And we also should join a neighborhood church, because we had been going to various chapels. Become a part of the neighborhood. We bought a house in San Diego and had the backyard for him. We joined the neighborhood church. In fact, in San Diego we always came back to the same church. Met a lot of good people there, and just had great times in San Diego.

Robby was really adopted by the wardroom. In fact, he was quite a good baby. You know, he wasn't crying all the time, and so whenever I had the duty, one night in four, Alma and Robby would come down. The wardroom bought him a high chair. So he had his own little high chair in the wardroom and everything else. He was just, just tremendous.

The ship went back up to the yards in San Francisco after the deployment. And Alma and I were down at Fisherman's Wharf, and I'm not sure exactly which place in that area we were having dinner. We were sitting there, and two guys came over. They were interested in talking about how good the Navy seemed and everything else. We started talking about my background, and a guy said, "Hey, how'd you like to have a job in civilian life?" I had never really thought of that. But it looked like here were two guys who wanted to hire me just because I had a good baby. [Laughter] But, of course, they had talked about my background a little bit, and I'd been a communications officer, so I had a little bit of electronics, things like that. But I turned them down, decided I wasn't quite ready to do that yet.

But, anyway, starting sometime in the spring of '59, I began to think in terms of, "Where do I go next, and how to get there?" I'd had a little time on a couple bridges, wherein I had been left up there all by myself and taken charge. So I decided that now was about time to strike out for an exec's job. I was lieutenant commander, and I really wanted to go to destroyers. So I wrote a letter to BuPers describing my desire to go to destroyers.

I got a very nice letter back that said basically, "Our plans are that when you finish your tour on Seminole, and we plan to keep you there for 28 months, you will then go the Fleet Training Group of San Diego for shore duty." I didn't like that answer, having been through several tours of amphibious training. Of course, you hear everything, but I frankly didn't think they had the best talent to become an officer there, and I felt I was pretty good. I just wasn't ready to retire, and I felt I shouldn't do that.

So I sat down and I wrote another letter. I incorporated all of the reasons why at this point in time I should go to a destroyer. And for the first time I wrote on a piece of paper, "I have an urgent desire for command." Then I let that letter sit for a while. In the meantime, I began to get a little disturbed that I was getting that kind of an answer out BuPers. So I told my skipper that I'd like to write an official letter, and would he endorse it. He said, "Sure, write it." So I wrote this official letter to BuPers, and I got back in short order from the same person two different answers. To the personal letter he said, "I told you once, and now I'm telling you again. You're going to stay aboard the Seminole for 28 months, and then you're going to Fleet Training Group San Diego."

To my official letter he said, "When we have found a relief for you, you will be transferred to a destroyer squadron, in training for executive officer of a destroyer." And they all came from the same guy.

Paul Stillwell: How could you figure that?

Admiral Gravely: Well, I figured like this. There are a couple of things. Number one is that a detailer has a job of putting a round peg in a round hole. And sometimes he'll put square pegs in those round holes. But he needs to fill the hole. When you write a letter to the Chief of Naval Personnel, maybe he doesn't see them all, but some level folks see those. Then that detail comes up, and he briefs them as to what he plans to do. They may have thought, "Well, this guy's got more on the ball than that." And I think that's what happened to me.

In addition to that, I had some rather good friends along the way, influential people.

Paul Stillwell: Was there any impulse that you could see at that time on the part of the Navy to groom some black officers for higher rank?

Admiral Gravely: No, there was no impulse in that regard. The impulse was that there were a lot of ex-reserve officers who had been in miscellaneous type jobs, and were now lieutenant commanders, and, "They're all going to get passed over for commander unless we can do something with them." And so there was a program called Training for Exec of a Destroyer, and it wasn't very widely known, but during my tour, and I spent six months doing this, I met several guys who had either been in the program or who were there at that time period. And so I just think that somebody looked and said, "Hey, we ought to at least give this guy a chance," and so I got it.

Well, I was there almost two years before I got off, about 21 months. I guess, it must have been about July or so of '59, my orders sent me to ComDesRon 7 staff for duty in training for executive officer.* We had the normal good-bye parties, and I really had a lot of good friends on Seminole. In fact, I think that my wife and I were probably closer to the Seminole group than we'd ever been with any other group of people, other than just one or two individuals. But we certainly were a close-knit group on board that ship.

---

* ComDesRon 7—Commander Destroyer Squadron Seven.

Well, I reported to DesRon 7, which was on the Lofberg at the time.* I've forgotten the other ships in the division, but I ran across my old nemesis, and that's called to some degree the temporary officer. A temporary officer was the chief staff officer and engineer of the squadron. My personal feelings are that they are very, very smart guys in their specialty, but unfortunately when you take them out of their specialty, they don't know what to do. Now, it's quite unfortunate that a guy can't just be an engineer and that's it, because he was a good engineer. But when he saw my orders he said, "My God, what are you to do?"

I said, "Well I thought that obviously there's such a program set up here, and that you would know what to do."

He said, "No, no, I never heard of this before, and what would you like to do?"

I said, "Well, I would imagine that someone should know something about what are some of the short courses I could take over at TraPac, number one.† And, number two, I probably ought to ride some destroyers and watch some execs in action." And he agreed that that would be a good thing to do. He said, "Now, take the TraPac book and go up there and see what courses you want to go through, and then maybe you want to ride a destroyer. Just pick any one of the destroyers in the squadron and go out there and get a ride."

So I thought about that for a while, and I said, "Well, you know, I can find the courses in the TraPac book that I think I need to do a little bit and get some training in. But I'm going to feel kind of like a bum going up and asking some exec can I ride his destroyer this week."

He said, "Oh, don't worry about it, they all belong to me. They'll take care of you." Well, that's what I did for three months. I took several of the three-, four-, five-day courses out at TraPac. Then I came back on a Friday, and if I saw somebody was getting ready to get under way, I'd go over there and say, "Sir, I'm staff DesRon 7, and I'd like to ride your ship next week if you don't mind."

---

* USS Lofberg (DD-759), an Allen M. Sumner-class destroyer, was commissioned 26 April 1945. She had a standard displacement of 2,200 tons, was 376 feet long, 41 feet in the beam, and had had a draft of 16 feet. Her design speed was 34 knots. She was armed with six 5-inch guns and ten 21-inch torpedo tubes. She remained in service until decommissioned on 15 January 1971. She was sold to the Taiwan Navy in 1974.
† TraPac—Training Command Pacific Fleet.

This guy might say, "Well, I really don't have any room." That was true in many, many instances—that they didn't have room. But there were a lot of other guys who said, "Sure, be happy to. Go and find yourself a bunk, and you got it made."

Well, I know that the commodore never knew this. And the skipper of the Lofberg at that time was Commander Prout, an officer who had been the first lieutenant in the Iowa, so I knew him.* And I don't think he ever knew this, but I was never assigned a bunk on board the Lofberg, and I was there for three months while that ship was in the yards at San Diego. I was never assigned a bunk. Now, I must admit, she was in the yard so I could go home every night. If you're attached to a ship, you need to have a little space to put things. And certainly if you're down there you don't want to sit in the wardroom all of the time. But I never was assigned a bunk for three months, and so I was a little disturbed about that. But that was fine. I got invited to the social affairs, etc.

Then one day I was called up to the commodore's room. Of course, he said, "How are you getting along?"

"I'm fine. I'm going to the short courses, I'm riding what destroyers I can." Generally when you have command of a ship, and you get so-called guests or a training officer, if he's a lieutenant commander, you give him quarters appropriate to a lieutenant. I slept in the bunkroom there in the top bunk, in that first compartment down in the bowels of the ship sometimes. I slept in anybody's room; it didn't matter. And, of course, I watched an awful lot of execs in action, and tried to learn from them, see what they were doing, things like that.

Paul Stillwell: Were they willing to help you?

Admiral Gravely: Most of the people were willing to help, but the thing that bothered me, more than anything else, was that there wasn't any glad hand when you came aboard. You know, "Yeah, there's a spare bunk back there in the junior officers' bunk room," you know, and that kind of stuff. And certainly, "Pay your mess bill before you leave." But I liked most of them, and I got along fairly well with the skippers. I think they knew

---

* Commander Russell K. Prout, USN.

what I was trying to do. I was not in the way—as best as I can describe it—when I came up on their bridge. That's the only way I can describe it: not in the way.

But, anyway, the commodore called me up, and he said basically, "How are you doing?"

"I'm fine."

He said, "Well, you know, we're getting ready to deploy, and I don't have room to take an additional officer. So what I plan to do is to send in a letter to BuPers saying you are qualified for exec of a destroyer, and I think you are. And probably they'll find a destroyer for you."

So I said, "Yes, sir."

He sent off his letter, and he transferred me to the tender to await orders from BuPers. But before I could report to the tender, I got orders back from BuPers which said "Go to Des Ron 5." And so, of course, I went directly to DesRon 5.

The commodore over at Des Ron 5 happened to be a guy that I had met in the amphibious forces, Commodore Nisewaner.[*] So we briefly knew each other, and I guess I'd seen him a second time in one of the short courses in electronic warfare, or something like that. So we had touched base, and I talked with him a little. When I got to his ship, the Somers, he was a little surprised to see me, but I told him that BuPers obviously didn't have a job for me, so this was what I was to do in the meantime.[†]

So, anyway, he said, "What have you been doing?" So I told him. And he said, "Well, here on the Somers we're going to be going to sea in a little bit, so you can learn a little bit here." And he said, "What I want you to do is, I'm going to give you the CruDesPac inspection lists, pre-deployment inspection, and I want you to take this book, and I want you to go down and inspect every department in this ship. In the meantime, I'm going to transfer you to the ship to work with the executive officer, and you can catch on from there."

---

[*] Captain Terrell A. Nisewaner, USN.
[†] USS Somers (DD-947) was a Forrest Sherman-class destroyer commissioned 3 April 1959. She had a standard displacement of 2,780 tons, full-load displacement of 3950 tons, was 418 feet long, 45 feet in the beam, and had a draft of 20 feet. Her design speed was 33 knots.

The skipper, Cummings, was a really great guy so far as I was concerned.* He did not make admiral, but he was a tremendous individual. Had a good wardroom. And, believe it or not, my roommate, and he gave me a room and bunk, was Larry Layman, who is an admiral today.† So Larry and I were roommates on that tour. The experience was a good one.

It was not the easiest thing in the world to be a one-man inspection team, particularly since the department heads didn't really have a lot of time. So usually I'd get assigned some guy who was fairly junior in the department, but at the same time I got it done. I stayed there with him for about a month and a half, when one day Commodore Nisewaner called me up and said, "Sam, I really don't understand this, because I thought you'd have orders by now, etc. But I'm leaving, and I'm going back to Washington, but I'd like to finish up all my unfinished business, and so what I'm going to do is write a letter to BuPers, tell them you're qualified for exec of a destroyer, and I imagine they'll find you a destroyer."

So he left, and I was still sitting there. The next guy was a guy by the name of Commodore Nash, and I knew Nash very well.‡ A very tremendous sailor. He was kind of happy with what I was doing, and he said, "That's the best way to learn destroyers. You know, seeing them in action, etc." I was on the watch bill of the Somers. Stood all OOD watches on there. There weren't very many lieutenant commanders in that day and age standing OOD watches. That's all right; that's how you learn things.

Paul Stillwell: You were getting some fleet experience, not just independent steaming.

Admiral Gravely: That's right, getting some fleet experience and loving it all the way. The biggest thing was that I had a bunk, and I had a seat in the wardroom. And I had good people to work with, and I enjoyed it.

Paul Stillwell: Had she been converted to a DDG at that point?

---

* Commander Edward J. Cummings, Jr., USN, commanded the destroyer Somers (DD-947) from 3 April 1959 to 28 October 1960.
† Rear Admiral Lawrence Layman, USN. In 1959 he was a lieutenant.
‡ Captain David Nash, USN.

Admiral Gravely: No, the Somers was a brand-new ship. The first skipper was Commander Cummings, and he was a tremendous help to me. His exec would let me do some navigating coming into port. The operations officer was Larry Layman at that time; I worked with him, and there was no problem there. I was pretty well qualified there in the ops department. Not for destroyer operations, obviously, but when you talk in terms of ops, ops is ops is ops. So there were no big things that I had to learn there.

Paul Stillwell: That was weapons and engineering.

Admiral Gravely: Weapons and engineering would have been the spots that I would have needed much more training, but I really didn't have sense enough to ask really very intelligent questions when I got there. I could follow the inspection form, and got a lot of good answers. But I watched the guys in action and everything else. Well, when Commodore Nash came aboard, as I've said, he was very happy with the arrangements, etc., but it was about Christmas, and he said, "Sam, I am going back to BuPers over the Christmas holidays on a little leave, and I will have you a job when I come back."

So I said, "Yes, sir. Thank you. I'll be happy, because I've done this for four and a half months now." Well, Commodore Nash came back just before New Year's, and I think he avoided me a little bit, but in any event when I did get to see him he said, "Sam, I just have not been able to do anything for you. As you know, we're going to deploy about the first of February. What I want you to do is to take the TraPac catalog, and go through there and find yourself enough five-day, two-week courses to stay here in San Diego for seven months, because we don't have a room for you."

So I said, "Yes, sir." So starting about New Year's Day I started looking through the TraPac schedule, and I had to have it all done by February the first. Sometime in January, when I had my list partially done, dispatch orders came in for me to go as exec on the Theodore E. Chandler.* The Theodore E. Chandler was a part of DesRon 5; it was in DesDiv 52. I was just flabbergasted, but happy as a lark.

---

* USS Theodore E. Chandler (DD-717), a Gearing-class destroyer, was commissioned 22 March 1946. She had a standard displacement of 2,400 tons, was 390 feet long, 41 feet in the beam, and had a maximum draft of 19 feet. Her design speed was 35 knots. She was armed with six 5-inch guns and five 21-inch torpedo tubes. She had a long career of service until being decommissioned 1 April 1975.

I made the mistake of going to the flagship of DesDiv 52. I was looking for the Theodore E. Chandler, and the exec sort of chewed me out for coming on board his ship and not knowing that it was not the right one. I said, "I know it's not the Theodore E. Chandler, but I thought you should have known where the Theodore E. Chandler was."

"Well, I keep up with this ship; that's it."

"Yes, sir." And I walked off the quarterdeck. And, of course, I did find the Theodore E. Chandler. Well, I reported aboard, and, of course, they escorted me up to the exec's stateroom. I thought that when I got there the ship was a little loose. I couldn't find the OOD, but some messenger grabbed me and took me up to the exec's stateroom. I said, "Sir, I have a set of orders, and I guess I'm your relief."

He said, "You know, I expected a relief, but I didn't know you were going to get here this quick."

I said, "Well, here are my orders."

He said, "Come on, I'll take you up and introduce you to the captain." So we went up, and I met the captain, Galen C. Brown.* Captain Galen C. Brown was one of the nicest people I have ever met in this man's Navy. He was not surprised to see me, or anybody. But the exec said, "Captain, let me introduce you to my relief." We shook hands. He said, "By the way, Captain, you remember I wanted to go on 30 days' leave?" He said, "Do you have any objection if I leave today?" Honest to God. The captain said, ""No." He took off.

Paul Stillwell: Great turnover period.

Admiral Gravely: I guess. [Laughter] Well, I have tried for the life of me to really figure out what had gone on on that ship, and I think I've come to some conclusions. The biggest thing was that the ship had gone through a yard overhaul during the fall before that and part of the winter. They had a FRAM inspection; that was the fleet rehabilitation and modernization program. And they busted that miserably. They'd had their overhaul, and then they came down to San Diego to go through refresher training. And they had had the refresher training, material, and administrative inspections, and they busted those.

---

* Commander Galen C. Brown, USN.

Then the next thing that was hell on them was a CruDesPac pre-deployment inspection, which they promptly busted.

Captain Brown had arrived about mid-December, so there wasn't anything you could blame him for. Each of the department heads had shifted. Some guys had fleeted up, other guys had left right after the yard period, so you really couldn't blame the department heads.* The exec had been the guy who had been through it all. I do know that Brown's predecessor, as a result of CruDesPac's inspection, got a letter in his jacket, and it took him, as I recall, five or six selections to make captain. He finally made it, but he bore the brunt of this.

Paul Stillwell: This wasn't exactly a bargain you were walking into.

Admiral Gravely: Well, I've always thought in terms of when I went aboard the Theodore E. Chandler there was no way for me to go but up, and Captain Brown admitted it. Captain Brown and I have talked about it many times.

Captain Brown had been in destroyers. He was exec of a destroyer, but he was exec of a destroyer during the Johnson regime as Secretary of Defense.† If you recall, the Navy just went through a traumatic budget cut in all this, and there were some ships that didn't get under way for months. And he had to have been caught up in that. So he wasn't the greatest ship handler in the world. Competent, yes. But I think that the best thing that I could say about Captain Brown, and he is a friend of mine today, was that he had really three or four good junior officers who were fairly competent ship handlers, and so they did a lot of it. Captain Brown let me handle the ship, which was the first since the Seminole and certainly the first time I handled a destroyer. And I got a lot of experience from it. In fact, it profited all of us.

The Theodore E. Chandler, as I said, deployed as part of DesDiv 52. I think she was in 52 then, because she somehow got into 11, and I'm not sure how we did that. But I came aboard, and the first thing that I did on my second morning aboard was to have

---

* "Fleet up" is a Navy term that describes a move to a more responsible position in a given organization.
† Louis A. Johnson served as Secretary of Defense from April 1949 until September 1950. He cut back substantially on defense expenditures, a program that had to be reversed with the beginning of the Korean War in June 1950. He was removed as SecDef a few months after the war started.

quarters for muster. I was somewhat shocked, because I'd been used to a guy who would say, "Report." So I stood in front of this group of department heads and said, "Report."

A couple of them said, "What the hell's he talking about?"

I said, "Normally you report 'all present and accounted for,' or so many men absent, etc. And you tell me anything you think I need to know at this point in time."

The guy said, "Well, we don't normally do that."

I said, "Okay, you guys go back down there, and let's muster these people, and let's read them the plan of the day, and quarters, etc. Then you'll come back in, and we'll do this again."

Paul Stillwell: You're in the Navy.

Admiral Gravely: Yes. I hadn't done it the other way. [Laughter] So we did, and we started our routine there.

Paul Stillwell: Did you have to teach them about 8:00 o'clock reports too?*

Admiral Gravely: We had to go through that one. My predecessor might have lost the bubble during the yard period, or something like that. I don't know what had happened, but they weren't quite the destroyer Navy that I was used to, or that I thought I was going to get used to, anyway. The other thing about the ship, so far as I was concerned, was that it was filthy, and Captain Brown wouldn't admit that. It was filthy. So I tell you, it took some detailed cleaning and scrubbing, and one of these days I'll tell you about the toothbrush brigade, because that's how we cleaned that son-of-a-bitch up, getting into corners and crevices and everything else.

Paul Stillwell: Do you think your predecessor was relieved for cause?

---

* The shipboard practice at sea is for the department heads to report to the executive officer as 8:00 o'clock in the evening approaches. They provide updates on the condition of their departments, and the exec then reports to the captain. In port duty department heads and the command duty officer do the reporting.

Admiral Gravely: Not officially, but I think that he got blamed for some of the conditions of Chandler, and someone had decided, "Hey, that's the guy."

Paul Stillwell: And that's why there was a job available for you.

Admiral Gravely: That's why there was a job available. I got what you call "Proceed Immediate" orders. They were dispatch orders, and you execute them in 24 or 48 hours, or something like that. And that's how I think I really got the job.

Captain Brown and I hit it off famously. He was just a tremendous guy. He knew how to handle people. He had a lot of respect for me; I had a lot of respect for him. In fact, I just visited him just recently since he retired out in San Diego. We went on a deployment. We had some close ones.

I remember that a carrier, and I think it was the Ranger, executed a left turn on us by Nancy one night and we were about 900 yards astern of him.[*] The only thing I can remember was ducking as we went that-a-way when she went that-a-way, and we had to, because it looked like the damn mast was going to be taken off by the fantail of the Ranger. But, of course, that's the way airdales run those things, you know. The hell with that little guy behind you.

Paul Stillwell: It's your job to stay out of the way.

Admiral Gravely: It's your job to stay out of the way. Did certainly our series of exercises and those things. Went on a deployment. Spent time on the Formosa Patrol. I can remember that it wasn't us, but we were there when one guy got the 100th warning from the Chinese about invading their territory while we were out there, and those kinds of things. Went down to Okinawa, where we did some shooting off in the White Beach area, not the White Beach itself.

---

[*] Nancy is an infrared signaling device visible only by special equipment; it thus differs from the normal flashing-light communication that can be seen by the naked eye.

Paul Stillwell: Were you picking up knowledge about the weapons and engineering departments as you went along?

Admiral Gravely: Well, I got a lot of time in engineering, going down there to look at their spaces and those kinds of things. I think what you're getting at is that ultimately you've got to take this exam for command. And that's another story. I'll tell you about that one too. Because I really didn't take it. Well, I got the command before I got to take the exam. [Laughter] So my commodore pinned a button on me that morning and said, "Now, I'll write the letter, if you've still got it on three months from now."

In any event, we went through all of the destroyer wickets that I can think of. Did the ASW bit. Certainly spent a lot of time in CIC, because that was my station during general quarters. Did some minor air controlling and other things to make me more proficient in that field.

Paul Stillwell: Then there's all the paperwork you have to deal with.

Admiral Gravely: There's the paperwork that you have to deal with, and the department heads, who would insist when something was late, "Well, that's just routine administrative delay." Give them the back of your hand, you know. But had a good group, and enjoyed the deployment.

Went into Hong Kong, and I never will forget this, because I was doing the navigating. The thing that I remember most about it was that I really didn't know where the hell I was. You know, I'd been headed in that direction. And finally I picked up a little pip on the radarscope. And I said, "That's it." Thank God, that was it.

Another time I'd been relying on CIC to do my navigating for me, and we were detached in the middle of the night to proceed to White Beach down in Okinawa. According to my plot, we were pretty close to there, but CIC's plot said we had about four more hours to go south. Well, I thought they'd been talking to the carrier, and been getting all directions from the carrier, I knew that carrier wasn't going to detach us with that long to go, but I made a recommendation to the skipper that we continue south. And so, of course, he took off and continued south. Finally, when we were just about out of voice communications range, the squadron commander questioned our movements, and we really got it all squared away. And we were right there, really, instead of our being four hours south if he'd followed me. You know, you make a glitch or two, but Theodore E. Chandler was the ship that basically did it for me.

Paul Stillwell: Why do you say that?

Admiral Gravely: Well, I got some chances later on that I'm going to talk about. For the first time I was really handling a destroyer in fast ops. I can't think of anything that we didn't go through. In fact, we even went through a hurricane. And about the time we were in the eye of it, Christ, I was up on the bridge with the captain, and everything else, and then, you know, everything's calm within the eye. And, sure enough, it is. And then when you come out of that, boy, oh boy, there you go for another two days of battling.

We had a unique happenstance in that we left Yokosuka with a carrier one time, and the carrier was off launching aircraft, and we were sort of doing some independent steaming, trying to stay within visual range of him. When he finished launching his aircraft he put the signal out for us to get around him and get in a bent-line screen.*

We started going over at about 15 knots, because we don't have very far to go. The Henderson, which was in our division, was running at about 25, the Duncan was doing maybe 10, and somebody else doing about 20. And suddenly we took a wave, and mount 51 caved into the chiefs' quarters.† There, as you were looking up like that, it was in the chiefs' quarters. I saw some chiefs I hadn't seen in a week or so. [Laughter] They were all over the place.

Of course, I was down there trying to supervise and make sure the damage control people got that squared away. The captain was on the bridge. And we finally went into the Yokosuka Naval Shipyard, wherein we got it fixed. It took a little time. But Captain Brown seemed to have been very happy with the way I handled my part of that. And so when I said I did it all, that was the first time I really had to supervise corrections of damage, really, except for little things.

---

* A bent-line screen is a formation of destroyers or other escort ships that steams in a bent line out ahead of an aircraft carrier or other major ship to provide antisubmarine protection.
† Mount 51 was the forward 5-inch gun mount on the bow of the ship.

Paul Stillwell: We're right at the end of the tape, Admiral, so we can resume the Theodore E. Chandler the next time.

Admiral Gravely: All right.

Interview Number 3 with Vice Admiral Samuel L. Gravely, Jr., U.S. Navy (Retired)
Place: Admiral Gravely's office in Burke, Virginia
Date: Thursday, 7 August 1986
Interviewer: Paul Stillwell

Paul Stillwell: Admiral, we're today resuming the discussion of your time as executive officer of the USS Theodore E. Chandler. What do you recall about the operations with plane-guarding carriers?

Admiral Gravely: Well, plane guarding with the carriers was sort of a new aspect, really, of shipboard life for me.* I'd been on a battleship, I'd been on a cruiser, I'd been on an amphib, and also I'd had some experience on the PC-1264, so it was quite different. But it was a most interesting facet, because I simply really enjoyed running at top speed. I'm not sure I really enjoyed sitting that close to a flattop, but I certainly got used to it. I can remember one of the things that frightened me, of course, was the time when the skipper of the carrier executed a left turn by Nancy, which we did not receive, and we were sitting about 1,000 yards, about 20 degrees off of his port bow, and you can imagine the turmoil on that bridge at that point in time as we tried to maneuver to avoid.

Paul Stillwell: That's an infrared signal light, isn't it?

Admiral Gravely: That's an infrared signal light, and generally you get an announcement over your pritac which says "Nancy Hanks." And when you got that word, then you had your signalman alerted to look for his signal bridge and expect a message to come in to you.

Paul Stillwell: And they have to have a special receiver to see it.

---

* A plane-guard destroyer steams astern—or off on one quarter—of an aircraft carrier in order to recover aircraft crew members who go into the water.

Admiral Gravely: We have to have a special receiver to see it. Unfortunately, they executed it without sending the signal, so far as I could tell. Certainly we weren't alerted to receive it. So when that turn was executed, and it was almost a 180-degree turn, and you can imagine, with us going at about 25 knots, how closely we were going as he sort of slowed down in the turn. Of course, the skipper was very alert to the right full rudder, which was the way we had to go to avoid. We went right full rudder, and I can remember that I thought his fantail was just right above our bow, but it was a maneuver which wasn't very smartly executed by the carrier, I didn't think. But I thought Captain Brown just really handled it beautifully. And we, of course, avoided a collision.

Paul Stillwell: Was it standard practice for either you or the captain to be on the bridge whenever you were operating with a carrier?

Admiral Gravely: Whenever we were operating with a carrier or in any kind of intense operations, the skipper was generally always on the bridge. I would go up to the bridge for most evolutions, and certainly I'd be up on the bridge when the captain felt that it was a ticklish situation, and he wanted somebody a little bit senior up on the bridge. We had practically all junior officers; they were very good, very competent, but he felt that as a lieutenant commander, that I probably had a little bit more experience. Not in destroyer operations but in just plain old operations, and he valued my judgment. So in any kind of an intense situation, whenever there were operations with other ships, or storms, or things like that, if the captain needed some rest, I was on the bridge. And generally I was on the bridge just about all the time when he was there.

But, of course, as exec you are an administrator more than you are an operator, so you spend an awful lot of time in the ship's office, or writing papers, or going through inspecting the ship, making sure that the bunks are made and people are up, the meals are served and on time, and those kinds of administrative functions. And I carried those on too. You make your 8:00 o'clock reports at night and constantly keep the skipper aware of what's going on around the ship.

One of the big problems, I think, with some ships, is just simply morale. You've got to have your ears open to make sure that things are going well. If you get any kind of word of some sort of dissatisfaction or something like that, you assess it, and if it's important enough, you tell the captain, "Hey, so-and-so is going on. Here's what I think we ought to do," and those kinds of things. Never keep the captain in the dark, or never let that poor guy get surprised.

Paul Stillwell: It calls for real judgment. On the other hand, while you're trying to keep him informed, you don't want to burden him with every detail.

Admiral Gravely: You do not burden him with details, but you've got to sort out the items that you hear, and those items that are going on and things that are transpiring on that ship. And if you think that the captain needs to know, then he ought to know. But you've got to assess it. Just like you say, you cannot give him every detail; he doesn't have time for it. There are certain things that you handle yourself. You've got to know what to handle, and you've got to know what is above your pay grade—things that he should handle. And I think that I was able to do that.

Now, one of the things I should have mentioned was that I got a considerable amount of XO-type experience on the Seminole. I think it really stood me in good stead when I got to the Theodore E. Chandler, so I knew how to handle men, and I knew the administrative details of the ship. I knew how to keep the ship clean and those kinds of things. My problem at that point was operating, and that's another reason I spent a lot more time on the bridge than maybe some execs might have spent. But I had to be up there to see how things were going, and see how they operated, see these fast maneuvers with ASW, and as well with plane guarding. We had shore bombardment, those kinds of things. I was up there watching and trying to learn.

Paul Stillwell: So you were learning right along with the JOs, probably.

Admiral Gravely: Yes, right. It was a real learning experience for me, because destroyers, I discovered, were a little bit different from other ships. They went faster, number one. Things happened so much more quickly. You had to be up there, able to see a situation forming, and take action in time. With an AKA you had plenty of time, generally to think it through, but here you had to be innate, and I like to think that I learned, or acquired, that ability along the way to guess and guess right, is basically what I'm trying to say.

Paul Stillwell: Well, the burden is ultimately on the destroyer to stay away from the carrier, no matter what the signal is. So you've got to have the experience to know what the light pattern should be and so forth.

Admiral Gravely: The burden is always to stay away from the carrier, and, as I recall, there was sort of an unwritten rule that you never cross within 1,000 yards of a carrier. You stayed at least outside of 500 yards on either side, as well as from the stern, unless you were to make an approach. And that was sort of the bible that I learned and the one that I used in all of my actions—that I was trying to avoid the carrier.

Of course, the other little thing that I think I acquired was the ability to operate from CIC. Now, as ops officer I spent a lot of time in CIC in an AKA. But on the Toledo, for example, which I would say I was assistant ops, that was sort of administrative, and I never got very much experience in CIC. I didn't stand watches there. But in general quarters on the Theodore E. Chandler, my station was in CIC. So I got a chance to watch CIC in operation, work with them. I knew how to handle telephone circuits or communication circuits and those kinds of things, but maneuvering board and those kinds of things, I picked that kind of experience up, knowing exactly what to do during ASW situations, etc.[*]

Paul Stillwell: I would think that that would prove especially valuable when you got to the Jouett, because you had to make the mental transition to seeing only the artificial world and not the real one.

---

[*] A maneuvering board is a sheet of paper containing a compass rose, concentric circles, and logarithmic scales. It is used for working out relative motion problems for ships that are maneuvering. In years past it was known as a "mooring board."

Admiral Gravely: Well, it helped an awful lot even before that, because, as you well know, I had some commands before Jouett, and this was basically the training ground that prepared me for the other things.

When I wrote my letters to BuPers concerning a destroyer while I was on Seminole, I asked for two things. One was executive officer of a destroyer or commanding officer of a smaller ship. I really felt I had the ability to be a commanding officer, but certainly I felt the training as an exec would be invaluable to me. And I was very happy that it went that way, because it gave me an additional chance to learn and to be better prepared when the days came. I felt, when I got those orders, that it would come and that I just had to make my number doing that job as exec for Captain Brown.

I think in summary that I did the job for Captain Brown. And I think Captain Brown will agree, because we are friends today, and I see him periodically out in San Diego. We felt that we had a very, very good ship. It was a clean ship. It operated well, we had some well-trained JOs, and I think I contributed to the training of some of those people. We had a good engineering department. She was just an all-around good ship, which we felt a considerable amount of pride in.

Now, the Theodore E. Chandler was not a young ship by any stretch of the imagination. Previous to my coming aboard, they had had a fleet rehabilitation and modernization InSurv inspection to determine whether or not Theodore E. Chandler would be worthy of the InSurv.* Now, as I understand it, the destroyer program had two phases, FRAM I and FRAM II.† A FRAM I destroyer went to a shipyard for a year and was completely built up from just about the bridge up and back and aft. That modernization was designed to last seven years.

The FRAM II ships went for a six-month conversion, and the modernization should last for five years. Well, Theodore E. Chandler had been certified for a FRAM I conversion. Under a normal set of circumstances, the FRAM I ship went into the shipyard, and all of the officers except for the exec, the four department heads, and maybe one or two junior officers, were transferred. The crew was cut down to about 125

---

* InSurv—the Board of Inspection and Survey.
† FRAM is an acronym for the fleet rehabilitation and modernization program. Under this program many U.S. destroyer-type ships of the 1950s and 1960s were substantially modernized by extensive rebuilding that incorporated later technology than that available at the time of original construction.

sailors. In the case of the FRAM II, all of the people remained aboard, with the CO handling the shipyard period.

Well, about this time we were fairly close to the end of the deployment, and we began to wonder how this would work for Theodore E. Chandler. Now, I was probably more concerned than most people about it, because I felt that there was no way that I would stay on board as the additional-duty CO. As exec, I felt that certainly someone would come on and relieve me. So I began to wonder a little bit about this time where would I go.

Paul Stillwell: Why did you have that feeling?

Admiral Gravely: Well, I had that feeling primarily because, so far as I could tell from naval history, no black had ever served as a commanding officer of a ship at this point in time. So I feel that I was sort of right in my thinking; however, circumstances later proved me wrong.

In any event, Theodore E. Chandler continued the deployment. We went to Hong Kong, of course, as one of our liberty ports. We spent a lot of time in Yokosuka. We went through one rough situation, which I explained earlier, when we took a strange wave across the bow, and mount 51 caved in. We were directed to go into Yokosuka for repairs, where we went in and stayed about a month. Very shortly after that, the deployment was over, and we came back into San Diego, where we were in for the normal upkeep and R&R period that occurs.* This was roughly about September or so of 1960. At that time the orders began to hit for our people.

Paul Stillwell: Did you talk to your detailer at all?

Admiral Gravely: The detailer was a guy that I had served with on the Toledo at that point in time. I wrote him a letter, and I basically said to him that I had been in the destroyer force for about seven or eight months at that time. The commanding officers' examination and qualification therefore required, as I recall, 18 to 24 months in the

---

* R&R—rest and recreation.

destroyer force with about 12 months as a department head or as exec. And in my letter I pointed out that I had been unable to do that, and so what I would like to do would be to possibly stay on Theodore E. Chandler some additional time, so I would meet the minimum qualifications and then take the command exam, or certainly, if I was to be transferred, to be transferred to another destroyer.

I got a nice letter from them, and basically the letter said, "We do not intend to move you." And I got to tell you, I was overjoyed, because I knew then that as soon as we got to the shipyard, then I would relieve Captain Brown and have the responsibility for taking the ship through the shipyard. Well, we did that. The ship went to the Hunters Point Shipyard up in San Francisco, and got there, I think, in January of '61 or something of that nature. And, frankly, we had a very small relieving ceremony, which was designed primarily to say goodbye to Captain Brown. It was not an official, formal change of command. We had the crew to muster inside a machine shop or something. It was a big, spacious room, and we sort of passed the baton at that ceremony.

I was, I must tell you, delighted, despite the fact that I knew that here I was commanding officer of a ship that was in commission in reserve. It wasn't going to go anyplace, but I've always been very, very pleased that I got the opportunity to do that, because of a couple of reasons. The first reason was that it gave me a chance to really, really learn a ship, because I watched that thing from the moment the first shipyard worker came on, with all of the cutting and everything else, until it was completely rebuilt. That took about 10 of the 12 months, really. I seem to have been able to really get along with the shipyard people. I had a very good rapport with them. I had very good rapport with the commander of the naval shipyard up there. His name was Admiral Curtze, and he really became just a personal friend of mine.[*] I really admired him. He had a hell of a job to do, and, of course, I had one too.

Paul Stillwell: In what ways did he particularly help you?

---

[*] Rear Admiral Charles A. Curtze, USN. Admiral Curtze has been interviewed as part of the Naval Institute's oral history program.

Admiral Gravely: Well, at the various briefings Curtze on a couple of occasions pointed out to the other shipyard commanders there—the shipyard commanding officers—a couple of things he thought that I was doing that was productive. Number one, I knew that no one likes to work in a dirty space. And then you suddenly wonder whose responsibility is it to clean up where the shipyard workers had worked. Well, the obvious answer is that every guy ought to clean up what he dirties. But then we're paying that shipyard worker an awful lot of money just to repair items and those kinds of things, and I didn't think we could afford to spend money to have this guy doing something that a couple of sailors could do.

So what I did was to establish cleaning crews. Which meant that I got the shipyard guy for his full eight hours that day, and that afternoon I had a group of sailors who had nothing to do as a night job except to clean up that ship. And that just worked beautifully, because those people were very pleased to come there. We weren't moving their tools, or doing anything like that. We were cleaning up the big dirty parts of the ship that I felt that I couldn't afford to pay them to do. I wanted to get it done, so we had a night crew.

The other thing, of course, was that we had office spaces ashore. And I think every sailor hates shore office spaces. So I spent an awful lot of time around there just looking at the ship, trying to see that it was being done right. I did not try to correct a shipyard worker. But if I saw something that I didn't think was going along quite like it should be going, I would speak to the supervisor or somebody else in terms that they would understand, and they would know that I was not trying to interfere. If it was wrong, they would correct the guy and make him do it right. Or they'd explain to me why he was doing it that way.

Paul Stillwell: The ship's supe can be a very useful guy in that role, so you want to develop a good relationship.

Admiral Gravely: Good relationship with the ship's supe. We also decided that we would have a picnic, which we invited the shipyard workers to. They came in droves. That Monday morning they were all at work with big smiles and everything else. In fact,

Admiral Curtze came to my shipyard party. So things went well during that shipyard period.

Well, subsequently my tour date, which was in the ODCR, was up, and I thought I'd better write another letter, because I had a very dear friend who was an additional duty commanding officer of another ship in my division.* That ship was up at Mare Island, and he got pulled off to go to Brazil.† So I began to worry, would I be able to go with Theodore E. Chandler when it came out of the yards so that I could then get my time in as well as take that command qualification exam.

At this time I wrote another letter to the bureau, pointing out that I had sufficient time on the ship, but as a result of being in the shipyard, I had not been able to meet the other qualifications for command, and I would just love to stay there to do that. So I got another nice letter, and it basically said, "Your tour date has been extended until March [or something] of '62," which was very fine, and I happily went about my job.

That fall, oh, something like about September, I was notified by BuPers that the destroyer/minecraft placement officer was coming out, and he wanted to talk in terms of the young officers that Chandler would be getting to build up the crew. Now, we went into the shipyard in January of 1961, so December time frame was about the time we were going to get out at the end of the 12th month, really after Christmas or January the first. And BuPers, in its normal way of thinking ahead, was going to tell me who would be coming on in the next four or five months.

The ship was in fairly good shape. It was fast approaching the date that we would go through a recommissioning ceremony, and the new commanding officer would come. We had an ops officer who'd been on there almost two years, and I expected that he would leave. But at the same time I really needed a hot ops officer who would come on board, because after refresher training and those kinds of things we would then be deploying again, and I didn't want the old guy to go through refresher training and the new guy take over without proper orientation and training. But, anyway, the officer from BuPers said, "Well, we really don't want to talk about those officers first. Let's talk about you."

---

* ODCR—Officer Distribution and Control Report.
† Mare Island Naval Shipyard, Vallejo, California.

I said, "Okay, where are you going to send me, sir?"

He said, ""You're going to command of—" Then he started flipping through a few notes there. Then he said, "Falgout, DER out in Pearl Harbor."* And I must tell you that I was so happy that I'm not sure I heard anything else he said after that, [laughter] because I was really, really overjoyed.

Paul Stillwell: You were taken by surprise.

Admiral Gravely: I was certainly taken by surprise, I was overjoyed, and I certainly felt that it had all paid off. Everything that I had done to sort of excel and those kinds of things, they really paid off. Here I was, going to my own command.

Paul Stillwell: How did that come about without you going through the command screening or the exam wicket that you'd been preparing for?

Admiral Gravely: Well, at that point in time, the practice of giving the exams had not been around long enough so that they'd been able to just get everybody to go through these wickets. And I don't think that in my own case, except after the ship had been operating for about three months, if I were to stay there, I could have ever been up to snuff to taking the exam. When I say up to snuff, I just simply mean that I was going to get a new commanding officer. He would have to observe me a little bit, then he'd have to recommend me, and those kinds of things. So it would have taken him, certainly, through refresher training. Then there would have been a board of COs who would have given me this exam.

Before that time it was a matter that was handled in BuPers, wherein they looked at Joe Blow, who'd had so much experience and those kinds of things, and not necessarily in the destroyer force, because I can remember destroyer skippers who'd never been on them before. But, anyway, that was a wicket he had to have in his jacket to make captain. So, based on what they saw in the jacket, they decided he was qualified.

---

* A DER was a World War II-built destroyer escort that had been equipped with additional radar to serve in a patrol role to detect incoming Soviet bombers.

I assume that someone in the bureau made the decision that my jacket was hot enough that probably I could handle it, and certainly they'd give me the chance. That's the only thing I can think of in that regard.

Paul Stillwell: I would like to go back and get a little more on the administrative side of your duties. You really had a double load there in the shipyard, because you were still the exec as well.

Admiral Gravely: Well, we worked that out fairly well in that I was the skipper handling everything that was done operationally. But my ops officer, a guy by the name of Mike Skubinna, took some of the administrative chores away from me.[*] At least I gave them to him. For example, he took the POD, plan of the day, which he religiously did. And, as you well know, in a shipyard the operations officer isn't doing much other than getting the spaces done and those kinds of things. So the ops officer basically did some of my chores as the exec.

You really are a commanding officer in all respects, and you're doing the commanding officer's job. Someone else has to do those little things. You sort of prioritized as what had to be done between those two jobs, which were most important. You did those; you gave those others off to someone else to do, and that was the way we handled it. Mike was a real sweetheart of a guy. He had not been in destroyers before coming to the Theodore E. Chandler. He'd been in amphibs and two or three other types, but he certainly was well trained and became one of the best ship handlers we had on the ship. Just a beautiful guy. So that was how that went about.

Paul Stillwell: You mentioned your concern about morale. I think that's particularly tough in a shipyard. In my experience that's the toughest period in the cycle of a ship, because she's torn up. You mentioned the dirt. There is not the satisfaction you get from operating.

Admiral Gravely: You're right.

---
[*] Lieutenant Myron A. Skubinna, USN.

Paul Stillwell: How did you keep people going?

Admiral Gravely: Well, first of all, everybody had a certain amount of pride in the job that he was doing on board the ship. Secondly, he knew that more than likely what was being done in that shipyard was something he was going to have to live with when that ship really started operating. So he would, to some degree, try to make sure that his spaces were taken care of, and his work was done over Joe Blow, or as well as it could be done. So I think that was one thing. We had ship's parties. We had softball teams and all the other recreational sports and things of that nature.

The biggest thing that helped us was the BuPers policy of changing our homeport, which meant that most of the married guys took their families up to San Francisco, and they lived in Quonset huts.[*] When you're with your family, a Quonset hut isn't the worst thing. So that facet of it was handled. We had a leave program. We also had a training program where we sent people off to San Diego every once in a while to various schools. I think that morale was fairly good during that period. Part of it might have been that I do have a way with people, I enjoy working with people, and I think people enjoy working with me. So it was a little of me, a little of, certainly, a lot of other things.

Paul Stillwell: Are there any milestones that you remember in the physical transformation of the ship? Did you have the laid-out plan of action and milestones and so forth?

Admiral Gravely: We had that. Of course, you know what jobs are going to be done. You get completion dates. You sort of make up your milestones, a chart, and those kinds of things on jobs, and we followed those very carefully. I would sit around and discuss how things were going continually with the department heads and about three other officers that we had.

---

[*] A Quonset hut is a semi-cylindrical metal building that can be shipped to an advance base area and erected quickly.

Paul Stillwell: Sort of an overhaul committee?

Admiral Gravely: Well, I hate to think in terms of committees. I'm convinced you don't run ships by committee. A ship is the responsibility of the commanding officer, but certainly we had wardroom meetings to sit around and talk in terms of jobs, and constantly they were appraising me of problems as they had them, and let me know how well work was going.

One thing, I happened to be going around the bridge area one day, right after we got our new signal bridge, and the signal house was on backwards. Now, I must tell you that I am convinced at this moment, and it took me a little while to be convinced of this, of course, but it had been tack-welded in place backwards, because the guy got it, say, Friday afternoon at about 2:00 o'clock. He probably just tacked it down so that it would stay there and wouldn't blow off. But you can imagine my chagrin when I went up there and saw that the signal bridge was on backwards. In other words, so that the open space was to the sea. We had a lot of little things like that that happened, but we got them taken care of.

One other thing happened a little bit before the detailer came, and to some degree I felt quite pleased when I heard it. I'm not sure whether it was Navy Times or whether it was the orders to officers that you only get on the Fox sched, but that list came out, and it showed a commanding officer coming to the Theodore E. Chandler. I happened to be up at a shipyard commander's meeting that morning, and Admiral Curtze said, "Sam, I just saw where there's a relief coming for you."

I said, "Yes, sir, that's fairly normal. The commanding officer of a destroyer is a commander, and I'm lieutenant commander at least a year or so away, and so I expected that."

He said, "Well, I do not think that that's fair. Here you've been here working on this ship for a whole year. You've done a great job," and all this kind of garbage. "I am going to call the Chief of Naval Personnel."* Admiral Curtze called the chief of Naval Personnel and told him about that. And I guess that's the first time, despite the fact that I

---

* At that time the Chief of Naval Personnel was Vice Admiral William R. Smedberg III, USN, who had been Gravely's commanding officer on board the battleship Iowa.

was certainly surprised when I heard it from the BuPers detailer, but that was the first when I had a rumor that I might be going to command, because I was told by Admiral Curtze that in his talk with the Chief of Naval Personnel that some good things would happen to me. [Laughter] So I knew then also that I obviously was doing the job that was expected of me by the shipyard commander.

Anyway, the new skipper, Joe Sperandio, happened to have been in the Hunters Point Naval Shipyard at that time.* He was exec of a destroyer which was going through a normal, about four-month, yard overhaul. So I got a chance to meet with him, and we talked about how we wanted things to go and everything else. I had not really known him very well, although we had met. We had met primarily because the CO of his ship had been navigator of the Toledo. In my calling on the skipper there, I had met him, and, of course, you see each other walking through the yard. When his skipper couldn't go to the shipyard commander's meetings, then he would be there, and so we would talk. But, anyway, we talked in terms of when he'd be available to relieve, what our plans were, and everything else.

He came over, and the date that sticks in my mind is something like November 14, although I can't swear to that date. But we did have a full-blown change of command, with all the sailors in dress blues. I did my little talk, he did his little talk, and he took over as commanding officer. The biggest thing that I can remember him saying to me was, "Sam, I've just heard such good things about Theodore E. Chandler, and I know that you're doing the job that I would want you to do on here. I'm the CO, and you're the exec. Just keep doing what you have been and keep me informed." And so we went on that basis.

Now, it got to be a little bit difficult and a little embarrassing for both of us, because you can imagine that for ten months maybe there were young sailors on there who have been saying, "Captain, should I do this? Captain, should I do that?" Well, we were standing on the bridge about the time we were really beginning to get under way, and a kid came up and said, "Captain, can I do this?"

I said, "Listen son, do me a favor. Now, there's the captain over there. Captain Sperandio is his name." Joe Sperandio took it all in good stead. He and I just became

---

* Commander Joseph L. Sperandio, USN.

great friends with one single idea in mind—that's to do the best thing for Theodore E. Chandler to get her ready to sail.

I went on one set of sea trials with Theodore E. Chandler, and, of course, by that time I had my orders which directed that I go to Pearl Harbor to relieve as skipper of the Falgout. Unfortunately, I had never seen a DER, and so I wanted to figure out how could I best at least see one, and get aboard and walk around before I got to command. I discovered that there were several with CortRon 7, I believe it was, because I became a part of CortRon 5.* I think it was CortRon 7 that was home-ported at Treasure Island. They had several DEW Line ships up there.† You know they had the AGRs as well as DERs which served on this line.‡

Paul Stillwell: Those were the old Liberty ships that were converted to the AGRs.

Admiral Gravely: That's right. So I decided that I would try to see one of those DERs over there. It turned out that I had a guy on there that I had not met, but I felt that our paths had crossed a couple of times, and that maybe I could induce him to let me come and see his. Now, the skipper of one of those AGRs had been exec of the Duncan, which was in my division when I was there. So there was no problem about talking to him, coming over to see the AGR, and in fact, I even had lunch with him. I knew how to get over to Treasure Island, where they were all home-ported.§ No problem there. But I could never, never convince this guy to let me see his DER, and I'm not sure why. He ultimately invited me to his home for dinner one night, where I met his family and talked to him. But he would not let me see that DER.

Well, in any event, I got off the ship and, of course, my family had remained in San Diego during this whole time, and I had been going home about once a month while I

---

* CortRon—escort squadron.
† DEW Line—Distant Early Warning Line, a chain of radar sites built 1,200 miles from the North Pole in the early 1950s as a means of detecting Soviet bombers approaching the United States over the Arctic.
‡ AGR was the designation for a large radar picket ship, a World War II merchant ship hull that had been converted for early warning duty with the addition of high-powered radars. DERs were World War II-built destroyer escorts that had been subsequently converted for radar picket duty.
§ Treasure Island is a man-made island in San Francisco Bay, located between San Francisco and Oakland. It served as the site of a world's fair in 1939-40, then was converted for use as a Navy base during and after World War II.

was up there in the shipyard. So I went down to San Diego, where my family and I packed. We decided that we would take a trip across to Virginia here to visit Alma's folks as well as mine, since we were going to Pearl wherein it would be that much further away. We felt we would be over there 18 months to two years and wouldn't get a chance to see them.

We had one of the most hectic drives across country that we've ever had, and hectic in several respects. One was that at this point in time I was beginning to expect a little bit more from civilian life. You see, in my normal transit across country I knew where to find the hotels and things, because you just couldn't go into any. But things had changed a little bit by that time.

Paul Stillwell: I think the Kennedy administration was making a conscious effort to see that things did change.*

Admiral Gravely: That's right. But even though things changed a lot on paper, they didn't change in real life. For example, in Albuquerque, New Mexico, in trying to find a hotel room, we went to about three, and whereas most of them would offer us two rooms, they wouldn't offer us two rooms together. Which meant that I'd be in one section of the motel with one kid, and my wife in another section of the motel with the other kid. Something that always seemed like a stumbling block to me, but somehow we managed it. I've forgotten what we finally did, but we did find whatever accommodation we needed to spend the night.

Of course, when you come across the southern route, then you begin to come through some real southern states. You come through Texas, you come through Oklahoma, you come through Arkansas, you come through Tennessee. I can remember distinctly that—and I am thoroughly convinced that the night we stayed in Memphis, I

---

* In the autumn of 1962, for instance, the administration of President John F. Kennedy sent federal marshals to aid James Meredith in becoming the first black student to enroll at the University of Mississippi. Riots ensued, and federal troops were stationed on the campus to protect Meredith until he graduated in 1963.

stayed in the same hotel that Martin Luther King got shot in.* Of course, this was before his time. Another real impressive thing about that motel was that it was typical of the motels of that day, or I should say those that have crossed the railroad track. Here it was December, with obviously snow and ice on the street, and there was no heat. The only way we managed to stay comfortable was to get under about six blankets with four us in the same bed with me hugging one child, and she was hugging the other child trying to keep them all warm. But, anyway, we managed to finish the rest of that trip.

Paul Stillwell: You got rebuffed trying to get ice cream cones, too, didn't you?

Admiral Gravely: Yes. We stopped in, I guess this was Arkansas, at one of the Tastee-Freeze places, as I recall. One of the kids wanted some ice cream. And I said, "Okay, I'll pull up here and get you some ice cream." When I walked into the place and asked for four ice cream cones I was told to go to the back. They wouldn't serve me. So I stood there for a minute and that sort of thing. Then I just said, "The hell with it," and walked on out. Went and got in the car, started driving off. But the problem was trying to explain to the two kids there why they couldn't get ice cream. But, in any event, that had happened to me before, but probably was the first they had ever had it happen to them.

Paul Stillwell: Had they, in effect, led somewhat of a sheltered life being in the Navy environment?

Admiral Gravely: Well, that's only part of it. You've got kids who are four and two years old basically. So kids four and two, you know, they're protected, number one. And number two, just like you're saying, they were fairly sheltered. Being in the Navy, certainly both kids had been in wardrooms where they ate with everybody, and they saw everybody, they walked over ships, and they enjoyed talking to people. People enjoyed talking to them, as much as four- and two-year-old kids can talk. Dad took care of everything, you know. So the fact that Dad finally can't buy ice cream came as a shock

---

* Civil rights leader Dr. Martin Luther King, Jr., was shot and killed on 4 April 1968 while staying at the Lorraine Motel in Memphis, Tennessee. The National Civil Rights Museum has now been built on the site and incorporates the room in which Dr. King stayed.

to some degree. But I tried to explain it to them, I guess. In any event, they knew they weren't going to get any ice cream.

Paul Stillwell: Had you seen any discernible changes within the Navy itself by that time as the result of the advent of the Kennedy administration?

Admiral Gravely: Well, there were several changes that had occurred somewhat earlier. Some were still taking effect about that time. Now, let's go back just briefly to about 1945, when I remembered that there was a directive which came out which said 5% of your crew can be black or Negro. About '46 that went to 10%. We also had, in some ships, a compartment right basically under the wardroom, which was the stewards' compartment. And those kinds of things slowly disappeared during this time. Now, as I mentioned earlier, I came back on active duty in 1949 to help recruit more blacks. So I began to see more black officers. I was a lieutenant commander. I saw more ensigns, more jaygees. There were certainly four or five people who were equal in rank to me, but you didn't find very many people who were senior to me at that point in time. Chaplain Parham made commander, as I recall, sometime in that time frame.[*] He probably was the senior black officer on active duty at about that time.

Paul Stillwell: Well, apparently most of the others that had been senior had gotten out by then, hadn't they?

Admiral Gravely: The Golden 13 went out en masse in about 1946. A couple of them stayed on for a little bit longer. Dennis Nelson ultimately got a regular commission, and he stayed all the 20. But Dennis made lieutenant commander, and then he just went through a series of passovers until he had his 20 years in and then was retired.[†] So there just weren't that many. The senior black officer during World War II in the Navy was a lieutenant commander, a guy by the name of Hope, who was a civil engineer.[‡] Wes

---
[*] Commander Thomas David Parham, Jr., CHC, USN, had a date of rank of 1 July 1960.
[†] Lieutenant Commander Dennis D. Nelson II, USN, retired in July 1963. He had been commissioned in March 1944 after a period of enlisted service.
[‡] Lieutenant Commander Edward Hope, CEC, USNR.

Brown, of course, was close to lieutenant commander, if he had not made it.* In fact, I'm pretty sure he was a lieutenant commander when I got to command of the Falgout.

Paul Stillwell: I think his date came pretty close to yours as adjusted, wasn't it?

Admiral Gravely: I was still senior to him.† Wes Brown graduated in 1949. So my date of rank was adjusted to '47. So I would have been at least two years senior to him.

We, of course, came home and ultimately went back in January, and then went on, caught a ship in San Diego. We drove all the way back to San Diego, caught a ship, and sailed to Pearl, wherein I arrived out there in January.

Paul Stillwell: That was an MSTS transport.‡

Admiral Gravely: MSTS transport, yes. I think we went on the Sultan or something of that nature. But anyway, there were four or five of these things. We had a good one, and had a good, enjoyable tour over there. My wife gets seasick, unfortunately, and so we used up a lot of Dramamine [laughter] on that trip. The kids just enjoyed the cruise.

Arriving in Pearl Harbor, the commodore and a couple members of the staff met us. They really took us in tow. They took us to a little place where we stayed for several days until we got quarters. Made sure that everything that we could possibly have wanted was taken care of. It was just a really great meeting. A guy by the name of Captain John Newland was the commodore.§ And Captain John Newland was another one of these just truly great sailors. I had the feeling that he really didn't give a damn what color I was. He really didn't care anything about anything other than the fact that I had been directed by BuPers to relieve the skipper of the Falgout, and he expected and

---

* Lieutenant Commander Wesley A. Brown, CEC, USN, had a date of rank of 1 July 1959. In 1949 he was the first black graduate of the Naval Academy.
† Gravely's date of rank as lieutenant commander was 1 March 1958.
‡ MSTS—Military Sea Transportation Service, a part of the Navy that operated ships for support functions. In some cases it chartered the ships, and it some cases it ran the ships directly with civil service mariners. In 1970 MSTS was renamed Military Sealift Command (MSC), the current title for the command.
§ Captain John W. Newland, Jr., USN.

probably felt that if BuPers had picked me to be the CO of that ship, then I was going to hack it.*

I visited with him two or three times, simply because of the fact that when I arrived in Pearl the Falgout was out on picket. We had lots of discussions, and he wanted to know if I felt I had any problems. I simply told him that probably I would not be his most outstanding ship handler at Pearl Harbor, because I had not had that much close-in ship-handling work. I had certainly put the Chandler up against a pier two or three times. But I hadn't worked it to the satisfaction wherein I was confident. So his first idea, he said, "Well, Sam, why don't you just take the Falgout as soon as it comes in, and there's a mooring buoy out here in the middle of this harbor. Pearl Harbor is round and thin. Nobody's going to be watching. But just go out there with ISE and just play with that thing as long as you want to."† In other words, he did everything to make sure that I would feel the confidence that I really needed to command it.

Oh, one other thing. I happened to be up at the commodore's office, and there was another skipper there, a guy by the name of Gordon Nagler.‡ And I know you would know who Gordon Nagler is. Gordon Nagler later became a three-star and headed the OP-94 command and control section. Gordon Nagler was skipper of the Forrester, which was one of the finest ships in that division. The commodore said, "Is there anything I can do for you?"

I said, "Well, Commodore, you know, I hate to tell you this, but I was in San Francisco, where there were several DERs there, and I tried my best to get aboard one just to see one. Is there some way I can see one?"

Gordon Nagler said, "Hell yes, there's some way you can see one. I got one down here. You can come and go down with me. We're going to lunch right now. Come on down and have lunch with me. I'll introduce you to the wardroom and take you

---

* USS Falgout (DE-324) was an Edsall-class destroyer escort commissioned 15 November 1943. She had a standard displacement of 1,200 tons, was 306 feet long, 37 feet in the beam, and had a maximum draft of 8 feet, 7 inches. Her design speed was 21 knots. She was armed with three 3-inch guns and antisubmarine weapons. From 1951 to 1954 the ship was on loan to the Coast Guard. She was recommissioned as a Navy ship on 30 June 1955 after conversion to a radar picket escort ship, DER-324). Following her active service she was decommissioned 10 October 1969 and stricken from the Navy list in 1975. She was sunk as a target in January 1977.
† ISE—individual ship's exercises.
‡ Commander Gordon R. Nagler, USN.

around the ship." Gordon did that for me, and I didn't expect that kind of kindness or anything. Obviously Gordon Nagler and I are just tremendous friends today, and I see him.*

Paul Stillwell: Did you get any briefings on the mission of the ship, say, from the CinCPacFlt level or whatever?†

Admiral Gravely: We didn't do them there. I got those basically from my squadron commander, Commodore Newland. I got a briefing on the mission, which was basically to go up there and serve as a lookout for all the airplanes that flew that mission. And I can't think of the name of the airplane now, but you worked with them. You were sort of a lightship out there, a beacon basically up there at a spot in the ocean where you stayed within a 25-mile circle. Despite the fact that that's historically where the DERs went, it was at this time that we were about to begin the nuclear high-altitude testing in the Pacific. The DERs would be utilized on a mission of basically surveillance down around Johnston and Christmas Islands. So instead of going north to the barrier for my first several missions, I knew that I would be going south to Johnston and Christmas islands.

Paul Stillwell: Was there any hoopla in the change of command?

Admiral Gravely: Okay, I'm going to get to that next. Well, the day the Falgout finally came into port I was standing there on the pier waiting for her to come in. My predecessor brought the ship in, very fine landing, etc. And I kept seeing that there was something strange about it. Finally it hit me with some realism that the 3-inch/50 gun mount up on the forecastle, was just cocked half off to the side. Well, ultimately I found out that this was part of the rough weather up there. That's how she had taken a beating, and this mount had been pushed over to the side. So the first chore, of course, was that we would go into the shipyard.

---

* Vice Admiral Nagler died 11 July 1998, subsequent to this interview.
† CinCPacFlt—Commander in Chief Pacific Fleet.

Well, in any event, we made our normal inspections and those kinds of things before the change of command. I think it was a Friday or a Saturday morning I relieved the skipper of the Falgout. You said, "Was there any hoopla, or anything like that?" I think every newspaper reporter within—certainly on that island—was there. It went on the international wires, and I have copies of stories that were written in Spanish, as well as a couple of other languages, about my taking over command. I guess it's been stated that this was the first time a black had command of the U.S. Navy ship since Robert Smalls captured a small frigate out of the Charleston Harbor and turned it over to the Union forces. So, yes there was quite a hoopla about it. There were all kinds of press people who wanted to come aboard and interview and everything else.

Paul Stillwell: Was this the first time you'd had that kind of attention focused on you personally?

Admiral Gravely: It was the first time I'd really had that kind of attention focused on me, although there'd been a couple of minor things, maybe one story about me. I can remember one when I was selected to go to the V-12 program. There were two or three minor stories when I graduated from Midshipman School, because I was one of the first to do that. And there might have been a couple of other instances that there was some press attention, but I was not prepared for what happened.

Paul Stillwell: Did that in any way interfere with you ability to run the ship?

Admiral Gravely: I don't think it did, because I was firmly convinced that that wasn't what the Navy sent me there for. I went down to see Commodore Newland, and I asked him, I said, "Hey, I've got some requests for interviews here and everything else, and frankly I don't think that I should accept these things. First of all, I don't have time." The second one was that we had a big request from a national black newspaper to interview me, take pictures, and everything else. I'd already turned them down, because they wanted to do it even before I got to Falgout, and I said I would not even consider it before I got there.

Anyway, when I talked to Commodore Newland about it after they put in their second request, he said, "Hey, your job is to run that ship. If you think that that is necessary, go ahead. If you don't, then turn it off." Of course, I didn't feel it was necessary, so I turned it off. Now, I got a little criticism in the black community for turning it off, but I didn't feel that that was my prime mission.

Well, of course, after getting on the ship, then my biggest job was to get under way the first time.

Paul Stillwell: Did you get a few butterflies at that moment?

Admiral Gravely: There were butterflies. There were a couple of other things. I read a couple of ship-handling books and everything else, and it told you to how to handle the straight-stick destroyers, but it didn't tell you to handle diesel engines that relied on compressed air for starts.

Paul Stillwell: And that ship had an enhanced sail area as the result of the conversion.

Admiral Gravely: As the result of the conversion it had a sail area that was just something else again.* But, frankly, moving it from the main pier there to the shipyard was just a short trip. And whereas the butterflies didn't leave before, by the time we got over there, and did it safely, it was no problem.

One of the things that began to bother me a little bit was that you had a lot of fine gentlemen, you might say, as officers, but the DER force at that point in time, so far as I was concerned, did not get the cream of the crop so far as qualified ship handlers and other things were concerned. You got a lot of good ROTC guys who were great at doing their specific jobs—as the engineering officer, as the communication officer, and those kinds of things. But you can imagine that you would have ten jaygees and ensigns, who had really never done as much ship handling as I, who hadn't done it very much at all.

Paul Stillwell: The blind leading the blind.

---

* "Sail area" is a term for the vertical hull surface of a ship on which the wind exerts force.

Admiral Gravely: Yes. I had a good exec, who knew how to handle the ship.

Paul Stillwell: Who was he?

Admiral Gravely: I'll have to think a while and get his name, because I had two execs during my tour there, and they were completely different kinds of people.

Paul Stillwell: That would be a really key guy in that kind of a situation.

Admiral Gravely: Yes, he was a key guy. Both of them had been officers on some of the destroyers, where they'd had some ship-handling experience, much more than I had. And both of them were fairly good. I believed always that I had to be the best ship handler in the crowd, so I tried to handle it most of the time. I had some rough spots, but no major damage occurred or anything like that.

In fact, I can remember that during another event when I was going into the shipyards I lost one engine; I can't tell you which one it was now. I was going into this shipyard, and I had a couple of choices. One was to run into the pier at the end of it, or run into the pier at the side. The ship was going off to the side, and we hit the pier. No damage other than we made a little bit more noise than you like to when you pull alongside the pier. And my wife and my two sons were standing on the pier. As I began to move off to get off the ship, they had the gangplank in place, and my son said, "Daddy, you're fired." [Laughter] Hey, can you imagine being fired by your five-year-old son for your poor ship handling? So you know you've got to improve.

So far as the mission was concerned, as I've said, we went down south to Johnston and Christmas islands four or five times, because the DER had really long legs on it. It had long legs primarily because of the diesel engines, which it had, number one. Number two, you could lie to an awful lot, and that's what you were expected to do. So, in that surveillance role, when someone would get a contact on an airplane, for example, you were to go over and give a warning that the guy was in a dangerous area. We had a

500-mile circle drawn around Johnston and Christmas islands, and we patrolled one aspect of that circle.

Paul Stillwell: Because the CIC was essentially your main battery.

Admiral Gravely: CIC was your main battery. Your secondary battery, of course, was the Mark I eyeball up there, because sometimes you could almost see things that CIC couldn't see.

Paul Stillwell: You had pretty capable radars in effect to have that kind of detection range.

Admiral Gravely: Yes. We had fairly decent radar. We also had a very, very good high-altitude radar, the SPS-8, as I recall, which we used for launching weather balloons. One of the things they needed down there was high-altitude weather, and we had a couple of aerographers aboard who had to launch the balloons. One day they let me in on a secret, and the secret was that there shouldn't be too much difficulty in getting these balloons to 100,000 feet. So from then on I accepted nothing less than that. And, of course, that kept them working a little bit, but 100,000 feet was what we aimed for and got most of the time. And got fairly decent weather data.

Operationally, I can remember distinctly my first encounter with the Russians. There were three Russian trawlers which were in the area, and I was given a steer by CinCPacFlt to go over and intercept them and give them the warning. I went over, and I found what I thought was the guy in charge. I gave him the order and turned off.

Paul Stillwell: By what means did you communicate with him?

Admiral Gravely: Flashing light, using international coded signals. And he turned off. Of course, that didn't mean he was gone, despite the fact I thought for a while he was. But we bumped heads with him a couple of times down there, and we'd give warning. He'd turn away, then creep in from another side. But we continually watched for that.

One other experience, which to some degree, I guess, I'm a little proud of is that we were down there for a Polaris missile shot, and our station was outside of 25 miles, I believe, of the burst.* And certainly we were to keep everything out of that area. We got down there. We picked up the submarine on radar, so were in position and everything else. When suddenly here came a small fishing boat, just plowing down in there. And, of course, you've got two concerns. How about the men on the board the ship? The biggest concern was that you had a job to get that guy out of there. It was just about time for the shot when I went in and warned him, but he wouldn't move. So I just decided that I'd get between him and the burst. So I guess I got in to about 18 miles. We didn't get any bad effects or anything like that, but the big job was that we kept him out so that he couldn't start yelling for damages and those kinds of things.

Paul Stillwell: Did those ships still have their ASW capability after conversion to DERs?

Admiral Gravely: Yes, yes. They had an SQS-4, I believe, was the sonar on them. And an SQS-4, after you've tried a couple of the sonars, it's kind of old-fashioned. Of course, we had a bigger one on the Theodore E. Chandler. Then we even got a bigger one that got hull mounted after the conversion. So I played around with some bigger sonars, and I really didn't think that our sonar was as reliable. You know, it obviously did the job during its day, but we came out with such better ones. You kind of doubted to some degree as to accuracy and those kinds of things, and whether you were really picking up anything.

Paul Stillwell: So you weren't expected to be used in that role.

Admiral Gravely: We were expected to use them in an ASW role, if necessary, but whereas we had a couple of training exercise with submarines, that was about as far as it went. We didn't get anything of any magnitude.

---

* On 6 May 1962 a Polaris missile, fired from the submarine Ethan Allen (SSBN-608), carried a live nuclear warhead into the atmosphere. It was the fifth of a series of nuclear weapons tests conducted in the Pacific test area near Christmas Island. For additional information see the Naval Institute oral history of Vice Admiral Lloyd M. Mustin, USN (Ret.), who had a major role in the test program.

Paul Stillwell: What do you remember about the nuclear tests themselves?

Admiral Gravely: Well, the biggest thing I remember is that I always wondered why they all went off at about 5:00 o'clock in the morning. After the first one, I knew, because we were given a set of glasses that everybody on the bridge had to use when the blast went off. And, of course, we put our glasses on religiously. I directed that everybody do it, and we all did it religiously.

The main reason they went off at that time of the morning was that they didn't want anybody looking at a blast. Because that was the brightest thing that I've ever seen in my life. I can remember distinctly that I took my glasses, out of which I could see nothing, and I could light a match in front of it, and I still couldn't see anything. But when that atomic bomb went off, it was like daylight. Obviously the big reason that they did it that time of morning was because they hoped everybody was asleep. But it was like a sun shining. So we didn't have a problem, although I understand that a couple of the ships, or at least one ship, had a guy who looked up at it with his naked eye, and he had a small hole in his retina as a result of looking up.

Paul Stillwell: Was there concern about radiation coming to the ship?

Admiral Gravely: Well, there wasn't that much concern, although I think you've almost got to be a nuclear engineer to know what to expect so far as radiation. Radiation, as I recall, doesn't travel that much through air. So I wasn't afraid as much from the blast aspect as from a nuclear radiation aspect. Radiation contaminates things when it hits, but I'm not sure what it does to the air, unless you've got a lot of particles in it. But then I really didn't want any of my people contaminated.

In fact, one of my biggest concerns occurred one night when one of the things that we were told in the op order to avoid was rain clouds and those kinds of things. I had a young officer on board who was a qualified OOD and the whole bit. In fact, he'd just recently come aboard from a destroyer. And I remember distinctly telling him, "Stay out of cloudbursts." I guess he couldn't avoid one, but anyway, he went into one, and we did get rained on. We took out radiac meters of various kinds.

Went through the ship with a fine-tooth comb, and unfortunately one of the meters just went all the way over. Frightened us about half to death, but I sent off a couple of messages concerning that. But we were basically told not to worry—that the radiac meters were probably malfunctioning. I guess that's what it was, but I made all those guys take off all their clothes and throw their clothes over the side. Go down and take baths and the whole bit. I wanted to make sure that nothing really happened. To the best of my knowledge, nobody got really radiated, if you want to use that word.

Paul Stillwell: One concern you had was about the ship handling. Another thing is you have to train yourself to sleep at night when somebody else has got the watch.

Admiral Gravely: Yes. In the case of the DER at that point in time, you didn't worry quite as much, because generally you were steaming independently. There wasn't another ship around. You didn't see very many ships transiting. So since you were alone all the time, the thing that bothered you most was a sudden shift in the weather, or things like that for which you thought you ought to be on the bridge for. Certainly you didn't think you were going to hit somebody. You were not maneuvering like you are in a destroyer when in fast task force ops. Christ, you're on the bridge all the time.

You felt you had competent people for independent steaming, and that's all our people qualified for. Well, my exec was qualified for task force steaming, and, of course, I was qualified for task force steaming. And maybe one ops officer, who had really even steamed in company with another ship before. So I could sleep a little bit sounder than when I got to that DD later on.[*]

Paul Stillwell: And you specify in the night orders the kind of situations you wanted to be informed about.

---

[*] This refers to Gravely's command of the destroyer Taussig (DD-746) in 1966-68.

Admiral Gravely: That's right. You specify in the night orders all situations you want to be informed of. You anticipate various things. Maybe a ship's coming up to join. Or maybe you're going to look for a tanker for starting at 5:00 o'clock in the morning, and so you'd specify those things. Of course, if there is a tanker coming up at 5:00 o'clock in the morning you've got to be up there before 5:00 too. [Laughter] But you do an awful lot of anticipating, and you try to cover those kinds of events in the night orders. Now, the purpose of night orders is not really to cover your behind. The purpose of the night orders is to alert the guy to be alert for such-and such so that he can alert you. Yes, right. A lot of people use them just to cover their own butt, but that's not it.

Paul Stillwell: You talked about the ship's mission in lying to. I would think that the <u>Falgout</u> would roll quite a bit, especially since she had been built up during the conversion.

Admiral Gravely: Well, rolling didn't bother you until it got really heavy. You know, a 30-degree roll, you're in trouble then. You can sit there in 20-degree rolls, 15-degree rolls. But when they got really, really heavy and big rolls, you would generally start moving along four or five knots into the sea. But what would hurt would be when you got a storm coming through there, and you didn't move out of that area. We had permission to move out of the area any time that we felt a storm was coming through there. Then to just sit there trapped in a storm, my God, you do take a beating there. But rolling isn't the worst thing. I think the pounding is what really beats you up.

Paul Stillwell: You talked about the damaged gun mount when she came in. That suggests that those ships were vulnerable to seas.

Admiral Gravely: They were very vulnerable to the seas. She, unfortunately, I think, had gotten caught in a storm. You know, you try to avoid those, but, let's face it, the weather's unpredictable. For example, who would have thought it would have rained like it did yesterday?

Paul Stillwell: That's right.

Admiral Gravely: But no matter how cautious you are, and how alert you are, there are things about storms that you just can't avoid at times.

Paul Stillwell: Was there any special stability considerations in that class of ship?

Admiral Gravely: Well, everything was special in that class of ship. The engine problems with the air starting. In other words, each time you went from all ahead to, well let's say, ahead one-third, and you wanted to go back one-third, you'd go through stop. They've got to stop that engine, and then they've got to start it again. As I recall, we used to think in terms of 16 starts. Sometimes you would use a little bit more air than you really needed, so that would cut down the number of starts. So if you're going to make an approach on a pier, you don't do it like you do in a normal destroyer. You want to make it the first time, or else you'll find yourself sitting out there and get going with the air to start an engine to move it around. The same thing with any other situation like that. It was top heavy. So you had a little stability problem from the top-heaviness of that class of ship. But whereas I was always cautious of that, I didn't consider that one of my top concerns at any time whatsoever.

Paul Stillwell: You talked about the officers perhaps not being as well rounded as you'd known in the destroyer force. How about the enlisted crew?

Admiral Gravely: The enlisted crew was fairly sharp. You got fairly decent people. I can remember specifically a damage control guy. And we used those guys, I got to tell you. You always got water, and you used them quite a bit. But I had a damage controlman, about a second class, who was seasick from the day that ship moved from port until generally it got back. But this young man would walk around with a bucket, and still did the job. You cannot ask for more dedication than that. He did the job no matter what the conditions. Of course, he slowed down a little bit every once in a while when he upchucked, but he did the job for me. I had a really, really top-notch signalman first class, I can remember distinctly, who was frankly what you might have thought of as a pre-World War II typical sailor. Here was a guy who drank like a fish ashore. If there was any trouble, it was going to be ashore. He'd come back on that ship for you and do a competent job. In fact, at that point in time you could bust, and you could re-promote.

Paul Stillwell: Suspended bust was probably an option too.

Admiral Gravely: Suspended bust.* And so you would suspend the bust on him for his conduct ashore, and then get him aboard and he'd work so fine for you till you gave it back to him. Then the next month you got in the same position. And you're not really playing with the guy's career, but he would do some stupid things. Like he'd get over there and get drunk, and wouldn't come back for two days and those kinds of things. You had to have some kind of leverage. But most of them were very, very good.

Now, he did shock me at one time on an incident. The op order required you to look through your crew to find out the guys who spoke various languages, because any nationality of ship might be sailing through that area. On this particular time we were going up alongside a Japanese fishing boat, and we wanted to make sure we had a guy who could speak that language. I had discovered that my signalman could speak it. Someone had put him down as a Japanese interpreter, primarily because of the fact that he had a Japanese wife. So we had a little set of warnings that we could give. And we had it written out on a cardboard in English, and then our interpreter would read it and give it to this guy in Japanese.

The warning basically was, "You are proceeding in a danger area. Request you move south, or west, or north," depending on what it would take to get him out of there. Or steer course such-and-such. And this guy, we flashed the sign out, and he just seemed to continue on. I was maybe about 100 feet away, yelling through this bullhorn to them in English. Finally I said, "Give it to him in Japanese," because, after all, he was a Japanese interpreter. And I was quite shocked when he gave them his Japanese. He said, "Mushi-mushi. Get the fuck out of here." [Laughter] Well, believe it or not, the guy

---

* "Bust" was a demotion to the next lower rate and pay grade. Suspending the bust essentially meant probation; the demotion would be carried out if the individual got into further trouble.

understood that. He moved. He turned and went off in the direction that we suggested. Maybe it took that kind of yelling to do it.

We spent most of our time in the DER down south in that situation, with the nuclear test. Now, the nuclear tests were completed, I guess, sometime in August or September of that year, 1962. It was about that time frame I think, because I can remember distinctly that I was down at Johnston when the last shot was made, and if I recall it correctly, the last shot didn't get off the pad. It blew up Johnston Island.*

We were out there, and I was beginning to creep home, just get a little bit of a head start, because I was ready to go home, when we got word that the island had blown up. Of course, we came charging back in there then. We were suddenly detached and all that, because I don't think there was any real danger or anything happened other than the pad blew up and the missile exploded on the pad. They didn't have a nuclear burst, I don't think. It was just the launch vehicle blew up.

Paul Stillwell: That was verging into the time of the Cuban Missile Crisis.† Did that affect you at all?

Admiral Gravely: The Cuban Missile Crisis didn't really affect us as the DERs. It affected us only from the standpoint that several of our DEs and other reserve ships were activated at that point in time. And I found it harder to get a berth when we came into Pearl Harbor, because there were many, many more ships in there at that time. But we got a little briefing by the commodore what the situation was, etc. We were certainly standing by in case anybody wanted us to move or go any other place or do any other

---

* On 25 July 1962 U.S. forces attempted to launch a nuclear weapon using the Thor intermediate range ballistic missile. The payload consisted of two re-entry vehicles, one with an instrument pod, the other with the warhead. The missile engine malfunctioned immediately on ignition. Range safety fired the destruct system while the missile was still on the launch pad. The Johnston Island launch complex was heavily damaged and contaminated with plutonium. Three months of repairs and decontamination were necessary before tests could resume.

† The Cuban Missile Crisis was triggered in mid-October 1962, when a U.S. reconnaissance plane photographed a Soviet nuclear missile site in Cuba and the presence of Soviet bombers. On 22 October President John F. Kennedy went on national television to announce a naval quarantine of Cuba, to be implemented on 24 October. On 28 October Premier Nikita Khrushchev of the Soviet Union notified President Kennedy that he was ordering the withdrawal of Soviet bombers and missiles from Cuba.

thing, but in reality it didn't affect us more than it just made a more crowded harbor in there.

Paul Stillwell: Typically in a small ship like, that the crew becomes pretty close and develops a lot of camaraderie. Did you see that on Falgout?

Admiral Gravely: Yes indeed. There was certainly a lot of camaraderie. There were guys who were quite pleased and quite proud of their ship. I enjoyed that ship. It was really an experience for me, and I guess the thing that I think I should mention was that from the day I came on board there was no doubt in my mind I could run that ship—from administrative or handling the crew business. I'd practiced it for a year, and I'd done it before that. I was a little leery about the ship handling, but except, as I said, for making a rough landing or two, I didn't have any problems.

One sort of interesting and humorous incident occurred. If you recall at that time, we had an athletic program—JFK's athletic program.[*]

Paul Stillwell: Right.

Admiral Gravely: Well, I didn't understand what was happening one morning, but I soon found out. We'd only been in port for a couple of days, so it was time for my 30 days' R&R or whatever we were going to have there. Practically everybody got under way. And then it dawned on me when I was called by the commodore, "Oh, by the way, Mr. Fay [who was Under Secretary of the Navy] is coming out, and he wants to visit a ship and see how they conduct their athletic program."[†]

Paul Stillwell: He was Kennedy's old shipmate.

Admiral Gravely: Yes, he was Kennedy's old shipmate on the PT boats, and he's also they guy who played football with him on the lawn of the White House in those days.

---

[*] John F. Kennedy emphasized national physical fitness when he became President in 1961.
[†] Paul B. Fay, Jr., served as Under Secretary of the Navy from 16 February 1961 to 15 January 1965.

And he wanted to see us operate our JFK program. So, fine. I made all preparations, and I purposely decided that certainly I would have the ship cleaned and those kinds of things, but I'd have my people ready to go out and physically show him how we did it. The commodore agreed with that. I had my bars on my khakis, of course, but I was ready to go myself. Didn't plan to, because the instructions specifically stated that if you were over 40, as I recall, you didn't have to do it. So this must have been in the summer of '62, because I had just passed 40.

So I was standing there all ready at the quarterdeck, and everything all shining and waiting for Mr. Fay. Up drove a big Cadillac with the Under Secretary in it. I went out and saluted, shook hands, piped him aboard. Took him down to the wardroom and briefed him on our program. He was very happy with it, and he said, "Yes, but, Captain, I want to see it. I want to see it in action."

So I said, "Well, it just so happens, sir, [laughter] we are testing our people this morning, and there's a few of them out on the athletic field." Well, the athletic field was really across the way from the pier. But it was far enough away that it would have been convenient to have taken a ride or something like that. As we stepped off the gangway, of course, the Cadillac pulled up there, and Mr. Fay said, "Well, son. Shall we ride over?"

I said, "No, sir. I think maybe we ought to trot over, and we'll both be ready when we get there." So one of the things that most people were pretty amazed at was me trotting alongside the Under Secretary of the Navy over to this athletic field. In the meantime, he had changed into his shorts, and he was prepared, shorts and sneakers, etc., skivvy shirt. We went over there, and he joined in each of these exercises with our people, and probably outdid most of them. Well, finally, it was about time when he should be going to a luncheon endeavor which he had, and I could sort of catch a high-sign from my commodore, and I went over to see the Secretary. I said, "Mr. Secretary, I think that they're probably about ready now to take you to your next engagement, which is a luncheon, I think, up at Com 14, or something like that."*

He said, "Well, let me tell you. I'm not about to leave here until I see you do your exercises." [Laughter]

---

* Com 14—Commandant of the 14th Naval District.

So I said, "Well, sir, you know, there's an out for me in that directive. It says if you're over 40, you don't do this. I'm over 40. In fact, I passed 40 about three days ago."

He said, "Well, I don't care about that. I want to see you do your exercises."

So I said, "Yes, sir." So I got down, and I was doing sit-ups. As I came up, I looked, and there was this guy running in my direction. I couldn't figure out what this was, but he was coming from the ship, and he was running. So finally, when I finished that, I looked and it was my corpsman. I said, "What the hell were you doing running over here?"

He said, "Well, the commodore told me that he thought I better get over here in case you had a heart attack."

Paul Stillwell: He was pulling your leg a little.

Admiral Gravely: He was pulling my leg a little bit. But, in any event, I did my full set of pull-ups, and then we went to pushups, and I did about half of those when the Under Secretary finally had to leave, and so we took him back to the ship. Unfortunately, when he left the wardroom going up to my cabin to change his clothes, he bumped his head on that ladder that we had, and it didn't gash, but I'm sure he had a headache for a day or so. I felt kind of bad about it, but I almost thought he deserved for making me do those damn exercises. [Laughter]

Paul Stillwell: You probably had to duck your head quite a bit in the ship, too, because you're tall.

Admiral Gravely: I did. Right. Well, I've got to tell you that carriers are the worst ones for me, because I've got to raise my legs up and then lower my head. And on the DERs, going up to the second deck, you had a little bit of a problem. Destroyers are not a hell of a lot better, but after so many of them, you know where to lower the head and the whole bit. So, anyway, that was certainly a major event for us.

The next major event was that there was another guy sent out from DoD, and I can't think of his name now, but I can remember that seeing the message which basically said that he was the equivalent to a major general, as I recall. and treat him as such.* He came out basically to interview me from a DoD standpoint. He was writing a book or something about integration of the Navy.

The cruise in the DERs went quite normally, except I did manage to go to the barrier on one occasion.† And I must tell you, I had one of the roughest experiences on that trip that I've ever had in my life. I sympathize with every CO that had to go up there more than once. I think everybody should have gone up there once, and once was enough. While we were up there, we inadvertently got into a couple of storms. I was sitting on this bridge at about 2:00 o'clock in the morning, when I thought the thing was going to break in half. That's how we were being beat. We managed to get out of that one with a certain amount of fairly careful ship handling. I had an old quartermaster on board who'd been up there about a dozen times. He was constantly whispering in my ear, "Captain, I think you ought to do this." And I thought he was right. [Laughter] And we managed that one.

The next thing that happened to us was that one afternoon we began to hear a knocking under the hull. This banging was going on under the hull, and I kept sending the engineer and his people down to inspect the engine rooms. It had to be something loose in that engine room. It sounded like a guy with a small hammer, about once every 30 seconds or so, maybe a little bit more frequently than that, but about that. But then, of course, it was coinciding with the roll of the ship. So we just kept inspecting, and couldn't find anything. Finally the next morning I decided that I had to send somebody over the side, because it was obviously under the ship, just to find out what this was. We had the guys dressed in their diving gear. It wasn't that bad weather or anything else. About that time a great white shark came through there. And I got to tell you, we abandoned that idea in a hurry. In the meantime, about a couple of hours later, the thing quit. As mysteriously as it appeared, it quit. So, to some degree, we forgot about it.

---

* DoD—Department of Defense.
† This refers to the North Pacific barrier patrol for the purpose of detecting incoming Soviet aircraft.

But subsequently, on that same patrol, we had a problem with our boilers. We had two small boilers which basically made the drinking water in connection with our evaporators, etc. And one of those went out. Actually, the second one went out. Well, with both boilers out you don't have water for drinking, you don't have water for showers, you don't have water to wash the dishes. Of course, we had a little bit to drink. Nobody got really thirsty up there, but certainly we couldn't do the heavy things that you normally did. So I decided that I had to go into Midway. And, of course, that was left to the CO's discretion. So we went on into Midway, and after getting in there and getting alongside, we got the boiler repaired, which is the reason I went in there. But I'd also asked to have divers there. When the diver went down and looked, I would say, I'd hate to guess, but anyway, a huge portion of the bilge keel had broken loose, and that was what was scraping along there. Then finally it broke off entirely. The purpose of the bilge keel, of course, is to stabilize the ship to some degree. So we just went without that the rest of the trip. I went back to the barrier, and then, of course, at the end of the picket came home.

Paul Stillwell: What sorts of things were you doing while you were up on the barrier patrol? You've touched on it briefly. Any specifics?

Admiral Gravely: Well, the biggest thing was communicating with the aircraft as they came by there frequently, and checking navigation positions. You checked yours, they checked theirs, and those kinds of things. Certainly you were vigilant for anything else that was coming in your direction. But it was sort of a lazy-type thing wherein your mission was basically to be a part of the guardian force up there that kept people from coming across the so-called barrier. Yes, DEW Line, early-warning line is basically what it was.

Paul Stillwell: Was there any trouble with navigation? Did you have overcast to keep you from getting star sights?

Admiral Gravely: You had overcast conditions an awful lot of the time. You certainly had nothing you could navigate with other than star sights and those kinds of things. Strictly celestial navigation. You were out in the deep ocean out there, and there's nothing else up there.

Paul Stillwell: Did you have Loran?

Admiral Gravely: You had Loran, but Loran isn't that reliable up in that area. So it was a case of—

Paul Stillwell: Approximations probably.

Admiral Gravely: To some degree. You certainly tried to verify your position with each airplane that crossed there, and between the two of you, you stayed fairly well on position. The exec was normally the navigator, with a couple of good quartermasters who had been in business for a long time. So you did a fair job of it. You didn't get lost coming home, I can tell you that. [Laughter]

Paul Stillwell: How capable was the communications suite in that ship?

Admiral Gravely: Well, it really didn't have much for communications. You had a couple of TED/RED series for your UHF communication with the aircraft.* Everybody has a ship-shore HF transmitter. You had those things. You were not equipped to communicate for a flagship, I can tell you that. You had the bare minimum, just like we did on all ships.

Paul Stillwell: Were you supposed to use high frequency to sound the alarm if you did see something?

---

* UHF—Ultra-high frequency.

Admiral Gravely: You were just going to get up on your HF and start yelling and screaming, unless you had an aircraft in the area someplace that you could contact, and tell them over your UHF. This was prior to satellite communications. But you had your minimum suite of communications gear that was probably as reliable as most that we had in those days. However, the DER wasn't the guy who got the most modern stuff at any point in time.

Paul Stillwell: Probably didn't have the on-line crypto at that time either, did you?

Admiral Gravely: I believe we did. Certainly we were beginning to get it.

Paul Stillwell: That was early in the era.

Admiral Gravely: Yes, that was very early in the era. We frankly didn't get that many classified messages anyway. I guess one of the problems so far as my communicator was concerned was that having been a communicator, I read the Fox file. I guess that caused him more trouble than anything else, because I knew when he'd missed a number.[*] [Laughter] And whether it was addressed to me or not, I knew when he'd missed a number, because I developed a habit, having been radio officer and communications officer, that I'd check the Fox file every day. And, frankly, I missed reading the Fox file when I came to shore, because on each of the destroyers that I commanded, as well as <u>Jouett</u>, the first thing in the morning that I did was to check the message board, and then I'd check the Fox file. Just got to be a habit with me.

Paul Stillwell: It's a way of keeping up with everybody else's business.

Admiral Gravely: Well, to some degree. Certainly the on-line thing you keep up with not only your business, but everybody else's, because it's all decrypted. But to some degree

---

[*] The messages on the fleet broadcast were numbered consecutively, so a missing number meant a missed message, and the ship had to find a way to get a copy.

with that thing is I can recall we got a few encrypted messages that you just couldn't talk about. But I knew what most people were doing, certainly at my level.

Paul Stillwell: What were the satisfactions you realized from being in command?

Admiral Gravely: Well, there were just so many satisfactions. I liked being the guy in charge. Somehow, giving orders sort of satisfied me to some degree. And I'm not a harsh guy with orders. I don't ask people to do impossible things, but just being able to assume and execute responsibility was satisfying to me. I felt that to some degree I appreciated the honors and other rewards that command gave you. I didn't purposely have people to make any special honors for me when I came aboard, or anything like that. But it is a sort of a nice feeling when you came aboard, and there were four side boys standing there and those kinds of things, you know.*

Paul Stillwell: It's a traditional respect and deference to a senior.

Admiral Gravely: Yes, right, right. And those things, well, they would have made anybody feel good, you know. Yes. "Oh, if my dad could see me now," [laughter] you'd say to yourself. Right. Because he was the guy who never thought you'd be much. Right.

Well, we went into Midway and went back on picket. When I got back from picket that time I was quite surprised. We moored, and, of course, mail call is the first thing. I didn't expect mail from home, because all of those letters would go to my family, but certainly you expect official letters, etc.

Now, the schedule for the Falgout was to go into the shipyard very shortly after January or so of 1963. And, frankly, I'd been at sea then since '57 continuously, continuous sea duty. So I expected to go ashore someplace. And I was expecting probably that I'd get transferred sometime during that yard period. So I expected to see some orders and those kinds of things. Lo and behold, I had three letters. I opened them

---

* Side boys are crew members stationed in two ranks at a ship's gangway on the arrival or departure of officers or officials for whom side honors are rendered. The number of side boys varies from two to eight, depending on the rank of the individual.

quickly, and I decided to do it in what I considered the order of their importance. One was from the White House. The White House letter invited me back to a cocktail party in celebration of the 100th anniversary of the signing of the Emancipation Proclamation.[*] Then I looked at my other two letters, and they were from BuPers, and one said, "You have been nominated for and will attend the '63 session of the Naval War College." And the second one said, "Contrary to what I told you in my first letter, you are not going to the Naval War College. [Laughter] And you will be advised later as to where you are going."

Well, in the meantime, the next thing you do, of course, is you immediately go in to see your commodore when you arrive in port. When I went in to see my commodore, and it was not Commodore Newland, who had been relieved, it was a new guy, whose name I can't recall at the moment, but certainly an outstanding gent who'd been in destroyers and everything else. Still a good fellow. But frankly, he was not as seagoing, I guess is the word that I want to use, as Commodore Newland. So he started by saying "Why did you go to Midway? Why did you leave the picket?"

I said, "Commodore, the op order says that it's a commanding officer's judgment if he feels he should leave station, and under no other circumstances, but at the same time, he can leave station if it's in his judgment. As a result of the problem with those boilers, I felt that I had to take the ship into Midway so I could give my crew water and creature comforts really. If we had been coming straight back into Pearl at this point in time, I would not have done that, because I'd have made them wait till we got back into Pearl. But we still had 10 or 15 days on that patrol, and I felt that we had to go in." Then I said, "Commodore, I want to tell you something. I really don't think that's my problem this morning. I think my problem is one of trying to say 'no' to the President."

He said, "What are you talking about?"

I said, "Well, I got these three letters today. I got these two from the BuPers. And frankly, one says you're going to War College, the other says you're not." I said, "But I've been invited to this Emancipation Proclamation celebration, and I really don't see how I can go to Washington."

---

[*] On 1 January 1863 President Abraham Lincoln issued the Emancipation Proclamation, which declared an end to slavery in all areas of the Confederacy that were in rebellion against the United States.

The commodore said, "Well, let me see that letter." He took my letter and looked at it. He didn't say anything to me, but he went downstairs to ComDesFlot 5.

And I said, "Oh?" Basically I was told to wait there. So I waited until he returned.

He said, "You're going to Washington."

I said, "Commodore, I really don't think I ought to go to Washington. There are a couple of reasons. Number one is that Washington is in blues. I am now a commander, and I don't have any striped blues."

He said, "We'll fix that." He called the exchange, said, "Commander Gravely's wife is going to bring his blues by this afternoon, and I want them striped by Friday," or something like that, because I had to take off very shortly after that.

Paul Stillwell: So you'd just found out you were selected?

Admiral Gravely: Yes, I'll go back to that. I said, "Well, what about my wife? My wife's going to want to go to Washington too, and I can't afford to take her. After all, I'm going to be transferred this summer and go back to Washington."

He said, "Don't worry about her, I'll talk to her." [Laughter] So, anyway, to make a long story short, I was given a set of TAD orders to come back to Washington, D.C., for this celebration. I, of course, came to Washington, and frankly the story gets humorous from there on out. It's humorous to me anyway.[*]

I said, "Commodore, I need at least a week. Who's going to come from Honolulu to Washington, D.C., and not stay Monday till Friday?" I said, "Is that okay—five days' TAD?"

"Okay, great." So the orders had to be fixed so that they just weren't open ended. I had to report someplace. I was told to report to OpNav for temporary duty in connection with a White House affair.[†] So I came into Washington, and got here on a Sunday or something like that. I had a brother who lived out at Cheltenham at that time. So I rented a car and went on out to my brother's house.

---

[*] TAD—temporary additional duty.
[†] OpNav—the extended staff of the Chief of Naval Operations.

The next morning I reported to OpNav. And there was a female commander there who I thought was giving me a rough time. She said, "Commander, you know, you've got to report in here every morning."

I said, "Well, let me tell you what my situation is. I'm here for a week, but really I'm here to attend a cocktail party at the White House, and I'm currently living out in Cheltenham, which is about 35 miles from here. I hope you don't want me to drive in to the Pentagon every morning just to check into your office. Can't I call you?"

"Oh, no, you can't call, but let me see your orders." Showed my orders. She put on that I had reported such and such a time, detached that Friday. And, of course, I didn't have to go in there anymore.

Paul Stillwell: What changed her mind?

Admiral Gravely: The White House. [Laughter] The White House connection changed her mind. But, anyway, I went to the cocktail party, and, of course, had on my blues. And for the first time I met President Kennedy, and I also met President Vice Lyndon Johnson.[*] I was quite impressed with both of them.

Paul Stillwell: What impressions do you have of each one?

Admiral Gravely: Well, both of them were certainly very, very fine gents. The President I thought was very cool, very coordinated. He knew what he was all about, knew what he was doing and everything else. President Johnson—well, he was Vice President Johnson, of course, at that point in time. I thought he sort of flustered about a little bit, ran in circles, shouted, screamed, you know, typical. I do not question his competence as President of the United States; I do not intend to even imply that. But two things that happened gave me this impression. One was the meeting with the President. Okay, I got to the cocktail party; I was alone. I was there for maybe 20 minutes, just sort of moving

---

[*] Lyndon B. Johnson (Democrat-Texas) served in the Senate from 1949 to 1961, when he became Vice President. He later served as President from 1963 to 1969.

around in the group. I saw Sammy Davis, Jr., there, for example.* I met the first black Army general.

Paul Stillwell: Davis.

Admiral Gravely: Davis. B. O. Davis, that's right.† I saw several other people of that caliber there, and I was just sort of taken aback to some degree to see that here the company that I was sort of associating with here, they were big people. But, anyway, I saw a Navy captain there, and obviously he was the presidential aide at that point in time. We've always had a big Navy guy. I guess they've got a Navy captain there now.

Paul Stillwell: I think the billet's been downgraded since then.

Admiral Gravely: Okay. I remember when we had a commander there, but anyway they had a captain.

Paul Stillwell: Tazewell Shephard was Kennedy's aide.‡

Admiral Gravely: That's who it was. [Laughter] How'd you guess? Tazewell Shephard—I talked to him for a few minutes, and the impression I got was that I was to somehow meet the President. Well, the President's wife came out, and the President came out. And I got to tell you, I don't know how many people were there. They took up a whole wing of the White House. With all those people, there was no way for me to get close to the guy. Then suddenly I looked over, and there was Tazewell Shephard.

Paul Stillwell: Giving you a hand motion.

---

* Davis was a singer and entertainer.
† In 1940 Benjamin O. Davis, Sr., became the highest-ranking black officer in the U.S. Army when he was promoted to brigadier general. His son, Benjamin O. Davis, Jr., who served in the Air Force, was later the first black officer to reach two-star and three-star rank in the U.S. armed forces.
‡ Captain Tazewell T. Shephard, Jr., USN.

Admiral Gravely: Yes, giving me the high sign—get over here and meet him. So, I thought, "Oh shit." I went over and I pushed through a couple of ladies there. Well, actually I saw which way he was coming, so I took a stand right there in front of the crowd there, instead of pushing people out of the way. Then finally I got a chance to shake the President's hand. His greeting was basically, "How are you, Commander?" I knew he was an ex-Navy officer. But that sort of set me on my heels a little bit, you know. Here's a guy that really knows what a commander looks like. But then I knew he should have then. "How are things going?" You know, blah, blah, blah. That was about it. And, of course, he had to move on, because there were people all around.

Well, I got out of that crowd. I was a little miffed at Tazewell for making me do that, but I guess I could see what his point was. In any event, subsequent to that I was over at one of the hors d'oeuvre tables, and here came Vice President Johnson. Big, "How are you, Commander? Great, it's nice to see a naval officer here." Then he called his wife's name, "Lady Bird. Come on over here and meet the commander." And Lady Bird came over, and I shook her hand and everything else, but that's the flustering thing and big noise and everything else. And I saw him a couple of times after that too, to get to meet him, to be with him. But that sort of took me aback a little bit too. But the biggest thing that took me aback I guess was being in the audience that I was in with the kinds of people there. I was really impressed by the big wheels and everything else.

Paul Stillwell: Well, it sounds like the whole thing was a symbolic gesture too.

Admiral Gravely: To some degree, right. Right. Well, I, of course, had been chewed out by my wife constantly that the invitation was for both of us, and that the Navy sent me but didn't send her. That's the only black mark the Navy has on its record as far as she's concerned. [Laughter] But, anyway, I went through that little thing-a-ma-jig, and then went on back to Honolulu.

Paul Stillwell: What was life like there for your family living in Honolulu?

Admiral Gravely: We had a great tour there in Honolulu. In the neighborhood in which we lived there were two or three other officers that I had served with previously, so we had friends in the neighborhood, etc. We lived below a Marine family, and the Marine wasn't quite ready for this. He gave us minor problems, but nothing we couldn't handle. We were both going through the same front door. He had to walk up a set of stairs, and I could just walk right in. But here was a guy who walked down the path from the driveway with me and wouldn't even speak, but that was no problem.

He unfortunately accused my son of something. It seemed like someone was either going into his mailbox, so we got a big complaint that my son was going into his mailbox. Well, my son was five years old, couldn't reach his damn mailbox. And whereas he created a little bit of a stink when I just took him out there and showed him my son had to be standing on a rock on his tiptoes to reach his mailbox, we kind of got that one settled.

One of my neighbors was a guy by the name of Earl Carter, a black officer. He was a lieutenant commander at that time, and so he and my family got to be very close friends. Pete Petersen was in the Marine Corps and was a captain, lived over in Kaneohe, and our families got to be close friends after that.

Paul Stillwell: Marine aviator.[*]

Admiral Gravely: Yes, Pete Petersen, who is a lieutenant general now. We met a really interesting group.

There were no major problems, a couple of little incidents precipitated by some unthinking people. For example, one was a time when my kid came home crying, and he said, "Dad, why is it I can't get a little Mickey Mouse thing?" something about milk bottles. You send in a top and you get a Mickey Mouse thing. Some little kid had told him that he was chocolate or something like that, and this was only for white kids or something of that sort. You know, those are little things that don't amount to that much, but at the moment they seem kind of big.

---

[*] In October 1952, Frank E. Petersen, Jr., was designated a naval aviator and accepted a commission as a second lieutenant. He thus became the first black aviator in the Marine Corps.

My set of quarters had a canvas over what you call the lanai. Most of the houses didn't, but apparently the guy who'd lived there before me had put up this canvas and left the top there. One of my neighbors thought he was going to give me a hard time, I guess. His kid happened to come around when we weren't there, and he climbed up on this thing and was going to slide on it, and slid through and fell on the cement there. And boy, I got this frantic call from this warrant officer, who was going to call the authorities on me. I simply told him that, "Hey, I kind of think I ought to call the authorities on you, because your son has no business on my back porch when I'm not there." Very shortly after that I got a little note apologizing with a bottle of wine, which, of course, that ended that. But, you know, nothing unusual.

Paul Stillwell: You found it a pleasant place to live, I take it?

Admiral Gravely: It was a pleasant place to live. I think Radford Terrace was the name of the housing unit that we lived in, and it was a very nice one. It was brand new at that point in time, and we moved in there about a month or so after we got there.

As I've said, the shipyard overhaul was the next facet of my being in Falgout, and frankly that went just very, very smooth. One of the reasons it went smooth was because in the ship's supe department there was a guy there who had been on the Seminole with me. You keep bumping heads with these guys, and you know, that's where an awful lot of work is accomplished and things. So he made it go very, very smooth for me.

One of the highlights, of course, was an inspection by Admiral Virden. Admiral Virden was a cruiser-destroyer group guy at that point in time and was previously Director, Naval Communications.[*] I'm obviously one of his successors in that job. I'd known him as a communicator all this time, and so I sort of looked up to him. He came aboard and inspected the ship, and I think he found it in fairly good shape, despite the fact that it was in the yard period. One significant thing so far as I'm concerned was that I was taking him through there, and we were putting down new tile. We got to a point wherein there was no more chipping, and new tile up against old tile. He looked at it and

---

[*] Rear Admiral Frank Virden USN, Commander Cruiser-Destroyer Force, U. S. Pacific Fleet.

he said, "Well, it seems like something is happening here, because I noticed that you're not tiling this over here. And this really looks good here, and that looks kind of beat up."

I said, "Admiral Virden, that's the point where I ran out of money." [Laughter] And money came to finish the tiling. Yup, right.

Paul Stillwell: How well did you and your exec work together as a team in that ship?

Admiral Gravely: Well, as I told you, I got a second exec, Jim Eller.* I think I was able to work much more closer with my second exec. My second exec had come straight from a destroyer ops. He had not been used to but one way of doing things, and that was my way of doing things. Very, very competent sailor. The other one was just as competent, but I think that you have to train people the way that you want them to be, and when you take over a guy that someone else has trained, they can only see one way for a long time. It is difficult to bring them around to your way of thinking. I think that to some degree I had a little bit of that problem. Now, there were no disputes. Nobody was mad at anybody. He did the job as best he could and as he saw fit. And, of course, he respected and did everything I asked him to do. I had no quarrels with that. In fact, I gave him a really outstanding fitness report. The other one, of course, being his first executive officer's type job, was willing to do it my way from day one, and we had just a great rapport. Jim Eller was just a tremendous guy and just really a fine ship handler too.

Paul Stillwell: Did you employ the good-guy, bad-guy routine that sometimes works in that CO-XO combination?

Admiral Gravely: Well, I don't think so quite that way. My XO was a bad guy, [laugh] so it made it easy for me be any way I wanted to be. But he was tough enough. He was demanding, and he managed to get people to do the job. He was one of the kind of leaders that does it without actually putting fear in people. There are a lot of leaders who can only lead by fear, and he went almost to that point. But stayed just far enough on this side of it that it wasn't that they were frightened of him, but they did it because they

---

* Lieutenant James B. Eller, USN.

really respected that guy. I know a couple of guys that I've met subsequently, and maybe I worked beside of them but not necessarily under them or any other way, who relied strictly on fear. Man, that used to upset me a little bit. But, anyway, we went through the yard period, etc., and finished that.

One of the interesting things about my dealings with the officers is that I had this one officer whom I told you I had a little problem with, who ran through the rain cloud. One Monday morning I got some minor complaint from the squadron chaplain that we were not ready for church service when he came aboard on that Sunday morning. So I listened to his complaint and everything else, and I went back to the ship to find out what had happened, and sure enough, we'd been a little remiss in that we weren't quite ready. We got ready as quickly as we could, but I was always convinced that the chaplain was sort of invited over here by you, the commanding officer, to attend to the religious needs of the sailors. And I've been convinced that some of them needed much more than others, and all of them needed a little bit, and so it was good to have the chaplain come. So I decided I would write an instruction on what would happen for church service. And basically that instruction directed the CDO to go back about a half an hour before, and make sure that everything was set up for church services.* Well, one of my officers, in fact, this particular officer, said to me that he was very sorry that despite the fact that he recognized that he'd been given some orders to do things, this was an order that he couldn't carry out. So I said, "Why can't you carry it out?"

He said, "Well, Captain I'm an atheist. And I can't have anything to do with church."

I said, "Well, I've got to tell you, I didn't tell you to have anything to do with church. I didn't tell you to go; I told you to be back there and make sure the thing was set up, and stay around here and officiate, and make sure it went off well."

He said, "Well, I'm afraid that I can't obey that."

I said, "Well, Tom, I understand that you have the duty Sunday, and if you don't do this like I told you, I shall kick your butt off this ship, and I got to tell you I think I'm big enough to personally do it." Now, this is a guy told me once he was an all-American end for the Naval Academy. But I was ready to do it if he was willing. In fact, I told him

---

* CDO—command duty officer.

that if I ever told him to jump over the side of the ship, that either I would see his heels as they went over, or I personally would kick his butt off. Well, we didn't have any more problems about that. However, that young man was thrown off the ship by my relief subsequent to that. There was something wrong with him psychologically. I don't know exactly what it was.

Well, we finished the yard period, and, of course, I then got my orders to go to the Naval War College. We had a normal change of command and the whole bit. No problems. And, of course, I left there. The news at that point was that George Thompson and I were going to integrate the Naval War College for the first time.* I was being sent to the senior course; George went to the junior course.

Paul Stillwell: Now, you'd had that discrepancy before where you had the two letters that said you were going and you weren't going. How was that resolved?

Admiral Gravely: I just got a set of orders [laughter] to go to the Naval War College. Yes, the first letter said, "You're going. Congratulations," and the second letter said, "You're not going." And suddenly I got the orders, so I didn't pay any attention to that.

I missed one thing that I wanted to cover here, and that is, as you stated earlier, I did get selected to commander while I was on Falgout. Well, the interesting part about that was that the message came out which listed the number of people who had been selected to commander, and as they kept bringing it up to me page by page by page from the teletype, we missed a page. It was the page that would have had my name on it or would not have had my name on it, depending on what it was. And, of course, communicators sometimes lose their lives simply from missing messages. I did not kill my communicator. But the interesting part to me was that whereas we missed that message, and we were waiting to see if we would get a rerun on it, I did get a personal message from Admiral Smedberg, who was Chief of Naval Personnel, congratulating me for making commander. Obviously, Admiral Smedberg sent messages to all of his former people who had been with him, but I was particularly pleased to get it. That's the way I got it, rather than reading it on the straight file.

---

* Lieutenant Commander George I. Thompson, USN.

Paul Stillwell: How much before the White House trip had that taken place?

Admiral Gravely: It must have taken place about two months, really, before the White House trip, because, as I recall, my date of rank to commander was something like November.

Paul Stillwell: So your number came up just about the time of the trip?

Admiral Gravely: My number? Well, I was senior enough so that I was immediately picked up in the first batch. But I had been selected for and had been promoted to commander, but I had not gotten blues striped simply because of the fact of where we were. My date of rank, as a commander, was October 1, 1962. And this was shortly before that when the message came out. So, yes, this was a few months before I had made the trip back there.

Well, I guess the next facet was good old Naval War College. Of course, the wife and I again took a leisurely trip across country, visited with our folks, and then went to the Naval War College up in Newport, Rhode Island. I was quite impressed with the Naval War College, with what they were trying to do there, and everything like that. But I frankly was not as prepared as some of my contemporaries who went there. The main reason is, and I'm a firm believer, that the Navy makes a mistake in sending guys directly from sea duty into the Naval War College without touching base with the Washington, D.C., community. At that time I'd had a two-year tour here as a very junior officer in a recruiting district, which was rather remote from the Washington scene.

Obviously, when you're selected for the war college, they send you various things to read, and they tell what other books and things you ought to read and everything else. But there's no way that you can get out of it what Joe Blow, who just came from BuPers, has in practical experience. Or Joe Blow who's been in OpNav. And so, frankly, I was a little bit behind the eight ball on that. It took one hell of a lot of reading. It took a lot of looking up things and trying to catch up. You were reading what was currently happening there. You were reading books.

I found it a little difficult, because the Navy and the defense establishment, so far as I'm concerned, is not an easy one to understand unless you've been there and you've worked in the environment. I came to the Pentagon, for example, really to work in the Pentagon as a captain. I didn't even know the corridor-floor rule. But some of these guys had. For example, Ace Lyons, who's presently CinCPacFlt, was a classmate, not from the senior course.* He was in the junior course. There are a couple of people. I just can't think of names right now. Well, Jeremiah Denton a classmate, for example, at the war college.†

Some of those guys had less experience in the higher hierarchy of the Navy than I did. But there were certainly a lot of them who had spent time in this environment, who, I think, found it a little easier. In the meantime, I thought that I should work on the master's program which was offered to you through George Washington University (GWU). I started working on the master's program, and just took one course, because I discovered that the amount of reading I had to do for the master's program, plus the amount of reading you had to do for the war college, plus the amount of reading you had to do to catch up, I didn't have any time for a family, who had made some sacrifices when I went to sea for seven years.

Because, as I said, I went to sea in 1957 in the Seminole, and when I came ashore it was in June of 1963. So I decided I'd better spend a little bit more time with my family. My wife, for example, is an avid fisherman, and you can imagine how much fun it was for her to fish up there at Fort Adams. We used to go down to Fort Adams on Saturday and enjoyed the fishing down there.

The war college was, again, quite a unique experience for me, but I enjoyed it. My classmates and other people were people that I enjoy as friends today. I was asked by the wife of one of the Navy captains in my class, who later became a flag officer, and he, in fact, was in my section, if I had been sponsored to the Naval War College by the NAACP.‡ I'm not sure what she meant by that, but she asked me that dumb question,

---

* Admiral James A. Lyons, Jr., USN served as Commander in Chief Pacific Fleet from 16 September 1985 to 30 September 1987. In 1963 Lyons was a lieutenant commander.
† Commander Jeremiah A. Denton, Jr., USN. Denton, who was a naval aviator, spent eight years as a prisoner of war during the Vietnam War. His memoir of that period is When Hell Was in Session (New York: Readers Digest Press, 1976). He subsequently served as a U.S. Senator from Alabama, 1981-87.
‡ NAACP—National Association for the Advancement of Colored People.

and I really didn't have an answer for her except to say, "Hell, I thought I was a naval officer just like everybody else that's here, and nobody particularly sponsored me here."

As I said, I did not complete the GWU course; I just completed the assignment. I did take a course in public speaking while I was there, and a couple of other things to improve. I wrote my paper on amphibious warfare, which I thought was something I was probably more ready to do than, say, a subject in ASW or command and control, which I didn't know very much about. But I'd been in the amphib force, and I really enjoyed my tour with the amphib force. I liked it, and thought that that would be the place where I should take my paper. And, frankly, there was a quote from my paper up there, which was given to me subsequent to that time by one of the professors who happened to read it before I got there as a three-star, and he remembered. So he took those lines out of there.

Paul Stillwell: One of the advantages, which you've alluded to indirectly, was that you met these people from other communities so that you got a broader view of the Navy there.

Admiral Gravely: You get a broader view of everything. You get a broader view of the Navy. You get a broader view of people. You get a broader view of the world around you. It's just a broader view of everything. I just met so many people who made it a broadening experience for Alma and me, including the foreign students who were there. And we just thoroughly enjoyed it. The quarters, no sweat. I was assigned a set of quarters just like everybody else. My neighbors became good friends; part of my car pool was the first public affairs officer to be Chinfo.

Paul Stillwell: Bill Thompson.[*]

Admiral Gravely: Bill Thompson and I were in the same car pool, for example. So it was an enjoyable experience. We stayed there for the year of the war college.

---

[*] Rear Admiral William Thompson, USN, served as the Navy's Chief of Information from July 1971 to February 1975. Thompson was a commander while a student at the Naval War College.

Paul Stillwell: What was the subject matter of all the reading you were doing? What was the range of it?

Admiral Gravely: Well, it ranged from plain old naval operations to the political and military. I read a lot on just plain old political policy. Certainly as many of the various current events as I possibly could. A lot of stuff put out by the State Department and those kinds of things. I was trying to get the big, overall picture.

For example, you mentioned the Cuban Missile Crisis. Well, driving a DER around in Pearl, you really didn't know much about the why and all what went on. So trying to backtrack and get more information on that and how we got out of it and read some of the various reports of those kinds of things. It was just a general, all-around, practically brand-new education for me is what you might call it. It was a big, broad experience really.

Paul Stillwell: Did you have a range of guest speakers also to supplement that?

Admiral Gravely: You're right. We had a big range of speakers from ambassadors right straight on down through the various chief of the services. Certainly you get the some of the top people. There were CinCs there, and just really, really top-notch speakers, all great guys.

Paul Stillwell: How much competition was there among the student body?

Admiral Gravely: Well, in those days, as I recall, it was referred to as a gentlemen's course. So there wasn't a hell of a lot of competition there. I was on a little committee with about eight or ten other people who sat around and discussed various problems, and, of course, we did papers and those kinds of things on our various discussions. We had both a military guy, who led, as well as a civilian, who was on the staff there to lead these discussion groups.

As I remember the kind of competition we had, basically there were always these guys who wanted to make sure that they stood up when the speaker turned to questions, and there were several of those. Two or three guys obviously were aspiring for admirals. A couple of them made it, a couple of them didn't. But it wasn't as competitive as maybe it got to be when Stan Turner was there.[*] It was still the gentlemen's course wherein you were there to study and in a relaxed atmosphere.

What made it tough for me, as it was, was the fact that I felt that some of my peers and other people had been in an environment which I had not been in, not being around the Washington area. With the experience of coming away from seven years of sea duty I didn't feel quite as up to snuff as I might be.

Paul Stillwell: So that was really a useful thing for you to have at that point.

Admiral Gravely: It was a very useful thing to have, but if I had to do it all over again, I would have come through BuPers first or OpNav first. I would have been better prepared, for example, after I finished my tour as director of the naval satellite communications program.

Now, in taking a tour in BuPers, George Thompson and two or three officers since George Thompson have always had a billet in BuPers—I believe that's where that billet is—where they've always been the guy who sort of represented the black community, who tried to get people to help them with recruiting. They did things to try to improve recruiting and those kinds of things. I regret now that I did not come into BuPers, although I'm not the guy who finally made the decision. I did tell a couple of people that I didn't want the job, but I probably should have said, "I do want the job." If I had come into BuPers and spent two years here, I would have gotten one hell of a lot more out of the war college. Now, I got what I went there to get, but I think I could have gotten even more if I had been a little bit better prepared for when I went there.

Paul Stillwell: Of course, you didn't know that until you got there.

---

[*] Vice Admiral Stansfield Turner, USN, served as president of the Naval War College from 30 June 1972 to 9 August 1974.

Admiral Gravely: No, that's right. That's right. I didn't know. It was a brand-new world for me, really. But, anyway, I went there, and, of course, I didn't suffer anything. I enjoyed it. I got what I came for and was very happy with having been there.

Paul Stillwell: How much involvement did you have with the war-gaming aspects of it?

Admiral Gravely: We didn't do any war-gaming in those days. When you talk in terms of war-gaming, I've been to the war college and I've played on their war-game machine, but I did that more as a group commander when I had Cruiser-Destroyer Group Two and worked basically for Admiral Ike Kidd, who used to take all of his troops up there every once in a while.* But I did not do any war-gaming per se as part of my class. I think the junior course probably played on that machine a little bit. After all, I was with the "senior gentlemen," you know. [Chuckle]

Paul Stillwell: So, really, your experience would be a determining factor in how much you got out of it. You weren't forced to.

Admiral Gravely: It was exactly that. You could have loafed through the course. Well, I think you had to go to class. But, other than go and be there, that was about the only requirement at that point in time. And, of course, a couple of presidents thereafter—I know Stan Turner was certainly one who recognized that, and he wanted to lay stiffer requirements on the students. I think that was absolutely correct. You make them do a little bit more than they were, because some guys just stuck around and did the minimum.

Paul Stillwell: Was Admiral Austin the president?

Admiral Gravely: Admiral Austin was the president while I was there.† Admiral Austin was a very, very fine gent. He had us over socially a couple of times. I liked him. The

---
* Admiral Isaac C. Kidd, Jr., USN, served as Supreme Allied Commander Atlantic, Commander in Chief Atlantic Command, and Commander in Chief Atlantic Fleet from 30 May 1975 to 30 September 1978.
† Vice Admiral Bernard L. Austin, USN, served as president of the Naval War College from 30 June 1960 to 31 July 1964.

guy, I felt, wasn't quite pushy enough to have pushed people to do things. I'm thinking in terms of pushing from just making them do. He probably went along with whatever the thing was before he was there, and there were no major changes. But Admiral Austin certainly was a competent president and did a good job there.

Paul Stillwell: How much did he make his presence felt to the students?

Admiral Gravely: Well, you saw him probably once or twice a week, and it depended on who the speaker was as to who introduced the speaker, whether the president introduced or whether the deputy introduced him. We had a two-star there, as well as Admiral Austin, who had three stars. And some speakers you knew that the two-star was going to introduce, and there were some speakers that Admiral Austin was going to introduce. Admiral Austin would never pass up—just like any other three-star—wouldn't pass up a guy who was senior to him, obviously. But, you know, you've got So-So here who is a major general or something like that, he'd get the rear admiral to do it. But we saw him, I would say, two to three times every week, so he was there, and his presence was known.

I must tell you that I really had only one problem at the Naval War College, and that was not the Naval War College. When I got my orders, I was a little shocked about the place I was going to, because I was coming to the Defense Communications Agency. Now, I knew I wasn't going to stay at the Naval War College, but I was shocked that here after over damn near ten years that here somebody was thinking about me as a communicator again.

The Defense Communications Agency was fairly brand new at that point in time. It was created about 1960, as I recall. Suddenly I was going to it, and obviously it was because of my communications background. But in 1955, when I went to Com Three, I was not a communicator and had never even been close to one since 1955, and here it was '64, and I was going back. Well, I was taken aback a little bit about that, but in the meantime I did get wiring diagrams of DCA, found out where they fitted in the Joint Staff, where they fitted in the Department of Defense, what the organization was like, and all that. So I was prepared when I got there.

The thing that got to me a little bit was that—and I'm not sure the Naval War College knows about this, because I'm not a complainer, but each year when the orders are issued, and they come out in the various publications, Navy Times, etc., every realtor in the Washington, D.C, area goes up and rents hotel rooms up there. They then talk to each of the students, and they let it be known that they're there to get you to come over there so that you can go and see about getting a house down here. I had decided at that point in time—this was '64—that I would not go, because I didn't feel that there was a person who would rent to me, other than the black realtors, and there were a couple of those who were going to find me a house.

So I came home from the school one day, and my wife said she'd just gotten a call from this real-estate agent who knew that I was going to Washington, D.C., and he'd like to have the commander come over and talk to him. He thought he could find a house for us if we wanted a house. So Alma and I sat around and kicked it around, saying, "Should we or should we not." And I kept telling her, "No. Don't go." But she insisted. My wife is a very insistent person. She said, "They would not call you if they're not going to find a house for you."

So we went over there to this real-estate agent, and she and I walked in with two kids. There were three guys in that office. I said, "I am Commander Gravely. You just called and told my wife that you'd find us a house." And the first guy disappeared. The first guy just went right through the place. "We came to talk about housing." Then the second guy left and left some poor guy in there who had to admit that he was very sorry, but they weren't in the process of renting houses to Negroes, as he said. Of course, Alma is much more of a fighter than I, because I was ready to walk out. She gave him a piece of her mind, and, of course, we did leave. But that was the situation we faced when we came here to Washington, D.C. It was trying to find a place.

Now, when I was here before, I lived in the BOQ, so it was no problem. But now I had two kids, so I had to find a house. We drove down from Newport, and I had the whole family here while we shopped around, trying to find quarters. There was no place in Virginia that I could find a real-estate agent that would deal with me. There was nothing that we could do in southern Maryland, and there was nothing we could do in Washington, D.C., except we could find a huge row house and rent a floor. Since I wanted an entire house, I could get that same row house, but they had stoves on every floor, because they had already divided it up into three or four apartments. Well, I didn't want that.

So I must tell you that we were in this town for about two or three weeks, the two of us. We couldn't find a cotton-picking thing. Finally I told Alma the only thing I could think to do was that she would go back to Virginia, down to her folks, take the kids, and that I would then find a place. Well, at that point in time, there were fair-housing groups, and most of these fair-housing groups were mixed-racial people, blacks and whites, who were working towards improving these conditions. I got in touch with one, and I'm sure it was not a Virginia group, but somehow we got in touch with a group that was from Maryland. Because I remember several times going to a woman's house who was on this group, and seems to me she lived about Rockville or someplace. They were trying to find us this place to rent.

Well, they found one. Of course, Alma and them were down in Virginia, and we found a place over in Arlington that was owned by a guy who had said he wanted to move back into Washington. He felt that it was unfortunate that all the whites were moving out of Washington, and they were at that point in time. But he felt it was not his bag, and he didn't think they should do that. He and his wife were going to move back to Washington. However, he would not vacate his place until his mother died. She was an invalid who was living with him; I would imagine she had cancer or something like that.

In the meantime, my wife was down in Virginia, and it was fairly close approaching September or something when kids have got to go to school, and I was living at the BOQ in Fort Myer.[*] Well, one day I got a call, and the guy's mother died. I was very sorry about that, but at the same time, as soon as the funeral arrangements, etc., were over, then I could rent that house.

Well, I guess that must have affected me to some degree, because I began having headaches, and my blood pressure started acting up, and, of course, I went to the hospital out at Bethesda to check. I have a thing called central hypertension, and all the tests in the world don't tell why. It just says you got it. So I went on this bunch of pills and

---

[*] Fort Myer is in northern Virginia, near the Pentagon.

everything else, which I take even today. The pills have been changed several times, but I still take them.

But, anyway, as soon as I got out of the hospital, I went back into DCA. I called my wife and told her I thought I'd found a place, and I'd like for her to come up and look at it. She got in there one Sunday night, and she looked, and she said, "This bedspread looks like mine. These curtains look like mine."

I said, "I've got to tell you, they are, because I just moved in here." [Chuckle] But, anyway, we got a house there in Arlington which we thoroughly enjoyed for the time I was there.

Well, DCA was the first time I can remember having problems in the military. DCA is a joint agency. You have all services there, and you have civilians there as well. I was assigned to an engineering group. I relieved a naval officer whom could call the construction engineer for the National Military Command Center. He followed all the joint papers through the works until they finally made the decision they would build it. The Army funded it, and they were about ready to hire a construction agency to do it. My job as project manager then became one of being in on the selection process of the contractor, and then after we got the contractor, to go in there every day to see what the phase of the construction was, to report on it—general program manager for the building of the National Military Command Center.

Paul Stillwell: If this was an Army project, why were you, as a naval officer, the program manager?

Admiral Gravely: Okay, it's a joint agency. So project managers from Navy did Army work. It was just my luck. But you're absolutely right. Why shouldn't an Army officer have done it? Don't ask me that question, but that's the way this thing was structured.

My biggest disappointment in DCA was that weren't used to me. As you know, I ultimately headed DCA, and I don't criticize them today; I criticize them as of that point in time. I was one of the first black officers to go to DCA, maybe not the first but certainly the first naval officer to go there and maybe one of the first officers.

When I went in there, and they had a huge bay in which they had so many people. They had another naval officer, a commander type, myself a commander type. We had an Air Force colonel; we had an Air Force captain, and then we had about ten civilians—all operating in this huge bay with desks. Well, that's the way it was when I went in there and reported. Of course, I told you I went to the hospital for a short time. When I came back from the hospital, they had built all this place up into cubbyholes. Every place was a little cubbyhole. I had a cubbyhole; the colonel over here had a cubbyhole. Actually, I had two Air Force colonels. This colonel had a cubbyhole. These were not permanent bulkheads; these were temporary bulkheads which had been arranged. There were nice little offices and all this and that. And that was the problem. I just simply said to him, "Why have we done this?"

He said, "Well, okay, we did this for two reasons. One is that we felt that the air wasn't circulating properly in this room, so now the air can roll under here and roll up above here, and blah, blah, blah. And the second reason was the noise level, just too much noise." So fine, I worked through that. And I've got to tell you that nobody snubbed me, nobody did anything to me, but that little thing got to me a little bit. So I did my job, and I had a civilian who worked with me that paid me the deepest of respect and everything else, and we got the job done. Later, I went to DCA probably two or three years after I had been there that time when I had gone into that big bay. It was a big bay again, so, of course, I said, "Hey, I see you got a big bay again."

"Well, yeah, we discovered that the air flows better if it just runs on an even keel, and there wasn't so much noise after all." [Laughter]

The head of DCA at that time was a guy by the name of General Starbird. And it's quite interesting in that General Starbird and I had met previously, because General Starbird had JTF 8, which was the joint task force which conducted the nuclear testing.[*] It was always interesting to go into a meeting with General Starbird, and General Starbird would remind everybody there that I was one of his ship captains when he commanded JTF 8.

DCA was a really interesting experience. I worked for an Army general. The next senior in the chain was an Air Force brigadier general, with a Navy captain as his

---

[*] Major General Alfred Dodd Starbird, USA, Commander Joint Task Force Eight.

deputy. I'd just never been in that situation before with all these strange people, civilians and everything else. So I found it took a little time to get used to it, but ultimately I discovered that they were people, and we all got along fairly well.

Now, the job in supervising this construction of the NMCC got to be very interesting because it's in the heart of the Pentagon there, right on the second deck there, and we had to tear out a lot of things. I'm used to watching people tear things. I watched them tear down a whole ship, but I found nothing really fascinating about watching them tear down old walls and all this garbage and even less fascinating when they were putting it back up. But I had to make certain decisions, like, "Do we need a ladies' head?" And they asked me if they needed a ladies' head. Well, there were ladies on the Joint Staff, so ultimately we decided we might have to put a ladies' head in there.

"How thick should these walls be, because, after all, certain classified information is going to be held here? How thick do you need the walls?"

Looked through the security manual, industrial security manual, you talk to people, and everything else. You decide, no, you need an 8-inch-thick wall here; you need a 12-inch-thick wall here. Okay, everything went along fine; we finally got it coming along quite well, till one day I just couldn't take it anymore. I went to my good Army colonel, my boss, and I said, "Colonel, I've got to tell you, I have been doing this job to the best of my ability, but, frankly, I am not the guy you need for that job." I said, "We have a guy in the Navy called a civil engineer, and I really think he'd be much more suited if you could get one of those over there to supervise this job than me. And in addition to that, I am currently working with a guy out of the J-3 organization, who's my counterpart, and he is a civil engineer, so why not get a civil engineer for that job?"

He said, "Sam, I'm glad you talked to me about that. I have decided that, and I don't know whether you know this or not, but we've just had a billet cut here." The IG had been through there, and they decided to cut some billets.[*] They had just lost the Air Force colonel who was running the National Emergency Airborne Command Post program, which is out at Andrews Air Force Base.[†] He said, "My intention is that you

---

[*] IG—inspector general.
[†] Andrews Air Force Base is located approximately ten miles southeast of Washington, D.C., in Prince George's County, Maryland.

take that job." Well, airplanes, brick walls, being a surface warfare officer, not quite up my alley either, but it sounded a hell of a lot more interesting.

So I said, "Great, Colonel, I'd just love to do that." And I said, "Oh, by the way, who do you want me to give this other one to?"

He said, "No, I think you ought to do that too."

Paul Stillwell: Oh, no.

Admiral Gravely: So then I became the program manager for the National Emergency Airborne Command Post, and also I was doing the NMCC job, which we were fairly well close to finishing up at that point in time. We were getting into probably about a year of my tour, and I was doing this all year.

Well, I really liked the National Emergency Airborne Command Post, because I discovered in briefings and going out to Andrews that every Friday they used to take training trips. Now, the training trip was simply flying for a certain length of time—four hours or six hours—depending on which route they flew. They had one route during the Kennedy Administration in which they used to fly straight up towards Boston, up in that area. Of course with Johnson in, they had to go towards Texas. But sometimes they'd fly four hours short of that, and then they'd go six hours and go the whole route. Every Friday I could fly in that airplane for four hours or six hours, and I really enjoyed that.

I was on this airplane one day and an Air Force major or lieutenant colonel or something said, "Commander, do you get flight pay, or do you get hazardous duty pay for flying as part of this aircrew here?"

I said, "Believe it or not, I don't get either one."

He said, "Well, I've got to tell you, you rate it. Anybody who's flying as much time as you do rates flight pay or hazardous duty pay."

I said, "Well, nobody's ever mentioned it to me."

He said, "Well, if you go back sometime and check with your service, you'll find they have an instruction out on it, and you rate one of those kinds of pay."

So I went back, and I began to check. Sure enough, there was an instruction which told me how to put in for flight pay. So I complied, including taking the flight physical, for which no flight physician would qualify me. But it didn't really make any difference whether you were qualified for flight training or not. It was a question of doing it. I finally put together a letter to BuPers requesting flight pay. About ten days later I got a call from the destroyer desk: "Commander Gravely, how would you like to go to sea? We have a destroyer out of San Diego that we're looking for a skipper for, and we've picked you. Now, we realize that you have a three-year tour over in DCA, and it would be kind of hard to get you unless you want to go."

I said, "Just tell me where it is and when to go."

Paul Stillwell: That solved the flight pay problem.

Admiral Gravely: So that solved all the problems, right, right. Well, you know, I chuckle every time I think about it, because I knew damn well they weren't going to pay a surface warfare officer flight pay for the job I was doing for DCA.

Paul Stillwell: Interesting how things come about.

Admiral Gravely: Yes, right.

Paul Stillwell: You, I think, overlooked one thing on that NMCC. You had a static-electricity problem to solve.

Admiral Gravely: I just hadn't gotten to that.

Paul Stillwell: Okay.

Admiral Gravely: That's over. I got out of DCA in 17 months; that's what it really took me. I didn't tell the story about the static electricity, but what happened was that after we got it built, the Joint Staff began to move and operate in the building. They discovered that there was a static electricity problem there, and the solution obviously was to get the static out of the room. Well, at DCA they had a system wherein each project manager had to write up a few briefs on what he was doing every day, and, of course, you had to have a title for whatever you're doing. So I came up with the title of "Project De-Static De-Rug." And I used to write what I was doing on this thing every day. Well, you can't have generals knocked on their duffs by touching doorknobs very often before people really get frantic.

Well, in the course of trying to find out how to do this, how to get the static out of this rug, I thought in terms of everything, but I decided I'd call some rug manufacturers, and there's one or two here in this area. There are also various rug cleaners, and, of course, there are lots of companies that sell rugs. So I called as many people as I thought necessary to get this out, and nobody knew. Finally one day, in calling a rug-cleaning establishment, the guy said, "Oh, I know how to do it."

I said, "Oh?" So I arranged to meet him and talk to him, etc., and found out that he would do it. The price seemed reasonable enough, and all I had to do was make arrangements for him to get into the Pentagon. Well, as serious as this problem was, it just really upset me to no end, because I made arrangements, and I touched base with everybody that I thought I had to touch base with, including members of the Joint Staff, as well as the duty officers, etc., up there. Then I made arrangements to get this guy entered into the Pentagon, and I rode down there in his little, cotton-picking truck with him. He and I went up there with a bucket—just a bucket. We got up there, and nobody would let us into the NMCC. So I explained to them again.

They said, "Well, I've got to tell you. We have a joint exercise going on right now, and there's simply too many papers around here that this guy might get a chance to view, and, we can't leave classified information, got to be very careful and everything else."

Well, I just simply said, "Gentlemen, I must tell you, I have ridden from Southeast Washington with this guy, and I can tell you, he can't read. He simply can't read, so he is not a threat at all." Well, in any event, they finally decided they could clear out their operation in a couple of hours and for us to stand there and wait, and then we could get in and do what we needed to do. So the guy agreed, and I said, "Hey, how are you going to do this?"

He said, "I have secrets too." [Laughter] "They won't let me see their secrets."

"Okay, fine." So, anyway, we finally managed it, and basically what he did was he went to a water fountain, filled his little bucket, and he sprinkled that rug with water.

Paul Stillwell: Big scientific method.

Admiral Gravely: Big scientific secret. And I'm not sure how they did it, because I just left shortly after that, but I think they watered it down for a while until finally we took out the tile. The tile was in squares, about 12 inch by 12 inch, over tile. These were rug things, and they had to leave it that way so they could get under the deck, because that's where the wiring for all this high electronic gear was and everything else. And it was a case of humidity that caused this. If you walk over there now, it's tile, but they put the rug down because they were afraid of the noise problem. But now we don't worry about the noise problem because we don't want the static back. But, anyway, that was one of the problems I solved, called "Project De-Static De-Rug." I will never forget that one as long as I live. I think a lot of people got a bunch of laughs out of me reporting on "Project De-Static De-Rug."

Paul Stillwell: What considerations were involved in the aerial command post? Were these trips designed to simulate missions and communications you'd need?

Admiral Gravely: They basically simulated the missions and the communications you'd need, although they didn't simulate that. They really did that. We had a series of UHF stations along the route that we checked into and checked out of every time we went down there. And, of course, these shore stations could relay then any messages they received right on back to the good old Pentagon here or anyplace in the world. But it was an actual check of the communications procedures, as well as the communications equipment, and everything as you flew along the way. They checked it out once a week with the actual aircraft there. We checked it four hours one time and six hours the next time. So it was a real live test of the system.

Paul Stillwell: Why UHF? Was that to minimize interception?

Admiral Gravely: No, no, no, no. UHF at that point in time was the basic communications from an airplane. I guess you could have done HF, but we used UHF, which was much more reliable than anything we had at that point in time. Now we have satellites obviously, and so you can do it differently. But UHF has always been a prime mode of communications form for airplanes, UHF or VHF—well, we've done some HF, but usually UHF requires a lighter, smaller transceiver, I guess you could call it. The antenna system is smaller.

Paul Stillwell: How was the inside of the plane configured?

Admiral Gravely: Well, the inside of the plane was configured, and they are today, so that if the President, in the event of a nuclear attack, had to take off and command and run this country from up in the air, he had the facilities there to do it with certain key members of his staff whom you take along to make any decision to run this country. At that point in time, you know, we had not only the three Boeing 707s that were the airborne command posts, we had two Navy ships which were specifically configured so that we could do that. They were home-ported out of Norfolk, as I recall—certainly in that area—the Wright and the Northampton. They got cut out of the budget very shortly after that, but they were specifically configured to take the Joint Staff and any other high-level officials aboard during a nuclear emergency, and the aircraft was the same.

There was always the idea at one time of having a train. You know, if the Army's got something and the Navy's got something, the Air Force has got to have something. So the Army's got to have a train. We've also talked in terms of big moving vans, and we've talked in terms of various other ways of getting the prime officials of our government to a safe haven to run the government. For example, as I recall, they had a response time of probably ten minutes or so that you'd have the helicopter on the White House grounds, bring him out there, and launch the 707.

Paul Stillwell: Was there some maximum duration that it was figured that the plane would be up?

Admiral Gravely: I have really forgotten so far as that was concerned, but it had a refueling capability, so you could keep it up there for one hell of a long time, as long as you could get tankers to it. So it could be up there for a nice long time.

Paul Stillwell: So it had places for these people to sleep?

Admiral Gravely: Oh, yes. It was a regular command center. It didn't have any queen-sized or king-sized beds in it, but certainly it was capable.

Paul Stillwell: Did you have to have liaison with the White House on that?

Admiral Gravely: I didn't. I would imagine that somebody from the Joint Staff did, but I did not. That was not my responsibility. My responsibility was to make sure that the communication equipment worked, and that it was operable, set on the right frequencies, and those kinds of things.

Paul Stillwell: I imagine you got the very best available for that one.

Admiral Gravely: We had fairly good equipment, right. As you well know, we have the rock, which is designed the same way. We've got Mount Weather, which is designed for the same thing. I forget the name of the place that the President goes on Sundays.

Paul Stillwell: Camp David.

Admiral Gravely: Camp David probably has equipment to handle all of those things, although I've never been to Camp David. In fact, interestingly enough, my relief on Falgout had been the commanding officer of Camp David, who then came out to take over Falgout. But Mount Weather and also Fort Ritchie. I've been to Fort Ritchie on several occasions. In fact, at DCA, in my office Fort Ritchie was programmed for by an officer in my office. The national command post afloat—NCPA, we used to call it—

there was a program manager in my office, just like I became the program manager for the NEACP and the NMCC. We had all the command centers in my office.

Paul Stillwell: You talked about the growth you experienced at Newport. I think this would have taken it even one step beyond in the inter-service relationships.

Admiral Gravely: Well, this was something that I really needed, despite the fact that at the Naval War College—what did we have, 120 students or so? Maybe ten of them Air Force, ten of the Army, one or two Coast Guard, and one or two civilians. This really put me in perspective so far as the Defense Department was concerned, because I never really thought of the services being anything but all Navy. [Chuckle] You know, I'd see an Army soldier once in a while. I didn't think they did much. But certainly this put me into the real world. It is a joint operation, and it really made me see that, hey, the Army has a job to do as well as the Air Force and everything else. I really learned a lot over at DCA, and I had a lot of respect for them by the time I left there. Certainly General Bestic was one of my bosses there and just a tremendous individual.* Taught me a lot.

Paul Stillwell: Kind of got you into the planning function, too, more than you'd had much experience with.

Admiral Gravely: Much more into the planning function from the old JCS papers with the red stripe, green stripe, that crap, which I didn't know that much about. And that was one of my faults with the Naval War College. A guy would say, "Well, this isn't green yet." I thought maybe he was talking about classifications. Remember, we had white paper for plain messages—

Paul Stillwell: Green for confidential.

Admiral Gravely: Green for confidential.

---

* Major General John B. Bestic, USAF.

Paul Stillwell: Yellow for secret.

Admiral Gravely: Yes, yes. I thought that's what they were talking about. They were talking about the stages in approving the paper. Green stripe? [Laughter] I was used to purple. You know, all the XOs who wrote used purple. When you scribbled something in purple, that meant, "Do it again." But I wasn't used to the Joint Staff colors. But that, as you said, really enhanced my education in the area of working with the Joint Staff, etc., in watching some of those guys move in that area who were very, very competent and knew what they were doing all the time. I enjoyed that.

Made a lot of friends, too, despite what I considered a difficulty when I first moved in there—or not a difficulty but a little problem that I thought I experienced, particularly in view of the fact that less than three years later that that obstacle that had been put up had all been removed. But some of the guys who were there when I was there were also there when I came back as head of DCA, and I felt quite proud and happy to see them, and I think they were quite proud and pleased to see that I had progressed along and had gotten to the point where I was when I commanded the place.

Paul Stillwell: Interesting turn-about.

Admiral Gravely: It was, yes. Come in as low man on the totem pole and come back in charge. Yes, that was something.

Paul Stillwell: Well, we're near the end of the tape, Admiral. Why don't we take up the Taussig next time?

Admiral Gravely: Have you got enough there for me to tell one more story?

Paul Stillwell: Sure.

Admiral Gravely: Okay. When I got my orders to the Taussig, the house that I'd owned in San Diego suddenly became vacant. So I decided that I would see if I could put my family in there early. Now, I left DCA in December 1965, but I got my orders about September or something, so I was there about 17 months. The biggest thing, of course, was my kids. I didn't want to put them in a school here and then take them out and then go over there, although they never had any problem with changes of schools, it was much easier to go in at the first of the year. The house was vacant, too, so I had to do something about that.

So a friend of mine who had been in my war college class called and asked me when would I be leaving; he'd seen my orders and everything else. He was the commanding officer of the naval air station up at Twin Cities. He said, "You've got to come through Twin Cities and visit with me and my family en route to San Diego. So I made him a promise that I would come up to Twin Cities, bring my family up there, and then go on out to San Diego, provided he would help me somehow get a hop when I left San Diego so I could come back to Washington, D.C. So fine, he agreed on that.

We went to visit him and the most interesting experience I ever had in my life was I met Hubert Humphrey there, because Hubert Humphrey was from there. He was Vice President at the time.* On a Saturday while I was there, he had to go down to meet him as CO of the station and invited me to meet Hubert Humphrey, and then I got a chance to talk to him and also meet him. And that was really an enjoyable experience, really.

Paul Stillwell: What do you recall about Humphrey?

Admiral Gravely: I just thought he was as bundle of energy, really, just a tremendous guy, very well spoken, talked all the time [laughter], but I enjoyed him, and I enjoyed meeting him. In fact, my wife met him too.

But, anyway, we left there. We had just a great time visiting with these guys, and this, as I said, was a guy in my Naval War College class. They had a good set of quarters, so we lived with them right in the quarters and the whole bit. Then took my family and put them in the house there, and then that Saturday night a guy called me and said that the captain had told him that I had to get back to Washington, D.C. He

---

* Hubert H. Humphrey, Jr., served as Vice President of the United States from 1965 to 1969. In 1948, when he was mayor of Minneapolis, he led a fight for a strong party stand on civil rights progress while addressing the delegates to the Democratic National Convention.

happened to be flying a cross-country hop, and if I wanted to go with him, he'd be happy to take me the next morning. Fine, so I climbed aboard and came back here and went on back to DCA and did the job, then moved back into Fort Myer and stayed at Fort Myer until the end of December, and then I went on out to San Diego, wherein that January then I was all set to go to the Taussig.

Paul Stillwell: So he kept his end of the bargain.

Admiral Gravely: Yes, he did. He really did. In fact, obviously all these people had children and everything else and just recently we heard from his daughter, who had just gotten married, and she was having her first child. Oh, we hear from them all. You'd be surprised.

There was a guy, I think I mentioned his name earlier, by the name of Roger Gibbons, who was my roommate at Hampton Institute, and we really became fast friends. One of his grandsons called me last night from Huntsville, Alabama, wanting my advice on whether or not he should come in the Navy.

Paul Stillwell: That's a satisfying moment.

Admiral Gravely: It is. It is. I've got to tell you, I advised this kid not to come in, and I generally don't do that. But this young man is 24 years old, he told me. He is college trained but doesn't have a degree. He is currently general manager of a Pizza Hut, so he's not making a pile of money, but he's been given an offer by them to buy one of their franchises. He doesn't have a dime to do that. I know he doesn't. But the only thing he can think of, so far as coming in the Navy is concerned, is coming in as an officer. Well, I'm not sure there's a program that he can get in under, number one. Number two, he's got his mind so much on making money, and he can't make it as an enlisted man, so there's no sense in coming in and screwing up, wrecking a whole lifetime trying to think he's going to make a whole lot of money as a second class seaman or something.

So my only advice to him was that certainly before just listening to me, he ought to at least go into a recruiting station and see what there is. In fact, he was going towards a degree in architectural engineering. And I said at the time I didn't think the Navy really needed very many of those; they need naval architectural engineers. Probably one or two in the civil engineer program, but all those people have got degrees. So that's what he's thinking about.

Interview Number 4 with Vice Admiral Samuel L. Gravely, Jr., U.S. Navy (Retired)
Place: Admiral Gravely's office in Burke, Virginia
Date: Tuesday, 12 August 1986
Interviewer: Paul Stillwell

Paul Stillwell: Admiral, we are just ready at this point to embark on a point in your career when you got command of a full-fledged destroyer after the Falgout. I'm sure that was a time of great satisfaction for you.

Admiral Gravely: Yes, indeed. I think I told about how I think I got to the destroyer as a result of my asking for flight pay, and having received a call from BuPers asking me if I was ready to go to command of a destroyer, and I was simply delighted. I transported my family to the West Coast and then returned to Washington, D.C., where I remained for about a month, then flew on out to San Diego to board the Taussig.* When I arrived, Taussig had just recently completed a yard overhaul, and she was one week into refresher training. She had had the first week, which was basically the inspections and alongside trials and those kinds of things, and so my first five days aboard Taussig were with the CO that I relieved. And we did what we could, so far as looking at the ship and records, but, of course, refresher training is quite a busy time, and so maybe he didn't show me quite as much as I would like to have seen, or certainly couldn't have been with me as much, because he had a job of running the ship. But I certainly was satisfied with everything I saw when I got there.

    I relieved on a Saturday morning, because I'm sure we were out for training until that Friday afternoon. And I must tell you, I was simply just overjoyed at getting a destroyer for the first time. Now, I certainly had driven Falgout for 18 months. I had enjoyed that, but this seemed to be a sort of a new facet of my life, because here I was on

---

* USS Taussig (DD-746), an Allen M. Sumner-class destroyer, was commissioned 20 May 1944. She had a standard displacement of 2,200 tons, was 376 feet long, 41 feet in the beam, and had a maximum draft of 16 feet. Her design speed was 34 knots. She was armed with six 5-inch guns and ten 21-inch torpedo tubes. She remained in service until decommissioned on 1 December 1970. On 6 May 1974 she was sold to the Taiwan Navy, in which she became the Lo Yang.

a full-fledged greyhound. It had legs, and it had guns, and it had all the things you dream about when you take over a ship.

My first Saturday, after the change of command, I was really overjoyed, as I said. And I did what most naval officers would have done on Saturday morning. That is, I went home and began to think about things like the exercise schedule for the following week, moving the ship from the pier, and the channel we had to go through—all because I knew I had to get under way on Monday morning. But the more I thought about it, I decided that, "Hey, I'd better go back to the ship and spend some time reading the op orders and familiarizing myself with ASW, which I will be faced with the next week." So that Sunday afternoon, right after church, I went back to Taussig, and I spent the afternoon there studying and familiarizing myself not only with the ship itself, as I walked through it, but primarily with the capabilities and those kinds of things, and what we would be doing during the next week.

Paul Stillwell: Was she substantially different from the Theodore E. Chandler?

Admiral Gravely: It was a FRAM II, versus the Theodore E. Chandler, which had been a FRAM I. The biggest thing there, of course, was the hull length, because the short hulls were FRAM IIs, and the long hulls were generally FRAM I.[*] That had to do with the fuel capacity, because when they lengthened those destroyers to make the long hull, they also added some additional fuel tanks in there. You can imagine that to see the skipper there on a Sunday afternoon was quite a surprise. In fact the OOD and CDO didn't even know I was coming down there.[†] But they were in fairly good shape; there was no problem there. I accomplished what I set out to do that afternoon. I was fairly ready to go the next morning.

The next morning, of course, we got under way, left San Diego, and began the exercise schedule. I can't tell you exactly what the particular phase was, but during the period of the refresher training we went through all of the facets that you would go

---

[*] The 2,200-ton destroyers were those of the short-hull Allen M. Sumner (DD-692) and long-hull Gearing (DD-710) classes, both built during World War II. The ships of the former class were 376 feet long, versus 390 for the latter. The extra length provided added fuel capacity.
[†] OOD and CDO—officer of the deck and command duty officer.

through with the gunfire support exercises; we went through the ASW. We operated as a task group with a mix of ships each afternoon and night, and did some of anything that you might anticipate.

Paul Stillwell: That's a busy but useful introduction for a CO.

Admiral Gravely: It is the best time in the world so far as I'm concerned to go aboard a ship. If I'd had my druthers, and if I could have directed when I went aboard that ship, I probably would have gone aboard two weeks before that. In other words, I would have wanted to go through the week of in-port inspections, and then handled the ship for the first week of the underway trials. I got the second week.

Now, there was a little bit that went on before that time in that when I reported to San Diego I had several short courses in my orders that I should have attended. Frankly, if I had gone to those short courses—there was about a month of them—then I think really I would have gotten there at a bad time. But my commodore and I sat down, and we talked about it. My commodore at that time thought that the best thing for me would be to report right away, see if we could get the schools canceled, which is what I did. And I am very happy that we made that decision.

The Thursday night, as I recall, of the refresher training we were operating with the Constellation, and that really became a very, very hairy experience. It wasn't hairy from the standpoint that I didn't think I could hack it or anything like that, because I was very comfortable up on the bridge of the Taussig. It had a rather small bridge compared to the FRAM I that I'd been used to. But, anyway, it had a good, nice bridge on there, good visibility, and the whole bit. But that night while steaming along behind the Constellation at 25 knots, suddenly I was listening to the land-launch frequency, and I heard the words, "Pull up. Pull up." About that time the Constellation pulled off to the left, and we immediately knew a plane was in the water. Apparently a plane that they were launching had gotten what they call a cold cat shot.[*] Didn't get enough pressure to take it off. The plant went off, and then, of course, plunged into the water.

---

[*] This is a reference to an unsuccessful catapult launch of an airplane from the flight deck of the aircraft carrier Constellation (CVA-64).

The thing that I remember most about it was the fact that at 25 knots, and something was in the water, you were pulling up on it quite fast, and we did. The minute that we got close enough that I could really get a good visual sight, and it was dark that night, I saw the helmet of the guy. I began aiming for the helmet. And then we got a little bit, not confused, but a helicopter saw the thing at the same time that I did. And in trying to duck the helicopter, pick up the helmet, and so forth we hit the helmet. No damage to anything. But I was a little concerned, because I had this helicopter up there too. But we went over, we got the helmet, and obviously there was nothing in it. But then we were detached and told to search.

We searched completely until the next morning bright and early, when I went off on my next mission. We found nothing other than a lot of sharks out there. We picked up everything that we saw in the water that might have been even parts of a human or anything like that. But unfortunately we found exactly nothing. I finally went to bed, and I got a call, because we had something weird that looked like an arm or something like that. It turned out to be a stick. But that was sort of my introduction to the good old Taussig.

But, in any event, underway training, as I said earlier, went along quite smoothly, other than that event.

Paul Stillwell: Did you have the mock battle problem as part of that?

Admiral Gravely: The mock battle problem came at the end. That's sort of your graduation exercise. That was also an interesting event.

Well, despite the fact that we had gotten out of the yard period in what we called good shape, apparently there was a spoke in the sonar dome. Of course, that's just a noise spoke, which appears there at various times. So we had been directed to go to Long Beach Naval Shipyard to correct that condition as soon as refresher training was over. Well, we came back into port on that last Thursday night before underway training ended, picked up my commodore, also the various people from the refresher training school who came aboard to conduct the problem.

About halfway through the problem, one of the exercises was a simulated steering casualty. Steering of course, had to be transferred back aft, and then after you successfully did that, then you would transfer it back forward and go on to the next phase of the problem. The unfortunate part for us, though, was that steering actually had a casualty at that moment, and control remained back aft. We just could not get it transferred forward. That was no major problem for me. Despite the fact that you like to be close to your helmsman so that when you give him orders and those kinds of things, we ran the problem successfully without the steering being on the bridge. If there was a problem at all, it was to come back into San Diego, let off the fleet training group people, and then after letting them off, then get under way, go back out the channel, and go up to Long Beach.

Now, that was fairly simple, I thought, but before going into Long Beach for the yard overhaul, you had to go into Seal Beach, which is quite a tight place. I brought the ship into San Diego. I anchored off of the refresher training landing, and we were going through the critique of the exercise, which we had done fairly well. In fact, they were quite complimentary about the ship handling with steering control aft while coming into San Diego.

About that time I got a call to come to the bridge instantly. I went up to the bridge, and, of course, we had sea detail set except for the critical people who were in the briefing. And, lo and behold, there was a tug pushing on my stern. I began to try to figure that one out, and discovered that the Constellation was coming in, and they had decided to just push me out of the way, not knowing that I had a steering problem. And there they were busily pushing. They were just going to push my fantail around. Well, there was only one solution to that; that was to put the fleet training group people off the ship as fast as I could get them off, and then just to get under way, which we did. We hauled in the anchor and then got under way.

Successfully maneuvered the Seal Beach problem. Went in to Seal Beach, unloaded ammunition, got under way from Seal Beach. Believe it or not, this was without tug and pilot. Then we moored in Long Beach. But I was quite proud of that experience, having handled that ship, particularly in Seal Beach without a tug and pilot.

I knew a couple of buddies who were in the area. One guy was one of the squadron commanders. I went over to just brag a little bit, and while I was bragging to him, he said, "Well, Sam, I got to tell you. All I can say is that was a stupid maneuver well carried out." [Laughter]

Paul Stillwell: Had you talked to your own commodore on how to handle it?

Admiral Gravely. No. Frankly, I'd been in to Seal Beach several times, and I was aware of how tight it was in Seal Beach. I had not really talked to the commodore as much, because frankly when we arrived there I expected the tug and pilot to be on hand. But I guess when you're a young skipper, and you know your business, you're a little impatient when things aren't quite ready for you. I knew I could do it, so I just did it. And it worked just like I said, with no problem.

Paul Stillwell: Or maybe you didn't know it couldn't be done.

Admiral Gravely: [Chuckle] That could be part of the problem. I should have said this earlier, though. I had been in Seal Beach once before in the Theodore E. Chandler, and somehow we had bumped up against the pier. You learn from watching other people make mistakes, and I was not about to make that mistake again. And I was a pretty cocky ship handler. I wasn't that way aboard Falgout, because I was still learning. But I knew that I could do it, and frankly the Taussig handled so much better to me. We didn't have the high sail area that you had to worry about. I got instant engines going back, forward. I didn't have to worry about air, those kinds of things.

Paul Stillwell: And a lot more power.

Admiral Gravely: And a lot more power. And so I was just ready for it. And we did it, and did it well.

Paul Stillwell: Well, there's a tendency to be a little flashy for the benefit of your crew too, so they'll have confidence in you.

Admiral Gravely: You've got to be a little bit, and you've got to know what you're doing, and you've got to make sure that that crew is behind you. A crew, no matter how good a skipper is, if he's not a decent ship handler, then they're going to look down at you. And I say decent, because the better you are, the better they're going to love you. Here are these other guys just going in, making one-bell landings and all the rest of that, and unless you can make some one-bell landings, you're down the totem pole.* I knew that from my past destroyer experience.

Paul Stillwell: Well, that's really part of the destroyer tradition.

Admiral Gravely: Part of the destroyer tradition is to do it quickly, do it snappily, and go do something else. And I was not about to let that tradition die.

Paul Stillwell: Did you unload ammunition at the pier, or did they have lighters out, or how did that work?

Admiral Gravely: No, you go in right up alongside the pier in a destroyer-sized vessel, and you just load right over the side. That's exactly what we did. It was about a five-, maybe six-hour evolution. Usually get in there in the morning, and you're out of there by 2:00 or 3:00 o'clock, or something like that. So we did that. If there are any problems at all, you get a little bit of a scream from the smokers, who can't smoke while you're alongside the pier, and they got to walk way across the pier and those kinds of things. But if done properly, it's a rather safe, routine operation. Certainly it's got to be done safely, and I was aware of all the safety precautions, and I had a bunch of good people on board who also were aware, and we did it right.

---

* A bell sound on the engine order telegraph accompanies each order to the engines. Thus, a "bell" is synonymous with an engine order. The fewer the number of bells in a given landing, the better.

Paul Stillwell: Was this all the result of the steering casualty? I mean, would you have had to go back into the yard anyway?

Admiral Gravely: We had to go back in the yard for the sonar problem.

Paul Stillwell: Right, you mentioned that.

Admiral Gravely: That's why we went back into the shipyard from refresher training. It was a job that the shipyard apparently had not done satisfactorily, and so ComCruDesPac directed that we go back up there, so they could do the job right. And we went up there for that job. The steering was fixed while we were there.

Paul Stillwell: That could have been done in San Diego.

Admiral Gravely: The steering problem probably could have been done in San Diego, but certainly the sonar problem could not have been done. It had to be dry-docked for the sonar problem. San Diego had a dry dock, and I can remember when I was there with DesRon 5 that the Lofberg, which was his flagship, was in the dry dock there. I don't think that dry dock was operating when I had Taussig. Now, it has been in and out, depending on base closures and expenditures and those kinds of things. But I do know that I had to go to Long Beach, because that's the shipyard it had been in when the sonar dome was fixed the first time, and supposedly done correctly. So we took it back up there. The sonar dome job, I would say, took about 30 days. So I was in Long Beach for about 30 days while they did that. Of course, this is on sort of a different time from when you're operating a ship, but I had spent a year in the shipyard, so I knew my way around shipyards. And we had fairly good relations with the people, so no major problems.

When we completed the shipyard work, we then, of course, had to get under way, go back into Seal Beach again, come out, and come on back down to San Diego, where we remained until it was time for a deployment. Now, when I got aboard Taussig the schedule was basically one of the refresher training period, a period of upkeep in San Diego, and a little time frame before deploying when you try to give max liberty and those things, and then you deploy. I had, however, gotten out of the deployment cycle with the rest of the ships in my squadron or division.

There were four ships in the division. Three of them had deployed earlier with the commodore. Taussig had to deploy with another group, and frankly it was not a division. I deployed with two ships out of two other divisions. I remember the Boyd perfectly as one of the destroyers. It was in the 600 class. The other one was the Rowan.

Paul Stillwell: This was a stragglers' group.

Admiral Gravely: Sort of a stragglers' group of three guys who didn't quite make it with their divisions.

Paul Stillwell: Did you have a unit commander at all?

Admiral Gravely: We did not have a unit commander aboard. The senior skipper was sort of in charge, and we remained together through Pearl, through Midway, and then the Boyd broke off and went to Yokosuka. The Rowan and I went to Guam, and he left Guam that morning and continued on to Subic. I remained in Guam for ten days.

But getting back a little before that, there had been some public affairs bit concerning my taking over as commanding officer of the Taussig. About two days before we deployed, I got a message from Chinfo, which basically said that Ebony magazine wanted to send some people there to interview me during the transit to Honolulu.* I personally had decided that I did not want to be interviewed, and I didn't feel that I had been aboard long enough to undergo what to me seemed like a little pressure. Certainly when a guy is interviewed, he's got to be on his best behavior. He's got to have all the right words at the tip of his tongue, and I preferred not to go through one.

But in talking over the phone with a friend of mine who was back in Chinfo at the time, he basically said that the decision had been reached. I should plan on them riding with me, and what they really wanted to know was what time the people should be

---

* Chinfo—Chief of the Office of Information, the Navy's public relations and media relations arm.

aboard. So I told them that I was departing at 10:00 o'clock, and they'd have to be there by 10:00, because I was leaving at 10:00. Well, sure enough, they were there. It was a writer and a photographer. Very, very good people. They integrated into the wardroom quite well. No problem, because we had them living in officers' quarters.

One significant thing that I do remember is that at noon I came down off the bridge. Of course, we had gotten under way without incident. We left at about 10:00 o'clock, so we were about two hours away. Things were calm. We had the three ships out. One was in front, one was on the port quarter, and one on the starboard quarter, something of that nature. We were just calmly steaming, no big exercise or anything else. So on those days I didn't hesitate to leave the bridge with the OOD up there, because he was quite qualified. I would then come on down and eat my meal in the wardroom with my officers.

When I got there, of course, they were all standing and waiting, and I came in. I noticed that we had empty chairs there, and neither the photographer nor the writer was there. So I asked them where were the writer and photographer. Nobody seemed to know, but they expected them at any minute. So I sat, and we began to serve. Well, on most ships the skipper is always the first guy to get served. And the minute the stewards came out of the pantry, I looked, and there was the photographer taking a picture. I think that they were a little taken aback, because it didn't work quite that way on the Taussig.

I don't know exactly how they had eaten before, but I had decided that we would have a buck system, which meant that a different guy got served first at lunch and dinner. The picture that I guess they wanted was of me being served by the steward. But then we sort of missed on that, because the buck was down at the other end. I was very sorry that I screwed up their picture, but I didn't really think that was necessary as part of the cruise. But they came in, we had a leisurely luncheon, and things went along fairly well.

They took pictures of me at every evolution that I can think of. The interview went, as you might anticipate: some hard questions, some easy questions, and some I really couldn't answer. But one of the things that happened was that basically how I kept in such good shape. I've always been fairly large, and frankly always been overweight, but I didn't show the weight as much as I do today. Then we began to discuss the

Kennedy athletic program, JFKs. And I said, "Oh, I take my JFKs every morning. I go back to the helicopter hangar, and I do pushups and so on."

This guy said, "Well, I would like to see that and take a picture." So I agreed that fine, I didn't have any problem of him taking a picture of it. Lo and behold, the next morning at about 5:30 I got out of the bed, and I came to the bridge for a few minutes, and was out on the fantail. I was out there hopping and jumping and everything else, and I did it for about a half an hour, and no photographer. You can imagine how angry I was, because that wasn't normally my routine [laughter], but I was doing that for him.

The other thing that happened that didn't cause me any major problems, but I guess I was quoted as drinking 25 cups of coffee a day. I did drink a lot of coffee, because when you're on a bridge like that, just the change of the watch will be a new messenger who'd want to get the captain a cup of coffee. Well, I did drink a lot of coffee. But I made the statement something like 25 cups a day, which, of course, came out in the story. After that I could not stand on that bridge for five minutes without somebody putting a cup of coffee in my hand. [Laughter] I never turned down one, but I don't think I ever got up quite to 25.

During the transit we, of course, had some ISE time with individual ships' exercises. We certainly operated as a task group playing leapfrog, and tictacs, and those kinds of things, and the normal routine that you would when you got under way. I almost had a little bit of a mishap going into Pearl. Of course, you come into port based on seniority, and I was number two in this group. The first ship in the evolution came into Merry's Point and nested ahead of two of the larger DEs that we had at that time frame. I've forgotten the class number, but, anyway, there were two DEs with the high bows.

Paul Stillwell: Probably Dealey class.

Admiral Gravely: Probably were. They had the nice high bows. He went in and moored ahead of one of those. Frankly, there was only one more berth ahead of him, and then you would have been into Merry's Point. But he got in. It took him a little bit longer than I had anticipated, because as we came in we were 1,000 yards apart. So I was at his spot in very, very short order. I got there to make the turn, and it was a right-hand turn coming into alongside that pier there. You had a nice run of, say, a quarter of a mile, or something, so you could really do it at a nice leisurely pace.

In any event, I got ready to make my turn, and I noticed that he wasn't ready to receive me. So there was a little problem in which I had to back out of it, and back and fill, and stand out there for a while. While I was doing that, I guess I was so anxious about getting into port and making a nice long approach that I didn't pay as much attention as I might have to the wind out there. Generally you've got anywhere from 10 to 25 knots of wind setting you on the pier. So when I saw that he was ready to receive me, I began to make my turn, and I had second thoughts about starting, but then I said, "Okay, I'm all right." And I started my approach.

Well, of course, with the wind affecting me, as I came almost abreast of the bow of the DEs that I was to be right in front of, I looked and I said, "My God, I will never, never do this safely without hitting the bow of the front ship." So I kicked my engines ahead two-thirds. I was just about in a position of stop. I kicked them ahead two-thirds, took a look back, saw that the stern was clear, and then started backing. Then I said, "My God, all back two-thirds," and that's not going to hold it. "All back emergency." And I went back emergency. I caught it right at the right moment. She slid in, phew, just perfect. One of the best landings I've ever made, but one of the most nerve-wracking ones, because it not only frightened me, but it also frightened some of the DesFlot 5 people who were on the pier, because they thought we'd had it.

But, no, it went in very nicely alongside. The magazine people were able to get a nice picture of me and the department heads underneath mount 51. Unfortunately, my engineer thought he'd lost control in the engine room and had dived down into the hole there, and his uniform wasn't as clean as the rest of ours. But he did get back up in time when he saw that it really wasn't his fault. It was my fault. But it was a good landing, and everybody really cheered to some degree, because they like the snappiness of that ship handling, although I was about scared to death. But, anyway, going back into Pearl, of course, was not exactly new for me, because two and a half years earlier I had been home-ported out there. So I knew my way around Merry's Point and those kinds of things.

We stayed there for the normal two days, as I recall, then all got under way together. The Boyd broke off and left and went individually to Yokosuka, and the Rowan and I went on down to Guam. Strictly a two-ship sail. He was the OTC for the move, and we did whatever exercises he wanted to do.* We had a little op order, which he prepared. We did electronic op orders, we did some leapfrog, very, very minor tictacs, because we didn't want to use up too much fuel and those kinds of things. Went into Guam, and again it was a case of going in for refueling, but in my case I had a ten-day upkeep period scheduled there. The other ship went on to the Philippines, and then joined the Task Force 77 or whatever was scheduled for him.

Our upkeep period there was quite fruitful. This was the first time I'd been in Guam, and I not only enjoyed the liberty, but I enjoyed being there. It was hot as Hades, but that's Guam. So there was no problem there. Did the normal amount of tourism and the shopping and those kinds of things. In fact, I have some cups from Guam, which I bought when I was there. We then got under way. We went to the Philippines individual sail, ISE, and arrived into Subic.† And no major problems.

The next schedule was, of course, to go to Vietnam wherein I would join the rest of Task Force 77 and operate as the task force commander saw fit.

Paul Stillwell: Were you supposed to catch up with the rest of your division at any point?

Admiral Gravely: No. No, there was nothing in there that specifically said that I would catch up with the division. In fact, during the entire WestPac cruise, I saw the commodore, as I recall, once. That's when he went over to visit the spotters over there, and I was shooting off of III Corps, and he came out for a short visit.‡ But that's the only time I saw any of them. I didn't see a single ship.

---

* OTC—officer in tactical command.
† Subic Bay is a protected anchorage on the island of Luzon in the Philippines. It borders the Bataan province and is about 35 miles north of the entrance to Manila Bay. During the Vietnam War, Subic had a strong role as a support base for the U.S. Navy. Included were a naval air station, piers, ship repair facility, supply depot, and recreational outlets for ships' crews.
‡ Spotters, either in the ground or aloft in aircraft, observe the landing spots of projectiles fired by Navy ships, then radio corrections to the ship for subsequent shooting. South Vietnam was divided into four corps tactical zones, numbered sequentially from north to south.

Most of the operations in Vietnam, they were kind of mixed for the ships. A couple of guys were assigned to plane guard and escort work for the carriers. Then you had three or four who were on II Corps, III Corps, IV Corps, usually one gunfire ship at a time. Then you had some on north SAR, some on south SAR, so it was a mixed bag.* Now, the beauty of all of this so far as I was concerned was that on <u>Taussig</u> I ultimately got to do one of everything. I went into III Corps. I went into IV Corps. I went into II Corps. I went into north SAR. I played around a little bit on south SAR. Did some work with the carriers. You name it, and we did a little bit of all of it.

Paul Stillwell: That's where the versatility of the destroyer pays off.

Admiral Gravely: That's the versatility of the destroyer, and the fact that you've got to be ready to do and change your maneuvers to one of these things no matter what. And I think we were ready. I had a good ship, to be honest with you. Had no problem. I fired one of my officers. He was a communicator, and he left his registered pubs on the quarterdeck in Guam. Being a former custodian and communicator at the same time, I knew that was not exactly what he was to do. It took a little time to get a new communicator, but I really got a beautiful, beautiful guy who was just great.

The next eventful thing really happened when we left Subic en route to Vietnam. Of course, it's basically a 270 course over there, and, of course, we got under way that morning and started off. We set course, speed 15 knots, one-boiler ops. Suddenly we began to get really rough weather out there. And, of course, we began to check and recheck weather and those kinds of things, and there was a typhoon which was to the south of us, which was headed in that direction. Now, normally you would expect that you got advance warning on these things, and we did have some advance warnings, but some of the navigational fixes on it weren't as good, and it was a little bit closer to Subic than even I anticipated.

I'm not too sure now in retrospect if I would have gotten under way at that point in time that I did get under way, but I had made a decision. We were anxious to go to Vietnam, and so we did. But as we drove to the west, we began to realize that we were

---

* SAR—search and rescue.

taking a little bit more a beating than I thought that the ship should take. And so we were about ready to divert when I got a message which told me to go into the vicinity of Scarborough Shoals, where there were three sailors in the water. That's about all it said. But divert and go up there.

Well, I turned north and started in the direction of Scarborough Shoals, and we were going at top speed, but at that point in time I realized that I had a couple hundred men on here as well, and also our plot on the typhoon showed that it was much closer and off the port quarter than I wanted it to be. Despite the fact that we were a little ahead of it, ultimately we were going to be in the dangerous semicircle.*

So I had to make a decision, and I made it primarily because sailors are inherently curious. When they see heavy seas, they want to get to the highest spot in the ship that they can possibly get to to look down on these seas. Then they can magnify how high they are. We were in some fairly high seas, and one of my radiomen slipped on the bridge and broke his leg. When that happened I said, "Well, I've got to come around and see if I can't come in behind this thing. At least it'll put me in the less dangerous semicircle." So I made the change in courses, slowed down, etc. Then, as the storm went north, I turned around and went north too.

Now, it was going sort of northwest, and I was going northeast, so obviously the distance was opening. The next morning we arrived in the vicinity of Scarborough Shoals, and I had no damage to my ship at all. Unfortunately, as I read on the Fox file, a destroyer coming down from the north had run into this typhoon and tried to come through it. That ship had suffered the loss of one man, and all kinds of damage to antennas, and two or three other things, so it had been beaten up the destroyer quite a bit.

Well, I got up to the Scarborough Shoals and started to look. We really didn't have much of a fix for where the guy was lost, but it was in the vicinity of Scarborough Shoals, and that's about all we knew. So you just go to a point, and then you sort of make an expanding-square search, or some other kind of search. Any kind of search you

---

* A typhoon or hurricane is a collection of rapidly circling winds. In addition to the rotation, the storm moves horizontally across the ocean. The half of the storm in which the direction of the winds coincides with the direction of horizontal movement is known as the dangerous semicircle because the two conditions reinforce each other. The other half of the storm is known as the safe semicircle, though obviously that is a relative term.

want. Of course, I wanted to cruise completely around the thing, and then pick a spot, and start searching as much as we could, which is what we did.

We searched the first day and nothing happened. Didn't see anything. We searched a second day, and about that time an oiler came up, and, of course, he took me under tactical command. It was a captain on there. He sent me searching a couple of ways. We searched and searched. The thing I remember most about this is that it was something like about the 26 of May of 1966 that it happened. Because on the 29 of May we found a Mae West. And written on that Mae West in grease pencil were May 26, May 27, May 28, and the guy was writing May 29 when something either pulled him out of that Mae West, or he gave up.* No one knows what really happened. But that certainly confirmed that there were people up there.

Now, I, of course, reported that, and then, after going alongside the oiler for fuel, because I needed fuel then, he released me to continue on my duties assigned. I went on to Vietnam.

Paul Stillwell: Had these guys gotten lost from a merchant ship or what?

Admiral Gravely: No. It was a different story from that. The one that I've always heard, and I've never seen anything in print about it, but apparently three sailors in Yokosuka were coming to the Philippines, and they bummed a ride on an A-6 or some other Navy airplane.† About in the vicinity of Scarborough Shoals the pilot lost control of his airplane, and he decided that the only thing that they could do was to jump. Apparently the copilot told them to jump. They jumped, and somehow the guy righted his plane and then continued on the journey. Of course, subsequent to his arrival, he reported men in the water, and I went up there on that.

Well, obviously there were men in the water because about ten days after I was there, an amphib or something came through there, and they found a body. I had the Mae West, so that clarified that there were people there. But it was quite a traumatic thing for

---

* "Mae West" was the nickname for an inflatable life jacket that fit over a man's head and chest. When not in use it was rolled up into a pouch that he carried on his belt. The life jacket was named for a buxom movie actress of the World War II period.
† The Grumman-built A-6 Intruder was the Navy's principal carrier-based bomber from the early 1960s to the early 1990s.

me to look at that Mae West, and also wonder about if I could have gotten there earlier, could I have found him. Or would I have been across that same spot a day earlier or something like that, but it's one of those things that you speculate about, you dream about, because I can always see that Mae West that somebody held up with those dates on it.

Paul Stillwell: But you can never know.

Admiral Gravely: There's no way of ever knowing anything about it.

Paul Stillwell: How much discretion did you have as far as avoiding the storm? Was Com7thFlt, for example, giving you any direction?

Admiral Gravely: No, nobody was giving us any directions or anything. In fact, the message that got us going in that direction came from ComNavBase Subic.* I don't think that other than the report that we made, and probably the oiler might have made more reports than we did, but that's about the only information. I told them I'd arrived here and those kinds of things, but there was no direction from anybody to look here or look there. It was my doing. I had the decision as to where to look and the whole bit. And we looked at a lot of charts in trying to figure out where, but, you know, you drop a guy from the sky into the water, and he can drop 1,000 places, plus the fact that the current and tide and those things moved him all about.

Paul Stillwell: Who was your normal operational commander? Was that CTG 70.8?

Admiral Gravely: Well, it would have been CTG 70.8 when you got in his area, but I still was basically under ComNavBase Subic.† I hadn't gotten out of his way yet, so basically ComNavBase Subic probably would have been the guy who directed me. Scarborough Shoals was just a little northwest of the Philippines as I recall.

---

* ComNavBase—Commander Naval Base.
† Task Group 70.8, a subdivision of the Seventh Fleet, was made up of the cruisers and destroyers that operated off the coast of Vietnam.

Paul Stillwell: So you hadn't gotten to the chop line, whatever that was.

Admiral Gravely: I really hadn't; I was in Seventh Fleet obviously. CTG 70.8 was worried about the bombing and those kinds of things over there in Vietnam. He was worried about north SAR, south SAR. I'm not sure that he was able to worry that much about one little destroyer who was coming over to join him. Then, of course, we began to get messages as to where to go as soon as that oiler released me.

Our first chore, as I recall, was to plane guard, and I'm pretty sure it was the Connie.* I joined with another destroyer; in fact, it was the guy who deployed with me, the Rowan. We were basically plane guard for the carrier. Then suddenly the other destroyer was detached, and he went on over to gunfire support. And I stayed there for a few days, and I was given the mission of gunfire support.

Paul Stillwell: Did you do any shooting up on Kahoolawe on your way out of Hawaii?

Admiral Gravely: We didn't do any at Kahoolawe. We had fired at San Clemente. So we had done some, and I had just a top-notch gunnery person aboard, who was really good. Had a fairly good navigational team and a good shooting team. We did it all, so far as I'm concerned, fairly well.

We had a couple of mishaps, which were quite unfortunate. In one of the gunfire missions we were off of Vietnam. We weren't at GQ, as I recall; we might have been at Condition II.† During a break in the shooting, one of the mess cooks, who was a loader, I guess, for the 51 forward, apparently went to sleep in the gun mount.‡ While he was asleep in the gun mount, the gun captain gave permission for the gun crew to come out of the mount and take a smoke. Now, they had coordinated this with the bridge, so there was no problem.

---

* Connie—the aircraft carrier Constellation (CVA-64).
† In Condition I, general quarters, the entire ship's crew is at battle stations; in Condition II, wartime steaming, only a portion of the crew is at battle stations.
‡ The ship's 5-inch gun mounts were numbered sequentially from bow to stern, 51, 52, and 53.

Unfortunately, that gun captain made the decision at some point in time to exercise the gun. In fact, he was raising and lowering the barrels, twisting it around. He was the only guy in there—so he thought. But the mess cook was in the gun mount, and as the guns were being raised and lowered, they crushed his head. I had a helicopter take him off. He was not killed instantly, but he ultimately died. I think it was from, basically, pneumonia or something, because it came right down over his neck. It was a real bad situation.

There was an investigation conducted. I'm not sure what all of the papers read, but I don't think I got any disciplinary action out of it. Certainly I know I held mast on the gun captain, but that was about the extent of it. It was a case of being on Condition II at least 24 hours, with some people, who when they got off instead of going to bed, sat up and played cards. Then they tried to man their stations at the same time when they were just so tired. It was quite a traumatic one for me, because I'd never really been involved in an accident with a guy on board ship.

Paul Stillwell: You feel a sense of responsibility even if you were not involved personally.

Admiral Gravely: You are responsible somehow. It's your responsibility. Now, what I wanted to do obviously was to leave port with so many men on board and take every one of them back. I really felt kind of bad that I wasn't able to take that guy back with me to port when it was over.

Well, we went through all of the normal events, going from one area to the next. We spent time in III Corps; we spent time in IV Corps.

Paul Stillwell: Did you shoot primarily spotted missions?

Admiral Gravely: We shot H&I an awful lot of time.* In fact, you could shoot H&I all night. We shot a lot of missions that were spotted. There were a couple that we were given the area in which to just put some rounds.

Paul Stillwell: What sorts of targets were you shooting at?

Admiral Gravely: We shot at some of everything, and there were troop concentrations. We fired at moving vehicles. One of my most interesting experiences came when we were given a mission of going up the Saigon River. We were told to remain at a certain position in the Saigon River and to shoot there. Gun 10, I think, was the publication at that point in time, and Gun 10 basically said under no circumstances shall you anchor in this river. And I had to make a decision, because there was no way I could stay up there without anchoring.

So I sent off a message to the group commander, 70.8, and I said, "I have been told that I am to remain here for ten days, except for those every third day or so come out and refuel and rearm. There's no way to successfully stay in this river for ten days without dropping the hook. Unless otherwise directed, I plan to anchor, taking all practical precautions in doing the job." I didn't get anything. I got no message at all. So I stayed there.

On one particular mission we were in the river, and we were told that there were some Communist boats coming down the river. Now, where we anchored was a point in this river where there were two forks. There was a little island in the middle, and there were these forks. The guy was on the other side, and you couldn't really see anything. But the idea was to shoot across him, basically, to drive him down the river until he'd come into the mouth of these guns. There were three boats, and that's exactly what we did. We sort of fired ahead of him basically; actually it might have been behind him depending on which direction you're looking at him. And we drove him down to where he was in the mouth of these guns. When the first boat came around the river, the weapons officer said, "Captain, I'm locked on and ready to go."

---

* H&I—harassment and interdiction, gunfire that is not aimed at specific targets and spotted. Instead, it is fired into a general area occupied by the enemy as a means of upsetting him.

"No. We'll let all three of them come around, and then we'll pick them off one by one. The second boat came around. The third boat came around. We were just beginning to pick up that boat, locked on, ready to shoot, permission was asked to fire, and I said, "Just let him come around a little bit more." At that minute a voice came over the gunfire support circuit and said, "Cease fire. Cease fire. They're friendly." I have always been just really undone with that one, because I'd been shooting at those guys for half an hour, and not trying to hit them, of course. Trying to drive them down there, so I could really pick them off, and then they turned out to be friendly.

Paul Stillwell: Who did that message come from?

Admiral Gravely: It came from the spotter, who was in an airplane. We had an air spotter who gave us that message. I think at that point in time, after really looking at them, and looking at them through the glasses and everything else, I'm pretty sure we saw an American flag, but they were in sampans, and I don't know whether they had the American flag up before they got around the bend. But I was shooting at them in accordance with the spotter's directives.

Paul Stillwell: How good was the visibility?

Admiral Gravely: Visibility was very good, except for the fact that they were hidden by the island until they came around the curve. So when they came around the curve of that island, they were less than a mile away. But in the meantime, in order to just shoot at them, my lifelines were smoking. There was the cord that was wrapped around the lifeline, and it was all burned up, because I was shooting just about a mile away. But, anyway, we didn't shoot them, because of this sort of freak of nature. But we would have bumped them off otherwise. We were locked on. Earlier that day, we'd hit a truck at about eight miles, so those kids were getting good. We were shooting anywhere from an average of 400 to 450 rounds in a 24-hour period. We shot as high as, say, 600 rounds in a day. Now, during that cruise we fired almost 9,000 rounds.

Paul Stillwell: That's a lot of ammunition.

Admiral Gravely: That's a lot of ammunition. But we were doing a lot of shooting in '66. I can remember being in IV Corps and shooting around in that area, just plain old flat land that's just for miles and miles of flat. You don't see much, but a spotter's giving you targets, so you let go.

Paul Stillwell: The navigation's kind of tough too.

Admiral Gravely: Navigation was fairly tough in all those areas, but we, except for IV Corps where the land is flat and the water is fairly shallow out in that area, in most of the area you could get fairly close in to the beach, and you had plenty of water. So we were in fairly good shape, and we had some good navigational points down there that we could use.

Paul Stillwell: Did you get over into the Gulf of Thailand at all on the other side?

Admiral Gravely: I just barely got into the gulf as part of the mission in IV Corps. But just a little bit into the gulf. But IV Corps was certainly part of that, and I got around there to do shooting on both sides for IV Corps. III Corps was basically on the Saigon River side and a little bit up, and then went up to II Corps.

Paul Stillwell: Did you work with the Market Time forces at all?

Admiral Gravely: Market Time was just beginning to be put up at about that time.* And Market Time, no, I didn't work very much with them. The DERs were beginning to come out in '66 and come out in that area. I'm not sure what they used. They used LSTs, I

---

* In the summer of 1965 U.S. ships and craft began working with the South Vietnamese Navy to establish the Market Time patrol off the coast of South Vietnam. Its purpose was to monitor coastal traffic and thus to prevent North Vietnamese craft from infiltrating South Vietnam to deliver weapons and other supplies to Viet Cong forces.

guess, before that.* But I didn't see much of them. I saw more of them in '68 when I came out the next time, but not much in '66.

Paul Stillwell: How good were the spotters you worked with?

Admiral Gravely: Well, the spotters, so far as their procedures and those kinds of things, I thought were very, very good. I can't tell you what it was so far as what they were seeing. You know, they told me I hit something, I said, "I hit it, I guess."

Paul Stillwell: You had to trust them.

Admiral Gravely: Yes, you made you reports, you know. Every night you had to make up your report on what you'd done etc., and send a message out that went to the world. I forget the name of that message, but it was a gunnery message that came out when you did your shooting over there.

We, as I said, did a little bit of everything, and I can't tell you what went on in what order, because I worked for a carrier, I went to II Corps. In fact, an interesting thing that occurred in II Corps was that I went up to relieve the Turner Joy, a destroyer up in II Corps. About three years later the skipper of that ship relieved me on Jouett, which was quite interesting.† I'll get into that probably a little later on, because I didn't know him very well, and when he came aboard Jouett I knew I'd seen him someplace.

What had happened was that I had looked dead across the bridge at him, because we had a strange situation wherein it was quite unfortunate when I was making an approach on him. He had a contact up ahead, and he decided that, well, maybe he should change course about five degrees to the left. And he told me that he was going to make a course change of five degrees to the left. Unfortunately he came five degrees to the right, and I was off his bow. We moved out smartly and got in and did everything perfectly,

---

* LST—tank landing ship, an amphibious warfare ship capable of putting her bow directly onto a beach, opening bow doors, and lowering a bow ramp to permit vehicles to exit.
† Captain Edward S. Briggs, USN, commanded the guided missile frigate Jouett (DLG-29) from 2 June 1971 to 25 July 1972. He was a commander while serving as skipper of the Turner Joy (DD-951).

but, of course, I was shaking my fist at him. And, as it turned out, that was the guy I'd shaken my fist at. [Laughter] But certainly there was no animosity; nothing was harmed.

Paul Stillwell: How many destroyers would work with a carrier in a given situation?

Admiral Gravely: It depended on what they were doing. During that period I was in Vietnam, there were times when you'd put three destroyers up front for a screen: Three Charlie Two, or whatever that formation is. There have been times when they had three destroyers. You had one destroyer who was really on plane guard, about 1,000 yards astern, another one about 2,000 yards back, basically keeping up. The second guy was sort of an emergency. And you'd have a third guy out there who would be doing some individual ship exercise, keeping the carrier in sight so that if something happened to one of the other guys, you could charge off and do that.

Paul Stillwell: Was there any disadvantage in that you weren't working with people from your own division, whom you would have known better?

Admiral Gravely: I didn't know them anyway, because I'd never worked with anybody from that division. So, no, there was no disadvantage from that. I think that as I saw it, you put three destroyer skippers out there in three different ships, and whether they are division mates or not, they will work well together after five or six minutes. The destroyer sailors are kind of versatile. They know their ships, and that's basically what it is. Knowing your capability, and the guy knows his, so you'll match them up fairly well.

Paul Stillwell: Did you get any doctrine from the carrier on his particular idiosyncrasies or practices?

Admiral Gravely: Well, you get a message welcoming you aboard, and here's where I plan to have you, and here's what I plan for you to do and something of that nature. You don't really go aboard the carrier and have any eyeball-to-eyeball contact with anybody except on some special operation that you're going to do. Then maybe you will get together for a meeting before getting under way, but after you get out there you join up, and you're expected to know your job. There was nothing like that.

We obviously got our time in port. I was stationed in Hong Kong for about ten days for R&R and duty as Com7thFlt directed. It was quite an interesting experience. My only problem with Hong Kong for ten days was that the sailors ran out of money in about the third day anyway, so ten days was obviously too much. But we did that.

Paul Stillwell: Anything you remember from being ashore there? That was a really neat place. I enjoyed that.

Admiral Gravely: Yes, I enjoyed Hong Kong, and I knew the defense attaché there, and so he invited me to his home for cocktails and those kinds of things. Going to that—what did they used to call that exchange?—basically the exchange there, and buying one of everything.

Paul Stillwell: They had the China Fleet Club.

Admiral Gravely: China Fleet Club, yes. I spent my share of money at the China Fleet Club, because I always wanted to have things for my family when I got back. Christmas was celebrated obviously on December the 25, but I think the big day was the day I got back from deployment.

There is one thing that I overlooked in telling the story of the Taussig. While I was here in '65 my baby sister died. And my baby sister had seven children, five boys and then two younger daughters. That was kind of traumatic, really. Young girl about 32 or so. One baby just under a year old, second baby not two months old. And she died and left these children. And, of course, the whole family was trying to decide for the husband what's best for him. And, let's face it, nobody can decide what's best for him but the husband.

Of course, in this idea I made the big pitch that he was a very young man. He was 33, 34. I felt that personally he needed some time to just get himself squared away, and that I would take his family with me when I went to the West Coast and try to see if I couldn't hold them a year or so until he got in shape. I made him a solemn promise that I really didn't want to steal his family from him, but I would like to see if I couldn't help him and do anything I could. He declined that offer, and said that, no, he felt that it was his responsibility to raise his children, and he wanted to start fulfilling it as best he knew how without a wife at that point in time. So he did.

But I kind of think I fell in love with the girls to some degree, because we had two boys then. Primarily because when we adopted the first child I insisted on a boy, and then somehow every boy needs a brother, and we so got two, and then finally we decided on a girl. Well, shortly after arriving at San Diego in January we started thinking in terms of a girl. And my home was approved for adoption about, say, three weeks before we were to deploy. Well, the procedure normally is if it's an infant, there's no problem about you going to the adoption agency, picking up this little baby and bringing it home. But it's different if the child is 17, 18 months old, and my daughter was, I think, 22 months old when she was placed.

Well, first of all, you've got to get acquainted. The child has a mind of her own, and she naturally doesn't take to people, particularly just picking her up and stealing her off. So the procedure was that she should come to the house, visit, play with the boys, play with her new dad and mom. And then you'd come there a second time, stay longer. And then the third time stay even longer, and finally she spent the night there. Well, we didn't have that kind of time. Everybody had made up their mind. In fact, we'd made up our mind, and they'd made up their mind that this was the girl for us. So instead she arrived to stay on the day before I deployed.

So here I was, going on a seven-month deployment, and my wife stepped on board with our new daughter. And I'd seen her really, you know, to spend time with her the night before and that morning, and then we'd take off on the deployment. But anyway, I wanted to get that in, because I had forgotten it.

Paul Stillwell: That was quite a chore for your wife at that point to have it all to herself.

Admiral Gravely: Yes, right.

Paul Stillwell: During the course of that deployment, then the article was published in Ebony. What kind of reaction did you get to that?

Admiral Gravely: Well, it was certainly shown on board the ship, and certainly those guys who had their pictures with the captain were very happy to see the article. There was certainly nothing unfavorable about it. I was, of course, deployed when it came out. So except for people sending me copies of it and those kinds of things, I didn't feel anything or see much of it. I did ultimately get a copy of the magazine.*

Paul Stillwell: Was there any discomfort in being singled out? You were not allowed to do you job with the same anonymity that your fellow destroyer skippers had.

Admiral Gravely: Well, I didn't feel any dissatisfaction with that. I to some degree hated the publicity. It seemed that from about the time that command of the Falgout came about, every time I turned around somebody was sending me a copy of a picture of me being in the paper or something. I kind of resented that to some degree. But most people who sent me copies of it sort of said, "Well, I see you made the papers again," and it was that kind of a thing. Of course, I guess I felt a certain amount of pride that they were good newspaper articles as a general rule.

It did bring on a little bit of uneasiness, because no matter how you tell the story of racial tension, and segregation, and discrimination, there's a bunch of people who will disagree with you and say that "Hey, you really didn't tell it right." Or the other group who said, "You didn't quite do it this way." You know, you can't please everybody in those things, and I ultimately learned, hell, that's not my job to please everybody. But sometimes I didn't even please myself in some of the interviews. But whereas I guess I enjoyed the publicity, I really tried to avoid it, and it was very difficult to avoid. I would not have had those guys to ride with me from Pearl, for example. But that decision was not mine; it was made for me.

---

* See "Proud New Victory for Navy Destroyer," Ebony, July 1966, pages 25-28 and following.

Paul Stillwell: Well, in a sense you were acquiring an obligation that reached beyond your ship. You were influencing all sorts of people indirectly.

Admiral Gravely: When you think about it from the times that we were living in, and we were trying to fight battles to win to some degree freedom for a group of people. Trying to make people more interested in education and those kinds of things. And they could look at me—the words finally dawned on me—as a role model, I guess. I felt pretty proud that I could be that kind of a role model, that people wanted to emulate me. But I never quite was able to really get it down in me that I was a role model. The other big thing is that I think that to some degree that I probably did things a little bit better than I might have, because I knew that I was being watched—or felt that I was being watched. I think that that was a feeling more than was actually occurred, because nobody cared what Sam Gravely was doing. But I think it had me a little bit more on my toes.

Paul Stillwell: Well, then it was a beneficial side effect.

Admiral Gravely: It was a beneficial side effect from both sides, yes.

Paul Stillwell: Taussig is a famous Navy name. Did you have any contact with the Taussig family?

Admiral Gravely: As I recall, we wrote a letter or something to some member of the family talking about Taussig and those kinds of things, but I don't remember any specific contact. The Theodore E. Chandler, for example, was named after a—well, there was a skipper, Captain Chandler, who would be the grandson or something like that, who had commanded the Chandler, and he came back and I saw his grandson someplace.[*] Captain

---

[*] Rear Admiral Theodore E. Chandler, USN, Commander Cruiser Division Four, was on board his flagship, the heavy cruiser Louisville (CA-28) when a Japanese kamikaze plane hit her on 6 January 1945 while operating near the Philippines. He was badly burned by the resulting fire and died the next day. The destroyers Theodore E. Chandler (DD-717) and Chandler (DDG-996) were named in his honor.

Joe Taussig, the lawyer, I met him as the result of that.* I used to get a letter from him, "Make sure you're taking care of my uncle's ship okay." But I've seen him since then, and we are fairly good friends.

Paul Stillwell: He's a good guy.

Admiral Gravely: He is. Just a tremendous guy, and a tremendous asset to the Navy. I don't know whether he's still in DoD now or not. He was in DoD.

Paul Stillwell: He's a special assistant to SecNav on ship survivability. He's very concerned about fires on board ships.

Admiral Gravely: Yes. He's a tremendous guy, and I've bumped heads with him several times afterward.†

I guess so far as Taussig and not so much descendants, but as you remember, there were two Taussigs.

Paul Stillwell: One was a DE.

Admiral Gravely: One was a DE, and there were any number of times that we got confused as to whether we were the DE or whether we were the DD.‡ In fact, one of the sort of disconcerting things to me was the fact that here I was driving this destroyer, and obviously I thought I was doing it very well, and one of the commanders of TG 70.8 came into Subic, and the senior squadron commander in that area decided that we would all be on the pier in Subic when he arrived. We were all standing there, having been

---
* Midshipman Joseph K. Taussig, Jr., USN, graduated from the Naval Academy in the class of 1941 and earned a Navy Cross for his heroism while serving on board the battleship Nevada (BB-36) during the attack on Pearl Harbor later that year. He subsequently lost a leg as a result of wounds suffered at Pearl Harbor and was retired in 1954 as a captain because of physical disability. During the 1980s he served as a civilian official in the Department of the Navy.
† Captain Taussig twice earned the Civilian Distinguished Public Service award, the Navy's highest award for public service. He passed away 14 December 1999. His remains were laid to rest 17 December 1999, at the Naval Academy Cemetery in Annapolis.
‡ The destroyer escort Joseph K. Taussig (DE-1030) was commissioned in 1957. She was named for Rear Admiral Joseph K. Taussig, the father of the Joseph Taussig mentioned above.

rained on at least twice, and ducked the rain, and he was late and everything else. When the ship moored and the gangway was put up, we began to crawl aboard the gangway, and here came this group commander in his tennis shorts getting ready to go play tennis. But he saw this mass of gold braid coming on there, so he immediately went back to his cabin, and was sitting in there. And he said, "Oh, you're the skipper of that Taussig, aren't you?"

I said, "Yes, sir."

He said, "Well, how does that DE run?" I almost wanted to punch him. [Laughter]

Paul Stillwell: This was your boss?

Admiral Gravely: Yes. [Laughter] Thinking I've got a DE, right.

Paul Stillwell: Did you make a conscious effort to keep in touch with the families while you were gone—family grams and that sort of thing?

Admiral Gravely: I have been somewhat of a little bit of a writer all of my days. And so I have always been a firm believer in family grams, trying to print the names of as many individuals as you can in one letter, making sure that the next letter had a different set of names, you know, to some degree. So we did maintain close rapport with the Taussig family. My wife, of course, maintained really close rapport with them ashore, and would constantly cut me in on what was happening at the various wives' clubs and those kinds of things. So we did it fairly well, I think, and certainly had contact with both sides of the Navy family.

Paul Stillwell: By the mid-'60s the Navy was doing a lot better than it had say 10, 15, 20 years earlier.

Admiral Gravely: Well, the family gram, I think, is a sort of a recent innovation. When you talk in terms of '60s, yes, but different compared with what went on during World

War II when ships left, and guys never heard from anybody for years and those kinds of things.

Paul Stillwell: So was the matter of looking out for families during a deployment.

Admiral Gravely: Well, we became a much more humane service, and you had to do a little bit of everything to maintain guys in the service. And certainly the family was a vital tie to this. There are still a lot of sailors who probably make up their minds to stay in the Navy primarily because Dad says, "Hey, you ought to do this," or "You ought to do that." Or Mom says, "Hey, that seems to be good for you." So the Navy has really taken a different view on families than they took in years gone by. In fact, all of the services today have great family programs, every one of them. Army as well as Navy. Families have always played a vital part, obviously, in any man's career. The services, unfortunately, didn't really take advantage of that fact until, just like you said, about the '60s, and they have certainly utilized it the maximum benefit since that time.

Paul Stillwell: How was the discipline situation on board your ship? Subic and some of those places can get people into trouble.

Admiral Gravely: Well, I'm sure that we had our share, but you've got to remember that, really, since the '60s we haven't had the old Navy type, who was always in trouble ashore. I had one in Falgout always in trouble ashore, but a great sailor aboard. You got a guy who if he was good aboard, he was good ashore. Certainly he'd get a little disorderly once in a while, or anything might happen. And I had my share of those. But for the most part, I had a very good crew, which was fairly high-spirited, with also high morale and those kinds of things. I certainly had to conduct mast, and I'm sure that I had a summary court-martial or two but not anything that I'm aware of that was not happening on other ships. I didn't have a discipline problem. I had a few guys, but not that much.

Paul Stillwell: With the exception of this communicator you mentioned, did you have a good group of officers too?

Admiral Gravely: I had a very good group of officers. When I got aboard, we had an engineer who was a lieutenant. He was qualified fleet OOD.* His experience had been in minesweepers prior to going to his first destroyer. Very good, very trustworthy. A guy that I hadn't seen in several years, but most of the people that I've sailed with to some degree I somehow either bump across them again, or I see them someplace, or they hear of me and I get word from them.

My weapons officer was a destroyer school graduate. He was Naval Academy and had been in destroyers before, so he was very good. My ops officer at that point in time was a good officer, but his background was not in destroyers, and he was on his first destroyer, so he had a little bit of a problem trying to qualify, really. But he became very good. I could trust him; there was no problem there. I had about five fleet OODs, and I was always convinced that I couldn't have too many. I tried to train these people as quickly as I could, and qualify them as quickly as I could. During that first cruise on Taussig I didn't have any problems.

I got a bunch of new officers about the time you'd normally get them, August, September. One of the most interesting and sharpest people that I've ever had in my whole career that I can think of, I had Admiral Kimmel's grandson, Tom Kimmel, and boy, he was just a sweetheart.† He was just really good. I've always been blessed with a bulk of good officers. You get one or two of the little guys that you're constantly on, you got to watch out for and those kinds of things, but I was never really plagued with anything other than just a very, very few of those types.

Paul Stillwell: I suppose if you fire one, that catches everybody else's attention.

---

* A fleet officer of the deck is one who is qualified for formation steaming with other ships in company; the other type of OOD is one who is qualified only for independent steaming operations.

† Ensign Thomas K. Kimmel, Jr., USN, graduated from the Naval Academy in the class of 1966. His grandfather, Admiral Husband E. Kimmel, USN, was Commander in Chief of the U.S. Pacific Fleet at the time the Japanese attacked Pearl Harbor in December 1941. After five years of commissioned service duty in the Navy, Kimmel resigned and subsequently had a civilian career in the FBI.

Admiral Gravely: Well, I almost got convinced that what you ought to do when you go aboard a ship is to fire an officer the first day or so aboard; then you've got everybody's attention. I didn't operate under that theory, however, but certainly when you do fire one, it catches everybody's attention. I'm sure they discuss it and everything else, and see that the captain means business, or please don't do that, you know. Don't do that and those kinds of things.

Paul Stillwell: What job did Kimmel serve in?

Admiral Gravely: Kimmel came into the gunnery department, and he was assistant ASW officer or something like that. I'm not sure. He remained on board there, as I recall, throughout the rest of my tour. But before I left there, and I stayed 30 months on Taussig, he was a full fleet qualified OOD. In fact, one night I saw him make one of the most beautiful approaches on a tanker that I've ever seen. Boy, he was good. He was a great guy.

We did all of the ops that you might want to think of. As I said, when we were up the Saigon River we came out every three days, and we either caught an oiler, which we had to have oil from, or we went to an ammo ship to reload ammo. And, of course, the supply ship would come around periodically and then we'd go alongside that. So we got plenty of experience of alongside movement and ship handling.

Paul Stillwell: How did you keep the ASW skills up? That wasn't among your various chores.

Admiral Gravely: Well, you couldn't really do it there. Once in a while there'd be a submarine out there that they would send you up to play with. And you'd play with it there for maybe a couple of days or something like that. But you didn't get very much submarine warfare out there. In fact, I think the waters are kind of shallow certainly in close, that you wouldn't do much, and let's face it, it wasn't that kind of a war, so you didn't have that much opportunity.

Paul Stillwell: You mentioned these SAR stations. What did that entail?

Admiral Gravely: Well, it was basically a search and rescue station wherein you'd normally have one of the DDGs.* One of the DDGs was normally the ship that had a squadron or division commander aboard, and you were along with him. The job, of course, was that you were available to pick up a downed aviator or something when one of those guys ditched at sea.

The interesting part about that, of course, to me was that you had a little spot that you maneuvered within about a 25-mile radius of. You ran it by. You sort of played games or tictacs and things during the day as much as you wanted to. Certainly some ISE. You stayed in close to shore, and then at dusk when the planes weren't flying very much, then you came on back outside, and you stayed out in the open ocean and tooled around out there together.

But the most interesting part about it to me was that the night the oiler came up you both took off, with you 1,000 yards, maybe 500 yards behind that DDG, running at 25 knots to catch that oiler. Finally, you'd pick up the oiler on radar, and at about five miles you'd see him turn around on your scope, and you were both barreling down on that guy at 25 knots. You were going in this side, the other guy was going in that side. You got in, you got your gas on board, and got out because of the guy coming in the from the south was going to catch him now. So that was quite interesting. I loved high-speed fueling, and, boy, we did out share of that.

Paul Stillwell: Did you guard the voice radio nets that the aircraft would be on?

Admiral Gravely: You guarded everything you possibly could on the bridge voice. And certainly you guarded the land-launch and any other frequencies that you thought the airplanes might be on, or that the op order told you to guard. Normal communication guard, you had pritac with your little destroyer, and you played on that. And, of course, the visual communication we're beginning to get away from, but you did have your signal bridge man always alert. You did quite a bit of practice in flag hoist during

---

* DDG—guided missile destroyer.

refresher training. And when you're having tictacs you would flag hoist and those kinds of things, but you really didn't rely on that for speedy communications, the kind you needed when you had to do something instantly.

Paul Stillwell: The flags are really a holdover from another era.

Admiral Gravely: That's a holdover from John Paul Jones, I guess. Before the radio and after the pigeon.

Paul Stillwell: The Oriskany had had a bad fire that year.* Did you have any connection with that?

Admiral Gravely: No, I'm not sure where the Oriskany's fire was. I really didn't get involved in that. I was trying to think of something else that we might have done out there, but I'll probably get to it, or think about it later. The big event, I guess, occurred towards the tail end of the cruise when we had an upkeep period in Kaohsiung.† In fact, we went into most of your ports out there during that time.

Paul Stillwell: Did you go to Japan also?

Admiral Gravely: I didn't go to Japan on Taussig. I went basically to Hong Kong, to Subic three or four times, to Taiwan, and the big one was going to Australia. We had the normal about five and half months or so out there. Of course, Hong Kong, as I told you about. We were station ship at Hong Kong.

Oh, I know one big event that occurred. We relieved the O'Hare, which was an East Coast destroyer. I forget the squadron that he was in, but his squadron came from the East Coast while we were out there. We happened to be in Subic, so their squadron commander came over and invited me and my engineer to come over and explain to them

---

* On 26 October 1966, while the aircraft carrier Oriskany (CVA-34) was operating off Vietnam, a parachute flare ignited a fire in the ship's hangar deck. Forty-four men were killed as a result of the fire. For details see the Naval Institute oral history of Vice Admiral David C. Richardson, USN (Ret.).
† Kaohsiung is the leading port of Taiwan; it is located on the southwest coast of the island. The city has a population of more than one million.

and brief them on the ops out there. We did that, and the O'Hare's squadron commodore, who was a big one for public affairs events, sent out a public affairs release to Norfolk talking about how the destroyer Taussig, a West Coast ship, had joined his squadron.

My commodore got a copy of that, and chewed me out about it. He was just kidding really, but it was quite interesting how suddenly I became an East Coast destroyer rather than a West Coast destroyer. But, anyway, getting back to the O'Hare, I came up to II Corps and relieved the O'Hare. In relieving the O'Hare my ops officer and a couple of other people went over to get a briefing, and get the gunfire, get the latest Gun 10 and op order and everything else. And when the ops officer came back, he came to the bridge. I was up on the bridge. We had picked up our boat, etc. And he said, "Captain, I have all the pertinent gunnery orders, the Gun 10 and all the recent corrections to it, and the II Corps parrot."

I sort of said, "What the hell is this II Corps parrot bit?"

He said, "Well, we have him down on the main deck level, right where the quarterdeck would be when we're in port. The II Corps parrot's down there."

So I said, "Oh, for Christ sake, don't tell me."

He said, "Well, sure, you can see him. He's down there." Well, frankly, I thought he was pulling my leg, so I just wouldn't go down there. But at lunch I heard some buzzing about this parrot. I went down to lunch, and then people were talking about it at the wardroom table, and I couldn't resist.

It was on the starboard side, so I went out that weather-break door there, and started walking aft, and everybody had told me he was on top of this spud locker in a little cage right there. Well, sure enough, as I stepped out there was a cage. And I started walking back. As I got there, I noticed that the door was open and there was a white sign there on a piece of paper. I went up to the sign, and it basically said, "Out to lunch." [Laughter] Well, one of my kids had let the parrot go.

But what had happened was that the O'Hare was up there on gunfire support, and this bird flew aboard, and someone caught it. It was one of these small lovebird-like things with a big beak and everything else. He caught it and put it in a cage, and basically this was the start of the legend of the II Corps parrot. It was to be passed from ship to ship to ship, just like Esther Williams's photograph.* And, unfortunately, the O'Hare started it, but my ship broke the II Corps parrot routine, because they let him go the first day.

The next time I ran into the O'Hare, the O'Hare came in to relieve me as station ship, and I went aboard the O'Hare. The skipper sent for me and everything else. I was going to brief him on station ship, etc. The next thing I know I was congratulated, and I was being given a cactus plant. What had happened was when he was in refresher training he went to Gitmo. Somebody went out on the beach and picked up a cactus, which they grew someplace, and every time they got a little bulb on it, he'd just take that and plant it in another pot. He had all these cactuses aboard, which he'd give out and take pictures of with everybody. And, of course, there was a big picture in the Chicago paper. "Captain So-and-so gives Captain So-and-so a cactus plant in Vietnam."

Well, I got my cactus plant. So we took my cactus plant back, and I guess I got kind of pleased with the darn thing, because one of the sailors took an unusual interest in it, and he would always make sure that it was moved to the wing of the bridge where the sun was. He watered it. He fed it and everything else. And, of course, we got into port, then he'd make sure that it was down in my cabin, and we kept up with the cactus plant. Well, anyway, so I had my cactus plant now.

We ultimately got into the part of the schedule wherein we had to go to Australia. The Boyd and Taussig were to be the two ships that would go down to join the Australian forces for this exercise called Sword Hilt. I was the OTC for the move, and so, of course, I took the Boyd down to Australia. We joined the Australian forces, and participated for about ten days in a very, very rigid and very, very high-class exercise. I was thoroughly impressed with everything that they did. I was impressed with every action that the Australians, the New Zealanders, and all took.

There was a Brit or two on the exercise. I had operated with Brits before. I'd seen an Australian up in Vietnam before, but I'd never really been in a close tactical environment with those navies. I think we conducted ourselves very well. In fact, we were complimented at the critique, which they called a wash-up versus critique, at the

---

* In the 1950s various Navy ships engaged in energetic rivalries to see which one could pilfer and then retain possession of a photo of Esther Williams, a movie star of the period. For details see Captain William C. Green, "My Affair With Esther," U.S. Naval Institute Proceedings, September 1990, pages 121-123.

end of the exercise. We went through varying evolutions there with refueling from a British tanker, which was a little bit different. The connection is about the same, but not quite the same. We did some gunfire support down there.

There was one minor problem in that you had a couple of places with the same name, and we went to the right place, but I could have just as easily gone to the wrong place and fired. I think they were both unpopulated, so it wouldn't make much difference where we were. They had a little tight formation that we all bunched into so that there could be a picture taken with the other ships. My position was right on the fantail of their carrier. There was another carrier astern of me, and he was about 300 yards off my fantail. If you're standing on the bridge of a destroyer and look back 300 yards, you know that if you slow a knot, that guy's going to overtake you. So, of course, I kept staying in formation. But it went very well. We really enjoyed it.

Paul Stillwell: A U.S. destroyer ran afoul of one of those carriers a few years later, the Frank Evans.[*]

Admiral Gravely: The Frank Evans got cut in half, as I recall, by the Melbourne. That was after I had left there, of course. I do know, just like you said, the Frank E. Evans was cut in half by the Melbourne. But they are very, very confident, sure shore ship handlers. They know how to do it right, they do it quickly, and then go on to the next evolution. That's the way we're supposed to react when we're down there, and we did our best.

Paul Stillwell: Did they have a briefing beforehand to get together on tactical procedures?

Admiral Gravely: No. There was no briefing. I just came in suddenly and joined them with the Boyd and said, "Reporting for duty, sir," and a guy gave me a station. I zipped over there, and the Boyd zipped over to hers, and there we were in the midst of it. We

---

[*] At 3:15 on the morning of 3 June 1969, during a SEATO naval exercise in the South China Sea, about 650 nautical miles southwest of Manila, the U.S. destroyer Frank E. Evans (DD-754) was struck and cut in two by the Australian aircraft carrier Melbourne. The bow section of the destroyer sank within two minutes of the collision, resulting in the loss of 74 of her 273 crew members. The bow of the carrier was damaged, but she suffered no personnel casualties.

did have the op orders, I think, in advance, so we had been briefed on what we were trying to do and what the exercise schedule was all about. But it was a very, very good exercise. I went through some places in South China Seas that I'd never been around. You know, like New Guinea and those kinds of places. We didn't go ashore there.

Well, when that exercise terminated, we went into Melbourne, and that was the first time that I had been down under. Melbourne was just a fascinating place to me. I had heard, of course, that there was some discrimination in Melbourne. Well, frankly, what it is is basically discrimination not so much against blacks or any other nationality as it is against their own aborigines, who are second-class citizens. Of course, if you were dark, then you were almost classed as an aborigine. But I was invited to some of the nicest affairs I've ever attended down there, and nobody even looked twice at me. I enjoyed it.

We threw a party, as I recall, and invited some high-level Australians and other people there, and they did the same. In fact, I went to a dinner down there which was similar to their Navy League, and I was sort of an honored guest and enjoyed it. We were scheduled to be there for about ten days. As I recall, we got there on something like a Friday, and we would have left the following Monday a week.

Unfortunately, on the Friday a week from the day we got in there, that changed. We had started our liberty at about 10:00 o'clock. We had split off into four sections. We had one section who went on liberty at 10:00, normally had another section that would leave at about noonish or so, and then a third section would leave at about 2:00 o'clock. The reason we staggered it like that was that certainly we wanted people to have maximum liberty, but I also wanted some people on there to escort the various visiting parties and everything else, and so we did it that way.

Well, about just before lunch that day, someone came in, and I guess my ops officer had been talking to one of the Australian officers and he said, "There is a hot message coming in for Taussig." So we began to speculate on what could be a hot message coming in. We had no idea. They didn't have any idea. All they knew was that there was some hot message coming in for Taussig. I began to think the worst, obviously, that we'd done something down there that offended somebody, and they were kicking us out of port, but then I couldn't recall anything like that. Well, we finished lunch, and about that time the exec came and said, "Captain I just let the next section go."

I said, "Okay." And I said, "Have you heard about the message yet?" No, he hadn't heard anything at all about it. Well, about 1:00 o'clock here came a flash message from Com7thFlt: "Get under way immediately. Proceed to the vicinity of Frederick Reef. The Tiru is aground. Render whatever assistance you can."[*]

Paul Stillwell: Tiru being a U.S. submarine.

Admiral Gravely: Yes, the Tiru was a submarine which had been with us on this exercise. Well, the Tiru left port, had gotten six or seven hours at sea, and he'd run aground on something up in the Great Northern Reef area.[†] Frederick Reef was a horseshoe-type reef, and he was about half across it at the point wherein he was bobbing and waving with each wave. Our mission was to go up there and render whatever assistance that we could.

Well, we left about 2:00, 2:30, something of that nature.[‡] We tried every method we knew how to get the entire crew back, but I had to leave 21 sailors ashore in Melbourne. We left the Boyd there, and I knew full well the Boyd would pick them up. We knew that since we were all going back to the States we'd join someplace, and the Boyd would bring my guys. Of course, I talked to the skipper and told him.

There were a couple of things about that that bothered me for years. One was I being the senior ship down there. Why didn't he pick the Boyd, which was the junior ship with the junior CO. At that moment it didn't concern me. Hell, it was a job; go do it. But I wondered about that for a number of years, and the second thing I guess it was that I wondered about at that point in time, was that, "My God, we've just been cut two days short. Will we make these up someplace in New Zealand?"

---

[*] On 3 November 1966 the diesel submarine Tiru (SS-416) ran aground on Frederick Reef. After the boat's own efforts to free herself failed, the civilian tugboat Carlock and the Australian destroyer Vendetta arrived on the scene. Working under the direction of the Seventh Fleet salvage officer, they successfully pulled her off the reef.
[†] The official history of the Tiru reports that she got under way from Brisbane, Australia, on Wednesday, 2 November, and ran aground the following day.
[‡] The Taussig got under way from Melbourne on 4 November.

Paul Stillwell: Why did you think it should be the junior rather than the senior ship?

Admiral Gravely: I've always felt that historically that's the way things happen. The junior is the guy who's called to do the dirty work, you might call it, although this was not dirty. This was just interrupting some liberty.

Paul Stillwell: One thing that's a little bothersome in hearing about it is that it took so long to get a flash message to you. I mean, you had all these inklings.

Admiral Gravely: Well, I had all these inklings, but then again, you've got to remember we didn't have satellite communications to the degree that we have it now. I'm not sure whether we were getting bits and pieces of it in, and not being able to get it all and got to get repeats, etc. But certainly in this day and time if it takes that long to get a message, somebody's in trouble. I don't think it would have happened today, but in 1966 it did occur that way, that I got rumors that I was getting a message in from Seventh Fleet. And then finally it took about two hours to really get in a flash message, which you ought to hear then in maybe three minutes or something of that nature.

Well, anyway, we got under way and started moving on up on north. For the most part we were traveling at 25 knots whenever the weather permitted. Of course, I wanted to get up there in a hurry. But that Sunday, when I was off from Melbourne, I was at 50% fuel, so I had to go in and tank up. So I went in, and I tanked up, and at that moment someone told me that they just heard over the news broadcast that the Tiru had been pulled off the reef. So I began to get in touch with some of the Australian authorities to find out if they still wanted me to continue to go up there.

The word I got was that, "Yes, we do. We want you to go rendezvous with him, and release the Australian destroyer, who has another mission tomorrow. And you will escort him back into Brisbane." So fine. I got under way from there and went on up and rendezvoused at first light with the Tiru and the Australian destroyer. I relieved him, released him, and then escorted the Tiru back into Brisbane. Having enjoyed my liberty time down in Melbourne, I now wanted to see what Brisbane was like, and I began to figure location versus speed versus, how long it was going to take, and everything else. I had it figured out that if we continued on at the current speed, that we'd probably be in there at about 2:00 or 3:00 o'clock that afternoon, which was just perfect. I could throw a night of liberty before anybody ever found out I was back in the town, and then I'd get my instructions later on to proceed. About that time the submarine suddenly slowed.

Paul Stillwell: With no explanation.

Admiral Gravely: No real explanation. Nothing happened. Of course, I tried to get some explanation from the destroyer commander over there, because they had a squadron commander on board. They'd already flown the guy in to start the investigation. And I really got nothing from him. And then they slowed some more. So finally he was at the point after slowing a couple of times that we were not going to get back till midnight. And that was about the time we got into Brisbane, about midnight. And I went over to investigate to find out the reason for the delay. I was trying to find out beforehand, if he was leaking or if they had a problem. No, they didn't have a problem; the commodore just decided that he didn't want to bring them into port during daylight hours with the press there to interview them.

Paul Stillwell: That would call attention to his misfortune.

Admiral Gravely: Call attention to the misfortune and everything else. But anyway, he got back into port, and, of course, I had to start liberty at midnight, but my guys [laughter] didn't mind that so much. They wished they had been there earlier.

But about that time, after the mission was completed, I got a message from CTG 70.8 which directed me to proceed to Fiji. And the Boyd, which got under way at its regular time on Monday morning, was to rendezvous in Fiji with me, and then we'd come the rest of the way back to the States. Well, we stayed in there until Wednesday morning, so I did get a whole night of liberty there and got most of the people off in Brisbane. We then sailed independently to Fiji, wherein later that day the Boyd came in and rejoined.

There was a celebration, and I cannot tell you what it was; I almost think it was their independence day. And, of course, got a chance to view a big parade and the whole bit, and drank some of the local liquor. They had a liquid drink there that looked and tasted like muddy water; you drank out of a half coconut. I can remember that they almost insisted, and you felt that you didn't want to hurt a native's feelings by not drinking this good stuff there, and so I drank one. And I got to tell you, one was enough. [Laughter]

Paul Stillwell: One was more than enough.

Admiral Gravely: One was more than enough. But it was some real potent stuff, which I understand was made out of coconut. Now, I've forgotten what they call it, guava or something like that. But the main reason you didn't drink any more was because you heard the story of how it was made. Supposedly the older ladies of the village, toothless of course, chewed on this coconut pulp, and then spit the saliva out, which they let ferment for a few days, rake off the bugs, rake off the bubbles and everything else, and then you really got good liquor. [Laughter] Now, obviously they don't make it that way in this day and age when they got machines to crush it, but that's the way the natives told me that they used to make it. And, my God. But anyway [laughter], one time was enough.

Paul Stillwell: Didn't you have some family members back home that were a little unhappy about your crew going to Australia?

Admiral Gravely: Not that time.

Paul Stillwell: Oh, okay.

Admiral Gravely: No, this was a subsequent cruise down there. We then got under way after the celebration. I guess we left there the next weekday after fueling and everything else was aboard. And, lo and behold, my cactus was gone. Nobody could find my cactus.

Paul Stillwell: Just like Mr. Roberts and his palm tree.*

Admiral Gravely: But shortly thereafter, that afternoon, I got a message from the skipper of the Boyd which basically said, "Mysteriously, a cactus appeared in my cabin. I understand it might be yours, and I would like some instructions on the care and feeding of cactus." [Laughter] So for the next five or six days there were messages going back and forth on the care and protection of the cactus, as well as what could they get for ransom for it, including ice cream, and the whole bit. We really went through a lot of stuff. Frankly, I'm not sure I really would have gotten it back except for the fact that somebody was getting wise to the fact that the cactus had to go through the agricultural inspection. Then nobody really wanted that thing, but we had decided that we'd take a chance on it. But I'm not sure the Boyd particularly wanted to take the same chance.

Well, anyway, in coming back I sent my commodore a message, because we were scheduled to get back on Thanksgiving Day. And I guess really the commodore sent me a message basically not directing, but certainly telling me in no uncertain terms that they wanted me in there on Thanksgiving Day. So we sat down and calculated it, because we'd been running on one boiler, trying to conserve fuel making max speed, which was about 17 1/2 knots to 18. That was the only way we felt we could make it unless we got a tanker. So I sent him back a message which basically said, "I need a tanker at such-and-such a point south of Pearl, and then I'll need another tanker about 400-500 miles west of San Diego."

Of course, getting one tanker was pretty hard, not less getting two. And so we finally gave up on the idea and I said, "I'll be in there the morning after Thanksgiving." And, of course, they agreed with that. Well, anyway, we got our tanker south of Pearl. Of course, it permitted us to top off, and I continued at the same speed and got in there.

Arriving in San Diego, I discovered that as we rounded North Island there were two boats sitting in the water. There was the commodore's gig and the admiral's barge, and these things had wives on board. And there was my wife. There was the ops

---

* Mister Roberts was a book of fictional stories written by Thomas Heggen on the basis of his World War II experiences as a Naval Reserve officer. Published in 1946, it depicted life on board an imaginary cargo ship in which the officers and crew flouted rules and regulations. It was later made into a successful stage play and movie, both starring Henry Fonda.

officer's wife and everything else—<u>Boyd</u> wives and our wives. I, of course, being senior ship was ahead of the whole gang.

Paul Stillwell: That was a proud moment, I'll bet.

Admiral Gravely: It was quite a proud moment, of course, you getting your wives to wave at you, but you got to remember that I got a daughter now who was not quite two and a half, but she was certainly older than 22 months, and I hadn't seen her. There was my wife and I was yelling at her, "Where's my daughter? Where is she?" She couldn't quite hear that, and I'm just wondering, you know, who was babysitting my daughter. But, anyway, the wives circled <u>Taussig</u>, and then they went aft, and they circled <u>Boyd</u>, and then they started to come up to go alongside the pier.

My group commander there was Admiral Goodfellow, who was just a great guy.[*] He was 70.8 when I was out there in Melbourne. So my wife said, "Admiral, now you know I wanted to be alongside the pier when my husband came in, but I think he's going to beat you."

And Scott Goodfellow said, "Alma, let me tell you something. First of all, I have never lost a wife over the side. And, secondly, no skipper's ever beat me into that pier yet." And he turned up. He said, "Whoops, Sam just did it." [Laughter] Because I was charging up there. Although there's a ten-knot speed limit in that harbor, you stretched that as much as you could when you were coming home. And, lo and behold, there was my daughter with somebody, holding her there and everything else.

Well, anyway, you can imagine that was a real, real happy time for me and a happy reunion. I got reacquainted with the family. I got a chance to talk to a daughter that I hadn't talked to in seven months, and hadn't talked too much in her whole life really, to be honest with you. And I had some nice Australian candy to give her and a Koala bear and all the rest of this. We just had a great time. At the normal time, when it was respectable, we went ashore. I've never been a big one for being the first guy off of the ship, so we stayed there for a short while and enjoyed ourselves in my cabin, and then I took my family home, where we started our leave like everybody else, and did the

---

[*] Rear Admiral A. Scott Goodfellow, USN, Commander Cruiser-Destroyer Flotilla Seven, 1966-67.

normal things that you do. I was greeted very shortly thereafter by my wife, who said, "I guess you know that the ship is taking the wives to Acapulco."

So I said, "No, Alma, the ship is not taking the wives to Acapulco."

She said, "Well, the commodore says you are, and you're going right after Christmas or in January."

I said, "Wait a minute, Alma. There's no way the commodore is going to make us take our wives to Acapulco. First of all, wives can't go on the ship."

She said, "Oh, no, no. The wives are going to fly down to Acapulco, and they're going to meet the ships while they're down there."

I said, "Alma, if we're going to Acapulco on a training exercise, that's a mission just like any other. If we're down there on a mission, and something happens and the ship has to leave, what are the wives going to do?"

She said, "Well, I don't know what the wives are going to do, but the commodore's going to take us."

I said, "No, you go back and talk to the commodore."

She said, "You talk to the commodore."

Well, anyway, to make a long story short, Commodore Langille had said that he had planned to, if he could get it approved, have an exercise down to Acapulco with about a five-day R&R time in Acapulco, and that the wives would fly down and meet us all there.[*] Well, I, of course, had said there was no way—operational commitment. So I couldn't back down. So there was quite a thing going between my wife and me, as well as the commodore, who had made the deal that all the wives come down.

In those days the destroyers were very close together. They had divisional parties and all those kinds of things. We had a divisional party, as I recall, in December, when somebody said, "Alma, are you going to Acapulco?" because she had told them she was going, then she told them she's not going. She was going back and forth for a half a dozen times. And I guess she said, "I really don't know."

About that time the commodore said, "Sam, come on over to the bar. I want to buy you a drink."

"Yes, sir."

---

[*] Captain Justin E. Langille III, USN, Commander Destroyer Division 213, 1966-67.

"How about a cigar?" Lighted up the cigar, took the drink. And he said, "Sam, take your wife to Acapulco."

"Yes, sir." So the decision was made we were to take wives to Acapulco. Well, lo and behold, the day came that we were going to sail. This was the first time I had really operated with all of the ships of the division. A submarine was tasked to go with us, and we had an oiler, which was going to play around with us, but not really going into Acapulco with us, because we needed fuel part of the way down there. Actually, we did some exercises off the San Diego op area for several days and then steamed on down there.

Well, anyway, I had a couple of things that happened that almost made it impossible for me to go in some respects. We were to leave on a Saturday morning at 8:00 o'clock. Then somehow the CruDesPac change of command came about that Saturday morning, so we were going to delay until after the change in command. And I'm happy that we delayed. But two mornings before that, some kid spoke to his division officer and said, "Boy, did I get high last night."

Well, to make a long story short, we discovered that we had a marijuana ring aboard. The first thing I did, of course, was to call the Defense Intelligence Agency, and they came over. They started to questioning people, and in the meantime, every time I turned around, they'd bring me a new guy; the last one was going to the brig. Frankly, I had something like about 22 to 23 people in the brig, and they were interviewing the last one ten minutes before it was time to get under way.

Well, I left, going to Acapulco, with 23 guys in the brig. And, of course, here again I was shorthanded, but we'd done that before. I wasn't worried about being shorthanded, but I was quite concerned about his drug thing. And the worst part about it, I guess, was my decision to send them to the brig, because you just can't keep people in the brig unless you got some real charges. We sailed, and I didn't have time to do that. Well, CruDesPac investigated it very quickly and briefly, and said that they were releasing So-and-so, and so many of them from the brig, and that they would keep them. They sort of took them. The men were not in confinement, but CruDesPac would maintain custody, which was fine.

Samuel L. Gravely, Jr., Interview #4 (8/12/86) – Page 262

But, anyway, we got down to Acapulco, had a tremendous exercise, played a little bit of everything. I haven't mentioned this before, but I had the DASH aboard, which whereas we had played around with it a lot during underway training, there was a requirement that the DASH be flown for so many hours per month.* We did that. This was the drone antisubmarine ship's helicopter. And we kept them quite proficient, had a very good operator. So we did keep up our proficiency, etc. So we exercised that during the trip down there and those kinds of things.

Paul Stillwell: Most people say bad things about DASH. How was your experience?

Admiral Gravely: My experience was that having a DASH aboard was just like having another friend, particularly during ASW. There were some malfunctions that happened to it. I can remember being with one of our destroyers when he lost control of his DASH while he was in the midst of an air study problem. He had to crank up at 25 knots to go catch that thing, so he could finally bring it aboard and land it, because it was going in the opposite direction. And he got it back and did land it.

I was standing on the bridge once with my DASH officer, who was watching another ship, and a ship that I cannot think of the name of. But, anyway, this other ship which was one of our nemeses, was flying his DASH, and the young officer said, "I wish that so-and-so would drop in the drink." And whsst. [Laughter] It was almost as if he'd pressed a button, and it did. So it was to some degree hazardous flying, not from a standpoint that you're going to hit something or anything like that. But they lost a few of them because it had to be perfect from an airplane-handling part. The CIC officer or whoever, your DASH officer, had to handle his part perfectly. It had to be functioning perfectly.

Subsequent to this Acapulco trip, ultimately we evaluated DASH as a spotting machine for gunfire support. Had a TV camera mounted on it, and we'd fly it off and take pictures of things, and it made a great spotting tool. Now, I think that really what

---

* DASH—drone antisubmarine helicopter. This was an unmanned, remotely piloted helicopter that was designed to fly to the location of a submarine and launch its weapons—either two lightweight Mark 44 homing torpedoes or a nuclear depth charge. DASH entered the fleet in the early 1960s but was never really successful.

killed DASH was being caught up into the manned pilot, or the pilot controlled-vehicle versus the non-pilot-controlled vehicle. The aviators think that if it flies, they've got to control it. And, of course, it was a CruDesPac weapon.

But I had very good luck with the DASH. We ultimately, like anybody else, lost one of them during the cruise. When I say cruise, I mean during my 30 months aboard I don't think we lost but one. But we didn't have any worse luck with them than anybody else. But the mission basically was to haul a torpedo out, then launch that torpedo out at a stand-off range for that submarine, which was way out maybe 5,000 yards or so, and we did that successfully many, many times.

The trip to Acapulco, as I said, went fine. We got into Acapulco, and the commodore called all the skippers over, and he briefed us thoroughly on Acapulco. He told us what conduct he expected from our crews and everything else, and how he expected that he was bringing sailors and diplomats down there and not rabble-rousers. Well, we went ashore and went on liberty and everything else. My wife and I had a good time, because we went to the Club LaBresis, or whatever the name of it is, along with the rest of the troops. We had a great time.

When I got back to the ship that night, there was a guy from the shore patrol over there with a report looking for a BT1, who was one of my sailors.[*] Then I began to see more and more and bigger people, like the naval attaché. Then somebody told me that it was the deputy or one of the assistant ambassadors. Well, we'd had a sailor to run amok down there. His problem was that, like any other guy, he didn't get what he thought he'd paid his money for, and this girl was running from house to house, slamming doors, and he was going through doors without unslamming them. [Laughter] So he'd created havoc down there.

When we finally collared him, of course, he was going to have a court-martial, whatever it took, and correct that situation. He, of course, ultimately paid for the damage that he'd done. But certainly we had damaged the Navy's reputation over there. So I was prepared to leave that next morning. In fact, I went over to call on the commodore to tell him that if he looked out his porthole, he'd see that I had the steam up, and I was

---

[*] BT1—boilerman first class.

ready to go if I had to." And I said, "Commodore, but don't forget now, my wife is down here, you know. She's down here because you made me bring her." [Laughter}

"Get out of my cabin!" And, of course, I didn't have to sail. But anyway we had a very, very interesting time down there in Acapulco. A great liberty port.

We then left there, and the fancy sort of a Queen Anne salute to the port at 25 knots just steaming all around in circles and everything else. It worked fairly well. One of my buddies went dead in the water about 500 yards in front of me. And, of course, we knew how to avoid it, so it was no problem. You're alert to those kinds of things; you expect the worst. It was a good exercise, a good trip down there, and, of course, we got home, and by the time I got home then I was faced with 23 court-martials.

Paul Stillwell: Well, that was really extraordinary for that period wasn't it? I mean, the drug phenomenon hadn't really caught on yet.

Admiral Gravely: Well, the drug phenomenon hadn't caught on as much as the fact that we had some users, but at that point in time we didn't tolerate them, and you got rid of them quickly. If a guy wanted to get out of the Navy, he said, "I smoke marijuana." And in short order he was gone, or even the other way was that, "I am a homosexual," and he was gone. "Here, I'm smoking marijuana." Phweet, in the brig. You obviously then took him out, and you followed the rules and regulations, but in short order he was out of the Navy. We then subsequently got to the point wherein, okay, we don't throw him in the brig necessarily—that's cruel and inhuman treatment, I guess—but we do ultimately prosecute him, and we may or may not throw him out of the Navy. But right now they're back to, you know, you do a drug and you're out.[*] So we go through phases in our Navy.

My problem, of course, was conducting all these dumb court-martials. And I got to tell you, certainly they weren't all court-martials. They were captain's masts, because I went through every jacket, every record that he'd done, the whole bit, mitigating circumstances, etc., and decided at that point in time whether there would be a court-martial or whether it would be a straight mast. We had so many masts, and we had

---

[*] In the early 1980s, when Admiral Thomas B. Hayward, USN, was Chief of Naval Operations, the Navy adopted a zero-tolerance policy toward the use of illegal drugs.

so many court-martials, and I guess there were only two guys that we really gave it to, who were the sellers basically. It turned out that it was a recalled reservist who had been aboard about a month or so, and he'd contaminated my whole damn ship, so to speak. It took a long time. We didn't do this in a day. But we finally got rid of all of that.

Well, we're now at the point wherein we were beginning to think a little bit about the next deployment, and also CruDesPac began to form the ships up a little differently. We were a group of multi-purpose ships; in my division there were four FRAM IIs. We also were the third division; in fact, we were in DesRon 5, as I recall, 51, 52, 53. But CruDesPac came out with the idea of some six-ship squadrons. And we formed an ASW squadron of six ships. We had two FRAM IIs, as I recall. We had two of the Dealey-class DEs, and I know we had one DEG, and I've forgotten what the sixth ship was.[*] But, anyway, we were a mishmash, but our basic mission was ASW, and whereas it was all the same mission, we all had different capabilities within that mission so far as the size of the sonars, and the kinds of sonars. In the meantime, the Taussig, and I hadn't mentioned this before, but Taussig also had the variable-depth sonar, as well as DASH.[†]

The other ship in that division which had the same capability that I did was the John A. Bole. We began to work together with the Yorktown, which was a CVS.[‡] My first meeting with the Yorktown was a little bit ahead of the rest of the group. We all knew that he'd be the guy we'd ultimately deploy with, and he'd be the guy we'd be working with, but even before that they needed a ship up in Long Beach, because the Yorktown was going on a family cruise. They needed a destroyer to play with them a little bit and to show the families what ops that the Yorktown would be undergoing with the rest of us.

So, of course, they had me to do a couple of things. I plane guarded for a bit. I went up ahead and set up a screen. And then finally I came alongside and took on a little fuel. Normal fueling is about 12 knots, as I recall, but we were getting a little late, and he was a long ways from Long Beach, so they wanted to know if we could do it at 15. I said, "Fine. Step it up to 15."

---

[*] DEG—guided missile destroyer escort.
[†] A cable reel was mounted on the stern of the ship, and this was used to lower the sonar down to variable depths in the ocean. That facilitated using the sonar in depth with different temperature gradients. In some cases the signals from a hull-mounted sonar bounce off when they hit a layer of temperature differential.
[‡] CVS was the designation for an aircraft carrier specialized for the antisubmarine mission.

"Hey, that's great. Can you do it at 18?"

"Hell, yes. Do it at 18."

"How about 22?"

"Twenty-two, go." The next thing I knew, there I was, alongside this guy, 25 knots barreling back into Long Beach. Of course, then he let me go after a while, and I took off and came on back to San Diego. It went well, I guess.

Paul Stillwell: That was an impressive show for the families.

Admiral Gravely: I got to tell you, they thought it was just standard routine. [Laughter] But the Yorktown became really a, not necessarily favorite ship but a favorite group to be with, because the good old admiral was just a great, fantastic guy, and I almost loved him, if you could love an admiral.

Paul Stillwell: Who was that?

Admiral Gravely: Ralph Weymouth.[*] He retired up in Providence, Rhode Island, and married a French girl. And, unless I'm mistaken, he became OP-98.

But, anyway, the time in San Diego became a series of inspections and those kinds of things, which we did fairly well. We did certainly our group of ship exercises and competing for the competitive year. I came back to Long Beach a couple more times for some reason.

Once I sent a diver down to inspect the sonar dome, and he decided he could push one of the plates in. So we had to come up to Long Beach for an emergency dry-docking to get some plates welded back on. When you can push the side of a ship in, you're in trouble, as you might suspect. We really weren't leaking, and I think it was just a mirage, but that was the report. So don't take any chances, get on back up here.

I remember one night, and this was a strange one, we were out with the division running exercises, and the commodore decided that he thought we ought to run a full-power trial. So we lined up about five miles on line abreast, and we started getting

---

[*] Rear Admiral Ralph Weymouth, USN, Commander Anti-Submarine Warfare Group One, 1967-68

on up to max speed. And so we were charging along at about 34 knots, I guess. And I got to tell you, that's pushing it when you say 34 knots. That was certainly max, if she was quite up to that. I was sitting up on the bridge, and I guess I'd been there for 10 or 15 minutes when the CIC reported a contact dead ahead. Well, we were moving along at 34 knots, and the contact was getting a little closer.

Finally our CIC said, "Collision course." Well, on a full-power trial you want to drive straight and true, and you do a little fishtailing no matter what, but you want to drive as straight and true as you can, if you want to get maximum with turns you're doing through the water. So I said, "Hang in there." And suddenly we were at the point wherein we were close enough that we could reach each other with flashing light. So we got a light from this ship, which turned out to be an AKA. It said, "Request you stand clear. I am running a full-power trial. My speed 16." [Laughter]

So I just said send him back, "Mike speed 34."[*] And I got to tell you, we could see he moved. [Laughter] I'm sure he didn't believe it. In fact, I know he didn't believe it, because it so happened that the ops officer on that ship was a young officer that basically was my protégé, or is my protégé, I guess, to some regards. He was the ops officer on there, and he reported us as a surface contact running at 34 knots, and his skipper didn't believe him.

He said, "It must be a helicopter or something. You guys are all screwed up."" And when he got that "Mike speed 34," he believed us and moved over.

Paul Stillwell: Who was your protégé?

Admiral Gravely: I don't know whether you have met Gordon Fisher. Gordon Fisher is currently CO of the NROTC unit at GW over here.[†] And just a fine young officer. He'd been an ensign about three or four months when I went to Pearl to take over the Falgout. Somehow we met, and I've tried to keep him on the straight and narrow ever since then. In fact, I talked him into staying into the Navy. He might have decided on his own, but I certainly helped talk him into that.

---

[*] In this context the signal "Mike speed" meant "my speed."
[†] Captain Gordon E. Fisher, USN, commanding officer of the Naval Reserve Officers Training Corps at George Washington University.

But, anyway, we went through a series of other little events like that but nothing really amazing. As I said, one time we evaluated the DASH as a helicopter spotter. We used the VDS on several occasions, and I must tell you that I felt the VDS was a great sonar, a great asset. As you well know, they're coming up with different kinds of towed arrays. We don't have the VDS per se, but we have all kinds of towed arrays that came about primarily because of some of the successes we had with the VDS.

Paul Stillwell: Did you deploy as an ASW group then?

Admiral Gravely: We deployed as an ASW group. After the normal routine in the San Diego area of certainly the ASW work, we worked together, the Yorktown and these six destroyers. We were always together after that time, although the destroyers were all home-ported in San Diego and the Yorktown was home-ported in Long Beach. But ultimately in January of 1968 we deployed as a group.

I guess, let's see, I should go back a little earlier, because the captains' list came out about that time. It came out before I deployed. I don't know exactly, I've forgotten what date I made captain, but I do remember that an old friend of mine on the Chevalier called me over to his stateroom one morning. The skipper of the ship Chevalier and I were very good friends, although he was senior to me.

One time when we were moored alongside of him, my exec in writing his plan of the day got a little bit too enthusiastic and overzealous, I guess, because one of the notes he put in the plan of the day was one which said, "We've got to clean up this ship or else we'll look like all the rest of the dogs alongside." The skipper of the Chevalier was the only guy who really took offense at it, and he called me over and showed me that thing and said, "Don't we have enough problems keeping our sailors from fighting and all this?" And I apologized to him and everything else.

But then the next time he called me over there, I wondered what we had done now. But, believe it or not, he was on a telephone line back to Washington because he'd heard the captains' selection was out, and, of course, they were reading off the names to him. He was writing them down, and my name was on that list, of course, which I was quite proud about. So, again, I get the word by a strange set of circumstances, really, about having been selected. Of course, when the list came out I was fairly senior on the list, so I put it on very shortly after I learned it.*

On the date the announcement came, I went home that afternoon and told my wife that, "I'm sailing in the morning, and somehow I've got to get my uniform striped by the next morning, stripe those blues." Of course, we were in blues in San Diego then. And we went downtown San Diego, and there are two or three of those tailor shops all over San Diego, you know. But nobody down there had any gold that they could stripe captain's blues on. And I had to sail the next morning at 6:00 o'clock, 7:00 o'clock, or something like that. So I said, "Well, honey I guess the only way we can do this is you got to do it."

And would you believe my wife stayed up all night taking a stripe off of one uniform to put the closest four that she could put that matched on the sleeve, and she striped my first uniform for me. The next morning, of course, I went down to the ship proud with four stripes on, and got under way, and left, going to Long Beach, in fact. But my wife striped my first captain's uniform.

I think it was December 28th of '67 was the date that we deployed. The six destroyers got under way from San Diego and rendezvoused with the Yorktown, and we came to Pearl. We operated as a group. In fact, while operating with a submarine off of Pearl Harbor, we picked up a nuclear submarine. We tracked this guy, and finally he took us up in the French Frigate Shoals. We lost him up in that area, but we did play around with him out there for about a half a day or so. And we managed that somebody had some kind of contact with six of us and the aircraft from the Yorktown. So we had a little something on him for a long time, but we did lose him up around French Frigate Shoals.

Came in to Honolulu for a short rest and recuperation, and then took off and sailed towards Yokosuka, Japan. Well, we were a day out of Yokosuka, Japan, when the Pueblo was stolen.† So that next morning we went by Yokosuka, Japan, at 25 knots,

---

* Gravely's date of rank as captain was 1 November 1967, which was assigned retroactively.
† USS Pueblo (AGER-2), an electronic intelligence ship, was seized on 23 January 1968 in the Sea of Japan by North Korean naval forces. The ship's crew members were held as prisoners until 23 December of that year. Of the 83 officers and men on board, 28 were intelligence specialists.

going up the Sea of Japan. We went up into the Sea of Japan and stayed up there with all the rest of the ships that were up there for, I think, about 45 days.

Paul Stillwell: Essentially a show of force.

Admiral Gravely: Essentially a show of force, and certainly so we'd people up there in case anything else happened. My big thing was that I thought that, really, a couple of 5-inch-gun destroyers could have gone with one guy basically going in and towing and another guy in there shooting them up. I asked the group commander to permit me to go in there, but he was much wiser than I, so we didn't do it. I really think it could have been done. I am convinced, though, that the political situation did not permit us to do it, and maybe we thought we could have done it, but the political situation was such we didn't do it.

Well, that was a very, very interesting tour to me, because I had spent time in Korea in both the Toledo and the Iowa, but certainly not with the responsibility that I had here, because both the Toledo and the other ship I was inside all the time. Here I was on an open bridge, and certainly I was seeing things that I hadn't. For example, I'd never seen it really snow at sea. In fact, I could remember that one of things that was a pastime was some kid to up on the forecastle and make a snowman.

One day I was trying to get mail from a helicopter, and suddenly we ended up in a fog bank. He said, "Stay out of fog banks," and I wasn't sure what I could do when I've got to stay on a steady course of speed and he wants to stay out of a fog bank. But we stayed up there for our length of time, and I still am convinced it was about 45 days. Then suddenly we were detached and, told to proceed to various ports that they'd picked out. Now, I wasn't really detached. I was told to plane guard for the Yorktown. One of the things I wanted to prove in my own mind was that a carrier forgets he's got a surface boy behind him, and I did. Maybe that's not universally true, but certainly in this case. I was behind the Yorktown, coming on down toward Sasebo, when he ceased flying his aircraft. So my OOD said, "Captain, can I ask him for permission to proceed under the assignment?"

I said, "Hell, no. You wait, he'll release you—I hope." [Laughter] But he didn't. You know when I got released? We were pulling into Sasebo, and I sent a message over, "Request permission to enter Sasebo in dungarees." [Laughter] I was detached so quickly. They forgot I was back there. Stayed back there for half a day, and nobody knew it. I was 1,000 yards behind him, but they'd actually physically forgotten that the destroyer was back there. So I was detached, and, of course, I went into Kaohsiung, and ultimately proceeded down to Subic. But I never will forget that the next time I saw the carrier skipper he was about ready to punch me in the nose, and he told me in no uncertain terms, "Don't ever do that again."[*]

I said, "What did I do?"

He said, "Well, you should have sent some other kind of message, or you shouldn't have sent a message at all. You should have taken off."

I said, "Well, you know, I was under your operational control, and I couldn't leave."

So he said, "Don't ever do that to me again."

"Yes, sir. I won't do that to you again." But he was very unhappy, because we came in by flashing light, and the good old admiral read everything that came by flashing light, and he was really upset that here was a guy letting me stay back there for six hours. But anyway, it worked out.

The ASW group in individual ships got out to Vietnam again, where we did more shore bombardment. We did plane guarding for other carriers. Did a little of the other thing. We basically chopped to 70.8, who was responsible for the surface ships out in that area.

Paul Stillwell: Was it essentially the same plane guarding for CVS as for CVA?

Admiral Gravely: Essentially the same thing. The planes are a little slower, so the speeds are down a little bit, but it's basically the same thing. No big difference in plane

---

[*] Captain William L. Bennett, Jr., USN, commanded the antisubmarine carrier Yorktown (CVS-10) from July 1967 to July 1968.

guarding. You plane guard for a big one, you plane guard for a little one. The big one might outrun you, but not that much difference.

Someplace along in there, and I'm not sure exactly when it happened, but we were at sea, and I guess one morning one of the sailors saw a small parrot on the lifeline, similar to the one that the O'Hare had. He asked me if I wanted him to go over and get him. I said, "Sure," because I had no idea he'd catch the bird. He went up there, and he caught this bird. I brought him up to the bridge, and we let him walk around on the gunwales there for a while. Of course, everybody was up there looking at the captain's bird. Finally I just told my engineering officer, "Why don't we build a cage for this bird." And then we started thinking of a name for it.

The call sign for a helicopter is "Fetch." And, of course, the commander is "Fetch Zero Zero." So that was the name of our bird, Fetch Zero Zero. We built a little cage for him and put him in this cage. I must have had him for three months or more, because he stayed on the bridge, nice sunshine and everything else, and then ultimately when we got into port or something like that, I'd keep him in my cabin. Someone fed him, they watered him, and everything else. And it was quite interesting, because the OOD was standing there with his arm up, right at the bridge there, and the bird pecking kept my OODs awake, you know. But, anyway, we really enjoyed Fetch Zero Zero.

Paul Stillwell: You've been a bird fancier for a long time.

Admiral Gravely: I've been a bird fancier for a long time. Many, many years, of course, it all goes back to my pigeons.

But anyway, we ultimately ended up in Kuala Lumpur, and when we got into Kuala Lumpur my relief came aboard. We had our change of command under way en route to Vietnam. The bird story, of course, is that Fetch Zero Zero, who was a regular member of that crew, to be honest with you, when we had the change of command we had it on the helo deck. And then when the change of command was through and we swapped off, we opened up the helo hangar and there was a big cake to cut, and there was the cage with the bird in it, Fetch Zero Zero.

Well, Admiral Weymouth, who was Commander ASW Group One, had heard a few things about Fetch Zero Zero, so he knew he was aboard and everything else, and he really admired him. In fact, he'd come on board, I think it was, and he'd seen him. He got quite a charge out of that. Well, came over in an orange flight suit, etc., and he'd taken that off for the change of command. Then he was back in the helo hanger changing to his flight suit and also sampling the cake, etc. About that time one of the sailors came up to me, and he said, "Captain, Captain, he's stealing our bird." Well, the helicopter was hovering over the fantail about this time. Admiral Weymouth knew that he was going to leave, and, of course, the helicopter couldn't land. He would have to climb the rope, as you call it. He had to be hoisted up. Well, Admiral Weymouth reached into the cage, took the bird, stuck it in his pocket, and walked on back. So when the kid told me that the admiral had our bird, I said "Son, go tell your captain, because I've been relieved, remember?" [Laughter]

Well, as luck would have it, I was getting a ride back to the carrier also, because I'm going to be CODed off the next morning.* Well, I went back, and I climbed up the rope right after Admiral Weymouth. They hoisted me aboard, and went on to the carrier. We got to the Yorktown, I got off. Of course, the skipper greeted me and everything else. Of course, he was an old friend of mine, the same guy who had kept me behind me for six or seven hours. And he said, "Well, you're going to sleep in my in-port cabin."

"Fine," and I started to leave.

Admiral Weymouth said, "Oh, no, come on up, come on up to my stateroom for a few minutes."

So I said, "Yes, sir." So I went on up to his stateroom, and he reached into his pocket and he pulled out the wettest [laugh] and the maddest little bird you have ever seen. He's had him in his hand, but that bird's had him in the hand too. [Laughter] But, anyway, he took the bird out and set him on the wardroom table. And at that time yes, the steward came up and brought him a glass of tea. The bird jumped up on his glass, and took a big swig, let out a big turd, and sat there a little while. Admiral Weymouth was just laughing and laughing. And, of course, I've got my tea, and I was drinking it.

---

* COD—carrier on-board delivery, an aircraft configured for carrier takeoffs and landings, dedicated to transporting personnel and cargo between ship and shore.

And he said, "You know what?" He said, "I liked your idea with him," he said, "I'm going to get me a cage."

I said, "Yes, sir."

He called up the damage control officer, and asked him to build a cage for the bird. Well, you got to remember that this is a carrier, not a destroyer. On a destroyer you build a little cage about 12 by 12 by 12 or something like that, great for the bird. The carrier damage control officer came over with a cage about three feet by three feet by three feet. Anyway, they took the bird, etc., and I just sort of moved around the carrier.

The next morning I was going to COD off at about 9:00 o'clock, so I was up and eating my breakfast and everything else. I had gotten to the point where I admired the little bird, and I went in to see Admiral Weymouth and tell him goodbye. He said, "When you get back to the States, would you check on the quarantine rules and write me a little letter, and let me know what I've got to do to bring him in."

I said, "Yes, sir."

Then, of course, I said I'd take one last look at the bird. I tried to find the bird, and I discovered that he was down in one of the ready rooms. Well, I went down to the ready room and sort of said goodbye to Fetch Zero Zero. Then I went up, and I said to the captain, "I've got to tell you, that bird has to have sunlight. You've got a nice air-conditioned compartment down there for pilots, dark and the whole bit, but the bird needs to be up in the sun. You ought to put him in a smaller cage, and put him up on the bridge."

He said, "Don't you worry about the bird. I'll take care of the admiral's bird."

"Yes, sir," and I got on my flight and flew back. Well, ultimately I got home, and I had just checked on the quarantine rules, and it was no major problem with bringing him in. He had to be examined and that kind of bit, but they'd let him in. Then I got a big long letter from Admiral Weymouth talking about how sorry he was he stole the bird, because the bird had died shortly after. The damn bird had caught pneumonia.

Paul Stillwell: From the air-conditioning probably.

Admiral Gravely: Yes, yes. Well, I was back now in the States, had my orders.

Paul Stillwell: Did you have any reflections on leaving that command? Were you sorry to go? You'd been so glad to get the ship.

Admiral Gravely: I really had mixed emotions at that point in time, and I have mixed emotions even today. I spent 30 months on that destroyer, and I know I did a good job on there. But I'm more convinced than ever that 30 months was too long. I am convinced that 18 months is too short, 30 months is too long, so it must be about 24 months to have command of a destroyer.

Paul Stillwell: Why do you say that?

Admiral Gravely: I just think that there are so many things that go on. I feel that every time you get a ship under way, you lose a little bit of the 100% luck that you started with. And I'm convinced that at about the 24-month point you get down to less than 50% luck, and something's going to happen sooner or later. You can get too cocky. When everything's going to work right for you, you screw it up. Or you begin to get cautious, and you screw it up. But I always based it on my luck theory—that at about the two-year point, you're below the 50% luck and you ought to go. I thoroughly enjoyed it. I had several—you could almost say several good crews. I had a tremendous XO my first half.

Paul Stillwell: Who was that?

Admiral Gravely: A guy by the name of Bob Wessman.[*] And Bob Wessman was just a great guy. Just a fine guy. A guy whose name I can't think of was his successor, who personally was not as good. Bob Wessman ultimately got his own destroyer and has since retired from the Navy. He is currently a minister. I'm not sure the other guy went much past commander either, but Bob Wessman and I clicked you might say, and we made a good team.

---

[*] Lieutenant Commander Robert L. Wessman, USN.

My first ops officer was a guy who was a wrestler. His first tour of duty, I think, in the Navy was in Yokosuka. He became a wrestler, so they transported him all over the world, wrestling, etc. He finally got to an AKA, and he did a little work there. But he had a good reputation. He did whatever job he was assigned very well. He then went to Monterey and spent a couple of years. So his problem was basically in really learning how to be in a fast-moving environment for the first time. He was special sea detail, and an OOD(F) on the Calvert, or at least on some AKA or APA, one of the two.

Paul Stillwell: Sounds a little like the skipper's career pattern.

Admiral Gravely: To some degree, but you've got to remember that I moved over to this DER, which wasn't quite as fast. But he wasn't quite as ready to move, and certainly wasn't as far along in his moving as I was, and I guess I wasn't very tolerant of that.

Paul Stillwell: I would think you'd have a little sympathy for a man in that position.

Admiral Gravely: Well, a little sympathy is about all I had, because it was a little difficult for me to have sharp weapons officers, sharp engineers, who were three or four years junior to a senior lieutenant who couldn't get the ship under way. And he did have a problem with getting it under way. In fact, with all due respect to him, he made lieutenant commander about the time he was leaving, and didn't make commander for ten years or something like that. In fact, he made commander just in time not to be thrown out on 20. Then he retired as a commander.

In fact, it was a little bit disheartening to see these fast-charging young lieutenants serving with the senior lieutenant who wasn't quite up to speed. It wasn't all his fault, because the Navy to some degree took advantage of this guy by letting him wrestle out in the world for almost two years before even sending him to a ship. But, oh well, that was the breaks of the game, I guess.

I guess we were off the Taussig. I remember I wanted to tell you one more about Taussig. We left Guam in '66, and there was a Polaris ship in there, one of the big boats, big boomers.* And the guy wanted to go out and play ASW for a little bit. So the day that I got under way I had an opportunity to play ASW with one of the big boomers. His rules of the game were simply that, "I am going to let you get contact, and you do all you can to maintain contact, but at 5:00 o'clock in the morning I want you to back off, if you still have contact. And I don't expect you will. At 5:00 in the morning I want you to back off, because I'm going to shoot an air bubble through this missile tube." It wasn't a dummy missile, but they just gave them a big blast of air, I guess.

Well, boy, oh boy. I don't recall exactly what time it was we started, but let's say about 10:00 o'clock in the morning. Would you believe, we couldn't lose contact with that guy. We couldn't. And I had my VDS down. We maintained contact with that guy until 5:00 the next morning, and at 5:00 o'clock the next morning I backed off like my instructions read, and then, of course, he blew his air bubble, etc., and then we steamed on. Now, how hard he tried to break contact, I don't know. I have no idea, but I assume that he tried his damnedest, because we did some violent turns in trying to keep up with him. But I had a VDS, number one, and on that VDS, as well was on the SQS-4, that thing made a big mark on that sonar scope. And we managed to hang on to that guy. I felt kind of cocky in my ASW, I got to tell you. I had a hold on that big mother for that long. That was a good one.

Paul Stillwell: Did you have any contact with the Soviets at all while you were in that ship?

Admiral Gravely: Yes, and I missed that opportunity to tell you, too, because that was one of my highlights, I really believe. At least I consider it a highlight. It was just hopping full of experience. But, anyway, the Soviets had their AGIs out there all the time.† The AGIs had a habit of getting close to, and somehow almost getting in the way. Well, I guess in some instances they got in the way of the carriers, but they constantly followed the carriers around, listened to their communications, and everything else.

---
* The nuclear deterrence submarines of the era carried Polaris ballistic missiles. The nickname for the ballistic missile submarines is "boomers."
† "Tattletail" was a nickname for small Soviet ships designated as AGIs. They steamed in proximity to American warships, observing their movements and, presumably, prepared to provide targeting information in the event the Soviets wanted to attack them.

Normally what we did was we sent a diesel-engine boat or ship somehow to trail them. We didn't have any DERs out there, but we had the ATFs and a couple other diesel ships that could keep up with them and stay with them for some time frame.* When we ran out of those kinds of ships for a short period, we'd then send a DD over. And the DD was to sit there and watch and report and those kinds of things.

Well, during one of the periods over there I had the Gidrofon, which was one of their AGIs, for about three days. Unfortunately, in lying to in a destroyer and turning over once every 30 minutes, or whatever you want to turn over your engines, you have a warping condition in your struts back aft. Engineers are very careful that when you then start up, they want to turn them over very slowly for a while until things sort of settle down, and then you can really get under way and move with no problem.

Well, in sitting there for about three days, we had that condition to arise wherein the engineer wanted to limit the speed. Well, unfortunately, when an ATF came out to relieve me, I felt that I should brief him, so I was all prepared to send my boat over to give them the current ops, tell him what had occurred, and everything else. But, frankly, it was a sort of a young wise lieutenant who said, "I don't need all that crap. Just tell me what went on, and blah, blah, blah." Well, we didn't really argue or anything like that, because lieutenants don't argue with commanders, you know.

But, in any event, I was sort of flabbergasted. And while I was sitting there and nobody was really paying any attention, the Gidrofon slipped off. The Gidrofon was about on the horizon now, and I had to turn him over to this guy who didn't want to accept the responsibility with him on the horizon. So I said, "All right, I'll get him again for you."

So I told my engineer, "I need to go. I've got to go."

He said, "Please don't go more than about 20 knots."

I said, "Screw it. I've got to go get that guy." At this point in time I looked, and the Gidrofon was astern of the carrier. Then I got a message from the carrier group commander which said, "Get him out of there." And, of course, smart salute, and I went up to 22 knots. And you could almost hear the engines going bump, bump, bump, bump. But I got 22 knots piling on to get this guy. I got fairly close to him, and then whipped

---

* ATF—seagoing fleet tugboat.

across his stern at 22 knots, put on left rudder, and then started paralleling his course, just coming in just slightly on him and moving on up his side. And so I was in there, and then I got just a little bit ahead of him—to the point wherein he thought we were going to collide.

He sent me a message that said, "You're maneuvering like a wild man," or some such crap as that. Then the next thing happened, he turned right and came under my stern. I whipped around hard to the right, and I had him trapped right between me and the ATF, which had come over to join us. And we proceeded on like that for about 10 or 15 minutes. He couldn't get out one way or the other, and ultimately I felt he was far enough out of the area that I could turn him over to the ATF. I then proceeded to join the carrier as his plane guard and never saw the Gidrofon again.

Interview Number 5 with Vice Admiral Samuel L. Gravely, Jr., U.S. Navy (Retired)
Place: Admiral Gravely's office in Burke, Virginia
Date: Tuesday, 19 August 1986
Interviewer: Paul Stillwell

Paul Stillwell: Admiral, just to go back a bit, I think there were some things that you wanted to tell me about concerning your time on the Taussig and your promotion to captain.

Admiral Gravely: Yes. Well, shortly after I got promoted to captain, of course, I realized that most destroyers of the type Taussig was did not have a CO who was a four-striper, so I began to wonder just where would I go when I left Taussig and when would I go. I'd been on there for almost two years when it was time to deploy, and I knew that my time was fairly short.

At the same time, I had a commodore who was a captain, and he resented the fact that there were two captains in that squadron—one as commanding officer of a ship, and he, of course, was a captain as the squadron commander. So, one day, while crossing the ship, he told me that he'd called the bureau to find out if they were going to take me off, because he preferred that there be a young commander on board. Apparently the bureau didn't give him any satisfaction, so I decided that I would call the bureau. I called my detailer to find out, if possible, where would I be going and exactly when.

Paul Stillwell: Were you eager to move? Did you want to make that second deployment?

Admiral Gravely: I wasn't eager to move. I was very happy there in the ASW group. I really think I'd found my niche there. I had a real good friend in the group commander, who liked me, who trusted me, and who knew that I was operating the ship as he wanted it operated in that division.

Paul Stillwell: This was Admiral Weymouth?

Admiral Gravely: This was Admiral Weymouth. So I was not concerned about going on a deployment, other than the fact that it was another six or seven months away from home.

Another thing occurred that I should alert you to, and that was that the first black naval ROTC unit in a predominantly black college was being established about that time. Unofficially I'd heard that I was being considered as a commanding officer of that unit. Ultimately, Jerry Thomas went down as exec of that unit, and I was no longer in the running.* When I called the bureau, in fact, I couldn't get the detailer himself. The secretary told me that, yes, I was being taken care of back there, and that I didn't have to worry. She said that SecDef was into my assignment, which really upset me a little bit, because I knew that something special was happening.† I was at that time the first black line captain, but I didn't particularly want any special treatment.‡ I just wanted to be treated as another naval captain and get a set of orders on my merit. Well, in any event, when I got back home after leaving Taussig, my wife and I decided that we would go north and take the Trans-Canadian Highway across, and come on down, because I did have orders which brought me back to Washington, D.C.

Paul Stillwell: Had you had an input to this set of orders, as opposed as going to the NROTC unit?

Admiral Gravely: I didn't have any input at all. No, all I could hear were rumors, and once in a while a friend would say, "Hey, I just heard that you're going to do this, or you're going to do that." The orders were a very, very good set. They were to head of the Naval Satellite Communications Program. Now, there was no problem with that except for the fact that I really was not a PG communicator, although I'd had a couple of

---

* Commander Gerald E. Thomas, USN.
† SecDef—Secretary of Defense.
‡ An unrestricted line officer in the Navy is one whose main concern is with control of forces afloat and is eligible to succeed to command at sea. This distinguishes the individual from members of the staff corps, such as medical, dental, legal, and supply officers. The restricted line includes such specialties as engineering duty, public affairs, and crypto.

tours back in the '50s on two ships, the Toledo and the Iowa, and, of course, ten years later I had had that tour in D.C. Here it just seemed to me that I was being bandied around a little bit back and forth in the communications, but not really enough in communications so that I really had a true grasp of communications. In any event—

Paul Stillwell: It may be useful at this point to just address the question of affirmative action and your philosophy on that.

Admiral Gravely: Well, I'd rather not do it here.

Paul Stillwell: Okay.

Admiral Gravely: I will address it before we're through here.

Paul Stillwell: Sure. But you had this set of orders to Washington, D.C., so then it was a matter of going there from California.

Admiral Gravely: That's right. It was a matter of coming from California to here. Well, en route from California I became depressed, and when I arrived in Washington, D.C., I had real difficulty about going to the Pentagon. I didn't understand it, but my wife took me out to Bethesda, and I was admitted to Bethesda in a depressed condition. Well, I stayed in Bethesda for a couple of months, and ultimately I discovered that the problem was a medication called Reserpine that I was on for my blood pressure. I never will forget that name, because it really had me driven up a wall for a couple of months. And, of course, this was a tough time simply because of the fact that I was going into a fairly new job. I was reporting into a responsible job. At the same time I didn't have a chance to find a house for my wife and kids and things like that. I spent two months in the hospital while she sort of did those things.

Well, in any event, I ultimately got out of the hospital, and I reported to OpNav in a job called OP-94 Echo. It was the head of the Navy's satellite communications program.

Paul Stillwell: Did the doctors find some other medicine that would do the job without the side effects?

Admiral Gravely: Yes, it's quite unfortunate, though, but most of the medications that you take for one kind of an illness seem to have a side effect which gives you another one. Subsequently I was put on another medication. Then one day I discovered that I had diabetic tendencies, and we discovered that that was brought on by the second medication. So I went on another medication. And now I discovered that the medication I'm currently on lowers my potassium. And, of course, I have to take a potassium supplement. But those are the hazards of high blood pressure and the medications that are supposed to treat it.

Paul Stillwell: We talked the last time about the situation where the real estate agent went up to Rhode Island and was seeking your business. Had the climate improved by now, your getting back here to Washington?

Admiral Gravely: The climate had improved a little bit, yes. As a matter of fact, really, my wife went out and found the house we rented, and she had no difficulty at all in finding a place. We moved into North Arlington, into a rather nice and quiet neighborhood. The house was owned by a political appointee to the federal government, and I'm not sure exactly what he was doing at that time. As I recall, he went to Europe for a two-year tour, and I took his house while he was in Europe. We had no problem. We had a good set of neighbors, and everything just went fine with the house. No problem. My kids played little league football. In fact, I became one of the coaches of the team.

Paul Stillwell: You didn't mind that much.

Admiral Gravely: No. We thoroughly enjoyed it; it was a good time for all of us.

Paul Stillwell: Did you make any special effort to do extra study in this area of communications since you didn't have the official PG training?

Admiral Gravely: Well, I did a lot of things. I was able to go around to several of the comm stations. My boss, Admiral Fitzpatrick, was just a top-notch guy, who made sure that I went to Norfolk to talk to the guy who preceded me there, to follow the work that he had done. Whereas I did touch base with my relief prior to my taking over the job, he insisted that I go down to Norfolk.[*] In fact, he was the guy who had taken over as skipper of the Wright, and I went down and talked to him one day. I saw the comm station at Norfolk, and I had fairly good rapport with a group of people over at NavElex.[†] In addition to that, we brought in just a tremendous civilian. A guy by the name of Bob Langeleer, who was my deputy in that department. Bob Langeleer was a guy who had come out of the Army as a captain and was very, very knowledgeable in the area of satellite communications. He made it quite easy for me to become familiar with the job. In fact, he was a good briefer, had original ideas, and the whole gamut of things.

Paul Stillwell: Well, that was pretty new for the Navy overall at that time, so you were probably learning along with the rest of the people.

Admiral Gravely: You're absolutely right for the most part, because trying to get that program through OpNav was probably one of the hardest things I had to do, and it certainly was a good time for me, because I got an awful lot of visibility in that job. In fact, the first thing that I had to do in that job was that the Navy had relied on super high frequency, the SHF, and we had seven terminals which never worked. Not only that, they were huge, monstrous things. The antenna section weighed about 2,500 pounds. So you can imagine the capability of putting these on the ships. In fact, they had only gone on the larger ships. And they constantly failed. So a decision had to be reached as to what do you do about this. And I had the chore of circulating a message through OpNav, and I do mean carrying it by hand, and getting all the chops on it, to kill this SHF

---

[*] Rear Admiral Francis J. Fitzpatrick, USN, Commander Naval Communications Command, and Assistant Chief of Naval Operations (Communications and Cryptology).
[†] NavElex—Naval Electronic Systems Command.

program. In the meantime, with Bob Langeleer there, we then went to the UHF satellite program, which is the one that we have now. There were certain experiments being carried on with various satellites that were put up by Lincoln Lab, by the Air Force, and two or three other groups. We began to join into those programs and managed to really get into it.

Paul Stillwell: Did you work with NASA on this also?

Admiral Gravely: No, I did not work with NASA at all.[*] I did go down and see a couple of launches as a result of being in this program, but I didn't work with NASA at all. The people we worked with were the laboratories. For example, the Naval Ocean Systems Center, which had NELC as I recall, Naval Electronics Laboratory Command, at that time. I met some really good people out there, whom I know today. The NavElex people worked as a team. Even more so, I think, than ultimately we did.

Paul Stillwell: Did you deal with some of the private firms in this like ComSat or RCA?

Admiral Gravely: Dealt with a lot of them—RCA, TRW, and a lot of the private concerns, but you have to be very careful, particularly if you're on active duty. There's always the possibility of conflict of interest. Certainly there's no conflict when you go out and see the program, etc. But then you've got to watch the lunches and the cocktail parties and the other things that go along with it. In fact, I got some very, very valuable guidance from Admiral Fitzpatrick concerning that. Basically it was "Avoid the appearance of evil." And I have never forgotten that. "Avoid the appearance of evil." It happened because I was invited to an oyster roast by my contractor. I went to see him, to ask if he thought it was all right. He just simply said, "Avoid the appearance of evil," and I knew that wasn't the right thing to do. I have never forgotten that.

Well, the Navy satellite communications program at that time was rather frustrating. I decided one morning that I'd had enough, that I'd served a good 20 years, over 20 years, that probably I should retire and try to do something else. I put in my

---

[*] NASA—National Aeronautics and Space Administration.

retirement papers. I worked—and I should have said this—I worked really for two admirals. I worked for an admiral by the name of Bill Moran in that I was attached to his staff under the space program, of course, since satellites were under the space program, and Fitzpatrick as a communicator.[*] So I ran between two bosses.

I first handed my retirement letter to Admiral Moran, who sort of said, "Hey, I'm going to keep this in my desk for a couple of days, and a couple days later if you still think that way, we'll forward it on up."

He held it for two or three days, and then he decided to send it to Fitzpatrick, who called me down one day. He said, "Sam," he said, "I want you go fishing. And I want you to fish for four or five days, take leave, and then come back let me know how you feel about this." And he said, "I want you to remember one thing about fishing, that the purpose of fishing is not to catch fish." [Laughter] And, of course, I went off and frankly came back with renewed vigor after about four days.

Paul Stillwell: Which is what he had hoped.

Admiral Gravely: I don't whether he hoped that or not. In fact, I'm sure he did, because I really admired Admiral Fitzpatrick, and I think he was fairly happy with the job I was doing, knowing that my condition for at least the first part of that tour wasn't top-notch. In any event, I came back and I just went down there to Fitzpatrick and said, "Sir, if you don't mind giving me back that letter, I know what to do with it today." And I threw it in the wastebasket.

Well, I stayed there for about 15, 16 months. Then one day I got the magic call from the bureau, which said that I had been selected for major command. And you can imagine that I was overjoyed to get this news.

Paul Stillwell: Before we get into that, I wonder if you could address more of the substance of the satellite program, the kinds of things that had to be done to put it in place, the hardware and training, and all that sort of thing.

---

[*] Rear Admiral William J. Moran, Director, Navy Space Program Division, OpNav.

Admiral Gravely: Well, first of all, so far as the hardware was concerned, we didn't have any. So basically we had to manage to put in our R&D program funds to get some R&D hardware, and we used that R&D hardware actually for operational use at times.[*]

Paul Stillwell: Did that money come begrudgingly out of the budget?

Admiral Gravely: It was difficult to get, let's say that. I can remember briefing Admiral Cousins.[†] I briefed the Secretary of the Navy; it was Chafee.[‡] And I briefed a couple of hundred people on this program. It was a very, very difficult program for the Navy to really grasp. We could see it doing just simply great things for communications, but as I've always felt, communications doesn't go bang, and it doesn't make any wave through the water. It's a way of doing things, and the only time communicators really are able to even be seen or heard is not when they've sent a message perfectly, but when one has been missed. And you really get the noise from that. So, whereas it's new programs that have to do with armament, or arms, those kinds of things, you can generally convince somebody you need it, and you can keep, to some extent, the old program going along until everybody can see that.

One of the hard things about a new program in communications, you first must sacrifice the old to get the new. And so what do you do in the meantime? It was that kind of a thing: trying to shuffle dollars from where you're going to repair and maintain old equipment to buying new equipment. We had some tough people in OpNav in those days. They were good people. I think they sympathized with me, but at the same time it was, "We've got to keep the ships armed, and, okay, we'll communicate as best we can." It was that kind of a feeling.

Paul Stillwell: Was there any connection with electronic warfare in your job at all?

---

[*] R&D—research and development.
[†] Vice Admiral Ralph W. Cousins, USN, was Deputy Chief of Naval Operations (Fleet Operations and Readiness).
[‡] John H. Chafee served as Secretary of the Navy from 31 January 1969 to 4 May 1972.

Admiral Gravely: No, none with electronic warfare. When you say none, that's wrong too. But I and the electronic warfare people didn't work together, if that's what you mean.

Paul Stillwell: You have to avoid mutual interference for one thing.

Admiral Gravely: Avoiding mutual interference, and providing the Navy with anti-jam communications. So from that aspect, we got into it a little bit. But, for the most part, electronic warfare is handled by an entirely different section.

Well, getting the news that I had been selected for my major command was probably the happiest news I'd received in a long time, so I just looked forward to what somebody would decide that I should get. Well, shortly after that I got a second call, and that call had to do with the fact that I'd been selected to go to the Jouett, DLG-29 at that time.* I think it's CG-29 now. But I began to look at Jouett from the aspect of op schedule and those kinds of things. When I discovered that I was going there, I became a little disappointed, because the Jouett was scheduled to go through a yard overhaul for a year, and it was a modernization program. It was to get the fleet flag modernization and several other innovations that would take a year.

Well, I talked to my detailer again, and he said, "Well, I've got to tell you, you were specifically picked to go to that job, because we wanted a guy with a little knowledge of electronics." And, of course, that was about all I had was a little knowledge, but in any event, going back to sea I was quite pleased with. So I just sort of eagerly awaited the day that the orders would arrive. Well, the orders arrived, and they shocked me a little bit, although I can easily see now why they read that way. But here I was, going to a ship that had a Terrier missile, it had the ASROC, it had nuclear capability, and I ended up with five days of damage control school.† And that concerned

---

* USS Jouett (DLG-29), a Belknap-class guided missile frigate, was commissioned 3 December 1966. She had a standard displacement of 7,900 tons, was 547 feet long, 55 feet in the beam, and had a maximum draft of 29 feet. Her top speed was 33 knots. She was equipped with a twin launcher for Terrier missiles, one 5-inch gun, ASROC, and six torpedo tubes. She was reclassified as a guided missile cruiser, CG-29, on 30 June 1975. The ship was eventually decommissioned and stricken from the Navy Register on 28 January 1994.
† ASROC—antisubmarine rocket. It entered the fleet in the early 1960s in new-construction ships and in FRAM I destroyer conversions.

me a little bit. I said, "Here I'm going out driving this new vessel, and I know nothing about the main battery here." But, after all, it was going into the yards for a year, and so obviously when I got there that would be the major thing that I'd be worried about, was making sure no fires, flooding, those kinds of things in the ship. So, after I looked at it, I was very happy about it.

I went to Philadelphia. I took their five weeks' damage control—fire-fighting school, really—and then went on out to San Diego. Now, I had a home in San Diego, but it was rented and in fairly good shape. So I decided not to go in my home, but rather to rent a place out in San Diego, which we did. There were no quarters available at that time, at least none available at the moment that I really needed them. So we took a home in Chula Vista, where we lived for the time I was on Jouett.

Paul Stillwell: Where was the ship in the yard?

Admiral Gravely: Well, that's the amazing part about it. By the time I got to Jouett, the shipyard plans had changed. Jouett had to be made ready to deploy in October, and, as I recall, I relieved sometime in May.* Now, the ship had come back from a deployment something like about January or February, so knowing that they were going to the yards, they'd made a considerable amount of preparation for going to the yard. They basically stayed alongside the pier. They had inspections and those kinds of things.

Well, on reporting and finding out that we weren't going to yards, and in addition to that, we were going to deploy, it meant first of all that there would be a couple of fleet operations. In fact, you had to almost complete your yearly schedule of exercises, because you certainly didn't get a chance to do many of those out in WestPac. So we put together a fast schedule to see what could we get out of the roughly three months that we had to work, because we knew that for a ship deploying in October that you would have your month's stay in port getting ready to deploy, September, which gave me really June, July, and August to do that.

Paul Stillwell: I'll bet you weren't disappointed with that change in plans.

---

* Captain Gravely commanded the Jouett from 22 May 1970 to 2 June 1971.

Admiral Gravely: I was not disappointed the least bit, and I was not disappointed that we had to really do some work during those next three months.

Paul Stillwell: Well, that was probably a good training period for you too.

Admiral Gravely: It was a beautiful training period for me, because we went in and out of San Diego, and I began to compare the maneuverability of Jouett with Taussig, and frankly I found Jouett much easier to handle from all respects. Just a beautiful ship. I loved it. I loved the ship handling with it. I can remember the first time we came back into San Diego after being out in the op area for three or four days. We were coming back in and had to go alongside the foot of Broadway. We took a pilot aboard as normal and had a tug standing by. For some reason, the pilot and my exec began a conversation up on the wing of the bridge there, and I kept waiting for the pilot to say, "Well, do you want me to take it?" And he never said it. So I just drove it on in alongside, and, boy, that really built my confidence up to where it should have been. And it was no problem. The pilot complimented me as well, and I was very happy with that.

Paul Stillwell: Did you get any kind of an availability period to compensate for not having the yard?

Admiral Gravely: We got an availability period up in Long Beach and spent, oh, three or four weeks, I've forgotten. We went to the dry dock. There was a spoke in the sonar dome on us for some reason,

Paul Stillwell: You knew about those.

Admiral Gravely: For some reason I always get these spoky sonar domes. When we went up there, they repaired the sonar and everything else. Of course, this meant another trip into Seal Beach, and out and back in, the whole bit. The only major exercise I can remember was one which we had with the First Fleet. Of course, the First Fleet was in San Diego at that point in time, and Admiral Isaac Kidd was the fleet commander.[*]

Paul Stillwell: Did you have any personal contact with him?

Admiral Gravely: I'll tell you about it. Yes, I did. This fleet exercise had in it, as I recall, at least two DLGs, and it had a cruiser also in for First Fleet's flagship. Admiral Art Esch ran the exercise, basically, for First Fleet.[†] But First Fleet wanted to go out and observe, and he did not want to be aboard his flagship. So I discovered that, and so I put a bug in the ear of one of First Fleet's people, and said that we would be very happy to take him aboard Jouett since he was sort of looking around for a typical flagship. Well, he took me up on my offer, and came aboard and rode the ship for four days. I think I made a credible impression on Admiral Kidd, because it was my understanding that a year later he sat on my selection board. So I didn't do things too badly.

Paul Stillwell: What are your impressions of him?

Admiral Gravely: Well, Admiral Kidd was a very, very knowledgeable guy, who wanted things done immediately. He also had sort of a supervisory nature in that I can remember transferring a missile, and I almost thought he was in the way of my people who were making the transfer, because he was right down there. [Chuckle] Not really screaming or shouting or anything like that, but giving a few orders here and a few orders there. I liked the guy, I really did. He had a very, very good staff. His ops officer made flag rank the same time I did. His chief of staff was a guy by the name of Thomas, who subsequently made flag rank, and Rich Fontaine, who made flag.[‡] So he had a top-notch staff. Very good people, very knowledgeable, never in the way, always just doing the job, and they did it well.

---

[*] Vice Admiral Isaac C. Kidd, Jr., USN, served as Commander First Fleet from 30 September 1969 to 1 August 1970.
[†] Rear Admiral Arthur G. Esch, USN, Commander Cruiser-Destroyer Flotilla 11.
[‡] Commander Richard K. Fontaine, USN; Captain John M. Thomas, USN.

Paul Stillwell: Do you have any specific recollections of the exercise?

Admiral Gravely: Well, the best one that I remember was that we had a phase in there wherein we were shooting missiles. And I've forgotten the name of the DLG, which unfortunately couldn't fire her missiles, so I got a chance to fire about twice my allowance for that exercise, as I recall about 16. And, frankly, that was the first time I'd ever seen a missile go off. You know, I'd been down to NASA, and I'd seen them launch down there, but that was quite an experience for me. In a DLG-class ship the CIC is usually where the captain does the conning from; the exec's out on the bridge. But for that exercise I had to change that, because I had to see the missiles go off and everything else.

Paul Stillwell: Did you later adjust and take up station in CIC?

Admiral Gravely: Well, I did, but I didn't particularly care for CIC. I always thought the commanding officer had the best eyeballs on the ship, and he ought to be out there where he could use them, and so I spent most of my time in both my commands on the bridge. And, frankly, I think it paid off for me ultimately, but we'll get into that a little later.

There was nothing unusual about the events around San Diego at that point in time. And, of course, we took off and sailed to WestPac. As I recall, we went alone, independently, with a stop in Pearl, where we stayed for two days. I went up to CinCPacFlt, got various briefings, and those kinds of things. And from there we went to Guam, wherein we had a fuel stop. And from Guam on into Subic, where we off-loaded and on-loaded our equipment and took our helicopters aboard. First trip to the line, and I may be getting these a little confused, but we went out as a PIRAZ ship.*

Paul Stillwell: Maybe you could explain in more detail what that entailed.

---

* The NTDS-based system was called positive identification radar advisory zone, almost always known by the acronym PIRAZ. For details, see Garette E. Lockee, "PIRAZ," U.S. Naval Institute Proceedings, April 1969, pages 143-146. The article includes a photo of an NTDS console.

Admiral Gravely: Okay. The PIRAZ ship was the guy who set up about medium way up north off Vietnam. He was responsible for the positive identification of any contact that came into the Tonkin Gulf. Normally you had either a group commander or a very senior commodore who was aboard, who basically was responsible for the ops up there, but the CO certainly was his right-hand man. So whenever anybody had any kind of a contact, it all came into Jouett, who evaluated it and made a decision on friendly or foe, etc. And we had a pretty good, pretty sharp radar group on board. And also ASW. We were the number-one ship up there, really, so far as I could tell.

Paul Stillwell: Who did you have on board as admiral?

Admiral Gravely: Well, I had two commodores, and frankly, their names escape me at this moment. I never had the admiral aboard. It was always the guy who relieved me who brought up the admiral. I will think of all of their names later, but Art Esch was certainly one of the admirals. Jouett's time, and we were there three times, there was nothing unusual except, I guess, the first time there, when they tried to release the prisoners up there at Son Tay.[*]

I was called down to Task Force 77's flagship, so I got in a helicopter and went down there. While I was down there, I developed what was called Plan Jouett. And Plan Jouett was basically an idea wherein the Jouett would go in as close ashore as possible, with all radars, everything all tuned, everything lit off, then turn, come out in the dark, gradually cutting off things as the range increased to where nothing was heard, and then zip back and just let go. And, of course, we'd have the airplanes in there too. But that plan was never used, and I'm not sure why.

One of the other things I should say about Jouett is that when I got aboard the—not mascot, but the little thing that you always put on your flags and everything else—was a jayhawk. Jouett, of course, somebody thought in terms of jayhawk, the little bird. Well, I discovered what the jayhawk was one day. It's just a little bird that preyed on other birds, and I didn't think that that was a proper name, or whatever the word is. So I

---

[*] On 20 November 1970 a U.S. commando force landed at the Son Tay prison, 23 miles west of Hanoi, North Vietnam, in an attempt to free U.S. prisoners of war reported to be held there. The commandos did not recover any POWs, because they had been moved to another location shortly before.

changed it, and we became the Jouett Jaguars, with a flag and everything to match. And I thought, frankly, that the spirit soared as the result of being connected with a beast like the jaguar vice being a small jayhawker. And, of course, we had our little tricks of the trade that we would be in on an unrep, make a nice fast approach, stay in until you were topped off, then you cut the lines, and, of course, you would break away at 25 knots, hoisting the flag with a little music for the troops on the other side. Little innovative things like that, which kept the spirits of the group going.

We had a couple of incidents, and I can't think exactly at which times these were, but normally on PIRAZ station you had a max gun destroyer with you. And that destroyer, of course, was usually one with six 5-inch/38s. We got to the point wherein we had DEs at times.

One of my favorite ones was that we were refueling one day when we got word that there was a contact sort of to the north and east of us about 30 miles away. I sent the helicopter, which had been flying around anyway at that time, to investigate. The helicopter reported on the radio that he was within about five miles of this contact, but it appears that if the contact had guns on it, and did we want him to go any closer. So I decided not to send him any closer to it, to come on back, and that as soon as we finished refueling we could come over there and investigate it ourselves.

So I put my max gun destroyer at 500 yards astern of me and went charging over there at 25 knots. And we got over there and it was a Chinese merchantman. It was completely white. I, of course, had my two ships at general quarters and we were all ready to go. I went alongside at about, oh, 120 feet or so, and we took pictures and those kinds of things. I was always sort of apprehensive that there was something pointed at me, and I couldn't quite make out what it was. I was always concerned afterwards that the first clap of thunder, and I think I would have let him have it. And I think he would have let me have it too. Well, it was all over, and I broke away, and dragged the destroyer right alongside so he could take a look as well.

Paul Stillwell: Did you ever see any guns actually on board this vessel?

Admiral Gravely: It didn't look like guns, but he had something that looked almost like a stovepipe that some guy stood behind.

Paul Stillwell: Like a mortar?

Admiral Gravely: Yes, like a mortar, yeah. That was probably what it was. And that thing was pointed at my bridge, and I could constantly see it aimed at my eyeballs, for some reason, every time I looked over there. But we were ready for bear if anything had happened.

Paul Stillwell: The U.S. had had this on-again, off-again bombing program on North Vietnam. What phase was it in when you were there?

Admiral Gravely: Well, we were still bombing, and bombing quite seriously at that point. They still had the ships down south doing some shore bombardment as well.

Paul Stillwell: So your job was to track these raids?

Admiral Gravely: Yes, track raids in and out, and make sure nothing followed them out, really. You were looking for everything out there. I guess, as I said, they had the prisoner thing during that time frame too, but I didn't get unusually involved in it or extraordinarily involved in it.

Paul Stillwell: Typically, ships like that get a lot of talent, both in the wardroom and enlisted. How was it on board the Jouett?

Admiral Gravely: Well, I thought frankly that we had probably one of the most competent wardrooms that I'd ever been associated with. Now, when you think in terms of I'd served on cruisers and I'd served on battleships, both times it was during Korea and the phase-down of Korea. You still had a lot of reservists and things like that. I had more regular Navy officers who were dedicated to being in the Navy, and who were going to make a career out of it. I did have two execs while I was on there, and both of them made captain. One was Nicholas Brown, and I'm sure you know who Nicholas Brown is.*

Paul Stillwell: The famous family.†

Admiral Gravely: Yes. Nicholas Brown, who was just an outstanding officer. The other exec, Zeke Newcomb, went down to Charleston, and he had command of a destroyer down there, did well.‡ Both of these former execs retired as captains, and both were just outstanding people. Good engineering group. I had one guy that ultimately I fired, but it was to some degree not because of his incompetence as much as the fact there was some disagreement with philosophy. I believed that every line officer should spend time on the bridge. This guy had been trained as a nuclear engineer, and he had failed the program, but he was a very good MPA, despite the fact he'd failed that nuclear program.§

Unfortunately, he made a couple of mistakes. One was he had no leadership qualities whatsoever. He couldn't give an order like "Right standard rudder" or anything like that. He knew how to fix the valves, but that was about all he could do. The major thing that happened was while we were in Long Beach. This was in his purview really, because we were supposed to get a boiler inspection before we left. He made arrangements for the CruDesPac boiler inspection team to come up and inspect our boilers. They arrived on a Monday morning, and they were there for about 30 minutes or so. I got word that they wanted to see me, so I had them up to the cabin. They said, "Captain, we came up from CruDesPac to inspect your boilers, and the boilers are not ready for the inspection."

I said, "Well, I'm sure if this is a surprise, they're not."

He said, "Oh, no. Your MPA had scheduled this about three weeks ago, and so we're going to have to give you an unsat."

---

* Commander Nicholas Brown, USN.
† The Brown family is prominent in Rhode Island and has a strong connection with Brown University in Providence. The father of the Jouett's executive officer was John Nicholas Brown, who served in the Navy in World War I and was later Assistant Secretary of the Navy for Air from 1946 to 1949.
‡ Commander Zeanious L. Newcomb, USN.
§ MPA—Main propulsion assistant.

I said, "Well, let me find the MPA and talk to him." Well, my engineer, who normally would have been there, had been sent down to San Diego for a short five-day course. It would have been no problem for the MPA to hack it, except the MPA wasn't there. And nobody knew where the MPA was. So I, of course, told them that, well, I had to accept the unsat, but I assured them that we'd have them back up in short order, and those boilers would be ready.

They left, and I guess it was about 11:00 o'clock I began to just take a routine stroll around the deck. And whom should I see but my MPA, who was walking a young lady around, giving her a tour of the ship. So he came up and he said, "Captain, I'd like you to meet my girlfriend. She came in from Brooklyn over the weekend, and she's staying so and so, and I'm taking her out to the airport to catch her plane back at about 2:00 o'clock, or something like that."

I just said, "Yes." I said, "When you get back, you might come in and see me." Well, at about 3:00 o'clock he came in to see me. By that time I had all his bags packed and sent him on down to CruDesPac. He had scheduled this inspection and then forgot about it, and in the meantime his girlfriend was much more important to him than the ship. So I just decided that I couldn't use him any longer. Not only that, I'd already given up on him on leadership and trying to get him up on the bridge. So I sent him down there.

My commodore, Stickles, whereas he sympathized with me, I know he felt that the guy should have been tried in another department.[*] Well, your OODs and things generally come from the weapons department, and he was not going to make an OOD; that was no place for him. Operations didn't want him. Nobody wanted him, so even though we disagreed, I got rid of him.

Paul Stillwell: This was the period shortly after you took command when Admiral Zumwalt became CNO and then started the program of Z-Grams.[†] What impact did they

---

[*] Captain Albert L. Stickles, USN.
[†] Z-grams were consecutively numbered policy directives from the Chief of Naval Operations, Admiral Elmo R. Zumwalt, Jr., USN. The Z-grams attempted to deal with such issues as enlisted rights and privileges, equal opportunity, and Navy families. Junior personnel viewed them much more favorably than did their seniors. See U.S. Naval Institute Proceedings, May 1971, pages 293-298.

have at the shipboard level?

Admiral Gravely: Well, Z-Grams, like any other messages generally, are interpreted by the officers, and it is handed down or not handed down depending on where it applied. I think it was Z-Gram 66 that affected us more than anything. Z-Gram 66 had to do with racial discrimination. The commodore sent out a message to all of the ships asking what were they doing to implement Z-Gram 66. One guy sent back a message which just really upset me. And I can't recall exactly what the tone was, but I do know that as a result of that I wrote a letter to the Naval Institute Proceedings, and it was published.[*] His views on integration were just so contrary to what I thought the norm was, not less what a CO's should be, that I thought I took him to task.

Well, anyway, I didn't have any racial problems on board my ship. Nicholas Brown was a man who believed that a man was a man, was a man. And Zeke Newcomb, my second exec, felt about the same way. They wanted to carry out my policies, and as best we could discuss them and do it, they did it. I was the commanding officer of that ship. Nobody doubted that. I didn't go around bragging about it, but I think in my walk and my nature of doing business, people knew that I was fully in charge. So there was never, never any problem.

How about the little fellow? It's one you might want to know about, the little fellow. I think that most of the little fellows felt that they were treated fairly aboard Jouett. I would hear of one or two minor incidences, and we'd investigate these things, and it was sort of a cum-ci, cum-ca thing. But never anything major. Okay.

Paul Stillwell: One of the problems for COs of that era was the feeling that the CNO was going around the chain of command, rather than down through it. In effect, giving rights to people that should ordinarily come from their own command.

Admiral Gravely: Well, you're absolutely right there, but, frankly, I didn't get that feeling aboard ship. I got that feeling more after I got into the CNO staff, and I did get

---

[*] Rear Admiral Samuel L. Gravely, Jr., USN, "Equal Opportunity in the Navy," U.S. Naval Institute Proceedings, August 1971, pages 91-93.

into the CNO staff about a year later. I began to see it, I guess, from a different perspective, and I thought that COs were being trampled on a little bit. But, then again, you know, when your boss man says do something, you do it to the best of your ability.

Now, I think that so far as Admiral Zumwalt is concerned, whom I admire, I felt that that was one of the problems. Admiral Zumwalt was instituting some new policies, which a lot of people felt they could drag their feet on, and when he sort of chomped down, they still dragged their feet, and so it was just an impossible situation. If you as a four-star can't get three-stars to carry out your orders, you're in trouble. And, of course, as we all know, there was trouble during the regime.

I don't think the young black guy, for example, was reading Z-Grams. He might have heard this or heard that, but the effect wasn't as great as I think some people think that it was. I do know that there were the race riots.* I didn't have any of those on Jouett, but a couple of ships did have race riots during that period. They began to appear about that time, but I think it was more from the new guy who'd had a certain amount of what he called freedom on the outside, who, despite the fact he had those same things in the Navy, found it hard to adjust to the discipline. For example, like 10:00 o'clock there's bed call. Or in the morning there's reveille. Well, you know, you're free to do a lot of things, but on board a ship you're not free to not get up at 6:00 o'clock in the morning, you know.

Paul Stillwell: Your petty officers can make an enormous difference in that kind of a situation.

Admiral Gravely: That's true. The petty officers can, and petty officers did. I can't give you a set answer for some of those things, and maybe I can talk a little bit more about them from the flag view, when I got to be a flag officer.

---

* Racial disturbances broke out in the carrier Kitty Hawk (CVA-63) on 12 October 1972; in the oiler Hassayampa (AO-145) on 16 October 1972; and in the carrier Constellation (CVA-64) on 3 November 1972. See Captain Paul B. Ryan, USN (Ret.), "USS Constellation Flare-up: Was it Mutiny?" U.S. Naval Institute Proceedings, January 1976, pages 46-53.

Paul Stillwell: Well, evidently, what you're saying, though, is that you didn't have any uproar of people on board your ship demanding rights as a result of these Z-Grams. You handled things through your chiefs and petty officers.

Admiral Gravely: I continued to handle things through my chiefs and my petty officers and those kind of people. And I think the people knew that's the way I wanted to handle things. In fact, I know it. I missed one thing earlier, and that is that, as I said before, this ship spent about four months in San Diego after having come back from a deployment. So there was lots of leave, lots of liberty, and lots of other things. And you get out of the habit of cleaning the ship daily and those kinds of things. You think about that when you're operating, but you don't think about that when liberty goes every day at noon.

Paul Stillwell: Right.

Admiral Gravely: Well, I'd been aboard for about three or four days, and I didn't raise any fuss or stink or anything else. But things weren't just quite the way I thought they should be. So I took about a day, and I inspected the entire ship. The next morning, right after quarters, I called all my officers together, from the exec down. I had them in the wardroom. We had a long discussion about what I thought was wrong with that ship, where I thought people weren't doing the job, and those kinds of things. Then, after I finished that, then I went down to the chiefs' quarters. I got all the chiefs together, and I gave them basically the same story. Then I said, "I better carry this on down further." So I got all the first class petty officers together, and we discussed where I felt the ship ought to be going, what should be done, what was the problem.

It was amazing to me the number the people who sort of shook their head, because they'd been seeing these things every day, but nobody had really paid any attention to them. I think they were a little amazed that here I come on there, a new guy, and in four or five days could find all this out. But, anyway, we got it squared away.

I had a chief petty officer who was probably one of the most outstanding chief petty officers I've seen in the Navy. A tremendous guy, and he was a black guy. Everybody on that ship had a tremendous amount of respect for him. He was an electrician. I went down into his spaces, and I discovered that the guy had a bad leg and hadn't been down to those spaces in three months. You can imagine how embarrassed he was when I pointed this out to him, and how embarrassed the electrical officer and engineer officer were when they found this out. But they hadn't been down there either. So we got a movement afoot to clean that bucket up, I got to tell you, in short order. And I'd had my experience in cleaning up ships from my good experience on board Chandler.

Paul Stillwell: I think this is almost inevitable with a new CO, that he's going to have a somewhat different set of priorities from the previous one, and the crew responds.

Admiral Gravely: The crew responds to that set of priorities when he lets it be known. Now, we could have continued on for four or five more months under the same set of directives, basically. But I just had to let them know that I expected better of guys who were being paid to do jobs, and they did respond. There's no doubt in my mind.

Paul Stillwell: Was there any laxity from the operational sense, from having been alongside the pier for a number of months?

Admiral Gravely: I think that there might have been a little bit, but people began to realize the seriousness of operating a ship under way, and they hadn't forgotten anything. They may be a little lax, but very quickly it all comes back, and they go ahead and do the job.

One of the bright spots of the tour was a young man whose father was Rembrandt Robinson, young Robinson.* One of the finest and most impressive young officers I've ever really had occasion to meet.† After firing my MPA, we got orders on a young officer who happened to have been in San Diego. This was the Robinson I'm talking about. He was at engineering school in San Diego. So when I got the orders, I called the engineer up, and said, "Hey, we have a new MPA coming, and he's right here in San

---

* Rear Admiral Rembrandt C. Robinson, USN, was a member of the Chairman's Staff Group in the office of the Chairman of the Joint Chiefs of Staff. On 8 May 1972, while serving as Commander Cruiser-Destroyer Flotilla 11, Robinson was killed in a helicopter crash in the Tonkin Gulf.
† The son was Ensign John Gregory Robinson, USN, who had graduated from the Naval Academy in the class of 1970.

Diego. I want you to go over and meet him, and find out what kind of fellow he is, and also tell him that we're deploying, I think, the second of October. And I want to make sure that if there's any gear that he wants us to take out, that it's aboard, and that we'll take it for him. And, secondly, there might be a possibility for him to come over and watch you light off just before getting under way." And so the engineering officer did that. And I guess we'd been under way for about an hour or so, and I happened to see the engineer and said, "Oh, how'd Robinson look to you?"

He said, "Well, he's a fine young officer, and I told him what you said about bringing his gear aboard."

I said, "Did he bring anything?"

He said, "Well, he sent his golf clubs."

And I said, "Oh my God, what am I getting?" [Laughter] That's the only thing he sent. But anyway, young Robinson did come aboard while we were out in WestPac, and I was just most pleased. Here was a young ensign, he was a Naval Academy graduate of that year, who in probably about I would say roughly three months' time I was able to have him and be proud to have as a special sea detail OOD—in fact, all special evolutions. I had no fear whatsoever that that young man handled the ship. He was just that good. I subsequently told his father about it, and I'll tell you about that too. I had Deutermann's son as an ops officer.

Paul Stillwell: Pete Deutermann.*

Admiral Gravely: Pete Deutermann.

Paul Stillwell: He made captain recently.

Admiral Gravely: He made captain recently. Pete was about ready to retire, I believe. He didn't feel he'd had a fair shake, and I hope I talked him out of it; in fact, I think I did. I was trying to think of a couple of the other young good officers that I had. I

---

* Lieutenant Peter T. Deutermann, USN. His father was Vice Admiral Harold T. Deutermann, USN (Ret.).

unfortunately had the young officer who ran the ship aground in Norfolk. What do they call that one? The hydrofoil.

Paul Stillwell: PHM?

Admiral Gravely: Yes, the PHM. I can't think of his name. He was my fire control officer, and was a real fine officer. In fact, he was good enough that he came in to be SecNav's PAO for a couple of tours. Did a bang-up job. But unfortunately had that occurrence down in Norfolk, and there, except there for the grace of God, go I.

One other incident I should tell you that occurred. I mentioned briefly about that first NROTC unit down at Prairie View. Well, there was a young naval officer by the name of Gordon Fisher, a young black officer, who I continually bumped heads with. In fact, I'm his sea daddy, as he calls me. But he went down there as an instructor on that staff, and in the fall of '70 was in San Diego as ops officer on a ship there. He came by my house that day, and brought with him four of the new graduates out of the first program down there. They were going to ships, and the squadrons, etc. And, of course, they were at my house. We had them in for hot dogs or something like that, and I never really expected to see them again.

But one day, while I was on line out there in WestPac, I got a message from a ship, which was my shotgun. It said that he was aboard, and he would like to come over and see the ship. Well, the normal circumstance was that the PIRAZ ship, being much more modern than the old DDs, which these guys were on, we would send the helicopter over in the morning and bring over one or two officers, and let them stay aboard all day, and let them go around, walk around, and see things and everything else.

Well, since I knew this guy and had met him, I sent a message to the commanding officer and said, "I understand So-and-so is aboard. Would appreciate it if you would let him come over for a day as my guest. I'd be happy to take care of him and send him back the next morning." The CO agreed and sent him over. Well, while I was on the bridge waiting for this young ensign to come aboard, I was wondering, "Now, what do I really do with this guy?" Because I really wanted to do something special for him, to be honest with you. So I thought about it, and finally it dawned on me. I had a young officer, white, who was my assistant CIC officer. Sharp as a tack. I really didn't know about this guy.

So I said, "Well, what I will do is I will bring this young assistant CIC ops officer up, and I'll put the two of them together." And I did, and I told them, "Listen, I want you to take this guy around, and I want him to be with you for the next 24 hours, except for a couple of times." I said, "He's going to be my guest, so for dinner tonight. I'll have him up at my in-port cabin for dinner, and, of course, after the movie, then he can sleep in my in-port cabin. I'll sleep here. But the rest of the time I want him with you, standing watches, the whole bit." And he did.

Well, everything went along fine with that part of the program. My habit was that I got up every morning about 5:30. I'd come out to the bridge, and if I hadn't had any calls or even if I had calls, I'd get a rundown from the CDO, talk to the CIC people, talk to my bridge people, etc. Then sixish I'd go down to the in-port cabin, and I'd read all the traffic, the Fox files, etc. And, of course, shortly thereafter the steward would come up and I'd have breakfast, then I'd go back to the bridge. Well, on this particular morning I did my normal routine, and about 6:15 the steward came in, and I was reading. He said, "Captain, would you like your breakfast this morning?"

I said, "Well, I've got guests, remember. I'll wait until the guests arrive." Of course, my guest was behind this closed door. Well, 6:30, he wasn't up; 6:45, he wasn't up; 7:00 o'clock, he wasn't up. At 7:15 I just could not take it any longer. I just never believed that ensigns should sleep that late, so I went banging on the door, and called and told him it was time for breakfast. Of course, he got up, came on in after dressing.

Well, we began to discuss a little bit about his job, how did he like it, and what was he doing. It turned out he was the electronics material officer. So I said to him, "Do you have any gear down?" Well, I'm not sure exactly how many of pieces of gear this destroyer had on it, but he had 90% of his gear down. And I said, "My God, how do you guys operate over there?" I said, "For Christ sakes, I've got two radio electricians on board. I've got three or four chiefs. I've got the whole works. I would have sent people over there."

"He said, "Well, we didn't want to worry you."

I said, "Don't give me that. How about MOTU"* Well, he didn't know anything about MOTU. He just religiously reported all this gear down every day. In any event, I gave him a little lecture. Told him I'd help him find MOTU, etc., and told him I'd send some people over to help him with his work. I said, "What's your routine like on that ship?"

He said, "Well, what do you mean?"

I said, "Well, what time do you eat breakfast?"

He said, "Well, I usually go in the wardroom about 7:15."

I said, "Well, where's the captain when you get there?"

He said, "Oh, the captain's sitting there about ready to finish his breakfast."

I said, "Well, what do you do next?"

He said, "Well, I sit there until it's time for quarters, then I go out and muster my people and make my report to the department head. And then I go to the EMO shack, and I start whatever work I have to do."†

I said, "Well, listen. Why don't you change your routine a little bit? What I would like to see you do tomorrow morning is that when the captain comes down to breakfast—and I don't care what time the captain gets down there—I want you in there about ready to finish your breakfast. And when you finish your breakfast, I want you to get up and go to the EMO shack. And the captain's going to say to you, 'Where are you going?' And you tell him that you are going back to the EMO shack to lay out your work for the day." And, you know, I told him a couple of other things. Well, anyway, that's the way it happened.

About three months later I happened to see the commanding officer in Subic, and he said, "What the hell did you do to that young man?"—I can't think of his name right now.

I said, "I didn't do anything to him. I talked to him a little bit."

He said, "That guy is doing so well now until I'm thinking about sending him to comm school when we get back, and he would be my communications officer." Well, I've always said that here's a guy who came from a small town in Texas, wherein when

---

* MOTU—mobile technical unit.
† EMO—electronics material officer.

he graduated from midshipman school, or from college, really, and got his commission and went back there and had that gold bar on. And he probably bought himself a car; he was the biggest man in that town. And so he became an overseer. And his idea of overseeing was that, "Hey, I'll go down and see what the people are doing at about 8:00 o'clock. I'll go back and rest a little bit, and right after lunch I'll go back down there again and check on them." And that was about the way he expected to run that ship. But I think he got the idea that he was not really an overseer—that it was his damn job. [Laughter] And I think from there he really improved. Now, this guy really got turned around as a result of that day over there, and was a success until something else happened to him. One day he was on board inspecting the ship. The captain for him and said, "I notice you are inspecting the ship. There are a couple of things I want you to do differently."

"Captain, I've been working this ship for two COs before you, and this procedure worked well for them. I think they'll work well for you."

"So change your procedure."

He said, "Captain, I disagree." And the captain fired him. He was never the same after that. You do things the way the CO wants you to, no matter what he tells you. Well, if things are going to happen to people, they happen to those kinds of guys.

Paul Stillwell: I think the time you spent advising him is a marvelous story of applied leadership.

Admiral Gravely: Yes. [Laughter] I did everything but spank him, to be honest with you.

Paul Stillwell: What other sorts of operations did you have over in WestPac besides the PIRAZ?

Admiral Gravely: Well, that was basically the only thing that the ship's purpose was. I went down to Singapore, as an R&R port, and the defense attaché in there was a guy that I had known for a long time. Apparently some spy ships and things had been picking up radiation and messages from him, so I went halfway around the south side of Singapore with them and surveyed the island with all my gear up and everything else to find out if we could hear the same thing. We did and advised him what frequencies and those kinds of things that we thought the people were listening to.

Paul Stillwell: Did you have a shellback initiation as part of your trip to Singapore?*

Admiral Gravely: Yes, we had one. Those things I'd been through when I went down in Taussig, and I've never been a strong believer that we ought to have those things. I don't care how much control you try to use, some of those things get out of hand. In fact, it did not get out of hand as bad on Jouett as it did on Taussig, because I was quite concerned on Taussig in that, you know, at some point in time a guy gets to be a man. He likes his hair cut so, and when you shave it, you just take away his manhood so far as he's concerned. We did a little bit of that on Taussig, but I took no cutting hair or anything you do it was make believe, and nothing worse than that. We did have two guys who decided that they were going to lock themselves in one of the radio shacks and wouldn't go through it. Of course, they were ostracized by the rest of the crew for a couple of days, but ultimately came out okay.

I had another little session with my Russian friends.

Paul Stillwell: This was in the Jouett?

Admiral Gravely: This was in Jouett, yes. One day I was receiving a helicopter aboard. A Russian AGI happened to be in the area, and so he decided to take a station about, oh, I guess he was about 2,000 yards ahead of me, and just sit there on a collision course. And here I had to hold course and speed while I took this helicopter aboard. There was nothing, really, to do. I had to order maintain course and speed. I took my helicopter aboard, and I guess towards the tail end I kicked up to about 25 knots, and made the distance close a little bit faster. Suddenly he just gave one blast and was gone. [Laughter]

---

* In the Navy's traditional equator-crossing ceremonies, the novice pollywogs are initiated by the shellbacks who have crossed the line previously. One member of a ship's crew portrays the role of King Neptune, who is welcoming the newcomers to his realm.

Sort of like a yelping dog, really, because Jouett was a pretty good-sized ship, as you well know.

I guess the only other thing that really happened besides the normal port visit to Hong Kong, where we went. We went to Hong Kong; we went to Kobe, Japan; we went to Sasebo; we went to Singapore, and that took up most of the port visits in WestPac.

But about the time that we deployed, we received a message from CruDesPac, which basically said that for a couple of years ships had not been permitted to go down to Australia. However, they were planning on opening that up again, and if any of the ships would like to go down to Australia, they'd like to have the CO put in a schedule change for the end of deployment. Well, I had been down to Australia in Taussig and thought that it was a great liberty town, and I thought that the people deserved a visit down there for those who had not gone, and so, of course, applied for this. Well, it was all approved.

The one untoward thing that happened was that while I was in Subic, just before leaving, I got a call from my wife who said that there were a couple of complaints that I was keeping the men away from home 15 or 20 more days, and so there were wives who were going to see CruDesPac, and they were seeing the chaplain and everything else. I asked if she had any idea who the wives were. She said, "Well, I really don't think I should tell you, but it was Mrs. So-and-so and Mrs. So-and-so."

I said, "Okay, I'll take care of it." So when I got back to the ship after talking to her, I remembered that there was a Z-Gram out which basically said that 5% of the people could be off the ship in liberty ports and things like that while we were deployed. So I told my exec to make sure that we had 5% of our people who went home early, and to make sure that Chief So-and-so and Chief So-and-so were on that list of the guys that were given the right to go home. Now, they objected. They didn't really want to go, but we sent them anyway.

The only thing about the Australia cruise was that I got a message back which basically said that I was free to go to Australia, and they gave me the schedule and everything else. But they did not want me to go direct from Subic to Melbourne, because I would be below 40% fuel. I thought about that, and I thought about the little jaygee who'd probably written that message who didn't realize that at the 50% point I had over 250,000 gallons aboard. But I sent him back a message and I said, okay, if it was acceptable that we would go on the West Coast of Australia to port, then to Melbourne. Then we went to Hobart, Tasmania, and then came on up to New Zealand. So that was acceptable. And I must tell you that that was really some cruise. We visited Fremantle and Perth, which are actually adjoining cities basically. I guess Fremantle is the port, and Perth is the city just inside.

Paul Stillwell: On the Indian Ocean.

Admiral Gravely: Yes. Spent about 36 hours there, then went into Melbourne, where we stayed six days. Just a beautiful place. I remember going in there at a time when the tugs were on strike. So it was a case of going over the reef to get into Melbourne. But we had no pilot or tug, and so I had to take it alongside the pier. And, of course, I'd had a lot of practice, so there was no problem there. Stayed there for six days, then went down to Hobart. Go ahead, ask a question.

Paul Stillwell: Were there any political ramifications of sending more U.S. ships there at that time?

Admiral Gravely: Not at that time, no. There were no political ramifications that I remember, and certainly we didn't feel anything about it. It just so happened that Australia was having a tug and pilot strike or something like that, and so it was impossible to get anything other than the pilot to bring you in from sea, and you weren't able to get one going in, but <u>Jouett</u> again was no problem handling the ship. So I just went on in there.

Paul Stillwell: Since they were encouraging more ships to go, I wonder if the governments were trying to build up solidarity between the countries.

Admiral Gravely: I don't think so. I think what had happened was that we'd been through a period of a couple of years when we were at odds, and I don't know whether it was about lamb or what. You remember, we went through that problem with lamb coming in and out. Nuclear powered ships going in and out. We went through that, but most of that was subsequent to this. No problem there.

I went down to Hobart, Tasmania, and just a beautiful place. We enjoyed it. Next went to New Zealand, Wellington, New Zealand, I guess. And finally capped that with a visit to Pago Pago, Samoa, where I went for fuel, and spent a night in Pago Pago. We got under way the next morning and came to Pearl. Well, of course, I'd been at Pearl many times. We only had four hours there, just long enough to fuel, and liberty we really didn't care about.

But that morning for some reason I began to think in terms of the flag list and wondered if it had come out. I didn't have any idea or even expect to be on it by any stretch of the imagination, because I was fairly junior at that point in my career. But at the same time I was curious about who had made it. So I had made arrangements to call on ComCruDesFlot 5, and that morning I went over about 8:00 o'clock after breakfast and waited in his office until he arrived, and we sort of discussed it. I asked him if he had heard anything, and, of course, he had not heard anything.

In the meantime, I wanted him to do for me what Jack Langille and Admiral Goodfellow had done, and that is I wanted to have a couple of barges come out and meet the ship on arrival in San Diego, and bring out some wives, and I'd even gotten permission for the wives to come aboard, and then we would steam up into the San Diego harbor, with ten wives aboard, I believe, five in one boat and five in another one. Well, I went over to make sure that those arrangements were made. Finally, after maybe 35 or 40 minutes, I was through, so I came on back to the ship.

As I got back to the ship, I noticed that they rang the bell, "Bong-bong, bong-bong, bong-bong. Jouett arriving." And quickly I said, "My God, I wonder who that OOD is." I got out of the car, and I walked up the gangway, and there were all my officers lining the quarterdeck—six side boys and the whole bit. As I stepped up, my exec, Commander Newcomb, grabbed my hand and shook it and said, "Congratulations, Admiral. You made it, you made it."[*]

---

[*] In the Navy's hierarchy of honors and ceremonies, a captain rates four side boys and a four-bell salute. A rear admiral rates six of each. The crew of the Jouett was thus honoring the commanding officer for being selected as a flag officer. The Navy announced its selection of 49 new rear admirals, including Captain Gravely, on 28 April 1971.

I said, "What do you mean?"

He said, "Well, we just heard that you've been selected for flag rank."

I said, "Oh, no, no." You know I'm too junior. I don't really expect it at this point in my career, but thanks anyway."

He said, "Well, come on over to the in-port cabin. We've got something up there for you." And so I went up, and actually it was the commodore's cabin. And in the commodore's cabin there were two bottles of wine. One of them was a bottle that a guy had given me down in New Zealand to drink with my wife when I got back. And I said, "Oh, God. Let me tell you guys something. You know, first of all, you cannot drink on board a Navy ship. And, secondly, let me tell you something, nobody's going to celebrate my becoming an admiral until I see it in print." So we broke up the gang, and they were all a little unhappy. What had happened, apparently, was that we had two officers who were leaving the ship as soon as we arrived in San Diego. They were going off to new duty. They'd been over to the CinCPacFlt Staff to be debriefed of their SI clearances.[*] And one of the people there said he had heard over the radio that the first black in the history of the U.S. Navy has just been selected for flag rank. And, of course, they said, "Well, it can't be anybody but you."

I said, "Well, you're wrong. It could be Dave Parham." Dave Parham was a senior Navy captain and a chaplain. And, obviously, it could have been Dave. But in any event, we made preparations and got under way. Well, we'd been under way, I guess, about 15 or 20 minutes when I got word that both CinCPac and CinCPacFlt wanted to talk to me over the ship's phone. So I went down to the radio shack, and, as normal, communications at a critical time failed, because I could never talk to either one of them. One was, oh, geez, the cigar-smoking admiral.

Paul Stillwell: McCain.[†]

Admiral Gravely: Admiral McCain. And the other one was our submarine admiral.

---

[*] SI—special intelligence.
[†] Admiral John S. McCain, Jr., USN, served as Commander in Chief Pacific from 31 July 1968 to 1 September 1972. His oral history is in the Naval Institute collection.

Paul Stillwell: Admiral Clarey.*

Admiral Gravely: Admiral Clarey, that's exactly right. Admiral Clarey and Admiral McCain. They both wanted to congratulate me, because the message had come out, and it was official at that point in time. I was told at that moment that that's why they wanted to call me. In the meantime, while I was in the radio shack, I was looking at the Fox file, and we were getting all kinds of news and everything else, and, Christ, the admirals' list was coming in and everything else. And, I guess, I was simply overjoyed, and I was happy. I started thinking about a lot of things, like, you know, why did I deserve this? Why had I been selected? I guess the person I thought about most was my mother, because, as I said, my mother died in 1937, and my mother was a big influence in my life.

Paul Stillwell: She always had great aspirations for you.

Admiral Gravely: She always had great aspirations for me. She not only had that, but she was <u>the</u> influence in my life. I just wish that my mother could have been there at that point in time. It was quite interesting to me, my dad was alive, and I didn't think about Dad very much. It was my mother that I thought about.

Anyway, I went back on up to the bridge, and I said, "XO, you remember that wine you guys had down there?" I said, "Well, it's official now. So maybe we ought to go back down there and drink it." [Laughter] So we broke the two bottles of wine and had it. I left one guy up on the bridge and said, "He can drink his a little later." But, anyway, we did.

Well, coming back to San Diego we had to do a full-power trial, because the yard period that had been delayed was scheduled now to start shortly after we got back, sometime in July or something like that.

I got a couple of messages that concerned me a little bit. One was that I was to be interviewed by the press on the moment that I arrived. ComCruDesPac warned me in a message that to remember the most important thing about the ship was not that I had been

---

* Admiral Bernard A. Clarey, USN, served as Commander in Chief Pacific Fleet, 5 December 1970 to 30 September 1973.

selected for flag rank, but that the ship was coming back from a deployment. I wrote him back and I said, "I agree. And, let's face it, I am also coming back from a deployment and haven't seen my wife and children in seven months."[*]

Well, despite that, the press briefing had to take place. The second thing was that somebody got the wise idea that the press should be flown out about 25 or 30 miles before I got into San Diego. That they should come aboard at that time, and then we'd start the interview. I just totally objected to that and told them that I felt that I did not want to be bothered with the press while I was bringing my ship back into San Diego. I would agree to an interview afterwards, but certainly not during that time. I guess the third thing was that I was to send off a dispatch on my feelings on being selected the first black flag officer in the Navy. And it is quite interesting how that occurred—not so much what was in the message as the writing of the message. Because when that message came in, my exec said, "Captain, why don't you and I go down and we'll do it?"

I said, "Well, how about the PAO?"[†] He thought that was great. The PAO was a Jewish officer. And I said, "Oh, by the way, bring down the weapons officer." The weapons officer was an Indian. So the message that Sam Gravely put out as being from the first black officer was written by four people, really: an American Indian, an American Jewish type, and an American Caucasian, and the American black who got selected. So we put out message together and sent it out. I've looked at that message since then, and I said "truly" I think five times and I only—have you ever read that?

Paul Stillwell: I read it in Commander Durrell's manuscript.

Admiral Gravely: Yes. But "truly" is in there for about four times, I read it. But, anyway, we finally got into San Diego. And, of course, we took our pilot aboard, and then the wives came aboard. We had, as I said, ten wives who came aboard and greeted their husbands first. Of course, my wife was one of those five, and then she came on up to the bridge. I showed her how to handle the ship, because I handled it all the way in. The pilot, we just pushed him aside.

---

[*] Rear Admiral Douglas C. Plate, USN, Commander Cruiser-Destroyer Force, Pacific Fleet.
[†] PAO—public affairs officer.

I was quite amazed at the crowd of people on the beach, standing on the pier. My daughter was holding a little sign. And they got all these signs, "Welcome aboard, Admiral," and everything else. The press had always generally overwhelmed me. I've never gotten used to reporters, or for some reason, and I'm not sure why. They just overwhelmed me. That's all I can say.

Paul Stillwell: Well, they're an intrusion at times.

Admiral Gravely: They are. They try to be as nice as possible, and they try to put you at ease and those kinds of things. But I just am not one of those people who fare well in interviews. Well, the interview went off. One of the things that really got to me was as soon as that interview was over, that I told my wife and the kids that we were going up to my cabin for a few minutes, because I had some candy for my daughter and those kinds of things.

Lo and behold, after so-called "getting rid of the press," here was some guy in my stateroom. He wanted to get a special interview. So I booted him out of there. And then, to top it off, a guy followed me home to get an interview. I guess I obliged him, but the press was overwhelming.

Well, now I was an admiral, and the mail started coming. And I have never, never in my life, even Taussig or Falgout, gotten as much mail. It came from everybody. It came from old friends; it came from interested people; it came from foreigners. Cuba, a Cuban newspaper. People sent me clippings and things like that. It was quite unfortunate, but I had so many letters until I couldn't answer them all. I tried. I started a program that I would answer about 25 letters a day. Well, you can imagine, having just gotten back from a deployment, that people were taking leave. Well, I decided I didn't want to be in the first leave party. Let the exec go first, and that I'd take something on the tail end. So the exec was gone and half the officers and half the crew.

Well, we got some new crew members aboard, and I got a really, really sharp yeoman aboard. I was up there writing letters, trying to write about 25 a day, and all I was doing was two or three lines, thanking people. But you want to let them know that you received their letter. In any event, this yeoman said, "Captain, hey, I can help you with those."

I said, "Oh?"

He said, "Yes, I've been here for two or three days now. I know how you're going to write, what you're doing and what you're saying. Why don't you give me that bale of letters, and I'll write a rough for you, and then all you got to do is initial it off, and I will then smooth it for you to sign." So I thought that was a bang-up idea, because for the most part they were people I didn't know anyway. And in case of any really old friends, then I could smooth up that rough letter that he'd given me with some special words in there. Well, this program went on through Friday, and on Saturday morning, I guess, I came down thinking that there'd be a couple of letters, and there were no letters. Then Monday I got back, there were no letters. Monday afternoon I called the yeoman up and said, "Hey, what are you doing about writing these letters? If you're not going to write them, give me the mail bag."

Well, he said, "Captain," he said, "I got to tell you." He said, "I put those letters into a burn bag; that was the only thing I had to hold them." A big brown 50-pound bag. "And I had that in the ship's office. And we had cleaning up the ship for inspection on Friday. And damn if the bag didn't get thrown out with the trash." [Laughter] So there went the end of my letter writing. And, to be honest with you, several years later I had a couple of guys who wanted to know what, you know, did I receive their letter, and I had to tell them I did, and I tried to answer them, but unfortunately they got away. Out of this batch of mail, and I was quite surprised and felt quite good about it too, there was only one letter was derogatory.

Paul Stillwell: How many would you say you received? Thousands, hundreds?

Admiral Gravely: There were thousands of letters. I would guess closer to 1,500 to 1,800 letters, and only one was derogatory, which supposedly was from some electronics type over in North Ireland, who basically said that I certainly wasn't the guy and blah,

blah, blah. And frankly, I turned it over to the FBI, or to the NIS people, and that was the last I heard of that one.* In fact, I answered his letter too.

Paul Stillwell: Did you feel overwhelmed by all this attention you were getting?

Admiral Gravely: Yes, I was quite overwhelmed. And in fact, I always am when there's a lot of attention paid. I certainly don't crave it. I don't really enjoy it. I thought that, frankly, for the press I had almost paid the price with seven or eight days of riding me as I went out to Pearl in the Taussig, but I guess every new venture requires new attention, and certainly they considered this an accomplishment to which they wanted to write about.

Well, I got my orders at about that time, and I discovered that I was coming back to relieve my former boss, Admiral Fitzpatrick, as Director of Naval Communications. I had mixed emotions about it, but I was quite pleased. I felt that the job in the Pentagon, despite the fact that I was only there about 15 or 18 months, had certainly prepared me, and I was in much better shape than I would have been if I had not had that job there. So I got the family together, and we prepared to come back. Now, part of the change of command ceremony, of course, was a frocking. I was frocked when I left Jouett. And that was quite a day.

By this time, First Fleet was Admiral Ray Peet, who had relieved Admiral Kidd.† He was the guest speaker who frocked me.‡ My daughter put my hat on, and it was quite a day. My wife pinned on one shoulder board and everything else. I got relieved, as I recall, on the second of June, and obviously, shortly before I was relieved, the Navy captain who was to relieve me came aboard. And I knew that despite the fact that I did not know him, that I had seen that guy.

It turned out it was Captain Eddie Briggs who relieved me in Jouett; he was the guy who was riding the Turner Joy when I mentioned earlier that we were coming up,

---

* NIS—Naval Investigative Service.
† Vice Admiral Raymond E. Peet, USN, served as Commander First Fleet from 1 August 1970 to 15 May 1972. Admiral Peet's oral history is in the Naval Institute collection.
‡ "Frocking" a naval officer refers to the practice of allowing him to wear the insignia and assume the title for which he was recently selected. The officer does not receive the pay for the higher rank until a vacancy appears on the lineal list so he can be officially promoted.

and he was to make a left turn and turned right. We got quite a laugh out of it, because it certainly wasn't anything done intentionally or anything like that. It was just a boo-boo. He admitted that under a normal set of circumstances he would maintain course and speed, but with the contact up ahead, he made a decision to come a little left. And when he translated that to his OOD, somehow the guy picked it up as come a little right. [Laughter] But, you know, we got quite a laugh out of that. Eddie Briggs was just a jewel of an interesting guy, who obviously was everything I'm saying, because ultimately he made three stars, and served as SurfLant.*

Paul Stillwell: What was the next step for you?

Admiral Gravely: Well, one of the things that happened, of course, after being selected for flag rank is that they normally bring you back to Washington, D.C., for what is affectionately known as "charm school." And in my case I was no different, so we got the message and the TAD funds, etc.† And I came back to Washington. I told my wife that I anticipated that my orders would be in Washington, so please don't ask me to pay her way over here. Then we'd stay over there for five days and then go back, and then come back again. So she understood, and I came here for the five days of charm school.

The first thing that I can remember happening, which really wasn't related to charm school, was that I got a call from Rembrandt Robinson. At that time he was on the Joint Staff. As I mentioned earlier, it was his son who came aboard Jouett the year before as my MPA. Rembrandt wanted to find out something about his son, how I felt about him, how was he doing, and everything else. So we sat there for a while and started talking. While we were talking he said, "Sam, I want to show you something."

He said he had the first fitness report he got after coming out of midshipman school and going aboard a ship, and he had his son's first fitness report. His son apparently had thought at that time in terms of coming out of the Navy, and said, "Dad, you know, after all, you're an admiral. I certainly can't surpass that, and I'm not sure I

---
* Vice Admiral Edward S. Briggs, USN, served as Commander Naval Surface Force Atlantic Fleet from 1982 to 1984.
† TAD—temporary additional duty.

want to even compete in the same community in which you've made your number, so I'm thinking about coming out."

And he said, "Son, I want to show you something. Here is your first fitness report, and here's mine. And your fitness report is so much better than mine, there's no telling where you will go." [Laughter] Well, as I told you, young Robinson was a truly outstanding officer. I don't know where he is today, but I certainly hope he's still in the Navy, because I think he's got a long way to go.*

Well, Rembrandt also told me about another thing, which I didn't know, which had occurred while I was on Jouett. We went into Hong Kong. In fact, Pete Deutermann was my ship handler at that point in time. Whereas we had no problem about getting in there, we had to come in, turn around, and then moor to a buoy. While we were making our maneuvers and coming up to the buoy, the Kowloon Ferry came up, and in sort of trying to see what was going on, and they wanted to get closer to the ship, they came too close. And the ferry scraped my stern. We moored, no damages, nothing.

Of course, the tug people came aboard Jouett very shortly after that to say, "Hey, if there are any damages, we're willing to pay," and all the rest of this and everything else. The last thing the guy said was that, "You know, nothing really happened here, other than the scraping incident, but I can assure you this afternoon it's going to be in the Communist paper that American warship sinks tug in Hong Kong Harbor."

Paul Stillwell: An unprovoked attack.

Admiral Gravely: Yes, right. So the first thing that came to mind was, of course, that this was an incident that needed reporting in an OpRep IV.† So Deutermann and I sat down. We wrote out the proper message and everything else and got it off in good order. I can't tell you what happened to that message, but the first thing that happened was that I got a message from ComNav Marianas wanting to know if there were any damages. And I'd put in there, no damages. If there were any injuries. And I'd already put in there, so,

---

* John Robinson retired as a commander in 1993, a few years after this interview.
† OpRep—operational report.

you know, it was just a case of repeating over and over again to this guy as to what had happened.

Paul Stillwell: What was your connection with him?

Admiral Gravely: Well, Hong Kong, I believe, is in the Marianas sort of chain, I guess. Not the chain of islands, but certainly it might have come under him for area coordination or something like that. But, anyway, and, of course, he was an addressee on the message, but he questioned. The next thing that Rembrandt told me was that—well, I knew about Marianas, but Rembrandt told me that it got to the White House situation room. And somebody wanted to know, "How could that dumb captain hit a Chinese ferry going into Hong Kong?" And Robinson said that he was very happy that he was there. Not so much for me or anything else, but to explain to people how things like that happen, and to make sure that they all knew that I had done everything possible. That it wasn't my fault. We had the pilot aboard. We had the flag showing, the whole bit. The guy came too close in trying to look, and he was probably looking while he should have been steering. But, anyway, I got over that one with no problem, with no investigation or anything like that.

Charm school, as you well know, is an activity wherein the incoming flag officers are briefed by the highest authorities in the Navy and the DoD. They get some Army, Air Force types who speak, and they are basically trying to acquaint you with the job that you are going to do on the flag level, and tell you how to do it, bring up some new policies and those kinds of things. Well, that was routine. It was very good, and I needed that, because my time in Washington prior to that was a tour in recruiting and a short tour in DCA when you're not on that level, and the tour in OpNav. So I needed that, and I enjoyed it.

On the third afternoon, on that Wednesday afternoon, generally, and I don't know whether they do it that way today, but there's usually a party hosted by the CNO for all his flag officers. Well, this party was being hosted, of course, by Admiral Zumwalt, who was the Chief of Naval Operations, and the party was held at his quarters, which at that time were on the Naval Observatory.* I had probably been to only one or two flag officers' quarters in my entire career. So I was not going to do anything wrong. I was going to do everything exactly right. In addition to that, I was in civilian clothes just like we were told to be, and I didn't want to have any problem about getting in the gate.

So that afternoon, about 15 minutes before the party, I parked outside of Rock Creek Park there, just across the street from the Naval Observatory to watch people go in, so I could make sure that I did it just like they did it and did it right. Well, after seeing two or three cars that I knew were new flag officers turn into the place, I, as soon as the traffic would permit, turned in also. It was a simple procedure. You go to the gate and show your ID card. Somebody checks you off on the guest list, etc. And then you're told to go. You've got about a quarter of a mile drive, maybe a little less than that, but in any event you make the drive, then you've got a circular driveway.

I was behind about four cars at this point in time, and I noticed that a car pulled up in front of the place, stopped. There were two sailors, one let out the guy's wife, and one let out the guy on the other side and gave him a little piece of paper, and took the car and drove it the rest of the way and took it to park it. This went on for three times ahead of me. But the minute that I drove up there, one of the sailors said, "Move it. Move it. Take that car to the rear. Take that car to the rear." I was about to get out of the car, and I thought, "Well, I really don't want to create a disturbance in front of the CNO's house. There's no sense in explaining." He said, "Take it to the rear," so I drove it around to the back. Well, I pulled into the parking lot and a chief petty officer came up, and he said, "You're Admiral Gravely, aren't you?"

I said, "Yes."

He said, "Well, you're not supposed to do it this way, sir. What you're supposed—"

I said, "Wait a minute. I've tried that already, and it doesn't work. Now, if you have no objection, I'll leave the car here, and I'll come back and get it when I'm through."

---

* Through the end of Zumwalt's tenure as Chief of Naval Operations in 1974, the official residence was a Victorian mansion on the grounds of the Naval Observatory in Washington, D.C. After Zumwalt left, the house became the official residence of the Vice President of the United States. The residence of the CNO is now Tingey House in the Washington Navy Yard.

He said, "Okay, fine." Well, anyway, I left the car there and started walking around to the front, and this little sailor who had given me the high sign about moving the car was standing there, and he was talking over this walkie-talkie. So I imagine at that point in time the chief was really giving him down the country, because he was beginning to get a little redder in the face and everything else. As I stepped up he looked me in the eye, with a nice sharp, snappy salute, and he said, "Pardon me sir. I didn't know you were Admiral Gravely. I thought you were a chauffeur."

I took my first step, and I started thinking, and I said, "Well, son. Please don't worry about it. But I want you to always remember, chauffeurs wear caps." [Laughter] And frankly, that was to be the title of my memoirs, if I'd ever had them written.

Well, anyway, the briefings were very well done. I got a lot out of the briefings, and I enjoyed them. We ended on Friday now, and it was time to go back to San Diego. Got back to San Diego and about that time my orders hit, bringing me to OpNav. I guess if I had any concern at all, it was, despite the fact that things had eased considerably so far as the housing situation here in the Washington, D.C., area for me, I was a little bit concerned about coming back and finding a place.

Well, I guess a day or so before we left home, a neighbor who happened to have been an Army major, and he was a neighbor who lived in North Arlington when I was there, wrote me a letter and he said, "When you arrive we plan to go to Texas," which is where his wife is from or something, "and we're taking all the children. So my house is vacant for the next month, and you're certainly welcome to use it." So you can imagine how helpful that was. So we moved into his house and started to look for a house; I decided that we would buy something. We bought a house in Falls Church. And the house that I bought in Falls Church was owned by the company that the renters were from, or the people were from when I was in war college, who just sort of disappeared.

Paul Stillwell: Sort of an irony there.

Admiral Gravely: Yes, there's an irony there, and it also shows you how fast things turn around, because we're talking about seven years now, how the process had completely reversed. We bought this house in Falls Church, which I really enjoyed. It was in an integrated neighborhood. Of course, this was unheard of in Northern Virginia in the old days, but it was there, and we kept the house for about ten years and finally sold it.

The job in OpNav was a very, very interesting one, because at about that time the Navy had decided to work to reorganize from the communications division to what they call command and control, C^2. In fact, if I'm not mistaken, the Navy had probably the first C^3I business, because on that staff we had the communications, the cryptologic guy.[*] We had the intelligence guy and all those things that are elements of command support. Admiral Fritz Harlfinger was in charge of that. He was a former Director of Naval Intelligence, and he was just simply a wonderful guy to work for.[†] Easy to work for. You did your job. He did his job.

Paul Stillwell: He sort of made himself a czar in that arena, didn't he?

Admiral Gravely: He became the first czar of the command and control group, and really did a bang-up job. He was a two-star when he came there but got the third star very shortly after that. My job basically was to ensure that the communication assets of the Navy were not only maintained, repaired, and those kinds of things, but also to put out policy procedures, etc. That was an interesting job. I had plenty of good talent on the staff. I had three chiefs of staff while I was in that job. All three of them made admiral ultimately within the next year or so. So I had good people to work with.

The job was a little bit tougher, I think, than it is today. The main reason I think it was a little tougher was simply because of the fact that the flag officer was double-hatted. You were not only the Director of Naval Communications from the OpNav side of the house, but you were also commander of the Naval Telecommunications Command from the other side of the house.

Paul Stillwell: Could you explain that disparity of what the two involved?

---

[*] C^3I—command, control, communications, and intelligence.
[†] Rear Admiral Frederick J. Harlfinger II, USN, Director Command Support Programs, OpNav.

Admiral Gravely: Yes. The OpNav job had to do with the policy aspects of communications, and the ComNavTelCom job basically had to do with the operation and maintenance of the comm stations, and also making sure that the shipboard equipment, etc., whatever, can meet the needs basically, and carry out the policies set by you in your other hat. It was quite interesting that once in a while you would find yourself writing a message to yourself, and then you had to go over to the other side of the house, and then answer that message. And sometimes you couldn't answer it as easily as you thought you could ask the question. But it was quite an interesting job. Kept you hopping.

Paul Stillwell: Well, there are plusses and minuses to being double-hatted. The plus is that you can resolve any argument yourself. You don't have to try to convince somebody else.

Admiral Gravely: Well, that's true to some degree, but generally there are info addees on a message like that, so no matter which way you answer it, you're going to upset somebody. One of the other facets of the job, which was a little bit disturbing for me, was that you couldn't devote full time to either one of them. And they were far removed. For example, the OpNav job was in the Pentagon, and the other job was up at Nebraska Avenue, which is quite a distance between. So I, feeling that basically the OpNav job was the most demanding, spent most of my time in the Pentagon, but I spent anywhere from one to two days a week out at Nebraska Avenue.

For the first time I began to get a lot of demands on my time from outside activities. Whereas I've never really been a great speaker, I was certainly in demand for speeches with various black groups, NAACP groups, high schools, and those kinds of things. I tried to honor as many of those as I possibly could. One of the things I regret is that President Tubman in Liberia died right after I took over the job.[*] I was offered a chance to fly over as part of the entourage that we sent over for the burial. I had to respectfully decline, because I felt that I was just brand new in this job, and I'd better stay on the job and learn it. I regret that to some degree now, because I had never been to Africa, hadn't been before, and I don't know why I want to go, but I have a feeling that

---

[*] William V. S. Tubman served as President of Liberia from 1944 until his death on 23 July 1971.

you ought to see a little bit of everything in this world, and one of these days I'm going to have to take my wife and we're going to go.

Paul Stillwell: There had to come the realization now that you have grown beyond yourself. You're not just a naval officer, you're a symbol.

Admiral Gravely: Well, you never feel that. But I think in some respects it's true. You are a symbol. And I guess people took you to be a symbol. For example, you know, I can't think of a thing that I didn't get invited to come to. One of the things that happened to me practically every year that I was a flag officer was I was decreed to be one of the 100 most influential blacks in this country. They carried that in Ebony each year, and I made that magazine for about ten years. Nobody cares about me now that I'm retired, but I think I'm probably as influential today as I was then. [Laughter]

Paul Stillwell: You hope so.

Admiral Gravely: Yes, right.

Paul Stillwell: Well, you were on a TV program, too, "What's My Line?"

Admiral Gravely: Yes, I got roped into that one somehow, and they guessed me before it was over. And I was quite surprised that they did, but there were always very sharp people on there making those guesses, and this woman nailed me right to the cross. Well, I did a little of everything. I can't think of too many things that I was asked to do that I didn't do. I tried.

Paul Stillwell: How did you keep a proper sense of humility while all this is going on? You didn't want your head to get too big.

Admiral Gravely: Well, the hat never really got too big for me. I guess that was just something was ingrained from birth, I guess, or something like that. I'm sure that I might have appeared at times to have let it gotten too big, but I tried not to. I remember that I was accused publicly of not attending a certain function, because I felt I was too big for it. I had to write the reporter who wrote that in her paper, I was very sorry that I had to decline, but in declining I declined primarily because I had to go to my stepmother's funeral. I never heard anything from her, but I can imagine how badly she must have felt about that one.

But the job, of course, was looking out for the interests of the Navy in the communications arena, trying to do the best you could to make sure that we were foremost in the communications world. Of course, you've got your joint programs, you're working with the Army, Navy, and Air Force.

In improving communications we decided on a couple of routes. One was we appointed a committee called the CIACT, CNO's Industry Advisory Committee to Telecommunications. Some very, very big guys were on that committee and I see one or two of them every once in a while, but they were big wheels in the civilian community as well as a couple of retired folk. I'd have to get a list of the names for you if you want that. When this group finally submitted its report, it came out with several recommendations.

But two of the best ones, so far as I was concerned, was that the Director of Naval Communications should always be an upper-half rear admiral, which said I was too junior for the job really. The second thing they said was that the Director of Naval Communications should be able to go to sea, because historically our communicators had come into the communications jobs, and then sort of got locked in. That was about as far as they went. And normally when it came time to cut people, these were the easy guys to cut, because they didn't have the sea experience. So in saying that I needed to be upper half, that was fine with me, and also that I needed to go to sea was also fine. So I was very happy with that report.

I can remember going with Admiral Harlfinger, who decided that he would take his bearings, as he called them, to see the fleet. We all went to New Jersey to the Air Force base up there.

Paul Stillwell: McGuire.*

Admiral Gravely: Yes, McGuire. We went to McGuire Air Force Base, and we boarded a C-47, and went to Rota, Spain. And from Rota flew over to Naples, where we met with Admiral Ike Kidd.† Admiral Ike Kidd made some rather historic remarks, but he sounded to me at that point in time almost like the typical three-star admiral, as he was then. But the guy who really doesn't understand communications, because Admiral Kidd said, "Sam, let me tell you about communications."

"Yes, sir."

He said, "The problem with communications is you send too many messages."

Not trying to be smart or anything like that, I just simply said, "Well Admiral, I don't send them, I carry them, and the bag is heavy." And I said, "In addition to that, I've read your op order. And the guys who require the messages are the fleet commanders." And when you get right down to it, that's true. Every guy who wrote an op order would put in it that he'd want to hear from you if you were away from the task group. I want to know where you are at 8:00 o'clock, 12:00 o'clock and at 2000. And probably every hour after that, or every hour. Or I want to know your fuel capacity. When you're down to 80%, 70%, 60%, 50%, so on and so forth. So in this search on how to stop sending so many messages, we've got to look to ourselves, because we as fleet and group commanders are the guys who are requiring as many unnecessary messages as there are. But in any event, we both lectured each other [laughter], and obviously he won the lecture, but that's the way I felt about it.

Paul Stillwell: You probably had to implement more and more satellite usage during this period also, didn't you?

Admiral Gravely: Well, we did. What happened at that time was that, as I told you earlier, that Bob Langaleer, who had been my number-two guy, had come up with the idea of UHF satellite communications. While I was on Jouett, and still in San Diego

---

* McGuire Air Force Base is adjacent to the Army's Fort Dix near Wrightstown, New Jersey.
† Vice Admiral Isaac C. Kidd, Jr., USN, commanded the Sixth Fleet from 29 August 1970 to 1 October 1971.

before deploying, I tested the first fleet broadcast receivers and antennas on board the Jouett. We took them aboard; they sort of fastened them on four corners of the ship, and we went to sea, and we tested them for about a week. So the Navy was gradually getting into the communications at that time.

Obviously the idea was that you had to put more and more in the program, but the unfortunate part about it here again is that there were decisions being made which said, "Hey, before you can implement satellite communications, you've got to get rid of some of your HF, and use some of your HF maintenance money into buying new equipment." Which was damn near impossible. But at the same time, yes, I got more and more involved. Certainly we got the fleet sat program going and those kinds of things, which are going great guns today, and this is the major source of naval communication. So, yes, I was quite a bit into the start of this, and also into putting the Navy in the forefront in satellite communications.

The tour at OpNav went normally. I guess the question I was asked the most concerning that tour was, "How often did Admiral Zumwalt call you up to discuss racial problems?" Well, he really didn't need to, number one. And number two he didn't. For example, the Kitty Hawk revolt went on during my time. I wasn't involved at all. He had several advisors who advised him on that, Bill Norman being one who was a young lieutenant commander. Bill Norman was the CNO's right-hand man.* So the things that went on racially, whereas I was never really involved certainly in helping the CNO making a decision. He had people there who could help him make decisions.

Paul Stillwell: So you didn't feel left out at all?

Admiral Gravely: I didn't feel left out a bit. I was there as a Navy communicator, and not as the Navy's racial expert, which I simply wasn't anyway.

Paul Stillwell: Presumably, if you had wanted to make an input, you had that opportunity.

---

* Lieutenant Commander William S. Norman, USN, was CNO's special assistant for equal opportunity.

Admiral Gravely: If I had wanted to make an input, I had no problem with being able to do it, and could have done it. And I guess Bill Norman and two or three of the other young officers who were around came to me periodically to ask questions and to see how I would go on certain things. But the biggest one being the <u>Kitty Hawk</u>, and I just simply was not involved. In fact, in several of the others I saw the reports, but that's about as far as I got.

Paul Stillwell: Did you applaud Admiral Zumwalt's initiatives and the climate he was trying to create?

Admiral Gravely: I applauded Admiral Zumwalt for everything he was trying to do. I feel that if I were to be critical of anything that he did, I thought that—and I think he did it ultimately the only way he could—well, in trying to hammer things down it almost seemed to me as if he sat in a little corner someplace with some junior advisors, who gave him advice contrary to the way these old sea lords had been doing things for years and years and years, and then he just suddenly hit them with a message. Rather than getting that group together and sort of coordinating things and seeing what you could work out. I don't think he did enough of that. Now, I may be wrong, but that's just my view of it.

Paul Stillwell: Well, and there's the famous meeting that he had. It almost came across like a rebuke of senior flag officers.

Admiral Gravely: Well, there were two things that went that were to some degree rebukes. Certainly that was one of them. I sat in there and listened to all of that, and wondered what the hell I did to rate this kind of a whipping? The second one was the sensitivity training sessions, and they were pretty hard for me to swallow. They were hard from the idea that they were a young group up there telling me that I was to blame for all of the Navy's problems. Well, frankly, I thought I was the result of them. [Laughter] You know, it got to me a little bit. In fact, I wondered why I even was sent. But, anyway, I went there. There were a lot of things like that that might have been handled a little differently, and might have been much more successful if handled a little differently. You had two or three different types of people. You had an old group that had been in the Navy and seen how the Navy had been working for years and years, and they weren't about to change.

Paul Stillwell: Since before World War II, really.

Admiral Gravely: To some degree, yes. Right. Since before World War II. Who, first of all, couldn't tolerate reserves being part of it. And not only blacks and other people being part of it. But you also had another group, who were coming up, who'd been parties to the sit-ins and those kinds of things who were going to make the people change, no matter what. The kind of discipline that the Navy had wouldn't permit those two factions to sit side by side, and so that brought on some of these revolts. I think it should have been explained better. I don't think that the young group who came in insisting that this was the only way to do it were necessarily right. And the old group who said you can't do it any way but this way weren't right either. I think that somehow there's been a meeting of the minds here within the last few years, and I think things have improved tremendously.

Paul Stillwell: I suppose one of the problems was that there wasn't sensitivity for how hard it was to bring along this group that had been in the Navy since the late '30s.

Admiral Gravely: Well, I'm sure there wasn't, because nobody realized how hard core that group was. As I said, they didn't like reserves either. But reserves at least looked like them, and they couldn't tell a reserve until they looked at his ID card, I guess, or something. It was not the most pleasant of times, but, then again, it was not the worst of times either.

Paul Stillwell: Well, the thing we'll never know, of course, is whether it might have been worse had there not been a Zumwalt and his approach.

Admiral Gravely: That's right. You'll never know that one, and I certainly admire and respect Admiral Zumwalt. I find it difficult to say whether I think he went about it the right way or the wrong way, although I guess I've said I didn't think he did it right. It is kind of difficult to be on either side of that damn pendulum. He had opposition not only from below him, but he had opposition from above him.

Now, the interesting thing to me is that John Warner, of course, relieved Chafee as Secretary of the Navy.* And, of course, John Warner is now senator from Virginia. John Warner was trying to get Zumwalt to go slower, and he has been accused at certain times of impeding racial progress. When you are doing something, and somebody says "Go slower," no matter what it is, you're impeding. I'm not sure that he impeded racial progress as much as he was trying to do it cautiously. But caution was not the name of the game in those days, so they were both wrong.

I have been to John Warner's place in his company on a couple of occasions. I see him now, because he has a farm down in Middleburg, as you well know. But I remember that when I discovered that I was going to command of Cruiser-Destroyer Group Two, I got it from John Warner. Which has always interested me. Most of the good things that happen to me I get it from somebody above me, not the normal detail route, you know. But my wife and I were guests at John Warner's house in Washington. He had an apartment there in Georgetown, and he said to my wife, "I see Sam is going to get a little salt water sprinkled on his tail."

My wife said something about, "I hope they're not going to send him on another deployment." And I was so mad I could have clobbered her. [Laughter] Because I had spent an awful lot of time in the Pacific Fleet, and I really wanted to get a group out of the Pacific Fleet. I had no problem with going to Group Two, which was what I went to, other than the fact that Group Two was not a deploying group. So I was a little upset from that side, because I think any naval officer worth his salt, when he gets to be an admiral and is a group commander, wants to go out and operate. Certainly training is one thing, but operating is another, and I wanted that.

Well, after the tour was over there in OpNav two years later I was given my orders, and I went up to relieve as Commander Cruiser-Destroyer Group Two. I relieved

---

* John W. Warner served as Secretary of the Navy from 4 May 1972 to 9 April 1974.

an old friend, Admiral Wentworth, who went down to take over CruDesPac.* Jake Finneran was the fleet commander, just a tremendous naval officer.† And I knew Jake Finneran from destroyers. In fact, it's quite interesting that you don't necessarily know everybody as individually, or know them well, but, you hear about them, and you feel you know them. And that's the way it was with Jake. I knew him very well.

Group Two, when I got there, was in Newport, Rhode Island. But the move of the ships from the northern training grounds had begun, and when I got there the ships were in the process of changing homeports from Newport to Norfolk, to Charleston, and to Mayport, Florida.

Paul Stillwell: This was part of the contraction of the defense establishment. For example, the closing of the Boston Navy Yard.

Admiral Gravely: That was part of that, and behind it, I guess, was that we had an argument that we'd be closer to the training grounds. Also, Boston was really a tough area to operate in during the wintertime. I mean, you'd get more ships down closer to the sunny South and those kinds of things. And so that was part of the rationale behind it. In the case of Cruiser-Destroyer Group Two itself, the staff was to move to Charleston, South Carolina.

Now, we had several exercises scheduled. And, of course, what it meant was that in order to put on an exercise, you generally took an airplane and you flew to Charleston or to Mayport or Norfolk, and you'd written your op order and those kinds of things. Then you went down and held a quick briefing, and then you went to sea. So you didn't get a chance to see the ships daily, like you would like to have had. Suddenly you've got a bunch of ships, and you've got them out at sea operating and those kinds of things. We operated not only with American ships, but we had, oh, the five NATO ships.‡

---

* Rear Admiral Ralph S. Wentworth, Jr., USN.
† Vice Admiral John G. Finneran, USN, commanded the Second Fleet from January 1973 to August 1974.
‡ NATO—North Atlantic Treaty Organization, which was established in 1949 as a means of coordinating defense against a potential attack from the Soviet Union.

Paul Stillwell: StaNavForLant.*

Admiral Gravely: Yes. I operated with them a couple of times. And several other mismatch ships. I call them mismatch, they weren't strictly destroyers, but, of course, when you're used to operating with destroyers all the time you feel that that's the only thing you've got.

Paul Stillwell: Well, the British had helicopter cruisers, for example, the Tiger and the Blake.

Admiral Gravely: Right. Well, we had amphibs and everything else. Another thing that we were doing at that time was that the in-port exercises became a big thing. And I did some pioneer work in going down to Norfolk for example, with five ships, all alongside the pier, and conducted a full week of training with these ships. Quite interesting, and I think we accomplished much, but certainly it's difficult to imagine that you've got a collision when you're in port and you can't see a hole. Or it's also difficult to say I'm going to get under way and leave here and not making any preparations.

Paul Stillwell: Well, this was during the great fuel crunch.† Did that dictate your operations?

Admiral Gravely: That dictated a lot of the operations, the fuel crunch and other things. And, of course, as much as anything was the fact that we were getting down in numbers of ships. I mean, we were at 500 at one time, about 400 and something another time. And with the fast tempo of those ships that were really operating out in WestPac, and also in the Med, you had to give these guys in port some time there. To not only repair, but to maintain their ships, as well as some leave and liberty and upkeep and those kinds of things. So it dictated a different kind of operation.

---

* StaNavForLant—Standing Naval Force Atlantic, a multi-national group of ships that operated together under the auspices of NATO.
† In the winter of 1973-74 OPEC, the Organization of Petroleum Exporting Countries, initiated an embargo on delivery of Middle East oil to the West. The result was a dramatic jump in oil prices and long lines of cars at U.S. gasoline pumps in early 1974.

Paul Stillwell: Why did Group Two have a different pattern of operations than the others, being a non-deployer?

Admiral Gravely: I can't really answer the question as to why, but historically it had been that way since I don't know when. That did ultimately change about three or four admirals down the line after me, because Group Two did become a deployer, and I think it's a deployer now.

Paul Stillwell: Did you consider it a readiness and training group?

Admiral Gravely: It was basically a readiness and training group, and no matter which one of the other groups the ship belonged to when they were in port, I could get any ships from any group to operate with me that needed training. We had routine ops down in the Caribbean. I worked with Jake Finneran down in the Caribbean, and also went to Rota, Spain.[*] I flew to Rota, Spain, and this was under Stan Turner, who since ships didn't have that much time to spend at sea, decided that we should train on the way back.[†] So I went to Rota, Spain, picked up a group and brought them back into the States. There was also a move afoot to take the guy who was down in the Caribbean, and see if Group Two couldn't take over the job of ComSoLant as well.[‡] I was not successful during my tour of doing that.

Paul Stillwell: Well, you probably had to coordinate your efforts with the fleet training group, didn't you?

Admiral Gravely: Well, we did more fleet operations. The training group, as you recall, will do refresher training and basic exercises. I was sort of at a level two.

---

[*] In March of 1974, the interviewer was a Naval Reserve officer on temporary active duty as part of Admiral Finneran's Second Fleet Staff. At that time the Second Fleet flagship and Admiral Gravely's Cruiser-Destroyer Group Two flagship were together at Roosevelt Roads, Puerto Rico, and then at sea during a NATO exercise.
[†] Vice Admiral Stansfield Turner, USN, commanded the Second Fleet from August 1974 to July 1975.
[‡] ComSoLant—Commander South Atlantic Force.

Paul Stillwell: Okay, operational training.

Admiral Gravely: Operational-type training. Missile shoots, obviously, had to be coordinated with those people down there, but that was about all that I coordinated with them.

Paul Stillwell: How much time did you spend at sea in that job?

Admiral Gravely: Well, you were at sea for anywhere from a week to two weeks, probably once every month and a half. The rest of the time you spent back in port, writing op orders and those kinds of things. And getting ready, and evaluating the last exercise.

The other chore, of course, was that there was an outfit called the Destroyer Development Group, which was up in Newport. A decision was reached that when Cruiser-Destroyer Group Two went to Charleston that the Destroyer Development Group became a part of my assets. So, of course, in that outfit you were looking at destroyer tactics, and writing tac notes and those kinds of things, so that happened. Shortly after I got to Newport, we had a major exercise scheduled. I had just moved up there, so I had my kids in school and everything else. Well, there was really no need to hurry to Charleston, so I remained in Newport for a whole year and then moved to Charleston at the end of that year.

Now, moving to Charleston was not easy for lots of people for lots of reasons. The Newport group of destroyer-force types really didn't want to leave there. They loved Newport, and Newport loved them. Blacks generally didn't want to go to Charleston because of the racial conditions that they felt would be there, and they didn't want to go for that reason. I personally didn't want to move at that moment, because I'd just got to Newport. [Laughter]

But, anyway, we went to Charleston, conducted a couple of exercises. One of the things that I decided to do was to go over to see the commandant down there and then talk in terms of some possible quarters down there. I didn't realize that quarters would be a problem. In any event, I went over and talked to the commandant about the quarters, and he said he had a reserve destroyer squadron commander who had a set of quarters, and that he had planned to move him someplace else, and that I would take over those quarters.

Well, at first note that sounded fine, but I went down there and I took a look at the quarters, and there were six sets of quarters, which were the old antebellum-type homes. Looked like they had been built prior to the Civil War. And the set of quarters that the old reserve squadron commander had were a duplex, with fairly modern quarters, but at the same time these stately quarters over there were designed basically for flag type. Well, at that point in time there were only about three flag types down there who had these quarters. SubGroup 6 had a set. Commander of Mine Warfare type had a set, and the commandant had a set. The shipyard commander was a captain, who was in one of those sets. The supply type was a captain, and he was in one of those sets. And then there was one other guy, as I recall. Maybe there were five, but I know there were sufficient quarters down there.

So I talked to the admiral about getting one of those things, because I felt that if I went down there as a black officer, and the people in the community saw that I was getting second best, that I felt that I'd be sort of laughed out of the community. Well, we talked about them, and shortly after that I left, and I visited the shipyard commander, who, as I said, was a captain. Well, frankly the guy made me a little angry. And in talking, we were talking about quarters and so forth. He'd been there for seven years and lived in that set of quarters for seven years. Well, you know, if you like shore duty, fine, but in my view I had moved seven times in seven years, and damn it, it was time for him to move too. So that's the set I decided I wanted. Well, I made a statement, which I regretted later when I told the commandant that, "Hey, you know, I really want one of those sets of quarters. And that's the set of quarters that I want. And I think I rate them. I'm senior to most of the people." And I was senior to mine warfare, and I was senior to SubGroup 6. I said, "I want that particular set of quarters."

He said, "Well, the major claimant for that set of quarters is BuShips, and we'll have to go to BuShips and do that."*

---

* BuShips—Bureau of Ships.

Well, I could care less about that, but I said, "You know, Admiral, I would gladly move to the set of quarters that you want to give me if there were six admirals down here. But since there aren't, I want one set, and that's the set I want." Well, that came back to haunt me a little bit, because since I was so set on that set of quarters, somehow when word got to BuShips that that's the set I wanted, BuShips turned a flag officer around who was in San Francisco going to Honolulu to take a job, and called him back to put him in that set of quarters. In fact, he was down there for the rest of my tour.

Finally, I simply said, "If it's that hard to get the kind of quarters I think I deserve down here, then I'll leave my family here in Washington, D.C." So the year that I remained in Charleston, my family stayed here in Washington, D.C., and I commuted and lived in a BOQ. I've always regretted making that decision. I probably should have taken the other set of quarters, because my relief did take the other set of quarters. As I said, about three tours later Harry Train was the guy who really stood up and put Group Two in the set of quarters that he needed.[*]

Charleston, despite the fact that I'm sure there was racial prejudice down there and everything else, I didn't have any major problems. I can remember driving into the gate about the first or second time I was down there, and as I was driving through the gate I was called to pull over to the side, and the guy said, "You don't have a pass."

I said, "Well, that's right, but I've got stars on my car, and I didn't think I needed it."

He said, "Oh, no. Everybody here needs a pass."

I said, "Fine."

So I went on into the chief police officer in there. And he said, "Well, you have to have a pass."

I said, "Well, let me tell you something. I'm Commander Cruiser-Destroyer Group Two, and I'm moving down here, and I'm going to be here for a while, so I'd appreciate it if you'd give me a pass." So he gave me a pass which said, "Anytime, any spot," and two or three things like that. So, you know, I was going to be there, and I didn't need a damn pass, but they said I did. I guess that was his way of being a little

---

[*] Admiral Harry D. Train II, USN, served as Supreme Allied Commander Atlantic, Commander in Chief Atlantic, and Commander in Chief Atlantic Fleet from 30 September 1978 to 30 September 1982. His oral history is in the Naval Institute collection.

hard on me as the new boy on the block. Well, that was sort of minor harassment, and the type of things that would happen to the young black sailor in Charleston that he could never either handle or know why or any of those kinds of things and then cause some minor problems. I, as a rear admiral, obviously didn't have any problems.

I guess during that tour the only one thing that didn't go what I considered very well for me, although that's a hard thing to decide, but I was head of a selection board at that point in time. It was selecting commanders. And it was quite interesting that in trying to make decisions on selection of people the number of proponents for one field or another. In other words, the submarine guy, he's got to select 100% of his people, and the aviator's got to select 100% of his people, and obviously I wanted 100% of the surface types selected. That was one of my toughest jobs in the entire Navy, trying to handle that as head of that selection board, and fight off submariners as well as airdales, who really didn't fight as hard as the submarine guys, but for some reason Admiral Rickover had everybody convinced in the submarine program, I believe, "Hey, you do it the way I tell you, and I want 100% of those people selected," and so we had a real tough selection board. But we finally got through with that one, although I'm not sure I made very many people happy with that job.

Working for Stan Turner was very interesting. As you well know, Stan Turner was probably one of the smartest naval officers we've ever had. He went on to become head of CIA, etc.[*] I admired him. He was fair. He directed the job to be done, and he expected it to be done.

Paul Stillwell: Do you have any specific examples of your dealings with him?

Admiral Gravely: Well, there was an exercise that we held down at Camp Lejeune.[†] We got a group of amphibious ships and Marines.

Paul Stillwell: Solid Shield?

---

[*] Admiral Stansfield Turner, USN (Ret.), served as Director of Central Intelligence/Director of the Central Intelligence Agency from 9 March 1977 to 20 January 1981. The first part of his tenure was on active duty, prior to his Navy retirement on 1 January 1979.
[†] Camp Lejeune is a Marine Corps base in North Carolina.

Admiral Gravely: Solid Shield, that's the one I can never think of. But I was the destroyer group commander for Solid Shield. Stan was a strong guy for good communications, and he wanted to constantly talk to his group commanders, and so we were constantly sitting up in the radio shack there sending messages back and forth, telling you how to do it. I'd worked with Stan a little bit before, of course, when he was OP-96 and I was 941. If I had any problem with Stan at all, it was Stan's, I think, lack of sympathy for what can be done in a certain incident.

Stan Turner directed me to go down to SoLant and to find out how we could integrate ComCruDesGru 2 and SoLant. Admiral Adamson was ComNavSurfLant.[*] SoLant was an asset as much of SurfLant as it was of Stan Turner, and SurfLant didn't want them integrated. So here I was, a two-star working for two three-stars who wanted opposite things. And no matter what answer you came out with, you upset one of your bosses.

Paul Stillwell: You were caught in the middle.

Admiral Gravely: I really got caught in the middle, because I had to tell Stan, "It can't be done." And he was quite upset with what I had to tell him. Now, I'm not sure what he did, but I do know that SoLant and Group Two haven't been integrated today. So it was a pretty tough chore, and sort of really put me in the spot between my two bosses, because I worked for both—operationally under Second Fleet and administratively under SurfLant.

Paul Stillwell: Had you gotten along more harmoniously with Finneran?

Admiral Gravely: Well, I got along harmoniously with Stan Turner.

Paul Stillwell: It was just this specific issue.

---

[*] Vice Admiral Robert E. Adamson, USN, served as Commander Naval Surface Force Atlantic Fleet from 1975 to 1977.

Admiral Gravely: Just that specific issue. And when you compare the two, I don't think Stan would have said, "Do it," knowing full that he had to coordinate it with the other guy first. Unfortunately Stan Turner and Rojo Adamson didn't really talk. I was given the chore, and then when they integrate the two and for me to take over SoLant responsibilities, you know, "What the hell are you doing, Sam?" [Laughter] It was one of those kinds of things. So I felt that wasn't handled quite right, and it was difficult. Well, I shortly got transferred, and so did Turner, and we just simply didn't solve it while I was down there.

Paul Stillwell: How would you compare flag command at sea with individual ship command? I've heard some say that there's not as much satisfaction when you don't have your own ship.

Admiral Gravely: Well, those people are right. There's nothing like being on a bridge watching a young commander not do it right. And nobody does it right unless they're doing it your way. [Laughter] No, as much as I enjoyed being a seagoing flag officer, there was not the personal satisfaction that I had when I commanded any one of the ships that I commanded. Being close to the individuals is what I really enjoyed and working directly with the individuals. You just don't do that in flag rank. And you have to be very careful, because despite the fact that you've got a seat on the bridge, and you're ready to jump up, you've got to remember that it's not your ship. And so that was kind of hard, but I lived through it.

Paul Stillwell: Were you OTC on some of these exercises?

Admiral Gravely: I was OTC on all the exercises except for those exercises that I had maybe Second Fleet along. Generally, there was no other flag officer who was out there who was senior to me except for Second Fleet when he participated with me in a major exercise. And we did participate in some, Solid Shield for example. And at that point in time, as I recall, Kidd was CinCLantFlt for a while. Yes, because I had both Cousins and Ike Kidd.* Ike Kidd came down on Solid Shield, and I saw him when he got on those.

Paul Stillwell: How much did you do personally at the OTC? How much did your staff do?

Admiral Gravely: Well, that depends on the admiral. Basically the way we did it was that the staff would come up with a proposed op order, doing most of the writing, etc. Then brief me on that op order, and I would cut out those parts I didn't like, and put in new parts that I might like better, and approve what I saw there. We would discuss it, say, every three or four days. There'd be some parts that they'd want to bring up, and then when it was finally put together, as I said, each staff officer would brief his part, and we'd knock out or add to, do it the way we wanted.

So far as the actual handling of the ships was concerned, if there was task force maneuvering and things like that, I generally was either on the bridge or in CIC, where we had our little cubbyhole, and would direct when we made our turns, or when we did various other maneuvers. One of the staff's officers would come up with those recommendations, and I'd either follow it or do it as I thought best. But a flag officer is quite busy at sea. In fact, so is the commanding officer really.

Paul Stillwell: What sorts of ships did you have as flagships?

Admiral Gravely: Generally you had a destroyer. I had a couple of DDGs at times, depending on where you were operating from. I had DLGs like the Standley and the Wainwright at various times. The regular flagship down in Charleston was a tender, and, of course, you left the administrative staff there when you went to sea. You took maybe four or five officers with you and conducted the exercise with those four or five guys, plus a few enlisted types as well. Usually on a destroyer you ate your meals in their wardroom just like anybody else. You were always a guest of the captain. He, of course,

---

* Admiral Ralph W. Cousins, USN, served as Commander in Chief Atlantic Fleet from 31 October 1972 to 30 May 1975. Admiral Isaac C. Kidd, Jr., USN, held the billet from 30 May 1975 to 30 September 1978.

sat at the head of the table. And it is quite unfortunate that a destroyer, a DDG, for example, is really not capable of handling a flag and his staff, so somehow you make room, double bunking and those kinds of things.

Paul Stillwell: The Charles F. Adams class was tight to begin with.

Admiral Gravely: Yes. That was one of the ships that I had as a flagship out of Mayport. Yes, it was.

Paul Stillwell: Could you talk some about the administrative side of the job too? You had the various destroyer squadron commanders reporting to you.

Admiral Gravely: Well, you had the various destroyer squadron commanders reporting to you, just like you said. We used to have periodic meetings on board the flagship to let them talk about their problems, etc., and then see if we couldn't solve them. The biggest thing we had though was the thing at least once a month wherein we all gathered at the little club down there. There was a little club right on the pier down in Charleston, and we sat around and tried to discuss things there. And obviously I'd go aboard ships, sometimes for formal inspection, but most times for just informal inspections and informal chats with the various COs. So from that aspect I was quite busy. We also had an engineer, of course, who was responsible for not only the engineering plants of most of the ships, and designed primarily to help those guys. So he was periodically going around, and when he found problems, he'd come up to me, and, of course, I'd go to the captain. We'd see if we couldn't find ways to solve this guy's problems.

We didn't do a lot of scheduling or anything like that, because that was basically handled by the SurfLant staff. But if there were modifications that we thought necessary, then I sent off a message to SurfLant to see if we couldn't get a guy's schedule changed to suit his needs, and make recommendations on the condition of ships, and recommendations on other things. You did an investigation or two.

Paul Stillwell: Any of those you particularly remember?

Admiral Gravely: Well, one a young skipper who was in the Baltic, and he ran aground up in there. When he got back I had to conduct the investigation on him. And it was quite unfortunate, but I kind of think his career was wrecked as a result of it. He was a young charger, made commander early, and probably had made lieutenant commander early, and didn't make captain at all. But he had an unfortunate grounding up in that area.

Paul Stillwell: The Propulsion Examining Boards were coming along at that time, increased emphasis on engineering readiness. Did that have an impact on your group?

Admiral Gravely: No. PEBs came on basically after Cruiser-Destroyer Group Two, as I recall. They really hit about the '75-'76 time frame, and it was at the point when I was leaving, as I recall. I don't remember getting involved in the PEBs at all. In fact, I know I didn't.

Both of those hats, of course—as I said, I had the Cruiser-Destroyer Group Two, and then when I moved down to Charleston had the Destroyer Development Group—kept me quite busy, because, here again, you had two staffs located in different buildings, at different places. The Cruiser-Destroyer Group Two staff was located on board the tender, and the Destroyer Development Group was located in a building down the pier. And that was not too hectic of a problem, but I had good chiefs of staff in both places, so I didn't have to be unusually concerned with them.

And, of course, when I went to sea the other chief of staff had to handle it anyway. So I thought we did it fairly well. There was a move afoot which ultimately culminated in the Destroyer Development Group moving up to Norfolk to be closer to SurfLant, so that SurfLant could put in his feelings from the entire surface force of the Atlantic Fleet, rather than one group commander handling it. And I think at the same time that was about the time they began to think in terms of Cruiser-Destroyer Two coming a deployable asset. In fact, Gordon Nagler, I think, was the first group commander to take CruDesGru 2 on a deployment.[*]

---

[*] Rear Admiral Gordon R. Nagler, USN.

Paul Stillwell: Were surface-to-surface missiles having an impact yet in your tactical development?

Admiral Gravely: We were certainly playing around with them, although not quite as much as they did subsequent to that. I always felt that if I had a surface contact that I would have hit him with one of the Terriers.* Of course, the Terrier did have a surface capability as you know, because one of the exercises that you used was that you had a surface drone out that you were to shoot at. We did that a couple of times during my tour on Jouett. But they weren't in being as much as, you know, Harpoon and those things that came along later.†

Paul Stillwell: Do you recall any specific tactical developments from that time?

Admiral Gravely: Nothing specific. I'm trying to think.

Paul Stillwell: Anything on towed arrays, for example?‡

Admiral Gravely: Well, we had a couple of towed array ships that I participated in various exercises. And whereas they were using some tactics, I don't think it was specifically developed by the Destroyer Development Group while I was there. But we did use towed arrays in a Springboard exercise down in the Caribbean. We had a couple of those things.

They are good ships, but I kind of fear for them in a real shooting war, when you got one guy out there almost unarmed.§ And he's sitting out there all by himself 15, 20

---

* The Terrier, a radar-beam-riding surface-to-air missile began in the late 1940s as an outgrowth of the Talos supersonic test vehicle. Its first shipboard launch was in 1951
† Harpoon is an antiship missile with a range of approximately 75-80 nautical miles. It can be fired from surface ships, submarines, and aircraft. It reached initial operational capability for shipboard use in 1977 and for aircraft in 1979.
‡ A towed array consists of passive sonar sensors, as opposed to those mounted directly on the ship's hull. By being on a towline, the passive array has the advantage that it can be lowered through thermal layers that would otherwise inhibit sound propagation and reception.
§ T-AGOS is the designation for ocean surveillance ships operated by civil service mariners of the Military Sealift Command. They are equipped with the surveillance towed array sensor system (SURTASS), a submarine detection system.

miles away. Really, you almost got to leave somebody back to protect him. You know, he's got that big towed array that he's moving around with. They don't go at big speeds, you might call it, when he's got that thing towed behind him.

Personally, despite the fact that I know that towed array is much more sensitive and everything else, I've never really seen anything wrong with VDS. I know we're not using VDSs anymore. I don't think any of the ships have VDSs now, but that was a very, very good towed array, so far as I'm concerned. And, of course, you could drive that thing at 27 knots. Catenary came up a little bit, but still you could still move and maneuver with it, no matter what. The only time I've ever seen a mishap on the VDS was when I had Taussig, and Frank Knox and I were operating together. When the exercise ended, well, Frank Knox couldn't lift his, so he had to do it manually, and that takes forever. But that was the only failure that I saw while I operated it.

Well, getting back to the Cruiser-Destroyer Group Two, I happened to be in Norfolk. I was doing something, I've forgotten what it was. I went by the Second Fleet flagship to see Admiral Turner, and he congratulated me. He said, "I just saw something on your orders, and you're going to Third Fleet." Of course, I was quite overjoyed, and I reminded him that it was my understanding that before you got three stars that you were normally interviewed by SecDef and two or three other people. He said, "Well, I don't know about that, but I just saw your orders this morning, and you're going to Third Fleet."

Well, I was quite happy with that one, and I came home. I came through Washington before going to Charleston. I told my wife, "Hey, don't tell anybody, but we're going to Honolulu for our next duty, and I'm going to command the Third Fleet." And she was quite overjoyed. The next morning I got a call from the flag detailer, and he said, "Admiral, I want to tell you and congratulations. Your orders have just been approved by SecNav, and you're going as commandant of the 11th Naval District." I don't know how I felt. [Laughter]

Paul Stillwell: You were thinking, "What about the Third Fleet?"

Admiral Gravely: Yes, yes. What about Third Fleet? What about the third star and the whole bit? But he wasn't the guy to ask, so I didn't ask him. So I just got off the phone, and I told my wife, "Hey, change that. We're going to San Diego again as Commandant of the 11th Naval District." Well, a little disappointed, but—

Paul Stillwell: But you liked San Diego.

Admiral Gravely: Yes, I liked San Diego so that made up for it. Well, I got relieved by Admiral Bruce Keener, who got selected that spring, and he came down to Charleston and relieved me.* I then made preparations to do something with my house, of course, and also to move on out to San Diego.

Paul Stillwell: You didn't have any problem with quarters there.

Admiral Gravely: No. Well, it was primarily because of the fact that there was a set of quarters that was designated for the commandant, and that was it. It wasn't a case of moving to where there were no designated quarters for you, and then some guy having to designate a set.

Well, there was a little minor problem, and it wasn't San Diego's fault. Wasn't anybody's fault, I guess. But I got detached in June to relieve a guy who wasn't retiring until August. So, of course, I came home. Well, I needed a little time, but I certainly didn't need 60 days, which was almost what it amounted to. And ultimately that hurt me, because that was the year that they set up top boundary on how many days you can have. Do you remember that one?

Paul Stillwell: No, I don't.

Admiral Gravely: Well, what basically happened was that I'd always planned to have 60 days on the books when I retired so that I'd stayed above 60. And then suddenly your top

---

* Rear Admiral Bruce Keener III, USN.

number was what you had as of that September or something like that. Which meant that I had about 39 days when I retired rather than what I wanted, 60.[*]

But, anyway, we sold our house here. I guess we sold our house and drove out to San Diego, and I mapped a route wherein we could hit guesthouses all the way across country, guest quarters or BOQ, etc. And that was quite interesting. We went from Washington to San Diego, and I guess Phoenix, Arizona, which does have an air base there, was the only place that I didn't stay in a military BOQ or quarters. Well, we went out to San Diego. Of course, we initially stayed in the Admiral Kidd BOQ for 15 or 20 days until I relieved Admiral Gilkeson and then took over that job.[†]

San Diego was probably the most interesting place I've ever been, and I've always liked it. And so I was just simply overjoyed. I did have a feeling that this being my third two-star job, and certainly my contemporaries and who were even junior to me, had been selected for three stars that I was probably being sent out there to retire.

Paul Stillwell: Well, that was a traditional retirement-type job.

Admiral Gravely: That was a traditional retirement-type job. And whereas the commandant had been in place since 1921, there wasn't a single Com 11 who had gone to three stars. And so that just reinforced it. But I did find out one thing, and that is that despite the fact that none had ever made three stars, two were at least nominated. One commandant was nominated to go to Taiwan as Commander Naval Taiwan Defense Force to a three-star job. But, unfortunately, his wife was down with cancer and so he declined. He stayed there until he retired. The second one was coming back to Washington, D.C. to a joint job. And when he got to Washington, D.C., to the joint three-star job, it had been downgraded to two stars. So that was what happened to him. Somehow I decided that, okay, so if this is where I'm going to retire, fine, but at the same time I'm going to do this job as best I know how, and make the most of it.

Well, San Diego became one of the busiest jobs I've ever had from a social aspect. And to some degree that was basically the commandant's job out there. You

---

[*] Upon retirement an individual receives one additional day's pay for each day of unused leave still on the books.
[†] Rear Admiral Fillmore B. Gilkeson, USN.

were sort of an interface between the military and the civilian community. I certainly knew all the big people out there, went to all the right affairs. Hopefully did all the right things. I was giving something like about a speech a month, the whole bit. Had lots of good friends out there and met new ones. Pete Wilson, of course, was a good friend of mine.

Paul Stillwell: The mayor.

Admiral Gravely: The mayor.* And also the other Wilson, who was the congressman from there became a good friend of mine. From a Navy standpoint, Bob Baldwin was there and Emmitt Tidd was there. Baldwin had AirPac and the other guy had SurfPac.† So it was a really, really enjoyable tour.

Paul Stillwell: There is no more district commandant setup. Do you think that the Navy lost something when those jobs were abolished?

Admiral Gravely: Well, the job as commandant was abolished, but I think what they did is basically retitle him; he became ComNavBase.

Paul Stillwell: I see.

Admiral Gravely: And as I recall, you were commandant and Commander Naval Base before. Now, what the ComNavBase's area is, I'm not sure now, but certainly as commandant you had a large area. And you were the area coordinator for a large area. Long Beach, of course, was under Com 11, so I spent time up in the shipyard checking on how they were doing things. We didn't really inspect them, but to some degree it was an administrative inspection. San Diego, the naval base there, I was very closely aligned with him. We used to have what we used to call area coordination meetings about once a quarter. So we conducted about four or five of those. Had all the COs in, wherein we

---

* Pete Wilson was mayor of San Diego, 1971-83, and governor of California, 1991-99.
† Vice Admiral Robert B. Baldwin, USN, Commander Naval Air Force Pacific Fleet; Vice Admiral Emmett H. Tidd, USN, Commander Naval Surface Force Pacific Fleet.

tried to lay down policies and those kinds of things. You set the uniform of the day and that. Of course, for San Diego most of the year it was whites anyway, but certainly you changed that.

Paul Stillwell: Well, one thing that that has changed is that the reserve administration no longer comes under that. That was one of your jobs.

Admiral Gravely: That was one of my jobs as the reserve guy, and that has been changed. Whether that changed before or after they went to the ComNavBase system or not, I don't know.

Paul Stillwell: About '74, as I remember, was when they set up the reserve regional commands.

Admiral Gravely: Yes, right, right, '74 they set up reserve regional command, but I think that to some degree that I reported to the commandant even before that. I think they've taken away from the commandant. They've taken it away from ComNavBase for that.

Well, there was a reserve destroyer group commander by the name of Lyons, who was out there during my time. And we came back to the reserve headquarters there; Charbonnet was the three-star reserve type there.* I guess I didn't do much in the way of functions with them except a change of command every now and then. A speech here, some reserve function. Lyons really ran the outfit so far as I was concerned. Other than that, there wasn't that much of a close tie. Of course, there was a reserve training center in San Diego, and I used to go there once in a while to talk to the commanding officer, find out if he had problems and things like that. But not as close a tie as you might think.

Paul Stillwell: So it sounds like there were a lot of demands on your time in this job as far as getting out in the community and what have you.

---

* Vice Admiral Pierre N. Charbonnet, Jr., USN, Chief of Naval Reserve.

Admiral Gravely: The job required you to be constantly alert to problems in the community. There was a move afoot to build a new hospital out there, which I got quite involved in. Had a problem with Mexico in that a female had a son who got locked up in the Tijuana jail because of marijuana, and she went down there and broke him out.

Paul Stillwell: She disguised herself as a prostitute, didn't she?

Admiral Gravely: Well, it was a little of that and little of a couple other things. I heard about this situation through a minister there, as I recall. He was telling me about this woman whose son was down there in the Tijuana jail. She was from Atlanta, Georgia, and apparently worked for an airline and periodically got flights out there, so she was out there quite often. So one night my wife and I were thinking about it and said, "Well, my God, you can only go down to Tijuana and visit a son just so often. What does she do the rest of the day?"

We thought we ought to at least meet her, and see if there was any help we could offer. So fine. So one night I located her, and went down to visit her, and brought her up to the house, and my wife and she became just really fast friends. Well, she mentioned to me about this plan about trying to break that son out, because she had used every legal thing that she possibly could, and apparently about all the Mexican legal types were doing were just getting her money and doing nothing.

Her son was a Navy guy. He was about a second class, and he was on the East Coast and had been transferred to San Francisco. When he came through Atlanta, Georgia, coming west, the mother let him bring a 17-year-old boy out, and they stopped in San Diego for some reason, went down to Tijuana and got thrown in the pokey for buying marijuana. In fact, the guy they bought the marijuana from was probably the guy who fingered them.

Well, somehow the 17-year-old boy got out, but they just kept the other kid down there. Well, ultimately this woman came up with this plan basically that she would go down there dressed as a prostitute, if you want to have it, along with another girl, and they would spring him out of there somehow. Well, the plan was that three women would go down to the shore patrol headquarters, get a pass, and as they carried it out then about halfway to the jail one woman got sick. And so the mother feigned illness and had to be brought back. The other two girls continued on, but the mother had the third pass. So when they got to the jail they were admitted.

Of course, the Mexicans were chuckling because here was this guy who had two women down here at the same time, and they had conjugal privileges there, and you know what they imagined. Well, what happened, one was his sister and another was a friend of the family, and they had enough clothing for him under their clothes, that when they got into this jail cell he immediately changed to a woman's clothes, and, of course, now he had a pass. Well, I guess the watch changed or something, but anyway the two women went in there and three came out, and they all got back, and here they broke this kid out who had been in the Mexican jail for about two or three months.

Well, in any event, the mother was not very popular with a lot of people around there. The Mexicans swore that the shore patrol had more or less instigated this. But ultimately it was proven it was just the mother's plan, and she got him out. And, of course, he went on back to his naval duty station up in San Francisco. And he was held certainly unlawfully, really, and so there were no problems with him. He reported, and I guess he's still in the Navy now. Well, you got to remember when you're caught like that, there's nothing you can do about it as far as Navy discipline. You can't say that he didn't want to come back, because he wanted to get back.

The other big thing that I remember about San Diego was the Newport Beach-to-Ensenada boat race. It's a sailboat race that goes on each year. And each year the commandant goes down to Ensenada to present to the winner of that race one of the trophies, or one class of winners the trophy from the Secretary of the Navy. And, of course, I was granted the opportunity to do that.

There was nothing really unusual about that except there were a couple of funny incidents like the aide had been down the year before with Admiral Gilkeson. He said, "The way we did it last year was that in order to ensure that we don't have any problem down there, we go through each city en route, and we pay a visit on the mayor and the chief of police and usually present them with a plaque." So we decided to do that. And I never will forget the mayor, as I recall, wasn't there, but we left the plaque for him. The chief of police was apparently a guy who was appointed, and not a dedicated policeman like our people are. It was a businessman who ran a business as a normal chain of events, but he was a police chief on the side.

So we went down and met him at the police station, and he was so pleased with that plaque until he decided that he wanted us to see his business. So we agreed, and we went over to see his business. He was basically a jewelry store operator, and he had watches galore, rings galore, and everything that glittered. That was the way I described it. But he was so happy with that plaque until he decided that he'd present each of us with watches. And he gave me a watch, and he gave my driver a watch, and he gave the aide a watch. Well, I was quite grateful, and I put the watch on, and I started winding it and the stem broke off in my hand. [Laughter] And, of course, I just quickly covered it up and left it there and went on from there.

The boat race went on as normal. My wife wanted to go fishing, so the Mexican Navy put the two of us on a minesweep, and she and I went out fishing. They probably thought they were going to have 20 people, but there were only the two of us, and we had Cokes enough and sandwiches enough for about 20 people. We went out there, had a good time.

Being commandant was a fun tour. It really was. I really enjoyed it, despite the fact that it was historically a retirement billet, I don't regret going there one bit, because I just met so many good people and was able to do so many things that I'd never done before in my life. I really enjoyed it.

Paul Stillwell: In many ways you were a goodwill ambassador for the Navy.

Admiral Gravely: You are a goodwill ambassador for the Navy for an area. We had all kinds of visitors out there. Of course, SecNav was out there, Secretary Middendorf, and several other people.* We hosted cocktail parties. We hosted a cocktail party for Secretary Middendorf, and Pete Wilson was at the party. Another good friend of mine was a councilman by the name of Hubbard, who has since died, but I can remember that Councilman Hubbard was there.

---

* J. William Middendorf served as Secretary of the Navy from 20 June 1974 to 20 January 1977.

Paul Stillwell: Did you get into judicial review for people in the naval district?

Admiral Gravely: No, you really didn't. Most of the things were the responsibility of the operational commander. I got inadvertently into a couple of things. One was a young black officer who was in Midway, at the SOSUS station.[*] Admiral Watkins, who was the Chief of Naval Personnel, asked me to look into this thing for him.[†] It turned out it was a young officer who was in a program wherein we sent young petty officers to the engineering thing at Purdue.

Paul Stillwell: NESEP.[‡]

Admiral Gravely: NESEP. Yes, he was a young NESEP officer who unfortunately decided that he wanted to be a race relations expert when he got out of school. Now, the Navy sent him to be an engineer, as you well know, that program. And when he graduated he was sent to an engineering officer of a destroyer, which was the finest set of orders a young man could have. This young man just constantly said, "No, I want to be a race relations expert." So he came to the surface warfare school, a short course out there.

He dragged his feet, and finally they decided that he wasn't trying, so he ended up getting orders out to Midway to the SOSUS station there. Apparently he was there for about a month when the CO said, "You know, in the next two months or so we're going to have an operational readiness inspection, and I want you along with two or three other officers here to be qualified watch officers by the time this team comes off. And personally I don't think you're working at it hard enough."

So the young man said, "Okay, sir. I'll do what I can," or something like that. But, anyway, he just continued to drag his feet. So finally the CO recommended him for a court-martial, and I guess ultimately he was dismissed from the Navy. I got involved in the review process, whether or not they should try him someplace else. But, frankly, he

---

[*] SOSUS—sound surveillance system, a seafloor network of listening devices used by the U.S. Navy to detect noises from transiting ships.
[†] Vice Admiral James D. Watkins, USN, served as Chief of Naval Personnel from 10 April 1975 to 21 July 1978.
[‡] NESEP—Navy Enlisted Scientific Education Program, which is no longer in existence. Under its provisions the Navy paid for the college education of promising enlisted personnel, then sent them through the Officer Candidate School for training and commissioning as officers.

had, so far as I was concerned, used up all of his chances at success, and we had to do without him despite the fact that here was a guy who now had about six, seven years in the Navy. He was ex-enlisted and had gone to college, etc. I guess the Navy wasn't the best spot for him.

Had another strange incident. The commanding officer of the Naval Communications Station had his office right above the commandant's office there. And the young man who commanded that station had worked for me at ComNavTelCom and was just really an outstanding guy. I admired him, and so occasionally I'd go up and have a cup of coffee with him. They had a problem in that a young black girl had come back to her desk, and there was a cross burning on her desk. We got into that one, and I did some investigating there. And believe it or not—and it's hard to believe—but this woman imagined that she saw a cross burning on her desk. It was just the strangest thing I've ever seen.

Paul Stillwell: It hadn't really happened?

Admiral Gravely: It did not really happen. And I just don't know. Once in a while you get involved in things like that, and you don't know why or how.

Paul Stillwell: Well, we're right at the end of the tape, Admiral. Why don't we take up your three-star tours next time?

Admiral Gravely: Okay, great. We're getting close.

Interview Number 6 with Vice Admiral Samuel L. Gravely, Jr., U.S. Navy (Retired)

Place: Admiral Gravely's office in Burke, Virginia

Date: Friday, 17 October 1986

Interviewer: Paul Stillwell

Paul Stillwell: Admiral, since our last meeting I've been to the Midwest and interviewed five members of the Golden 13.[*] The name that kept coming up over and over was that of Dennis Nelson, the only one in that group to stay in for a full career.[†]

Admiral Gravely: Yes.

Paul Stillwell: What are your recollections of Dennis Nelson through the years?

Admiral Gravely: Well, I knew Dennis very well. In fact, I was stationed in New York with Dennis for about a year and a half on the staff of Com Three. I'd also met Dennis previously, because when I first was commissioned as a reserve officer back in 1944 and went to Great Lakes, Dennis was there as a member of that staff. Dennis was definitely one of the smarter of all of us, really. As I recall, he either had his master's or he did his master's while he was on active duty. He remained on active duty until retirement, which was something different from the other members of the Golden 13, as well as the entire 62 naval officers that we had in the Navy during World War II.

As I recall, Dennis was the only ex-reservist, other than John Lee, who might have been counted in that group during World War II, who stayed on.[‡] John Lee, of

---

[*] The Golden Thirteen comprised the first black line officers commissioned for active duty in the U.S. Navy. Sixteen Navy petty officers went through a special officer-training program in early 1944 at the Great Lakes Naval Training Station in Illinois. Of the group 12 received Naval Reserve commissions as ensigns, and the 13th became a warrant officer. See Paul Stillwell, The Golden Thirteen: Recollections of the First Black Naval Officers (Annapolis: Naval Institute Press, 1993).

[†] Ensign Dennis Denmark Nelson II, USNR. He eventually retired from the Navy as a lieutenant commander. He died in 1979 before he could be interviewed as part of the Naval Institute's oral history program. Nelson's master's thesis was published by the Navy Department in 1948 and later came out as a book, The Integration of the Negro into the U.S. Navy (New York: Farrar, Strauss and Young, 1951).

[‡] On 15 March 1947 Lieutenant (junior grade) John W. Lee, Jr., USNR, became the first black officer with a commission in the regular Navy. He served on active duty until his retirement as a lieutenant commander in 1 July 1966. His oral history is in the Naval Institute collection.

course, became the first black regular Navy officer when he transferred, and Dennis was very shortly after that. Dennis was the only one of the Golden 13 to stay in. Dennis probably did more for all of us than any of us, really, because he fought some really impossible odds to become a naval officer. As I recall, he was a little bit over age, which was against him, because Dennis was, I'm sure, in his 30s someplace. He transferred at a time when he was a lieutenant, which was almost unheard of to some degree at that point in time.

Dennis was in the public information area, wherein he was certainly able to do a lot of positive things. He worked with all of the major black groups of that time: the NAACP, the Urban League, and those kinds of things in his capacity as a public affairs officer. And I think that he knew at least a couple of Secretaries of the Navy, because he worked in the Washington area. So, overall, so far as the integration of blacks into the Navy, I think Dennis did as much or more than any of the rest of us. Of course, he also wrote the book, The Integration of the Negro into the U.S. Navy, which was sort of a bible to some respects for all of us. So Dennis, despite the fact he only got to the grade of lieutenant commander, was one of the stalwarts, I think, of the young black officers that we had during that time frame. Again, I knew him very well, because he was in Great Lakes. He had a program of teaching people who couldn't read at that point in time, the illiterates. In fact he established that program in the Navy and was working at Great Lakes when I first met him. And, of course, as I said, he stayed in during those hard years of '47-'48 when the rest of us went off to do other things, except for John Lee.

Paul Stillwell: Do you have any suppositions on why he didn't reach a higher rank than lieutenant commander?

Admiral Gravely: Well, I think that Dennis sort of sacrificed himself in some regards in that Dennis felt very strongly that he should have been at the scene of activity relating to integrating blacks into the Navy. I can remember at one time that Dennis probably should have gone to sea, and he insisted on staying at that scene in Washington. I think if he'd gone to sea at that point in time, he might have gone higher. The Navy wants seagoing officers and not people who stay ashore. As I recall, Nelson came to the staff of

Third Naval District at about the time when Nelson should have gone to a seagoing job. So that's the only thing I can say that is probably the reason that he didn't go higher. But, of course, as you well know, it just so happens that guys who are plodding ahead and were ahead of the curve, are usually the ones that take the brunt of the blow when we chop and stop things. So it could have been that. I don't know.

Paul Stillwell: Well, I've also heard, I guess, that his personality may have worked against him, that he was aggressive, and maybe that turned some people off.

Admiral Gravely: He was very, very aggressive, and straightforward. He was a no-nonsense guy. I can remember that on one occasion that when the average black, and not only black naval officers but black period, couldn't live at certain places. In my case I guess I took the easier route out in that my wife and I, when we drove across country would—if we knew that we could live at this hotel, we'd go to this hotel, but if we knew that we were going to be turned down, there was no sense in going there. Whereas Nelson put on his uniform. In fact, he drove across country once in whites. Stopped anyplace he wanted to, and it looked like some of those places they thought he was sort of an African prince or something, when he was just another black naval officer. And he got accommodations wherein I just went across the tracks at times. So it was some of that, and I'm sure that if some people who resented that kind of activity who knew about it, then that would have stopped him right there.

Paul Stillwell: Well, I've gotten the impression this was a very proud, very determined man. And as you say, he did pave the way, and perhaps did sacrifice himself so that others might succeed.

Admiral Gravely: That's right. I firmly believe that. He was just a tremendous naval officer. He was the kind of a guy that a lot of us went to for some type of advice and those kinds of things. In my own case, for example, he was probably 15 years older than I, and he was almost like a fatherly figure to me. And he knew how to get things done.

Paul Stillwell: You then may have been one of the primary beneficiaries of the work that he did.

Admiral Gravely: You're absolutely right. I may have been. We worked together a couple of times. Once in Com Three on the staff there in some recruiting programs and those kinds of things. Very, very smart, very, very intelligent guy. And, as I said, knew how to get things done. Yes, a great guy.

Paul Stillwell: Well, you did some trail blazing of your own, being the first black officer to achieve three stars and get command of a fleet. Could you describe, please, the sequence of events that led to that?

Admiral Gravely: Yes. I was commandant of the 11th Naval District. At that point in time the reserves in the area were under the cognizance of the commandant. I was going around to various reserve training centers, and I happened to be up in the San Francisco area about that time, inspecting a couple of those, when I got a call from the Chief Naval Operations's office. When I talked to Admiral Holloway himself, I found out wanted me to come to Washington, because I was to talk to the Secretary of Defense concerning my next job.* Frankly, I'd only been there for about 10 and a half, maybe 11 months, at that point in time, and I really didn't expect to go anyplace. I thought I would be there for at least a two-year tour, maybe a three-year tour.

Paul Stillwell: Had you expected to retire from the job in San Diego?

Admiral Gravely: I really had. I had anticipated that that was the main reason I was sent there, so I was quite surprised to be talking about another job. At the same time I said, "Well, okay, it'll be a communications job someplace as a two-star," because there was no hint at all that it was to be a three-star job. But then I thought it might be, because it mentioned that I had an interview with the Secretary of Defense, and I knew that

---

* Admiral James L. Holloway III, USN, served as Chief of Naval Operations from 29 June 1974 to 1 July 1978.

normally if you went to the three-star level that you were interviewed first by the SecDef, probably SecNav, and the rest of them.

Paul Stillwell: You'd gotten your hopes up before when you had the cruiser-destroyer group, so you were probably more cautious this time.

Admiral Gravely: Well, you're absolutely correct, because I did have my hopes up at that point in time, and was quite disappointed when I got the phone call which said I was going to Com 11, because I'd been advised that I'd been accepted to Third Fleet at that point in time. I told the CNO certainly I could be back there at any time, and I quickly came back to San Diego, and, of course, got on an appropriate airplane, came on to Washington, D.C., and went in on the scheduled time for my interviews. I talked, of course, with the Chief of Naval Operations. And for some reason, I guess, I felt that I would probably be interviewed by the Secretary of the Navy, and I was not. There was no requirement whatsoever. Then I went up to see Mr. Rumsfeld.[*]

Paul Stillwell: What was the substance of your discussion with Admiral Holloway?

Admiral Gravely: Well, basically that I had been nominated by him for a third star, and that I was going out as Commander Third Fleet. And, of course, it basically depended on my interviews, etc.

Paul Stillwell: Did he say on what basis you had been picked for the job?

Admiral Gravely: No, there was no discussion of the basis or anything else. Just simply that I had been nominated by him for the job. He did say that I'd done a fairly decent job out there at Com 11. In fact, he didn't say fairly decent, but an outstanding job at Com 11, and they felt that I rated a look at and possible promotion. Well, this was about the first time I found out that it was really the Third Fleet. However, Third Fleet, as I said, had come up a year earlier. I went in, and I was interviewed by the deputy first, the

---

[*] Donald H. Rumsfeld served as Secretary of Defense from 20 November 1975 to 20 January 1977.

Deputy SecDef—Clements, I believe his name was.* We talked in general terms as to what the responsibilities would be, and just simply that. He was a little bit pleased, I believe, at my answers, although there were a couple of things when he said, "Well, the responsibilities are greater than that."

Fine. I thought in terms more of the training aspect than I did the aspect of the defense of the continental limits of the U.S. So when I said training, because I knew that Third Fleet basically trained the ships for the deployment out to the Seventh Fleet. Then he wanted to make sure that I was aware that it was more. So fine, I was aware of that, but I thought that was a secondary mission rather than—really, it's the primary mission. But, in any event, after that interview I went up to Mr. Rumsfeld. That interview went rather straightforward, and some of the same questions were asked. He talked a little bit about my having been Director of Naval communications, and why hadn't I solved this secure voice program problem, which nobody had really done.

But he asked me one question, which made me think a little bit and basically that question was that if I had been promised the job of Commander of Third Fleet, and then was told that I would not get it, how would I feel about it. I simply said, "Well, I'm not sure, but I wouldn't go out and shoot myself." I didn't think that much of the question at that point in time, but suddenly shortly after that I knew what the problem was. The problem was that another three-star officer had been told that he would get that job, and then they had to backtrack. The reason I knew that was because I got his mail for about three or four weeks after I got out there. And it was quite interesting as to why he had asked me that question. The other officer then did get a three-star job, and I talked to him after that about it. He said he would liked to have the Third Fleet job, but it really didn't make any difference as long as he got the third star, which he did get. And, of course, he ultimately got four stars.

Paul Stillwell: That was Admiral Whittle, wasn't it?

---

* William P. Clements, Jr., served as Deputy Secretary of Defense from 1973 to 1977.

Admiral Gravely: Admiral Whittle was the guy.* Admiral Whittle and I were selected the same year, so we knew each other and the whole bit. And whereas I guess any two admirals who are two stars are sort of fighting each other, in other words trying to get the three stars first, we weren't enemies. We were good friendly competitors, I guess.

Paul Stillwell: Did any of these interviews touch on the ASW aspects of the job?

Admiral Gravely: Only from the aspect that this was a very, very vital and important aspect of the job. I guess it didn't come up too much, because, as I recall, Admiral Gayler was in town about the same time I was there, and I think that Admiral Gayler, who was CinCPac at that time, had been in and had basically touched on his problems in ASW with Mr. Clements.† I'd overheard a couple of things on ASW. Gayler had a nice loud voice, so you could hear him—overhear him—and I did. So I think that Mr. Clements felt that that problem was being handled very well and everything else. So we didn't talk too much about it, although it was my prime responsibility when I got out there.

I went out, and, of course, I relieved Admiral Coogan, who had for a very short while been both Third Fleet and ComNavAirPac.‡ I've forgotten exactly what happened to ComNavAirPac, why that job had been gapped for a little while, and why he had to fill both of them. But in any event, he did come back and fill that after I'd done it.

Paul Stillwell: How soon after your interview with Secretary Rumsfeld did you get the news that you were in fact getting the job?

Admiral Gravely: Well, it was very, very shortly after that, and I can't tell you exactly when, but I do know that I happened to have been out again, up in the Long Beach area, when the word was announced. I got a call from Admiral Holloway saying they expected

---

* Vice Admiral Alfred J. Whittle, Jr., USN, was assigned instead as Chief of Staff, Supreme Allied Commander Atlantic, working for Admiral Isaac C. Kidd, Jr., USN.
† Admiral Noel A. M. Gayler, USN, served as Commander in Chief Pacific from 1 September 1972 to 30 August 1976. His oral history is in the Naval Institute collection.
‡ Vice Admiral Robert P. Coogan, USN, served as Commander Third Fleet from July 1975 to September 1976.

to announce it at 10:00 o'clock California time, which was about 1:00 o'clock there. So within a week or ten days the announcement was made that I was getting the job.

It was quite interesting to me, because at that time I happened to be up there attending a luncheon with the commander of the Naval Base San Francisco. He was really concerned because he wanted to have Third Fleet in the San Francisco area for Navy Day. And his real concern was that he was not able to ask the guy and get a commitment out of him, because he didn't know who it was. And there I was sitting there talking to him, knowing who it was, and I couldn't say either. [Laughter] But it was announced just about the time we were finishing up our luncheon. And I said, "Okay, I'll do it for you." [Laughter] So it was quite interesting the way that happened.

Paul Stillwell: I'm sure there was a great pleasure and satisfaction for your wife in your getting this promotion.

Admiral Gravely: Yes, for the entire family really. We had been out in Honolulu before, at Pearl Harbor, and we were quite happy and eager to get back a second time, certainly with the third star. The relieving ceremony there was quite nice. We had a really, really nice crowd and lots of people, because I had made a lot of friends in San Diego, and friends from all over came to that.

The biggest thing was that the arrangements were such that on the ship on which I was frocked for two stars, the USS Jouett, we later used that for the change of command ceremony for Com 11. I was frocked with my third star on Jouett as well, so I have always considered that quite a significant happening. For the relief as Com 11 we had done it on a carrier over in the ComNavAirPac bailiwick, primarily because my predecessor was an aviator. This time as a surface force commander, I did it in a surface forces backyard. Admiral St. George was ComNavSurfPac, and he was the frocker, with me being the frockee, I guess.[*] It was quite an enjoyable ceremony. As I said, we had lots and lots of friends there and thoroughly enjoyed it.

---

[*] Vice Admiral William R. St. George, USN, Commander Naval Surface Force Pacific Fleet.

Paul Stillwell: There were rumors that your nomination was tied in with the presidential campaign in 1976. Did you hear those rumors? Did you put any credence in them?

Admiral Gravely: I don't remember hearing any of those rumors. Could have been, though. But I didn't really hear them. Now, it so happened that I knew President Ford, because I'd met President Ford out in San Diego that year.[*] And I guess he's the guy who nominated me. I'm sure he was. So I don't really know. But I don't remember hearing that much about it, and stranger things have happened, let's face it.

Paul Stillwell: Well, as we said before, you've got to be both lucky and good to get a job like that.

Admiral Gravely: You have to be lucky, and it's more being at the right place at the right time. And of course, having the right stuff. Okay, I was at the right place at the right time, and, of course, hopefully had the right stuff. But, anyway, I successfully got it.

Well, I went out to Third Fleet, and, of course, I relieved Coogan out there. I've forgotten what day it was. September or something like that. I do recall that my relief at Com 11 was one year to the day, and I went out there something like about the 12th of September, the 10th of September. Admiral Hayward was CinCPacFlt.[†] I had known Admiral Hayward, so that was fairly easy from that aspect of it.

I got involved in a couple of things that I really didn't think were mine, despite the fact the fleet commander thought were my bailiwick. One was the Kahoolawe situation, wherein the island of Kahoolawe was used as a target for naval gunfire support training. And we had a group of Hawaiians at that point in time who were anti the Navy using that island for that. They contended more or less that the island should be cleaned up, and somehow it should be turned over for use of native Hawaiians, and probably the Navy ought to pay reparations, etc.

---

[*] Gerald R. Ford served as President of the United States from 9 August 1974 to 20 January 1977. He ran for election in 1976 and was defeated by Jimmy Carter.
[†] Admiral Thomas B. Hayward, USN, served as Commander in Chief Pacific Fleet, 12 August 1976 to 9 May 1978.

Paul Stillwell: Sort of comparable to the Culebra situation in the Atlantic.

Admiral Gravely: Comparable. It was basically the exact same thing. I'm not sure about the water supply on Culebra, but there was no water at all on this island. You brought a desalinization plant in there or something like that. But, then again, the readiness of the forces out there certainly deteriorated, because the Navy had no place to do the shooting in the gunfire support area, which was what was done all the time. Well, originally Com 14 had been the biggest defender of that.* And, of course, he was the guy who went to court, and all the rest of the garbage. But then the people from Com 14 were transferred over to Commander Third Fleet, and as the user of the facility, then I became the defender of it.

One of the most interesting things that occurred during that time frame was that the Kahunas, or whatever you want to call them, who were proponents, wanted a meeting on the island, which I had to arrange, and we carried Congressman Heftel down there.† The agreement basically was that there'd be no press—that only the Navy, members of the Congress, Congressman Heftel, and the proponents for the island would be taken over there. So we did this, but we stopped in Maui to pick the councilman from Maui. When we arrived the councilman was not there, and it turned out that he felt he could not go, which meant that there was an extra seat on the airplane. There were two press people, one a reporter, and she had a photographer with her, who decided that that seat then belonged to at least one of them. The young lady went over to Congressman Heftel while I was standing out sort of waiting to see if the councilman was coming, and demanded from Congressman Heftel that she be given that seat.

He promptly told her that, no, this was a Navy helicopter, and she would have to get her seat from the admiral. Well, knowing full well that the agreement was that there would be no press, I refused to take her. So I went over where she was climbing into the airplane, and I said, "I'm sorry, Miss, but I cannot permit you to go in that airplane." The woman turned around and slugged me. And she was about ready to slug me again when I

---

* The Commandant of the 14th Naval District had been based in Hawaii, but the naval districts were being phased out.
† Cecil L. Heftel (Democrat-Hawaii) served in the U.S. House of Representatives from 3 January 1977 until his resignation 11 July 1986.

just sort of put both hands on her arms, and just lifted her off of the step of that airplane, and said, "I'm sorry, Miss, but I can't let you on there." She then sat underneath the airplane where we couldn't take off. So we promptly got the police to get her out of there.

Everything would have been okay, I guess, except for the fact that her photographer, and we had photographers too that were Navy, but her photographer was the one that took the picture. [Small laugh] The picture made it look like I slugged her. In fact, I got a call from my brother when he saw the picture in The Washington Post, and, "Hey, you don't slap women." And, of course, I had not done it.

Paul Stillwell: Did you get the impression that the whole thing was staged?

Admiral Gravely: The whole thing, I think, was staged. It was quite interesting to me the minute I got home her lawyer called, and wanted to talk to find out if I had planned to sue and those kinds of things. But I personally felt that it looked kind of strange for a 250-pound admiral to be suing a 100-pound woman because she slapped him. But, in any event, I really was taken aback by that reaction there. But the only thing that I really objected to was the picture and the publicity and everything else. Well, I guess the Honolulu news types were a little unhappy with me, because the first thing they wanted when I got off the helicopter back on Pearl Harbor was an interview. But I just slipped off the airplane and went on home. Of course, I guess I should have satisfied them, but I'd had my fill of the press people at that point in time. And so I did nothing.

Paul Stillwell: And you probably had the idea that they didn't want to talk about the substance of the issue either.

Admiral Gravely: They didn't want to talk about that. All they wanted to talk about was me. You know, was I going to sue her and all those things?

Paul Stillwell: Wasn't there also a concern in this whole discussion about Kahoolawe that the shooting was interfering with bird migration?

Admiral Gravely: Well, there are all kinds of concerns. Bird migration. The racing pigeon fans, of whom I am one, wrote an article which basically said that it was interfering with the homing pigeons' instinct, and they weren't coming home on time. Lots of other things. All kinds of things. In fact, when the story came about the homing pigeons losing their way as a result of the shooting—in fact, I even got into that argument, and wrote a letter to the <u>Honolulu Times</u> or whatever the name of the paper is. A letter to the editor, which we could probably get a copy if we wanted it.

Paul Stillwell: What was the ultimate resolution of the issue?

Admiral Gravely: Well, it was not resolved while I was there, and I don't think it's fully resolved today, although there is certainly less noise being made. Certainly you don't have Ritter, who was one of the head guys, and his group stealing onto the island like they used to do. In fact, if you recall, there were three of them, as I recall, who surfed out there and ended up with one dying. One drowned. There was a time when Ritter got on the island and stayed on there for about 30 days. We couldn't find him. And then, when we finally did capture him and bring him off the island, he got off with a bag of goats. There were about 30 little goats in a knapsack. Of course, that upset the commander in chief, but there wasn't much we could do about it.

Paul Stillwell: But the upshot was the Navy was able to continue using the island.

Admiral Gravely: The Navy continued to use the island throughout, and I believe they are using the island even today. There's less stink about it now than there was at that point in time.

Obviously there was more to the Third Fleet job than Kahoolawe. The job basically was the readiness and the training of the forces that all belonged to Third Fleet: scheduling the various exercises, going out on the various exercises, and I did go occasionally, riding one ship after another. The ASW readiness. Arranging for lots of ASW training, etc. Conducting three or four fleet exercises a year. Several of them were multinational in that we worked with the Australians, with the New Zealand types. We also had the French in on a couple of exercises, who came up from Tahiti. In fact, I went down to Tahiti and down to Australia on a couple of occasions to brief on exercises that were coming up in which their forces were involved. We had Canadians in on our exercises. I don't think we had a Brit during my two years out there, because most of the Brits were on East Coast exercise, but there had been times when we operated with the Brits as well.

Paul Stillwell: Are there any particular highlights of these exercises that you recall? Anything unusual or striking?

Admiral Gravely: No, they're rather routine exercises to some degree, but at the same time they were devoted to increasing the readiness of all of the forces of all of the countries. The biggest one, I guess, is the multinational exercise that we conduct. I was very fortunate in that that is normally run on a two-year cycle, but the year after I left we knew that the Australian carrier would not be available, so we were able to conduct two in a row. So I conducted two of those exercises. I'd have to think a little bit to give you the exact name of it, because it's named the same thing every year.

Paul Stillwell: Well, there's one called RimPac.

Admiral Gravely: RimPac is the one that I'm talking about. So I managed to do two RimPacs, which was to some degree a feather in my cap.

Paul Stillwell: Was there some thinking about how that carrier capability would be replaced? She was certainly aging at that point.[*]

Admiral Gravely: Yes, she was aging. We really didn't get into that. It was a concern, but it wasn't a major concern in Third Fleet. We wanted a ship, and a ship that was operationally fit to do a job, and it was at that point, despite the age and things like that.

---

[*] Construction on the British aircraft carrier Majestic began in 1943; because of a reexamination of post-World War II priorities, the ship was not completed until 1955. In 1956 she was transferred to the Australian Navy and became HMAS Melbourne. She was decommissioned by Australia in 1982.

Paul Stillwell: Was the multinational planning done at a CinCPacFlt level, or even higher perhaps?

Admiral Gravely: CinCPacFlt basically got permission to do the exercise, but the planning for that exercise went on the Third Fleet. It was my officers who planned that exercise, planned all the series of events, and etc. Certainly we got help from CinCPacFlt on scheduling things and the like. But the planning of that exercise happened right at Third Fleet. In fact, I signed the op order. Permission to conduct it, I'd go to CinCPacFlt, and, of course, he would touch base on the international aspect, of course, even with the U.S. scheduling. So we did the planning of the exercise.

Paul Stillwell: How much were you personally involved in the workups of ships going to the Seventh Fleet? Did you board those for inspections?

Admiral Gravely: I did not go aboard necessarily every ship that went out there, but we conducted the series of training exercises which declared basically that that ship was ready to go to Seventh Fleet. And whereas, again, I didn't conduct every exercise, or go aboard every one, the ship went out as a result of our saying he was prepared to go, right. So it was one of those things that you didn't get directly involved in every one, but you were a contributor in his readiness.

Paul Stillwell: But you still had opportunities to go to sea.

Admiral Gravely: And you had opportunities to go to sea. Yes, generally, you wouldn't go to sea from standing in Pearl Harbor, for example, or watch some guy get under way. You'd probably pick a time that you could COD in and fly in when the guy was out at sea. You know, various times, you wanted to see various things. You did not necessarily want to do them all on board one ship. You'd take the helicopter, and you moved about and went from ship to ship. So I did do that.

Another one of the functions, of course, was that the Antarctic Support Forces were under the cognizance of Third Fleet. So I went down to Antarctica once or twice. I've been down there about three times, but I went down there as the commander of Third Fleet once, and I also came up to Port Hueneme, where their headquarters are, and I guess I was involved in a change of command there. I participated in the Rose Bowl Festival. And incidentally, getting back to it, the thing that Commander San Francisco Naval Base wanted was Third Fleet there for Navy Day. I was there for Navy Day in San Francisco, and used one of the DLGs as a flagship.

Paul Stillwell: Was that a special one because it was the bicentennial year?

Admiral Gravely: You're right. It was. We had probably about 20 ships in there, which is many more than normally go in there for a place. I was there for about a week, as I recall. I can't think of anything special we did, although I do know I hosted a dinner. Dianne Feinstein wasn't the mayor at that point in time, but she was invited to the dinner, and several other of the notable types in the San Francisco area were invited.[*] I also was crowned as one of the Rose Festival honorees, or something like knight, I've forgotten, at the Rose Festival.

Paul Stillwell: Did you make a fair number of public appearances in that job?

Admiral Gravely: Yes, quite a few. Lots of speeches and lots of public appearances up and down the West Coast. Navy League functions. The American Battleship Association did something up in Honolulu, and I was the speaker, because I'm an ex-battleship sailor, as you well know. It turned out that I saw for the first time in many, many years Admiral Stephan, my old exec on the Iowa.[†] Great guy, really. I enjoyed working with him. The rest of the tour on Third Fleet was quite routine in respects to how things are done.

---

[*] Dianne Feinstein, a Democrat, was mayor of San Francisco from 4 December 1978 to 8 January 1988; she has been a U.S. Senator from California since 10 November 1992.
[†] Rear Admiral Edward C. Stephan, USN (Ret.).

I did have the one traumatic thing which happened in that I lost my son out there. He got killed in an accident on Ford Island.* And one of the things that was really traumatic about the stay out there was not just my son, but it was quite ironic, but there were three deaths on Ford Island—actually, four deaths in those two years. Ford Island is not that big a community, so it has quite an impact on you. One of my officers' sons committed suicide out there. He didn't do it on the island, but everybody on the island knew him, and he was only about a 17-year-old kid. Of course, my son's death was quite traumatic. Then there was a kid who was hit by an automobile. And the last one was we had a guy who had been relieved on Ford Island who was coming back to, I believe, San Diego to a job there. He had a heart attack and died at a neighbor's house one night. And so, oh God, you know, you almost looked on Ford Island as a bad spot to be. But no, it was not. It was a good spot and we enjoyed it.

Paul Stillwell: This was your son Robby. I think he had just gotten a car, hadn't he, for the first time?

Admiral Gravely: Well, it was a strange set of circumstances. When we left San Diego, Robby came back to Virginia Union to go to college. And he spent a year there wherein he didn't do very well. So I was all set to take him out of school and bring him back home. They just said that he wasn't really mature enough to be on his own. Well, his mother convinced me that, well, we ought to try more time, and we did. So he started his third semester there, which was his second year, and he went till Christmas, came home for the Christmas holidays. When he came home for the Christmas holidays he hadn't done any better, so I said, "Give me your ticket. Not going to send you back anymore."

While he was there he went to work, and just like you're saying, he bought his first car. He had a little problem with it in that the wheel bearings burned and had to be repaired. On the day that he was killed he had—actually the night that he was killed—he'd picked it up earlier that day, and so he was driving it basically for the first time. I can imagine that he was running around Fort Island, sort of checking it out, and unfortunately he got to the curve that he couldn't really make, and so it went over into the

---

* Ford Island is in the middle of Pearl Harbor, Hawaii.

water. Another really unfortunate thing is that he drowned rather than killed himself in a car accident, because the car went upside down in about three feet of water in a lake there. And, of course, that was just a real tragedy.

It was even more traumatic for me because it happened my wife was in the hospital at Tripler, having just had her feet operated on, a bunion-ectomy, and this happened at about 1:30 in the morning, or at least I knew about it about 1:30 on a Saturday morning. So I had to get to the island to tell her at that time of morning. And a second thing was that you we had a whole weekend wherein we couldn't do anything so far as arranging things. I guess even more traumatic than that was the fact that it was my birthday. There are three of us who were born in June: my birthday is June the 4th, my son David's birthday is June the 9th, my daughter's birthday is June the 13th. It turned out he was killed on my birthday, buried on my son's birthday, and only four days away from my daughter's. So once a year you're constantly reminded of these things. But anyway, we decided to bury him out at the National Cemetery in San Diego. The three of us, my daughter, my son and I, brought the body back and buried him there. Of course, my wife wasn't able to travel at that point in time.

Paul Stillwell: Did religion provide a source of solace in a situation like that?

Admiral Gravely: Yes it did. I guess the thing that did it even more, but it made you question it more, was that—and I don't remember the passage right now, but it turned out that my son was either getting kind of religious or something in that there was a bible in the car. And it was turned to a passage that I can't remember the exact passage right now. I can almost see it. And so, yes.

I guess the biggest thing that happened to me was that the word obviously got over to Tripler by the time I got over there. So while I was in there waking my wife and telling her, and we're both trying to console each other, in walked a minister. He gathered us together, and we sort of said the Lord's Prayer, and he prayed a bit. That did me as much good as anything else. There are times when you need that.

That did almost change my mind on what I had planned to do further, because I certainly was looking forward to when I completed the Third Fleet tour, and this was the end of it, of coming back. I knew I'd come back to Washington. I think that I really wanted to be the OP-03, which is a surface force guy.* I couldn't think of anything else that would have been available to me, although I knew that the DCA job would be available to me.† So I got wind that I was being nominated for DCA. At one point in time I, as soon as the problem with my son came, I had almost decided that, "Well, I'm going to retire. I'm going to just get out of the entire environment and everything else. But, frankly, the job at Third Fleet had been such a big one, and I'd enjoyed it so much I said, "Well, the Navy really needs to have a guy, Navy type, in the DCA job."

Paul Stillwell: What had stimulated your thoughts toward retirement?

Admiral Gravely: Well, I just felt that that was just such a blow for me, losing that boy, that everything in the Navy just reminded me, really, of him. I just felt that, "Okay, it's time to go now. It's time to get out of the environment and go home." The Navy hadn't done anything to me, but his untimely death had just demoralized me, really. But, then again, when I discovered that I'd been nominated for the DCA job, I felt that I really owed the Navy something. That they had given me an opportunity in the Third Fleet job, one that I really enjoyed. I felt that I'd done some good there. And I felt that, "Okay, now the Navy is offering me a chance to do them some good here in this joint arena in the DCA job. So I will come back and do that one, and I'll stay at least a couple of years anyway." And, of course, I did.

Paul Stillwell: I wonder if we could explore in a little more detail, if we could, the good that you did do in Hawaii and the specific accomplishments that you'd like to put on the record?

Admiral Gravely: Well, I don't think there are anything specific that I can think of that's different from what any other Third Fleet commander could have done.

---

* At that time OP-03 was the Deputy Chief of Naval Operations (Surface Warfare).
† DCA—Defense Communications Agency.

Paul Stillwell: You said that you got the briefing with Clements that the defense of the United States was a big role. How did you execute that responsibility?

Admiral Gravely: Well, you basically executed that responsibility through the commanders of your various naval bases, etc. Also, in fact, it was the whole Pacific Coast, really. And you had a two-star Canadian officer, whom you worked with so far as that was concerned. I met with NORAD on one occasion, and I also went down to Phoenix to meet with that air group down there.[*] What is it, 25th or something like that? I forget the name of the Air Force group that's in Phoenix. The normal routine things that you would do in preparing for the defense and those kinds of things. No special exercises devoted to it, but certainly when an exercise was in that area, that's part of the things that would be written into that op order that you had as a goal to accomplish. That was about it, I guess.

Paul Stillwell: What was the status of the Western Sea Frontier at that time?

Admiral Gravely: Well, the Western Sea Frontier, as you recall, went out of being a long time ago, even much earlier than that. So did the Eastern Sea Frontier. I remember when I was at Com 3 that there was an Eastern Sea Frontier, but that had gone by the board. In fact, the naval districts were going by the board and became the commanders of the naval bases. So the responsibility for that defense and everything else, which might have been relegated to the sea frontier commanders, now belonged strictly to the fleet commander, who had the Second Fleet off the East Coast and Third Fleet off the West Coast, as I recall.

Paul Stillwell: Was there any residual force from the sea frontier that you could work with?

Admiral Gravely: No, there was nothing that I can recall that was there.

---

[*] NORAD—North American Air Defense Command.

Paul Stillwell: That was just one of the organizations that was part of the Third Fleet.

Admiral Gravely: In all respects, yes. That was just a part of Third Fleet. That's right. For example, I didn't have anything in San Diego or anything in San Francisco. My staff out in Hawaii just played the whole role, that's all.

Paul Stillwell: Did you have a specific section devoted to that?

Admiral Gravely: Not a specific section. You probably had that as part of the overall operational officer's task. But he didn't have any special, well, maybe one guy, who would do some part of that, and then he did something else and those kinds of things, but you took it as a whole, not so much bits and pieces. Yes.

Paul Stillwell: How much operational control did you have over Third Fleet ships?

Admiral Gravely: Well, you had absolute control over the Third Fleet ships. Certainly the CinC could take it away from you, but you didn't have any problem with anyone else. The ship belonged basically to you, and the commander took his orders from you. He chopped to Seventh Fleet at an appropriate time, which was sort of routine if he was going to the west. You had absolute control.

You had a little bit of, not a problem, but the one thing the Third Fleet Commander always wanted, and any other guy in that position wanted was when a ship was turned over from SurfPac, that the ship was ready to operate rather than having to go back for repairs and those kinds of things. So every once in a while there was some concern that the ship really wasn't ready for Third Fleet ops, so you had to look at it very carefully, and decide whether or not you wanted to turn it back to NavSurfPac. We'd get together on those kinds of things, and decide, okay, he needs another four weeks in the yards, or four more weeks under the type commander to work up to the point wherein he's ready for Third Fleet ops. Third Fleet ops were basically the fast-paced things, versus the slow things that you'd do in refresher training, which you do under the type commander.

Paul Stillwell: So you would do multi-ship training.

Admiral Gravely: We were doing basically multi-ship training things. The ISE, we might get a little bit of that, but that's only because the guy is in multi-ship training, but he's got a few minutes here when he can do things alone. But for the most part it's multi-ship exercises when you're at that point in time.

Paul Stillwell: The deployed Seventh Fleet has quarterly fleet scheduling conferences. Did you have that formal setup?

Admiral Gravely: Yes, right. We had the same formally set up. And we conducted them mostly in San Diego, in conjunction with the type commanders there, and we worked up our schedule together. Basically, to some degree, it was as much each type commander's scheduling conference as it was mine, because the ship belonged to him until the thing was ready to move over to Third Fleet. So he would schedule his type commander's maintenance schedule, and his RFTs and those kinds of things, and then we'd take it on and tack on our part of that exercise schedule.*

Paul Stillwell: Did the type commanders all come together for these conferences or send representatives?

Admiral Gravely: They sent representatives, and they met there. No, the type commanders themselves did not just sit down and bat it out, but I knew when it was going on. Of course, I could always come to San Diego if I wanted to. Now, there was a quarterly PacFlt conference wherein we invited the type commanders as well as the rest of the COs in the San Diego area, and I'd come back to San Diego and conduct those quarterly training schedules basically, if you want to call it training. Did that quarterly.

---

* RFT—refresher training.

Paul Stillwell: The type commanders report to the fleet commander in chief. Did they also have another reporting requirement to you, or a liaison requirement?

Admiral Gravely: We had a liaison requirement. A type commander was a three-star, just like I was. So he didn't report to me. But certainly we got together and tried to come out with coordinated reports. And so I worked very closely with St. George and with Coogan. We all tried to work together. But so far as getting together—no. The staffs more or less ran it.

Paul Stillwell: What was your working relationship with Admiral Hayward? What impressions do you have of him as the fleet commander in chief?

Admiral Gravely: Well, Admiral Hayward was just a tremendous naval officer. He was obviously very sharp. He certainly had to be to have been selected as Chief of Naval Operations. He was an active guy, and he wanted things done. He held various briefings and conferences for his type command. In fact, we went to Guam a couple of times wherein there was a meeting between the Third Fleet Commander and the Seventh Fleet Commander with CinCPacFlt. We went there a couple of times. He was very nice to me, and that usually if I wanted to take a trip, he made available to me one of his aircraft, which I could take my staff and we could all go together. That made it quite easy, because if you took an airplane, then you could obviously relax and study and work on that airplane, whereas you couldn't do that very well on a commercial airplane. Admiral Hayward, I guess the thing I'd like to say is that he really had it all together, and I was quite impressed how well organized, how great he was able to meld things together and make things happen. Just a tremendous naval officer, right.

Paul Stillwell: During my one brief meeting, I was very impressed by his pleasant personality. I wonder whether that came across to you also.

Admiral Gravely: Yes, he was very pleasant. He was a strong enough guy so that he knew how to snap up a guy who was a little lagging. I can remember that he was quite unhappy when Ritter came back with those damn goats, and he let me know that, "Hey, you didn't quite do the job here. Don't let that happen again." I was mad really. I felt that I had let him down; however, I'm not sure I could have counted the goats in that bag either. [Laughter]

Paul Stillwell: He's also a witty man with quick, humorous comebacks.

Admiral Gravely: Right, right. Quite a wit. A very, very funny guy. Well, Christ, here's a guy who was valedictorian of his class, or something like that, in high school. You know, those kinds of guys aren't dummies by any stretch of the imagination. When you've been smart for 40 years, you just have to be smarter [laugh] each year, right. So he was great.[*]

Paul Stillwell: You were a phenomenon in being the first black two-star admiral. Did you continue to be a celebrity in that regard as the first three-star?

Admiral Gravely: Yes, that came up all the time. And, you know, there were certain things that somebody would need a guy to give a speech for. And, fine, okay. Here's a two-star over here, or here's a three-star Air Force guy. Well, we've had several three-star Air Force types, and we need the first three-star Navy type. Well, I was that for a long time, and even today, as you know, there hasn't been a black three-star since then Navy wide.[†] So there are a lot of people now who won't accept active duty three-star. They want a retired flag officer, despite the fact I can't even wear the uniform. Well, I can, but I don't wear the uniform. I outgrew it, frankly. [Laughter]

Paul Stillwell: It was during the period that you were at Third Fleet that the Golden 13 survivors began to get together for the first time in 30 years. Were you tied in with their reunions at all?

---

[*] Admiral Hayward has subsequently been interviewed as part of the Naval Institute's oral history program.
[†] Since the time of this interview in 1986 the Navy has selected several more black officers as three-star admirals. In 1996 Admiral J. Paul Reason, USN, became the first four-star admiral when he took command of the Atlantic Fleet.

Admiral Gravely: Not so much as an active duty officer. However, at that first get-together in San Francisco, I was there present for that. I came in from Hawaii. Admiral Holloway was there, and I think I came as much for that reason, because I wanted to hear what Admiral Holloway was going to say, as I did for the fact that the Golden 13 was there. Obviously, another reason was that I knew all of the Golden 13 and hadn't seen them for years, and wanted to just touch base with them again. So it would have been about '77, I guess, that they got together for the first time.

I've seen them at several functions. In fact, they had a meeting in Boston, which was at Baugh's home, and I was the speaker for that meeting that year, and I've forgotten when that was, but it was since I retired.[*] You know, I was closely aligned with many of the Golden 13, because Dalton Baugh was in my company as a recruit, and also in my service-school class down at Hampton Institute. Johnny Reagan was in Hampton, in service school, as an electrician.[†] And then when I came to San Diego, was here in San Diego when I got here. Cooper, as I recall, was on the staff down at Hampton when I was there.[‡]

Paul Stillwell: Yes, he was.

Admiral Gravely: So I knew many of those guys. I met Jesse Arbor for the first time about that time frame.[§] Most of them I had either bumped heads with before or seen or something like that. So I knew them.

Paul Stillwell: You've described the process by which you came to DCA. Could you describe some of the functions that go with that job, please?

---

[*] Dalton Louis Baugh was a member of the Golden Thirteen. He died in 1985, before he could be interviewed by the Naval Institute's oral history program.
[†] Ensign John Walter Reagan, USNR, was a member of the Golden Thirteen. His oral history is in the Naval Institute collection.
[‡] Ensign George Clinton Cooper, USNR, was a member of the Golden Thirteen. His oral history is in the Naval Institute collection.
[§] Ensign Jesse Walter Arbor, USNR, was a member of the Golden Thirteen. His oral history is in the Naval Institute collection.

Admiral Gravely: Well, the job at DCA is a sort of a multi-faceted job, really. The first thing, you are the Director of Defense Communications Agency, which runs the defense communications system. The defense communications system provides all of the strategic and long-haul communications for the Joint Staff, and for the services, etc. It's the strategic point to point.

Historically, the services have had all of their own communications arrangements and everything else, but about 1950, I guess it was, it was decided that, hey, we need one agency at least to provide the long-haul stuff. And maybe the services can provide their own tactical communications. This would cut down on some of the duplication. Well, that's what the purpose of DCA is, to provide that long-haul strategic communications for the services so that you don't have all of the duplication and everything else, which we had historically.

Now, as such, DCA came up with the idea of the defense communications system, which does that. The defense communications system has two or three different kinds of communications. For example, it has satellite communications. It uses the telephone lines, and the telephone company's commercial communication, I guess you should say, and, of course, it has its own communication service, the service communication, which all sort of join together to link into this system.

The other thing, of course, is you are the manager of the National Communications System, which is to some degree a consolidation of the Department of State, and the various other departments of the government who all come together, and they meet periodically to decide what their communication requirements are, and also trying to keep from duplicating and those kinds of things. We generally do not get involved into the tactical communications, which are strictly service related.

Paul Stillwell: There are also administrative service-related communications as well.

Admiral Gravely: That's true. But that's generally that particular service's communications, and DCA only gets involved when it comes on a long-haul, point-to-point circuit. When you're talking in terms of an administrative message that goes from the CNO out to Pearl Harbor, well, it goes over a DCS line until it gets to Pearl Harbor.

And at some point it goes through the main frame. When it passes through the main frame, then it becomes Navy again. That's right. But tactical and administrative traffic, for the most part, involves servicing. Except that administrative traffic is strictly the end of the line, basically.

Paul Stillwell: To what extent did the establishment of DCA succeed in meeting this objective, that is, eliminating the duplication?

Admiral Gravely: Well, they did it only because it was done by edict, and they have done it quite well. There's always been a certain amount of disagreement, because the services would like to do it all themselves. There's always been an argument between the services and JCS, for example, or any joint agency. The services feel that they can satisfy their needs much better. The services feel that they are kind of unique. The Army is different from the Navy, blah, blah, blah. So they have unique requirements. And when it is determined that that unique requirement would be satisfied by this guy over here, the big monster called DCA, and the Army would say, "Hey, he can't do that, because he doesn't know what my real requirement is."

Paul Stillwell: A real concern, though, is that they don't have the degree of control they want.

Admiral Gravely: The degree of control that they would like to have, they no longer have. So you've got a tremendous job of coordination, and patience, and those kinds of things.

Paul Stillwell: It calls for some skills in diplomacy.

Admiral Gravely: It calls for diplomacy. It calls for skills in really negotiating. And it calls for being able to put the fist down, too, and saying, "Hey, that's where the crap ends."

Paul Stillwell: What are some of the issues that you recall addressing?

Admiral Gravely: The hardest job for me was one in which the Defense Science Board had during its summer meeting decided that the Defense Communication Agency should be more in the acquisition business. Basically in the long-haul communications DCA is responsible for it with a budget and everything else, but there are certain communications they don't really acquire and pay for, etc. But, anyway, they wanted DCA to become DC^3A, which would also put DCA's nose a little bit under the camel's tent in that it was getting a little bit into the tactical communications area.

And I was tasked by Dr. Dinneen to come up with a plan for doing that. Dr. Dinneen was the Assistant Secretary of Defense for Command, Control, Communications and Intelligence.[*] I put that plan together. But, of course, any plan which is going to do something new will cost somebody people and dollars. I thought we put together a plan which would carry out that function at a minimum cost and with a minimum number of people. But you've got to remember where you get your dollars from, okay. Your dollars come out of the services' budget, and the people come out of the services' hide. So there was quite an objection to that.

Ultimately what really happened, I believe, was that JC^3S, which was a group of people on the Joint Staff who were formed to do the function that the Defense Science Board felt should be done, without giving that power to a separate agency or the DCA. Currently, I have watched some of the jobs that the DCA has been tasked to do lately, and the DCA is being tasked to do some of those jobs. And we still have a JC^3S, because the function can't be done by the JC^3S. It has to be done by someone else. So really the Defense Science Board recommendations to some degree are being implemented, but they are really coming out of DCA's hide to do it, and DCA is having a problem, but they're doing it. Now, that was the hardest job that I had to do, because it required a considerable amount of negotiating. I didn't really successfully negotiate it.

There was another problem. The services have all yelled and screamed about their requirement for secure voice communication. And we got into that one. It was a

---

[*] Gerald P. Dinneen served as Principal Deputy Under Secretary and Assistant Secretary of Defense for C^3I from 1977 to 1981.

problem, basically, that we just have not been really able to successfully coordinate with the NSA types.* It's not NSA's fault, because NSA feels that they are satisfying a requirement that's been laid down to them. The services and DCA has always felt it hasn't been done fast enough, or quick enough, or as complete as it should have been done. Today, probably 15 years after we said we had a requirement for secure voice, we don't have one. And we just can't seem to get one. I don't know why. I guess those were the two biggest problems. The break-up of AT&T didn't happen on my watch. I should say this, that my predecessor testified quite a bit on that, and I guess we were deliberating during my two years there.

Well, I stayed there for two years, and about, oh, six or eight months away from the end of that two-year period I decided that I would retire. I would be 58 years old that summer. I knew that under any set of circumstances, no matter what happened to me, that I probably would not get a fourth star, because as you well know, mandatory retirement age is 62. Secondarily, the Navy and all the other services try to pick people young enough so they've got about four years. They can do two two-year tours someplace as a four-star officer, and I was too old for that. So I decided that, well, I had devoted 34 years of naval service, and I was coming up on my 58th birthday. So I put the letter in, and I retired on, I guess, July 31, actually as of August 1, 1980. Then I came on out into civilian life.

Paul Stillwell: What have you been doing since retirement, Admiral?

Admiral Gravely: Well, I did a couple of things. One is that when I first retired I didn't plan to do anything in the line of work. I had purchased a mini-farm, as I call it. It's about three acres of land. I didn't plan to do much more than a garden, some fruit trees, and that kind of thing. I've got chickens and pigeons; pigeons, of course, are a hobby of mine. I've always contended that that's going to be my backup communications system. Because, as you well know, we had them for communication systems for years in the Army Signal Corps, and the Navy had used them too. But, in any event, for about nine

---

* The National Security Agency (NSA) is the U.S. Government's primary organization in the field of communications intelligence.

months I just sort of took care of that, worked around my yard, and those kinds of things. I got kind of frustrated, and a little bit tired of doing nothing, and whereas I didn't actively go out and seek work, a guy who knew that there was a job available, came out to find me one day and told me about it, and so I went to work for a defense contractor. The job was basically one wherein the requirement was for a guy who had a background in intelligence more than communications, although communications was certainly an asset. But it was primarily for a guy in intelligence.

Paul Stillwell: What company was that?

Admiral Gravely: Okay, a small company called CTEC. CTEC had been in the OSIS business, the ocean surveillance information systems, had designed and built that system. I knew about the system. I had used the system previously; even as a ship driver you use it to some degree. But I kept having this conflict-of-interest feeling. What had happened was that when I first retired, I went over to see a member of the Judge Advocate General's Corps, and asked him, "Hey, I want you to explain to me what I can really do, and what can't I do."

    The first question he asked was, "Do you like to go to the Pentagon?"
    I said, "Yes."
    He said, "Well, don't."
    I said, "Oh?"
    He said, "Well, I know that you want to go into the Pentagon, and you've got friends there and you're just going to visit them. But then that's going to be interpreted as selling. And you can't do that." Well, I guess as a result of that, every once in a while I was asked what was going on in the Navy, and I would go to the Pentagon and find out. Then I kept getting this conflict-of-interest feeling. So I was all set to quit, and I did.

    But, just before quitting, I had met the president of another company, which was a small minority company, and he said he needed some help, and I could certainly help him. Well, I quit CTEC, and went to work for this other company, Automated Business Systems and Services. And I got to tell you, it was much more of a conflict because of the kind of help he needed [laughter] was more so than the other guy. And so I worked there for a year, and finally decided that I just couldn't live in this environment wherein I felt that I was in conflict of interest. Nobody was going to interfere with my retirement pay or anything else, so I decided that I would leave that type of life.

I then came to the Armed Forces Communications and Electronics Association, where I've worked since December of '83. I've been in the business of education and training, and certainly there's no conflict there. In this job I have three basic functions. One is I run what is considered to be a professional development center, wherein we teach one- to five-day, short, continuing education courses. I schedule about 20 of those courses a year. I really don't do the teaching myself, but I find what we call a course coordinator, who puts it together. He ends up with four, five instructors, and then I make the arrangements for locations, get the material cleared, and those kinds of things. So we do that.

Paul Stillwell: Who are the customers for those courses?

Admiral Gravely: The customers are three types, and we have three different price ranges. One are military-government people, who come in large numbers. We have the AFCEA members, which are 750 corporations which are associated or corporations who are members of this association. Then we get a considerable number of other types, who are not members of this organization, but they are people who are interested in our course, because they are in some instances defense contractors, and in some they are not. But those kinds of people. So we're getting, basically, civilians and military-government types to the courses.

The courses, depending on what they consider the value of them, will run anywhere from, say, 40 to 150 students. And it is quite interesting that I try to sort of maintain a budget around here, and I want to know what my revenue is going to be. But the most difficult thing is to predict how many students you'll get, number one. Plus even harder, is what the breakdown of students is going to be in that number. You know, because we get different price schedules for all. But anyway, that's one of the jobs.

The second job is one that is certainly of much interest to me, and that's called the AFCEA Educational Fund. The job here basically is number one to solicit money from the corporations and members of AFCEA. And the second job is to handle a scholarship that we run for ROTC students. We select each year 15 Army, 15 Navy, and 15 Air Force. There are five each incoming sophomores, incoming juniors, incoming seniors in the ROTC schools, and we award them scholarships of $500, $750 and $1000 respectively. That's really a rewarding experience from the giving of the scholarships. It's another thing entirely to ask people for money, being begging all the time. But that's an important program. We also give out a certain number of awards. And that is basically for ROTC students. We give an award each year to the military academies, to their top guy in the electronics field, and those kinds of things.

The third one is what we call a career-planning center. And in the career-planning center we generally try to match retiring military people to jobs in industry. I get the requirements from industry for the kinds of people they need, and I also get résumés from the military people who are retiring, and I try to match those and send them to those corporations and say, "Hey, here's a guy who's suitable for you." If they hire him, then AFCEA gets a 5% stipend of the first year's salary, basically, of that guy. So those are the three functions. In the case of the career-planning center, that is one of the things that DoD says in an instruction that an association such as AFCEA should be involved in. So in the case of the other thing, conflict of interest certainly is a supporting role here that I'm doing. So, I enjoy that, frankly.

Paul Stillwell: How much contact do you maintain with the National Naval Officers Association and other black groups within the Navy?

Admiral Gravely: Well, the only one I know of, really, is the National Naval Officers Association, and I'm a member. It's $25.00 a year, and so I join each year. I get a call maybe once a year to speak to a group, and to tell them a little bit about my experiences. I also get a call maybe twice a year from the recruiting command to do basically the same thing. They've got a big pitch for minority officers, and I'll go around. I guess the last one of those that I did was down in South Carolina, where I went to each of the minority schools around there, the colleges as well as a couple of high schools down there for a couple of days. And I got a call just three or four days ago about coming out to San

Diego. In fact, I think it's May of '87 for something for the NNOA. But that's about the extent of it. I still know quite a number of young black naval officers. So I see them occasionally and talk to them occasionally and those kinds of things. But that's about the extent of it.

Paul Stillwell: You've had a long view of the Navy. What is your assessment of the job the service has done in providing career opportunities for blacks?

Admiral Gravely: Well, I think that the Navy has done an outstanding job when you consider that I knew when it wasn't doing any job at all. I get a little concerned that there are people who come in and see what the situation is, that they then assess it as, "Hey, the Navy is not doing very much." But then when you look at 40 years, and, you know, they've done quite a bit. And you say, "Well, 40 years is a long time. They should have done more." But you've got to remember what they did 100 years ago. So you're really assessing a period of from 1776, so you're doing over 200 years in this assessment.

I agree with the concerns of most people, that more could be done. I get a little concerned with a couple of things that I see the Navy doing. One is the requirement that there be a black officer in all the recruiting districts—all stations, really. And I get concerned because what we're doing is we're taking the young officer who ought to be out learning his trade, and then bringing him in here for two years of shore duty which doesn't really qualify him to be a naval officer. Now, okay, he's doing a vital job for the Navy, but doing vital jobs for the Navy don't really add up at the end when picking commanders, commanders of destroyers and those kinds of things. You need to be in destroyers to do that, and those are the things you need to do to get promoted.

A guy will always look at me and say, "Well, hell, you did it."

And I say, "Yes, well, I did, but how many officers will complete 60 or more correspondence courses these days?" I don't even know if they're teaching them. I guess they still have correspondence courses. But the people who are going to do what they're required to do and, in addition, do more. So that's part of the problem.

Paul Stillwell: What are the areas where you think the Navy might do more?

Admiral Gravely: Well, I'm not sure that there are many, many more things that the Navy can do. I'm not a guy who says, "Hey, give some opportunity over here to people who really aren't ready for that opportunity." I say, "Hey, maybe you can do something to make them more ready and give them more opportunity at that point in time." I'm not really sure what there is that we can do. We are constantly going out trying to recruit. We constantly get good numbers in. I'm curious why sometimes we get these numbers in, and then turn around and at Pensacola they fail, for example.* I do know that the flunk-out rate at Pensacola is just astronomical compared to other racial groups. And what that's all about, I can't answer the question, because I've never really been down there to see it. Now, I hear all kinds of reasons. I hear discrimination and those kinds of things, but, you know, there are an awful lot of things that are passed off as discrimination which I'm convinced aren't discrimination.

Paul Stillwell: It becomes a convenient excuse.

Admiral Gravely: It becomes a convenient excuse in many, many, many cases. Now, don't get me wrong; I'm not saying in all cases, because I think discrimination does play a part. One of the things that concern me is that—and it happened when I was the Third Fleet Commander. One of my officers, Fred Bailey, went out to drive a ship; it was the Preble, in fact.† And I happened to be coming back from San Diego. A young black officer from his ship asked me for a ride on the airplane, and so fine. We sat, and we talked. Then he went back to his seat. Ultimately, I had him in my little compartment on this airplane for one of the meals. I said, "What are your aspirations, Jaygee?"

    He said, "You know, I think I'd like to be an aide."

    I said, "Hey, that's great. Let me tell you, I think that an aide is a guy who probably has one of the best jobs in the Navy for a young officer to learn. He's walking around with a flag officer, he's meeting them, and everything else. He sees how they

---

* The Navy's primary flight training site is the Pensacola, Florida, Naval Air Station.
† Commander Fred W. Bailey, USN, served as commanding officer of the guided missile destroyer Preble (DDG-46) from July 1978 to June 1980.

comport themselves, and he can learn. He gets into high-level discussions, and all this. But, you know, I wouldn't have you for an aide."

His eyes bugged, and he said, "Well, why wouldn't you?"

I said, "Well, first of all, you've a beard. You've got to shave your beard."

He said, "Well, Admiral, I wouldn't shave my beard off for you or for anybody."

I said, "Son, that's the reason you can't be an aide. Now, why won't you shave your beard?"

He said, "Well, my beard connotes my blackness." Well, damn it, if a beard has to connote blackness, then there's something wrong with us, you know. Because I could look at him and I could tell by the skin; I thought that connoted blackness.

But we have some of those kinds of things which I think are anti really one people in this good country. The NNOA is a good example, really a good group. They do things to help other black officers. But then it tells you that we're separated. It's that kind of thing that bothers me. And what else can be done about it? I don't know.

Paul Stillwell: What are your basic views on equal opportunity as a concept, affirmative action, and so forth?

Admiral Gravely: Well, equal opportunity is something that I think that this country has to practice. But I think at some point in time we've got to get to the point wherein equal opportunity is so routine that we don't have to call it equal opportunity, that it's just a matter of fact. I almost think that we've called attention to equal opportunity long enough that we ought to be at that point. I'm hoping that one of these days we will get there. But when, I don't have any idea. Equal opportunity offices and those kinds of things, I just feel that we've still got so far to go, because we should have been out of that range a long time ago. I don't know.

Paul Stillwell: Well, affirmative action is even a step beyond that. Are you hoping that we can do away with that?

Admiral Gravely: I'm hoping that we can do away with all of that. Yes. In fact, I may be wrong on this, and I've got to find it out, because next week I'm supposed to be the speaker on the NAACP program. And, frankly, it's only about a five-minute talk. But I think the NAACP has basically changed its focus. It's changed its focus from saying ultimately we ought to be two people up here who are equal—to we ought to be one people up here. I think that's what they're saying. That's the new focus, and I'm so happy to see that, because I think that we ought to be one set of Americans.

Okay, well, some are going to be dark, and some are going to be light and all the rest of that kind of crap, but that's the way it is in, say, South America, where we have, in some countries, one strong organization. Now, I've forgotten who it was that was a guy who just said recently, "You can't do that." I think he's wrong, because I think we can have one country of people, who may be mixed in the color of their skin, but they're one people otherwise, speaking the same language. All got the same goals and everything.

Paul Stillwell: The Navy is always vulnerable to talent-seekers from outside in business and industry trying to get the good people. I would think that capable black people might be especially vulnerable, because they help these companies meet some of these equal opportunity goals. How could the Navy protect itself and keep the good young black people?

Admiral Gravely: Well, that's a tough one here at this point in time. It is tough primarily because, just like you're saying, these companies do have equal opportunity goals. Particularly defense contractors, which have to satisfy the DoD goals for equal opportunity, or else they don't get these contracts. So they are going to go out and actively seek people who are trained, blacks and otherwise. There's not much the Navy can do about it, because the Navy cannot automatically give Joe Blow here, who's a young black second class petty officer, more money than it's giving Joe Smith out here, who's a third class or second class white petty officer. Can't give him more time off. The little things that I could do if I were running a company. I could pay them more money and those kinds of things. The Navy's just lost with that kind of competition.

The thing of it is that well, I guess, we've got to instill in these people that, I do mean not just the black people but all of that, that, "We really want you. Here's what we're doing for you." And remind them every once in a while that there are lots of benefits here.

One of the interesting things to me, and I really don't know why I didn't do it, but I was a young lieutenant commander on board a ship, and we happened to be up in San Francisco. I was in a restaurant, and there were two high-level industrial types who found out that I had some communications experience. They basically came over to talk to me because my wife and I were sitting in this restaurant eating. We had our son with us, who was about two years old at that point in time. They were so tickled at how he was so well adjusted, or appeared to be well adjusted and everything else, so they came over and started up this conversation.

Now, you got to remember that this was about 1960, 1961, and a black who was in maybe a restaurant stood out a little bit. But in any event, I was offered a job that would have paid me about four times what the Navy was paying me at that time. But the one thing they couldn't guarantee me was the security that the Navy offered me. And they couldn't guarantee me the well-being and everything else that I felt I had in the Navy. So I didn't do it. I think that we've got to instill some of this in our younger crowd. I don't know, our football player, for example. I personally am very unhappy with the decision that was reached.

Paul Stillwell: Napoleon McCallum.[*]

Admiral Gravely: Yes. I personally don't think that that guy ought to be able to play football and have a Navy career. In fact, I figure he ought to be at sea anyway as a young ensign. I'm a little concerned at the decision on our big basketball star.[†] Now, he's

---

[*] Ensign Napoleon A. McCallum, USN, graduated in December 1985 from the Naval Academy, where he had been a star running back on the football team. He subsequently reported to a ship home-ported in California and for a while juggled his Navy duties with playing football for the Los Angeles Raiders.

[†] At the time of the interview, Midshipman David M. Robinson, USN, was a standout basketball player for the Naval Academy team. He subsequently graduated from the academy in 1987, served two years of active duty as a naval officer, and then resigned in 1989. He then embarked on a long, productive career playing for the San Antonio Spurs of the National Basketball Association.

outgrown us anyway, so maybe we ought to let him go. Because physically there's nothing you can do with him. What is he, 6-10?

Paul Stillwell: At least.

Admiral Gravely: [Laughter] It's hard to get him in an airplane. It's even harder to stuff him in a submarine, too, you know. So I don't know, but certainly I don't think that that is conducive to retaining anybody.

Paul Stillwell: Well, what the Navy needs to do to hold on to people is convince them that this really is an area in which they can grow and prosper, and that they've got the individual's long-term interests at heart. By contrast, the people on the outside want to use people for a short time and then get rid of them.

Admiral Gravely: It is interesting to me since I've been out here the number of people who get hired basically because a defense contractor has a contract with the government that lasts for, say, two years. At the end of that two years we no longer have a contract, and he no longer has a job. And some of them even shorter than that. Well, that's amazing to me, but you're absolutely correct. That we've got a long-term interest in you, and that we're going to do things for you, and those kinds of things.

Paul Stillwell: I'd like to ask you in conclusion, Admiral, to reflect on this remarkable career you've had. You set out to become a motor machinist's mate, and you became a vice admiral—something that you couldn't even have remotely envisioned at the time. What are the highlights and things that stand out?

Admiral Gravely: Well, let me tell you. I really set out to do something different even from that. I set out, really, to satisfy an obligation that I knew was forthcoming. That obligation was to serve during World War II. I really did not expect that we were going to have a long war by any stretch of the imagination, but at the same time for my part I wanted to do as well as I possibly could. And the motor machinist route seemed to have been the most interesting one for me. And, of course, that's where I went.

As I reflect back on this, I really have always been very curious as to what would have happened to me, for example, if World War II had not come about, because I wasn't doing what I know today that I was capable of doing in college at that point in time. In fact, I had dropped out, and I was working as a coat-liner presser. I really got turned around when I got selected to the program at UCLA. Now, this was the V-12 program. There I began to realize that I not only had to compete in a world wherein I was involved, but there were a lot of other people were involved as well. And I realized that I had some of the same stuff that they did, the same capabilities, the same two legs, put my pants on the same, and can do that fairly successfully.

This was certainly more influenced when I went to the PC-1264, wherein I was accepted for the first time, really, as a young man who was a young naval officer, and I enjoyed it. I came out of the Navy, as I think I said earlier, for a couple of reasons. One was that, first of all, nobody asked me to stay. And secondly, I didn't believe that there was the opportunity that did present itself after I came back. And the major reason, I guess, was that I had not completed my education, and I felt that I should come out and do that. I've often wondered what would have happened if I had of stayed in and tried for one of the college training programs that the Navy offered at that time. I personally don't think I would have gone as far, and I don't think I would have gone as far, not so much that I wouldn't have been probably better qualified, or as well qualified. But I think that part of my success came about as a result of the timing.

As a result of when I went regular Navy, I became two years less senior, and it gave me two more years in which to better prepare myself. I've always certainly been quite pleased with the success that I had. I attribute it not so much to me as to, certainly to the people that I've worked with, who've worked for me and again worked with me. This is whites as well as black. I certainly enjoyed every minute of it. I would do it again if I had to. I don't think I would change much of it if I had to do it again, but I'm quite happy that it worked the way it did.

Paul Stillwell: Well, there's a role that maybe has been thrust upon you that goes beyond what you've achieved yourself in that you serve as an inspiration for many others coming along. How do you accept that role?

Admiral Gravely: Well, as graciously as I can, I guess. For example, and you're right, there are certainly people out there who feel that I am sort of a role model. I had a young man to come by the house just about a week ago, who it turns out happened to have gone to a school with my son David. He now is a schoolteacher and a football coach at one of the county schools, Loudon County I believe, which is our neighboring county. He's asked me to come out to speak to his kids in January, and I'm quite happy to do that. If there is something that I can tell them, and I'm not sure what there is, or sit down and answer a question or something that will cause this guy to reflect and prepare himself a little bit earlier, I'm just very happy to do that, really.

You know, a lot of wonderful things have happened to me. I have a street named after me in my hometown, and in fact, I have a street sign from it, which I have in my dining room: "Admiral Gravely Boulevard." You know, that's impressive. I really appreciate what that group did for me. I've become citizen of so many cities from the plaques and things that I've gotten from various people. I sometimes am impressed with myself [laughter], although I hope I don't show that too much.

Paul Stillwell: Wives have a way of deflating that balloon.

Admiral Gravely: They certainly do. They certainly do. That has been really, I guess to some degree, one of the prime reasons for some success on my part. I was very fortunate. I married a really wonderful woman. You know, it's quite interesting to me that when I look back on it, there was no long courtship. None of that. I met this young lady in 1940 on the campus. I managed to see her for a total of five or ten minutes. I guess I went back there once after that and saw her, because she was really one of the girls who lived on the floor with my sister.

Then when I got into the service and I started looking for people to write, I found out very quickly that the best time of your day is mail call, and the only way you can get letters is if you write letters. And I just happened to begin to write a lot of people. She was one of them and I heard from them. So I happened to be down at Hampton and went up to Richmond. The school was 22 miles away, so I went down there once more. No, we continued to correspond, and then finally in 1945 in December I made a commitment basically that I would go down to Roanoke to visit her during the holidays, but I wasn't able to do that because my leave didn't occur until January 1 rather than Christmas. It occurred during New Year's. And in the meantime she'd come back, and she was closer to Richmond. She was teaching school. So I went down there. And would you believe that less than a month and a half later we were married? It's amazing to me, and it has lasted for 40 years.

She has just been a tremendous young lady, and one that I admire, because she's done some things for me that I wouldn't do for myself really. But she's just a great gal. And that's been part of it, having the right kind of a partner. We didn't have any children. We adopted three children. And those guys and the gal were just tremendous people. They went around at times when things were really tough. In fact, I can remember driving through Tennessee when I couldn't find a place for them to sleep, and I finally found a place wherein we were practically frozen. The two boys and my wife and I were all in the same bed one night, trying to keep warm, you know. So they've been all troopers, and I've been just quite happy with that.

Paul Stillwell: Admiral, your life and career have been ones of service and made many contributions, and I want to thank you for making this contribution. For putting your recollections on record. I'm very grateful for that and appreciate your cooperation.

Admiral Gravely: Okay. I was perfectly happy to do it.

Paul Stillwell: Thank you very much, Admiral.

Admiral Gravely: Fine. Okay, great.

Interview Number 7 with Vice Admiral Samuel L. Gravely, Jr., U.S. Navy (Retired)
Place: Admiral Gravely's home in Haymarket, Virginia
Date: Tuesday, 21 January 2003
Interviewers: Paul Stillwell and Rear Admiral Mack C. Gaston, USN (Ret.)

Paul Stillwell: Admiral, it's good to see you again. This is in your habitat with the birdhouse out back.

Admiral Gravely: Two birds in there only. I sold or gave away all the others, I guess.

Paul Stillwell: Oh.

Admiral Gravely: The guy couldn't catch them all, and he left two in there. So I've got two males.

Paul Stillwell: Okay.
   Well, our purpose today is to fill in any gaps remaining from our previous six interviews. Do you have any topics that you want to bring up?

Admiral Gravely: I'm finding it a little difficult to read some of that, because some of the corrections I can't seem to tie the events to the rest of it. You'll see it as I go along.

Paul Stillwell: Okay.

Admiral Gravely: Other than that, I don't have anything.

Paul Stillwell: Well, one thing I do remember, and I don't think we covered it that thoroughly in the oral history, concerned some of the values and lessons you got from your parents, particularly the work ethic. What do you remember about your father's teachings and examples in that regard?

Admiral Gravely: Well, my father was a hard worker, and I'm sure he got to the place in life that he got through hard work, because he didn't have very much education. He had only about a third-grade education. But he got to be a post office worker as a mail handler, and that was strictly laboring, carrying sacks of mail from one place to another, dumping them down so somebody else could work the mail. He taught me that whenever you see a guy's work station that doesn't have a bag there, put one there so he could keep going, you know. [Laughter] Because otherwise, he'll quit on you. Things like that.

I remember one thing. I was coming from what we used to call down corner. I passed a drugstore there, and the druggist called me and said, "Son, would you like to make a dime?"

I said, "Yes, sir."

So he said, "Well, would you mind sweeping my walk?"

I swept his walk, and he gave me the dime. When I got home, I told my dad about this. He said, "Son, I just got off the streetcar at that corner, and that place doesn't look like it's been swept to me. You give me that dime. And we're going to walk back around there and we'll see Mr. Harrison and see if he'll let us do it again so I can show you how." And, boy, he swept that sidewalk out to the middle of the street, where the streetcar came up the track, right to the gutter, curb, and everything else. I guess it took about an hour, when I thought I'd done it in about 15 minutes and done it right. He knew how to work much harder than I did, and he did it.

Paul Stillwell: And you never forgot that.

Admiral Gravely: I never forgot it, and not only that, the next time I saw Mr. Harrison, he said, "How would you like to come back here and work every Friday and Saturday night?"

"Yes, sir." So he gave me a job, basically cleaning up the drugstore.

Paul Stillwell: One thing that we sort of skipped over previously was the tour you had with the fleet training group after you left PC-1264. You talked about the housing situation but not about the job itself. What did the job entail?

Admiral Gravely: Well, basically, I was a communicator. I was a communications watch officer, and I had to look through all the messages that came in to make sure that the pertinent ones got to the right people, routing the traffic. That's basically what we used to call it. And that was about the extent of it. But the housing, I told you about that—no BOQ facilities, couldn't go to the officers' club—those kinds of things. But I liked the job, and I liked the people that I worked with, but I couldn't stand the conditions.

In fact, I was walking across the shipyard one day down in Norfolk, and a guy came over and spoke to me. He said he'd talked to me once. And I asked him, "You know, what do you do around here?"

He said, "I play football in the afternoon. Come go with me and see what we're doing here."

I went down there and made his football team. I played football there for two years—one summer and the fall of '45, I guess it was, and stayed there until the ship departed. Then I had all these friends when I went back down there to the fleet training group, so I knew where to go to find the right people and where to find a place to stay and everything. It was nice. I enjoyed it.

Paul Stillwell: Were you strictly in the headquarters, or did you get out on any of the ships for the training?

Admiral Gravely: No, you didn't do any shipboard stuff. To be honest with you, blacks were not allowed on naval ships at that time as officers. Only steward's mates went to sea. In fact, guys who had been trained at Great Lakes and all that basically went to shore duty activities, not ships.

Paul Stillwell: So you had sort of broken the pattern with the PC-1264.

Admiral Gravely: Yeah, right. The 1264—the pattern was broken long before I got there in that it had been decided that we would commission two ships with completely black crews and white officers. One was the Mason, a DE, which had an entire black crew and white officers, about ten. And the PC-1264, which had five white officers and about 70 men, all black. I was the first black officer to go to sea as part of the crew of a ship, and I went to the PC-1264.

The Mason ultimately got one or two black officers, because one of the Golden 13 served on there. I forget his name.

Paul Stillwell: James Hair.[*]

Admiral Gravely: Yes, Hair. Hair served on board there. And then a young officer that graduated from midshipman school came there too.

Paul Stillwell: McIntosh, I think his name was.[†]

Admiral Gravely: McIntosh, yes. I remember him vaguely, and he served on board there as well. And, of course, when those ships were decommissioned, most people went to a receiving station to be ultimately discharged. The war was over, and most people had points enough, including me.

Paul Stillwell: Was the fleet training group sort of where you got into the communicator slot that followed you on several tours?

Admiral Gravely: I don't think so. What happened was that when I was at the recruiting station in Washington, D.C., and this is after I came back on active duty, and I put in for sea duty. And before going to sea duty, I went to a four-month comm school in Monterey. As soon as I got out of there, I was a communicator. [Chuckle] But I learned

---

[*] Ensign James E. Hair, USNR.
[†] Ensign John McIntosh, USNR.

the rudiments of the business there and then went to the Iowa, where I served for 18 months as communicator. Then, unfortunately, my next tour was Toledo for two years as communicator. And I was dyed in the wool by then. [Laughter]

Paul Stillwell: I remember a couple of years ago out in Coronado there was a wonderful tribute for you by the National Naval Officers Association.*

Admiral Gravely: Oh, yes, yes, yes.

Paul Stillwell: I met George Thompson there, and you and he had integrated the Naval War College in the 1960s.

Admiral Gravely: Yes, right.

Paul Stillwell: Could you talk more about that, please?

Admiral Gravely: Well, you know, integration wasn't a difficult thing in those days. I didn't have any problem with quarters; there was a house for my wife and me. I guess we had two kids at that time. We lived right amongst the other officers who were at the Naval War College. In fact, it was on the grounds of an old Kennedy estate, as I recall. And we lived next door to part of that estate. Fort Adams was there, and that used to be fun, to go down to the old fort and walk around in it and play with the kids. They had a ball. I remember once that I saw some pigeons up there. There was a young squab, and I went over and caught it. I said, "Oh, there's another one," and gave this one to my son to hold. I climbed back up there, and he let him go. And that was the end of that one. [Chuckle] And I didn't catch the other one. Fort Adams was a wonderful place. You could fish down in that area.

Paul Stillwell: What do you remember about Commander Thompson from those years?

---

* The tribute to Admiral Gravely was held Saturday, 12 February 2000, at the officers' club of the North Island Naval Air Station, Coronado, California.

Admiral Gravely: George was a young tiger, and I do mean tiger. I guess he finished the ROTC unit at UCLA, so we almost were friends from that matter, because I'd gone to UCLA. And George had "command" written all over him. Not only that, he had the experience, because he went to a ship, wherein they obviously integrated the ship's company, the officers. Big, outgoing guy, married to a beautiful woman, and everything else. George seemed to have done it all right at that point in time, and I don't know what happened to him later on. From what I gathered, he had done it all right. He had been up and down the East Coast a lot, because I spent about all my time on the West Coast, except for the PC-1264. George was gregarious. We used to go out every once in a while, but our wives wouldn't let us get together too often. [Laughter] Because we went to the clubs and things like that. He was a great guy.

Paul Stillwell: Was he in any sense a rival?

Admiral Gravely: No, he wasn't a rival. I was a little bit senior to him, you see. We didn't get to be quite rivals in that respect. I was shocked that George didn't make admiral.[*] But something else happened along the way that I don't know about, don't care to know about. But George was a great, great man.

Paul Stillwell: And his wife later married John Reagan.[†]

Admiral Gravely: Yes, right.

Paul Stillwell: She's a wonderful person. I hope you'll say something about her.

Admiral Gravely: Yes, Dede. Dede and Alma were great friends. And she was a beautiful girl; she was fun to be with. I've been with her on a couple of dinners and a couple of things like that when I'd be out in San Diego all by myself. Alma has been

---

[*] George I. Thompson eventually retired as a captain.
[†] After Willita "Dede" Thompson was divorced from her husband, she married John W. Reagan, a member of the Golden 13, the first black naval officers, who were commissioned during World War II.

places with people that she knew too. Dede was just tremendous, and I've never understood what happened to that couple. I've never understood it. In fact, I don't care to know.

Paul Stillwell: Well, Dede strikes me as very competent also.

Admiral Gravely: Yes, right, very competent. In fact, I think she's working someplace now in a telephone company.

Paul Stillwell: I think so, yes.

Well, in one of our interviews back at AFCEA, you were telling a story about when you had the Taussig, and there was a carrier.[*] You got pulled away by a Soviet AGI, and there was a tugboat there. Do you have anything to add to that story?

Admiral Gravely: Well, I'm not sure exactly where it was, but it was off the Gulf of Tonkin someplace. And, as I recall, this guy went off into the distance and just stopped. He just stopped and started sunning and everything else, and we sent messages to each other: "Hope you're enjoying the sun," and all the rest of this garbage. He stayed there a couple of days. Then I noticed that he had taken off. I didn't catch him. So the engineering officer tried to ring up 25 knots, and he couldn't get but 22. He was afraid he was going to rupture something. I'm not an engineer, so I didn't understand it all. So I said, "Well, okay, do the best you can." And I stayed right behind him.

But then we soon got up to the carrier, and suddenly I get a message from the flag officer on the carrier, "Get that guy out of there!" So I just followed him right on in behind the carrier. He went to about 1,000 yards behind the carrier, and he was just sitting there.

Paul Stillwell: Kind of a gutsy guy.

---
[*] For the beginning of the story, see the end of interview number four of this oral history.

Admiral Gravely: Yeah. I went up his starboard side, and I started easing to get in front of him. [Chuckle] And he wasn't about to allow that, so he tried to keep up with me. And then I got my speed back, and I whipped up, and I went left. And when he saw that I was meaning business, he quickly turned this way, and I turned and went that way.

Paul Stillwell: So he went behind your stern?

Admiral Gravely: Yes, and I walked him right on out of the area. [Laughter] The people had a good time looking at that show. The man said, "Get him out of there," and that's exactly what I was going to do.

Paul Stillwell: Did you have any other incidents like that?

Admiral Gravely: Not that particular incident or that kind of incident.

Paul Stillwell: The Soviets were pretty bold in some of those, and that's why it led to the Incidents at Sea agreement to cut down on that.

Admiral Gravely: Yes, right.

Paul Stillwell: When we finished up earlier, you were with AFCEA. Can you fill in the last 15 or so years, please, from the last time we did an interview.

Admiral Gravely: Well, I was working at AFCEA as the educational foundation guy, basically. The job was to raise money to be able to send kids to college—scholarships, etc. I think we had about a million dollars when I left there. Now I understand they've got enough money so they send Ph.D's to college. [Laughter] They'll send anybody to college that deserves and should get an education. AFCEA moved into its own building. They were renting this place over in Burke when we were there. But they built a building over here in Falls Church. They're still operating. They've had two or three directors since then. They've added to the glory of the AFCEA educational foundation. In fact, we got into another facet of the education, I guess, in that we began to find jobs for people. So that was part of the educational foundation. It went well, and, incidentally, I heard from Jon Boyes, who was president of that, this past Christmas.* He sent me a book for memos and things like that. I gave it to somebody else; I've got to read it.

Paul Stillwell: How long did you stay with AFCEA?

Admiral Gravely: Six years, I believe it was. I began to go through fainting episodes. I fell one time, and, God, they came down in the basement. I was working in the basement, and they found me lying on the floor. They rushed me to the hospital, and everybody checked my heart and the rest of it. I stayed in Fairfax Hospital for a couple of days or something like that. But I thought I had worked long enough, so I decided to give it up, and we came out here. This has been my home ever since.

Paul Stillwell: What sorts of things have you been doing here?

Admiral Gravely: Well, I started off by planting trees around here. If you'll look out there in that back, where all those pine trees are, I planted every pine tree up there.

Paul Stillwell: They're pretty tall by now.

Admiral Gravely: Yes, well, they've been there 19-20 years. I've planted every tree out here except for one or two. In fact, we just took down one the other day. You can see the log. It must have been about a 5-foot trunk, out front there. Afraid they were going to fall into the house. A tree that size, when it falls, it damages things, so I decided to get rid of it. Now I've got to figure out what to put back there.

    I raised pigeons, of course.

Paul Stillwell: Oh, yes.

---

* Vice Admiral Jon L. Boyes, USN (Ret.).

Admiral Gravely: I don't know if you've heard the story about my pigeons. Well, I was fascinated as a youngster by pigeons. A young man came into my neighborhood, and my mother knew all the ladies and everything else. He came with his mother; apparently the father was divorcing or something. They lived very close to me. So I was brought into the picture to sort of show him around the neighborhood. I got up there, and this guy was in the back, and he had a bunch of pigeons out there. They were what they called rollers. The rollers are fancy, beautiful colored birds generally. They fly and flop. They roll; that's just what the name is. And I just became utterly fascinated. So somehow I got a couple of males, and I got some hens. The thing of it is that I found out you could eat them, and squabs are a delicacy. My mother could really fix them. The thing that got me was that I was picking a thing about the size of a robin. [Laughter]

Paul Stillwell: When you got all the feathers off.

Admiral Gravely: Yes, when you got all the feathers off, it was about the size of a robin. So then I got fascinated by a larger bird, which was the homing pigeon. Little larger, fly, and return home after a while. And I could fly them around. One of my neighbors had some, and we had chickens as well. My father was a big one for chickens. In those days in the post office, chickens came through the mail. If they couldn't find the guy's house where the chickens went, then they'd raffle them off at the post office. And dad would say, "Well, son, I've got another hundred chickens for you to feed. Twenty-five cents." Twenty-five cents for 100 chickens. Boy, oh, boy. I took care of them.

    Well, one day we went out there, and about half of these 100 chickens were dead. I noticed they were all wet. My baby brother had been trying to teach them to swim. [Laughter] Thought they were ducks. Oh, Lord, I wanted to skin his ass.

    I was a big chicken, pigeon fancier—any other thing like that. And I've been fascinated with pigeons ever since then. I've read all the fascinating stories about the pigeons that were used by the United States Navy and Army in World War II. We had a pigeon place up in Fort Monmouth, where they bred them, trained them, etc. One time I went to Korea as part of the DCA contingent, and a guy said, "Oh, I hear you're a pigeon man."

"Yes, sir."

He said, "We have a pigeon corps too."

I looked, and there, standing beside the train, was a guy with a pigeon in a cage. He said, "When you take off in this helicopter, I'm going to let him go." He let him go, and when we got there, the pigeon was already there. [Laughter] By the time we got there and got off the helicopter, the pigeon was sitting on the roof, trying to get in.

Paul Stillwell: In the U.S. Navy the first carrier, the <u>Langley</u>, had a pigeon loft.

Admiral Gravely: Yes, right.

We had an admiral who was a big pigeon man too. I can't think of his name right now. He was during my day, and he was quite a pigeon fancier. In fact, I've screwed around with a guy here who was in the Air Force. He was a colonel, and he was a big pigeon man. In fact, he just sold all of his but 17 the other day, and he said he got $13,000 for them. Well, he had good pigeons; he had been raising them for a long time, breeding them, so he had some good stock and everything else, which the pigeon fanciers all wanted. And he had won a lot of the races. I never was much for racing. I just didn't want to spend all that time training them and everything else.

Paul Stillwell: Just liked to have them around.

Admiral Gravely: Yes, just breed them. That's enough.

Paul Stillwell: What have been some of your other interests since you got rid of the birds?

Admiral Gravely: Well, about two years ago I began to feel kind of sick. I discovered I had prostate cancer. I had to fight that one for a while. Then I had congestive heart failure. So we had to fight that one. And one of the things they did was to take me to the hospital. They dragged 22 pounds off of me in dialysis in one weekend. [Chuckle]

Paul Stillwell: That's amazing.

Admiral Gravely: I didn't look the same anymore, not with 22 pounds gone. I was weighing close to 250. I'm down to less than 200 now.

Paul Stillwell: And now dialysis is a regular part of your life.

Admiral Gravely: Yes. Now dialysis is a regular part, so that takes four and a half hours three days a week. I haven't gotten used to that yet.

Paul Stillwell: What can you say about updating on your children? Where are they now?

Admiral Gravely: Well, Robby died in Pearl Harbor.

Paul Stillwell: You had told me about him, yes.

Admiral Gravely: David went to Virginia Union, graduated, and got a scholarship to Kent State. I made a mistake; I bought him a TV and a car. I bought him a car when he graduated and a TV set to take to Kent State. That's all he did while he was there, was watch it. They finally told him that he wasn't doing well enough to stay, so, to make it short, he quit, or they'd have put him out. So he came back home, and his first job was in these kiddie machines that you play with.

Paul Stillwell: Video games?

Admiral Gravely: Yes. And I said, "David, if you want to be a computer guy, why don't you take this course in town here, about six months?" So we sent him there, and he came out, and the first job he got was $35,000. He's still there. He married and then bought a house. After, September, 9/11, a lot of people were laid off, and he was one of those.[*]

---

[*] On 11 September 2001 terrorists hijacked commercial airliners and crashed them into the twin towers of the World Trade Center in New York City and the Pentagon in Arlington, Virginia.

The next thing I knew, he was working two jobs. He was working a job for a contractor who has a government contract for nuclear weapons or something. And he stayed there, and then he took another job, working Friday and Saturday night at Holiday Inn as basically an accountant. Then he just told me that he got a call from some computer group in Falls Church that wants to hire him back and pay him a decent salary.

Paul Stillwell: Good.

Admiral Gravely: So he's doing fine. Unfortunately, his wife came up with a disease called deteriorating ankles. Her ankles are just shot, bones crushing and everything else. She went to the hospital, and they finally found that she had diabetes and had it kind of bad, because it had contaminated one foot. They ended up taking a toe off, her big left toe. But she's getting around, and she's doing a little better. They're great.

My daughter was a runaway when I retired, and I didn't see her for a couple of months after I retired. I found out that she'd been to Florida; she's been all over. She ran away one time with an admiral's car. She ran away at 14, stole his car, went to Lake Placid, and stayed up there with another girl for a while. And we didn't know where she was. We finally got a call from a guy who said, "Well, I can tell you where she is. She's living in my motel, and, damn it, I want her ass out of here. She won't pay anything." [Laughter] They strong-armed themselves into this man's motel and lived there. So I sent them money enough to come home. She came home and stayed a month or so, and she was gone again. She's been off and on a runaway since '70-something. But now she's settled down. Of course, in all this time she was away, she worked as a waitress. She finally got herself a goal of being a manager of a restaurant. She came back here, and she's working out in Reston now as manager of a restaurant out there and doing fairly well. Only problem is she didn't pay her rent for three months, and they're kicking her out of her apartment. I don't know where she's going to live. I don't know why it needs more than just that.

She has a pit bull, the bad dog that bites people, and that's part of the reason they're kicking her out. When I was out to see the woman, I told her that the law in Washington, D.C., basically, and the area immediately surrounding it, pit bulls are not allowed in apartments. And she wants to bring that pit bull home. My daughter can come home if she wants to, but that pit bull can't. I don't want a damn pit bull. I wouldn't have one to start with. So I don't know what she's going to do. She's got to get something here in the next day or so.

Paul Stillwell: Do you have grandchildren?

Admiral Gravely: No grandchildren.

Paul Stillwell: Well, I'm even with you on that. I have none either.

Admiral Gravely: Yes.

Paul Stillwell: Well, I remember very warmly that evening out in Coronado that was Admiral Gravely Night.

Admiral Gravely: Yes.

Paul Stillwell: Can you bring out your memories of that evening?

Admiral Gravely: Well, most of my memories hinged around the fact that there were a tremendous number of folk there that I'd seen on ships and been in ships with and in sister ships with and things like that. I saw a friend of mine by the name of Joe Baer.* He was the exec of another destroyer when I was exec of the Theodore E. Chandler. We were in the same division, and we deployed together, had a good time. He and I and his wife and Alma got to be very good friends. We used to go to restaurants in San Diego. But to see Joe after so long was something.

One of the most important people that I saw was Tom Kimmel, who was probably the top young officer that I can remember serving with. And another one was John

---

* When Gravely knew him originally, Joseph Baer, Jr., was a lieutenant commander. He retired in 1969 as a commander.

Robinson, the son of Rembrandt Robinson. John was in Brazil, and he came from Brazil to that function. I don't know where he is today; I wish I did, because I owe him a letter. You name it—just a number of people that I didn't know but certainly some people that I had seen.

There was a guy on the Lofberg, and this guy was the first young black officer that I saw on a ship—after I got on one.

Admiral Gaston: Was it George Gaines?

Admiral Gravely: That's him, George Gaines.* I met him in Hong Kong when I was in command of Taussig. He turned out to be a tremendous officer, but he got stuck in communications. So be it. Communicators didn't fare very well, and I was surprised that I fared so well. But it was hard work, dedication, doing the job, and constantly trying to improve in various areas. But that's about the extent of it.

Paul Stillwell: Well, it had to be heartwarming to see all those people there that had never served with you but were paying their respects.

Admiral Gravely: Yes, that's right. It was. It was a tremendous experience for me. And the biggest thing, of course, was to see my son there with me. He was there, and I don't think he made any remarks. I remember John Robinson was one of those JOs you'd just like to put your arms around and say, "Hey, you're a great guy, but you can't do that." In fact, I told a joke about him. We were in some port, coming back from a deployment. It got to be about midnight, and I found myself stumbling around the street with him. I said to him, "Didn't liberty expire at midnight?"

He said, "Yes, sir."

I said, "What the hell are you going to tell the exec in the morning when you get back to the ship and you've been out here after midnight?"

He said, "Well, I was with the captain." [Laughter]

---

* Lieutenant George L. Gaines, USN.

Paul Stillwell: That's like a get-out-of-jail-free card. [Laughter]

Admiral Gravely: Right. Yes.

Paul Stillwell: What are your thoughts on the degree of integration in the Navy of today?

Admiral Gravely: Oh, I think the difference today, versus back in the '40s when I first joined, is just tremendous, and it's magnificent. I think this country is one country. We're all people. We're all American extraction, and the government and everybody else has to make a place for residents. I watched two movies that brought almost tears to my eyes last night. One was the story about Emmett Till.*

Paul Stillwell: I watched that program, and also Bayard Rustin was on right after that.†

Admiral Gravely: I saw that too. Those were the two programs. They kept bringing tears to my eyes, because I remember those days very well. Although I didn't realize that Bayard Rustin was a queer. Did you know that?

Admiral Gaston: No, I didn't.

Paul Stillwell: Mrs. Till just died about two weeks ago. What a courageous woman she was.

Admiral Gravely: Yes. I guess Emmett Till was saying, "Hi, Sweetie," or something to this white woman, and she told her husband. Two guys got together, went out, captured him, took him off, shot him, beat him half to death, disfigured all over. His eyeball laying on his cheek. His face looked like a ghost or something or a monster. They got off scot free. They never served any time. They were tried.

---

* Emmett Till was a 14-year-old black youngster who was murdered in Mississippi in 1955. The outrage over the killing and the subsequent acquittal of the killers was part of the growing civil rights movement.
† Bayard Rustin (1912-1987) was a pacifist and early leader in the American civil rights movement. He was an associate of Dr. Martin Luther King, Jr.

Paul Stillwell: And then they sold their story to a magazine and confessed in the story.

Admiral Gravely: Yes, confessed in the story—$4,000, I think.

Paul Stillwell: Yes.

Admiral Gaston: Believe it or not, a lynching of a black man happened in my hometown in my lifetime.

Paul Stillwell: What a terrible memory.

Admiral Gaston. I didn't see it. I guess he was probably 10 or 15 years older than I was.

Paul Stillwell: A few days ago I was up in New York and visited George Cooper's widow.* And this debate keeps raging on about affirmative action.

Admiral Gravely: Yes.

Paul Stillwell: She said, "They owe us. I don't want reparations, but they owe us." It's still a political issue.

Admiral Gravely: Yes, oh yes, yes. Well, I sometimes sit back and think—the University of Richmond gave me an honorary Ph.D. I couldn't walk on that campus when I was a kid. I went to college at Virginia Union; I didn't go to the University of Richmond. In fact, as quiet as it's kept, when the Navy sent me to the V-12 program, I first had orders to USC. I went to USC; I spent the night there. I lived in a room with five white guys. We got along fine and everything else. The next day the administrator came up and said, "I'm sorry, but we've got another school for you." They put me in a truck. I threw my stuff in the back of a truck, and they drove me over to UCLA. That's

---

* George C. Cooper was a member of the Golden 13.

where I stayed for two semesters. But everybody who asks me about that says, "Oh, that was before O. J. Simpson," the football player who murdered his wife. Yes, it was.

Paul Stillwell: Well, that honorary doctorate symbolized an enormous change.

Admiral Gravely: Yes, right.

Paul Stillwell: Well, I've about run out of questions. Do you have any other answers?

Admiral Gravely: No. [Chuckle]

Paul Stillwell: Admiral Gaston?

Admiral Gaston: What was the toughest thing that you felt, Admiral, of your whole career in the Navy?

Admiral Gravely: The toughest thing for me was getting to destroyers. I'd been sort of a big-ship man after the PC. The PC was special, but after the PC I went to the Iowa, went to the Toledo, and I went to the Seminole. And I just felt that that was probably the end, frankly, but things worked out.

I was in the process of filling out forms for various schools when orders came in. They were top-priority orders, which meant I had four days to get to Theodore E. Chandler, which was right down the pier. [Laughter] I walked over there on a Monday morning, I guess it was. Alma drove me down to work, and she and I said a little prayer on the pier. And I went aboard. It was amazing to me—the messenger and two young people. They were expecting something, but it wasn't me, I don't think. But, in any event, they finally went and got the exec and brought him down. The exec said, "Oh, happy to see you. I've been looking for you for months. I expected you to be here."

"I got orders yesterday, so here I am."

He said, "Well, let's go see the captain." Went up to see the captain, and the captain was a guy by the name of Galen C. Brown. I'll never forget him—just a tremendous individual. We were sitting up there, talking, he and I, the captain and the exec. The exec looked the captain dead in the eye, and he said, "Captain, you know, I've been wanting to go on 30 days' leave. Do you mind if I go tomorrow?"

The captain said, "No, be my guest." So he took off [laughter] on 30 days' leave, and I had just gotten there that morning.

Anyway, I saw him 30 days later. He said, "Well, how do you like my ship?"

I said, "Well, your ship is fine. I'm going to make it my ship here in another 24 hours when we get rid of you." [Laughter]

But everything went fine. Captain Brown and I became great friends. But I found out why the previous exec was fired. He was fired because he was the exec on there during the time that they'd had administrative inspections by CinCPacFlt and had a couple of inspections by a couple other people who found it to be the dirtiest ship in the fleet. So that was my first job. I went to work doing that and did it, and it turned out pretty well.

Out of that, of course, came the fact that I wanted to put what I do next. I knew Captain Brown, and after a while I knew that he was going to write me a good fitness report. I worked my tail off for him. But, in any event, we got to San Francisco for the fleet rehabilitation and modernization. I knew a guy in the bureau, so I wrote him a letter and said, "Hey, what are you people going to do with me now? You've taken the skipper off. I imagine you're going to pull me off too and cut the crew down to 100. I'm not quite ready to go ashore yet. What are you going to do?"

Said, "Oh, Sam, we've got a great thing for you. You're going to command of the Falgout." I almost cried. I almost cried. Well, that's that story.

Admiral Gaston: What was the most rewarding thing? If you could label one, what would it be?

Admiral Gravely: Most rewarding thing? I guess after the turmoil and some of the other things that I've been through, the most rewarding thing was to find out one morning that it had not all been in vain. I was in command of the Jouett when I learned I'd been selected for admiral. Boy, oh boy, that was a shock. It brought tears to my eyes. That was the most rewarding thing I ever had to happen to me.

Admiral Gaston: Did you have any thoughts that the Navy, before that happened to you, that the Navy would ever select a black man for admiral?

Admiral Gravely: I never had any thoughts that a black man would be selected for admiral. Now, I figured, I guess, sooner or later, they'd do it, but not in my time. So I was overjoyed, flabbergasted, any other words you want to use.

Paul Stillwell: Do you ever sit back and reflect on your place in history?

Admiral Gravely: I don't know. What's the guy that the service school is named after at Great Lakes?

Paul Stillwell: Robert Smalls.

Admiral Gravely: Smalls.* At one point in time, there was an effort taking place around here to get a ship named after Robert Smalls. So I talked to a woman who was in the process of trying to do this, and I didn't know this, but Robert Smalls—not only had he done the things that he said he'd done, captured a ship in Charleston Harbor, ridden it into port, turned it over to the Yankee forces, but when that was over and the war was over, he tried to get into the Naval Academy. They wouldn't have him. Here he was, the so-called main commander of the ship. So I don't have any second thoughts about it.

Paul Stillwell: My guess is that someday there will be a USS Gravely.

---

* Within the Great Lakes Naval Training Station in World War II, Camp Robert Smalls was the site of training for black recruits. It was named for an escaped slave who captured the Confederate steamer Planter during the Civil War and turned her over to the U.S. Navy. He served as pilot of the Planter and later of the gunboat Keokuk. After the war, Smalls (1839-1915) served in the U.S. Congress as a representative from South Carolina from 1875 to 1879 and from 1884 to 1887.

Admiral Gravely: I don't doubt it at all. In fact, I was told by a group that my name was before them not too long ago. They said, "Don't worry. Your place in history is secure." What does that mean?

Paul Stillwell: Well, I think that's true, yes.

Admiral Gaston: It's well deserved too. It's already there.
  Is there anything that you wish you had done differently?

Admiral Gravely: Yep, yep. First of all, I went to service school, and I didn't concentrate on service school like I should have. And I would have, because when I got out of service school, then, to be honest with you, I don't think some of the other things would have happened, like getting picked for the V-12 program.

Admiral Gaston: If you had an opportunity to start your life again, make decisions again as to what you were going to do, would it be different?

Admiral Gravely: No.

Paul Stillwell: I imagine there are few people who can say that.

Admiral Gravely: Yes.

Admiral Gaston: I'm one.

Paul Stillwell: Well, good.

Admiral Gaston: I wouldn't do any different. And he's one of the people that caused me to have the opportunity to do it the way I did it.

Paul Stillwell: Well, I think not only that, Admiral Gravely, but you've been an inspiration to a lot of people, brought them along.

Admiral Gravely: Well, one of my proudest moments has been basically that. I've had this to happen to me two or more places. When I was on the Iowa, we had run out of people for communications school. And it wasn't just the Iowa; it was Navy wide. So one of my skippers said, "Suppose I give you two new men every month. You keep those guys down there in the radio shack, and when you decide that you cannot make them radiomen, just transfer them back to the first division. If you can, you get them, and you get two more. We started like that, and I would always give them a lecture and tell them what I wanted them to do and how long they could stay there. If they did well, they could stay, or else back to first division.

Years later I met a guy who was a lieutenant commander, retired, LDO type. He said he never would forget talking to me aboard the Iowa. He said I talked him into becoming a radioman in the first place and staying there.

Paul Stillwell: Was he a seaman when he came to you?

Admiral Gravely: He was a seaman apprentice. [Laughter] He rode that thing right on up to lieutenant commander, LDO. I've seen a couple people do that.

Paul Stillwell: And I suspect that you've also touched a lot of lives of people whom you've never even met.

Admiral Gravely: Oh, yes, I wouldn't doubt that. I know I've touched the lives of people I didn't know.

When we came to San Diego in '70, I guess, I was on Jouett, and we came into port. A woman sent for me on the quarterdeck, so I went down there. Her grandson was on board. She brought me a cake. She made a cake for somebody she'd never met for bringing her grandson home safely.

Paul Stillwell: Well, thank you very much for this addition. And we look forward to wrapping up the whole project.

Admiral Gravely: Okay.

Paul Stillwell: Thank you.

Index to the Oral History of
Vice Admiral Samuel L. Gravely, Jr.
U.S. Navy (Retired)

Acapulco, Mexico
   The destroyer Taussig (DD-746) took part in an operation in early 1967 that included a visit to Acapulco, 260-264

Accidents
   A crewman was killed in a gun mount mishap on the destroyer Taussig (DD-746) in 1966, 232-233
   The guided missile frigate Jouett (DLG-29) had a slight collision with a ferryboat during a visit to Hong Kong in the early 1970s, 318-319

Adamson, Vice Admiral Robert E., Jr., USN (USNA, 1944)
   Served as Commander Naval Surface Force Atlantic Fleet from 1975 to 1977, 338-339

AFCEA
   See: Armed Forces Communications and Electronics Association (AFCEA)

Air Force, U.S.
   Operation of the National Emergency Airborne Command Post in the mid-1960s, 203-205, 207-208

Alcohol
   Robust beer drinking by midshipmen on liberty in 1944, 27-28
   Officers held a drinking party on board the attack cargo ship Seminole (AKA-104) in the late 1950s, 121-122
   In the early 1960s a crewman of the picket destroyer escort Falgout (DER-324) drank too much ashore, 171-172
   In 1971 the officers of the guided missile frigate Jouett (DLG-29) drank wine to celebrate Gravely's selection for flag rank, 311-312

Algiers, Lieutenant Norman A., Jr., USN
   Served in the early 1950s as damage control officer in the heavy cruiser Toledo (CA-133), 86, 97

Allen, Captain Charles Vern, USN
   In the late 1950s commanded the attack cargo ship Seminole (AKA-104), 117-118, 122, 126, 128

Ammunition
   Seal Beach Naval Weapons Station provided ammunition for the destroyer Taussig (DD-746) in the mid-1960s, 219-221

Amphibious Warfare
   Training courses ashore at Coronado, California, in 1957, 112-113
   Operations in the late 1950s by the attack cargo ship Seminole (AKA-104), 114-115, 120

Andrews Air Force Base, Maryland
   Base in the mid-1960s for the operation of the National Emergency Airborne Command Post, 203-204

Antisubmarine Warfare
   Role of the Submarine Chaser Training Center in World War II, 29-31, 33-34
   Use of the drone antisubmarine helicopter (DASH) by the destroyer Taussig (DD-746) in the mid-1960s, 262-263
   ASW exercises around Guam in 1966 involved a Polaris submarine, 276-277
   ASW exercises in the mid-1960s built around the carrier Yorktown (CVS-10), 265-266

Use of the variable-depth sonar in the mid-1960s, 268, 344
Introduction of sonar towed arrays in the 1970s, 343-344

Armed Forces Communications and Electronics Association (AFCEA)
Work in the 1980s on a variety of programs, 383-384, 401-402

Army, U.S.
Gravely's father served in the Army in World War I and shortly after, 1, 7-8
In 1940 rejected Gravely in his attempt to enlist, 6-7
In 1945 Gravely was arrested by Army MPs in Miami for allegedly impersonating an officer, 39-40

Austin, Vice Admiral Bernard L., USN (USNA, 1924)
Served 1960-64 as president of the Naval War College, 197-198

Australia
In 1966 the destroyer Taussig (DD-746) visited Melbourne and Brisbane, 253-256
In the early 1970s the guided missile frigate Jouett (DLG-29) visited Melbourne and Fremantle, 308-310

Australian Navy
In 1966 was involved in a combined exercise with the U.S. Navy, 251-253
In the late 1970s took part in multinational exercises in the Pacific, 366

Battleship Division Two
In the early 1950s the division commander and his staff were in the battleship Iowa (BB-61), 81-82

Bennett, Captain William L., Jr., USN (USNA, 1944)
Commanded the antisubmarine carrier Yorktown (CVS-10) in 1967-68, 270-271

Boyd, USS (DD-544)
Deployment to the Western Pacific in 1966, 223, 227, 251-259

Briggs, Vice Admiral Edward S., USN (USNA, 1949)
In the 1960s commanded the destroyer Turner Joy (DD-951) and in the 1970s commanded the guided missile frigate Jouett (DLG-29), 237-238, 316-317

Brown, Commander Galen C., USN
In the early 1960s commanded the destroyer Theodore E. Chandler (DD-717), 135-140 143, 146, 148, 411-412

Brown, Commander Nicholas, USN (USNA, 1956)
Outstanding officer who served as exec of the guided missile frigate Jouett (DLG-29) in the early 1970s, 296, 298

Bureau of Naval Personnel, Arlington, Virginia
In the early 1950s advised the battleship Iowa (BB-61) that the ship would receive a black officer, Gravely, and put him in a communications billet, 59-61
In the 1950s offered the opportunity for reserve officers to augment into the regular Navy, 75, 100
Gravely's contacts with the bureau over the years concerning his billet assignments, 105-107, 112, 128-129, 134, 146-148, 150-152, 154-155, 181-182, 191, 205, 215, 280-281, 288, 344-345

Charleston Naval Base
In the early 1970s Commander Cruiser-Destroyer Group Two relocated from Newport to Charleston, 331, 334-335
Gravely's difficulties in getting desirable quarters assigned by the Commandant of the Sixth Naval District in the early 1970s, 334-336

Chevalier, USS (DD-805)
    In the late 1960s operated out of San Diego, 268

Christmas Island
    Site of U.S. nuclear weapons tests in 1962, 165-169, 172-173

Clarey, Admiral Bernard A., USN (USNA, 1934)
    In 1971, as CinCPacFlt, congratulated Gravely on his selection for flag rank, 311-312

Clark, Vice Admiral Joseph J., USN (USNA, 1918)
    In 1952-53 commanded the Seventh Fleet, 62-64, 67

Classified Information
    Control of registered publications on board the battleship Iowa (BB-61) during the Korean War, 72-74
    Concerns for security during construction of the National Military Command Center in the mid-1960s, 203, 205-207

Clements, William P., Jr.
    As Deputy Secretary of Defense in 1976, interviewed Gravely about commanding the Third Fleet, 358-360

Cockell, Captain William A., USN (USNA, 1928)
    Served as commanding officer of the heavy cruiser Toledo (CA-133), 1953-1955, 94, 97

Collisions
    The guided missile frigate Jouett (DLG-29) had a slight collision with a ferryboat during a visit to Hong Kong in the early 1970s, 318-319

Columbia University, New York City
    Site of midshipman school for the V-12 officer program in World War II, 22-27

Communications
    Use of visual communications in World War II, 30-31
    Communications training course at Monterey, California, in the early 1950s, 56-57
    On board the battleship Iowa (BB-61) in the early 1950s, 59-68, 71-77
    On board the heavy cruiser Toledo (CA-133) in the early 1950s, 87-91, 94-95
    On board the attack cargo ship Seminole (AKA-104) in the late 1950s, 114-115
    On board the picket destroyer escort Falgout (DER-324) in the early 1960s, 178-181
    Role of the Defense Communications Agency as a joint-service operation in the early 1960s, 198, 201-204
    Operation of the National Emergency Airborne Command Post in the mid-1960s, 203-205, 207-209
    On board the destroyer Taussig (DD-746) in the mid-1960s, 248-249, 253-255
    Development in the late 1960s-early 1970s of the Navy's satellite communication program, 283-288, 326-327
    Role of the Naval Communications Command in the early 1970s, 322-327
    Role of the Defense Communications Agency as a joint-service command in 1978-80, 377-381

Constellation, USS (CVA-64)
    Operations off Southern California in the mid-1960s, 217-219
    Vietnam War service in 1966, 232

Cooper, Captain Joshua W., USN (USNA, 1927)
    Commanded the battleship Iowa (BB-61) in 1952-53, 65-66, 76, 81-82
    In the mid-1950s was chief of staff for Cruiser-Destroyer Force Pacific Fleet, 87-88

Cruiser-Destroyer Group Two
    In the early 1970s relocated from Newport to more southern homeports, 331
    Conducted a number of training exercises in the Atlantic in the early 1970s, 331-334, 337-344
    Administrative role for the commander and staff in the early 1970s, 341-342

Cryptography
    Encoding and decoding messages in the battleship Iowa (BB-61) during the Korean War, 67-68, 81

Cummings, Commander Edward J., Jr., USN (USNA, 1943)
    Commanded the destroyer Somers (DD-947) from April 1959 to October 1960, 133-134

Curts, Rear Admiral Maurice E., USN, (USNA, 1920)
    In the early 1950s commanded Cruiser-Destroyer Force Pacific Fleet, 94

Curtze, Rear Admiral Charles A., USN (USNA, 1933)
    In the early 1960s commanded the Hunters Point Naval Shipyard, 148-150, 154-155

DASH
    See: Drone Antisubmarine Helicopter (DASH)

Defense Communications Agency
    Role as a joint-service agency in the early 1960s, 198, 201-203, 210-211
    Construction in the mid-1960s of the National Military Command Center in the Pentagon, 201-207
    Role as a joint-service agency in 1978-80, 377-381

Defense Science Board
    Role in connection with the Defense Communications Agency in the late 1970s, 380

Destroyer Squadron Five
    In the late 1950s Gravely spent time on board ships of the squadron while in training to be a destroyer executive officer, 132

Destroyer Squadron Seven
    In 1959 Gravely spent time on board ships of the squadron while in training to be a destroyer executive officer, 129-132

Deutermann, Captain Peter T., USN (USNA, 1963)
    Served as a JO in the guided missile frigate Jouett (DLG-29) in the early 1970s, 302, 318-319

Disciplinary Problems
    In 1945 Gravely was arrested by MPs in Miami for allegedly impersonating an officer, 39-40
    In the early 1950s a seaman in the crew of the battleship Iowa (BB-61) went on unauthorized absence, 78-79
    Officers held a drinking party on board the attack cargo ship Seminole (AKA-104) in the late 1950s and were punished, 121-122
    In the early 1960s a crewman of the picket destroyer escort Falgout (DER-324) drank too much ashore, 171-172
    Drug abuse in the mid-1960s by the crew of the destroyer Taussig (DD-746), 261
    In early 1967, while on liberty in Mexico, a sailor from the Taussig went on a rampage, 263-264
    Court-martial for an officer at the SOSUS station on Midway Island in the mid-1970s, 352-353

Drone Antisubmarine Helicopter (DASH)
    Operated in the mid-1960s by the destroyer Taussig (DD-746), 262-263

Drugs
    Drug abuse problem in the crew of the destroyer Taussig (DD-746) in the mid-1960s, 261, 264-265

Education
    For Gravely in Virginia public schools in the 1920s-1930s, 2-3
    Gravely attended Virginia Union University in the late 1930s and mid-1940s, 5-6, 13, 44-45
    The V-12 officer training program in World War II included college, 16-21
    Course of study at the Naval War College in the early 1960s, 192-198
    Work of the Armed Forces Communications and Electronics Association in the 1980s on a variety of programs, 383-384, 401-402

Eleventh Naval District, San Diego, California
    Role of the district commandant in the mid-1970s, 346-353
    Naval Reserve connections within the district, 348, 357

Eller, Lieutenant James B., USN
    In the early 1960s served as executive officer of the picket destroyer escort Falgout (DER-324), 189

Enlisted Personnel
    In 1942 the Navy first allowed black sailors into general service ratings, 8-11
    Training and duty assignments for black enlisted men in World War II, 11-17, 27-29, 32
    In 1945-46 in the crew of the patrol craft PC-1264, 34-35, 39-42
    Crew members of the battleship Iowa (BB-61) in the early 1950s, 76-79, 415
    Crew members of the heavy cruiser Toledo (CA-133) in the mid-1950s, 87-90
    Crew members of the picket destroyer escort Falgout (DER-324) in the early 1960s, 171-172
    Crewmen of the guided missile frigate Jouett (DLG-29) in the early 1970s, 299-301, 314-315

Equator
    Ceremonies connected with the crossing in the early 1970s by the crew of the guided missile frigate Jouett (DLG-29), 307

Falgout, USS (DER-324)
    Picket duty out of Pearl Harbor in the early 1960s, 160-162, 172-173, 177-182
    Publicity in 1962 in connection with Gravely taking command, 163-164
    Ship handling, 164-165
    Diesel propulsion plant and auxiliary equipment, 164, 171, 178, 182
    Support duty in connection with nuclear weapons tests around Johnston and Christmas islands in 1962, 165-169, 172-173
    Seakeeping/stability qualities, 170-171
    Enlisted crew members, 171-173
    Visit from Under Secretary of the Navy Paul Fay, 174-176
    Lost a bilge keel while on patrol, 177-178
    Communications capability, 178-181
    Shipyard overhaul, 188-189, 191
    Wardroom officer makeup in the early 1960s, 189-191

Fay, Paul B., Jr.
    As Under Secretary of the Navy in the early 1960s, pushed physical fitness, 174-176

Fiji Islands
    Visited by the destroyer Taussig (DD-746) in late 1966, 256-257

Finneran, Vice Admiral John G., USN (USNA, 1947)
    In 1973-74 commanded the U.S. Second Fleet, 331, 333

Fisher, Captain Gordon E., USN
    In the 1960s served on board the destroyer Taussig (DD-746), later had other duty, including command of an NROTC unit, 267, 303

Fitzpatrick, Rear Admiral Francis J., USN (USNA, 1939)
   In the late 1960s-early 1970s served as Commander Naval Communications Command, 284-286, 316

Fleet Rehabilitation And Modernization (FRAM)
   In 1961 the destroyer Theodore E. Chandler (DD-717) underwent the FRAM I conversion, 146-156

Football
   Gravely played the sport at various times in the 1930s-1940s, 6, 26, 44-45, 82-83, 396

FRAM
   See: Fleet Rehabilitation And Modernization (FRAM)

Gardner, Commander Earle G., Jr., USN (USNA, 1935)
   In the early 1950s served as executive officer of the battleship Iowa (BB-61), 80-81

Gause, Chief Radioman D. C., USN
   In the mid-1950s ran the radio gang in the heavy cruiser Toledo (CA-133), 88-90

Gayler, Admiral Noel A. M., USN (USNA, 1935)
   In the mid-1970s, as CinCPac, was concerned about antisubmarine warfare, 360

Gidrofon (Soviet Intelligence Ship)
   Operated near a U.S. carrier formation in the Pacific in the mid-1960s, 278-279, 400-401

Golden 13
   Group of black naval officers commissioned in 1944, 24-25, 31-32, 159, 354-357, 397
   The group had its first reunion, in California, in 1977, 376-377

Goodfellow, Rear Admiral A. Scott, USN (USNA, 1940)
   Served as Commander Cruiser-Destroyer Flotilla Seven, 1966-67, 258-259

Gravely, Vice Admiral Samuel L., Jr., USN (Ret.)
   Parents of, 1-8, 13-14, 26, 29, 43, 45-46, 48-49, 54, 312, 394-395, 403
   Wife Alma, 26, 41, 43-47, 49-50, 56-57, 69-70, 76-77, 83-85, 97, 100-103, 110-112, 116, 127, 129, 157-158, 165, 183, 186, 192-194, 199-201, 240, 244, 258-261, 263-264, 269, 281-283, 308, 313-314, 316-317, 324, 330, 344, 351, 356, 361, 370, 392-393, 398-400, 411
   Children of, 70, 116, 120, 127, 157-158, 165, 187, 200, 212, 240, 259, 283, 314, 316, 369-371, 392, 394, 399, 405-408
   Growing-up years in Virginia in the 1920s-1930s, 1-10, 394-395, 403
   Attended Virginia Union University in the late 1930s and mid-1940s, 5-6, 13, 44-46
   Enlisted Navy service in 1942-43, 7-17
   In the V-12 officer training program, 1943-44, 16-28, 410-411
   Duty training recruits at Great Lakes in 1945, 27-28, 31-32
   As student in 1945 at the Submarine Chaser Training Center, 29-34
   In 1945-46 served in the crew of the patrol craft PC-1264, 34-42, 82-83, 396-397
   Service in 1946 with the Fleet Training Group at Norfolk, 42-43, 396
   Civilian life between 1946 and 1949, 43-48
   Service in 1949-51 as a Navy recruiter in Washington, D.C., 49-56
   In 1951 attended a communications training course at Monterey, California, 56-57, 105-106
   Served 1952-53 in the battleship Iowa (BB-61), 57-84, 415
   Served 1953-55 in the heavy cruiser Toledo (CA-133), 65, 83-100
   Augmentation into the regular Navy in the mid-1950s, 100
   Served 1955-57 on the staff of the Third Naval District, 100-112
   Duty from 1957 to 1959 on board the attack cargo ship Seminole (AKA-104), 112-129
   Interim duty in 1959-60 while in training to be executive officer of a destroyer, 129-134

In 1960-61 served as executive officer and acting commanding officer of the destroyer Theodore E. Chandler (DD-717), 134-156, 411-412

In 1962-63 commanded the radar picket destroyer escort Falgout (DER-324), 160-191

In 1963-64 was a student at the Naval War College, 191-198, 398-399

In 1964-65 worked in the Defense Communications Agency in the Pentagon, 198-211

In 1966-68 commanded the destroyer Taussig (DD-746), 215-281

In 1968-70 was coordinator of the Navy's satellite communications program, 281-288

In 1970-71 commanded the guided missile frigate Jouett (DLG-29), 288-319, 412-413

Selection for flag rank in the spring of 1971, 310-316, 412-413

Served 1971-73 as Commander Naval Communications Command and Director, Naval Communications Division of OpNav, 322-330

Served in 1973-75 as Commander Cruiser-Destroyer Group Two, 330-345

In 1975-76 was Commandant 11th Naval District, 345-361

Served 1976-78 as Commander Third Fleet, 362-377

Death of son Robby in Hawaii in the mid-1970s, 369-371

In 1978-80 was Director of the Defense Communications Agency, 377-381

Post-Navy activities, including work with the Armed Forces Communications and Electronics Association, 381-393, 401-404

Great Lakes, Illinois, Naval Training Station
Site of segregated recruit training in World War II, 9-10, 27-29, 32

Groner, Commander William T., USN (USNA, 1936)
In the early 1950s was executive officer of the heavy cruiser Toledo (CA-133), 91-93

Guam, Mariana Islands
Served as a stop-over when the destroyer Taussig (DD-746) deployed to the Western Pacific in 1966, 227, 276-277

Gunnery—Naval
By the battleship Iowa (BB-61) during the Korean War, 70-71
By the destroyer Taussig (DD-746) in the mid-1960s, 232-237
Concerns in the late 1970s about the use of the Hawaiian Island of Kahoolawe for Navy gunnery practice, 362-365

Hampton, Virginia, Naval Training Station
Site of service school for black enlisted personnel in World War II, 10-12

Harlfinger, Vice Admiral Frederick J. II, USN (USNA, 1935)
Served in the early 1970s as Director Command Support Programs, OpNav, 322, 325-326

Hawaii
In the early 1960s Pearl Harbor served as a base for DERs on radar picket duty, 160-161, 173-174
Life in Honolulu for the Gravely family in the early 1960s, 187-188
In 1966 the destroyer Taussig (DD-746) visited Pearl Harbor en route to a Western Pacific deployment, 225-226
Concerns in the late 1970s about using the island of Kahoolawe for Navy gunnery practice, 362-365

Hayward, Admiral Thomas B., USN (USNA, 1948)
Served 1976-78 as Commander in Chief Pacific Fleet, 362, 375-376
Personality and working style, 375-376

Heftel, Cecil L.
As U.S. Representative from Hawaii in the mid-1970s, was concerned about Navy gunnery practice on the island of Kahoolawe, 363

Helicopters
    Use of the drone antisubmarine helicopter (DASH) by the destroyer Taussig (DD-746) in the mid-1960s, 262-263

Henry W. Tucker, USS (DD-875)
    Fired on at Wonsan, North Korea, in 1951, 69-70

Holloway, Admiral James L. III, USN (USNA, 1943)
    As CNO in 1976, had a key role in Gravely's selection as Commander Third Fleet, 357-358, 360-361, 377

Hong Kong, British Crown Colony
    Visited in the mid-1950s by the heavy cruiser Toledo (CA-133), 94-95, 98
    Visited in 1966 by the destroyer Taussig (DD-746), 239
    The guided missile frigate Jouett (DLG-29) had a slight collision with a ferryboat during a visit to Hong Kong in the early 1970s, 318-319

Hope, Lieutenant Commander Edward, CEC, USNR
    One of the first black naval officers commissioned in World War II, 24, 159

Horrall, Lieutenant Commander Eugene F., USN
    In the early 1950s served in the battleship Iowa (BB-61), 60-61, 64

Humphrey, Hubert H.
    Served as Vice President in the latter part of the 1960s, 212

Hunters Point Naval Shipyard, San Francisco, California
    In 1961 did a FRAM I conversion on the destroyer Theodore E. Chandler (DD-717), 148-156

Iowa, USS (BB-61)
    In 1951 was recommissioned for Korean War service, 58
    Captain William Smedberg as skipper, 1951-52, 58, 63-65, 72
    Communications in the early 1950s, 59-68, 71-77
    Korean War operations, 62-71
    Duty as flagship for Commander Seventh Fleet, 62-64, 66-67, 73-74
    Captain Joshua Cooper as skipper, 1952-53, 65-66, 76, 81-82
    Control of registered publications on board the battleship Iowa (BB-61) during the Korean War, 72-74
    Home-ported in Norfolk in the 1950s, 75-77
    Enlisted crewmen, 76-79, 415
    Officer stateroom assignments, 80-81
    Operations in the Caribbean in 1954, 84

Japan
    Sasebo and Yokosuka supported U.S. warships during the Korean War, 65

Johnson, Vice President Lyndon B.
    In early 1973 attended a celebration at the White House for the 100th anniversary of the Emancipation Proclamation, 184, 186

Johnston Island
    Site of U.S. nuclear weapons tests in 1962, 165-169, 172-173

Jouett, USS (DLG-29)
    Characteristics of the ship in the early 1970s, 288-289
    In the summer of 1970 did training exercises out of San Diego, 289-292
    Deployment to the Western Pacific in 1970-71 to take part in the Vietnam War, 292-295, 303-313

Officers on board in the early 1970s, 295-296, 301-305
Engineering plant, 296-297
Enlisted crewmen in the early 1970s, 299-301, 314-315
Equator crossing and visits to Singapore and Australia, 306-310
Encounter with a Soviet AGI in the Western Pacific in the early 1970s, 307-308
Slight collision with a ferryboat during a visit to Hong Kong in the early 1970s, 318-319
In 1976 Gravely was frocked on board the ship as a three-star admiral, 361

Kennedy, President John F.
In early 1963 held a White House event to celebrate the 100th anniversary of the Emancipation Proclamation, 182-186

Kidd, Vice Admiral Isaac C., Jr., USN (USNA, 1942)
Commanded the First Fleet from 1969 to 1970, 291
Commanded the Sixth Fleet from 1970 to 1971, 326

Kimmel, Ensign Thomas K., Jr., USN (USNA, 1966)
Top-notch junior officer on board the destroyer Taussig (DD-746) in the mid-1960s, 246-247, 407

Korean War
Navy manpower needs jumped with the onset of war in 1950, 51-52
The battleship Iowa (BB-61) was recommissioned in 1951 and served in the Korean theater, 58-71

Kowalzyk, Captain Alexander M., Jr., USN (USNA, 1927)
In the mid-1950s served as Third Naval District chief of staff, 109

Langille, Captain Justin E. III, USN (USNA, 1946)
Served as Commander Destroyer Division 213, 1966-67, 260-261, 264

Layman, Lieutenant Lawrence, USN (USNA, 1952)
Served in the destroyer Somers (DD-947) in the late 1950s, 133-134

Leave and Liberty
In New York City and Pennsylvania during World War II, 25-28
In Miami in 1945, 29-30, 33, 39-40
In Japan during the Korean War, 65
In Australia in 1966, 253-254, 256
In Acapulco, Mexico in early 1967, 263-264

Lofberg, USS (DD-759)
In 1959 Gravely spent time on board while in training to be a destroyer executive officer, 129-131

Long Beach Naval Shipyard
Did repair work on board the destroyer Taussig (DD-746) in the mid-1960s, 218-219, 222

Martin, Captain Farar Benjamin Conner, USN (USNA, 1927)
Commanded the heavy cruiser Toledo (CA-133) in 1952-53, 86-87, 90-91, 94

Matthews, Rear Admiral Herbert Spencer, Jr., USN
In 1951 attended a communications training course at Monterey, California, 56-57, 106

Mau, Lieutenant George W., Jr., USNR
Served as first lieutenant in the attack cargo ship Seminole (AKA-104) in the late 1950s, 112-113, 120-121

McCain, Admiral John S., Jr., USN (Ret.) (USNA, 1931)
    In 1971, as CinCPac, congratulated Gravely on his selection for flag rank, 311-312

Medical Problems
    Gravely's difficulty in the 1950s in passing vision tests, 107-108
    In the 1960s Gravely was hospitalized for depression caused by his blood-pressure medication, 200-201, 282-283
    Gravely's battles with prostate cancer and kidney problems following retirement, 404-405

Mexico
    The destroyer Taussig (DD-746) took part in an operation in early 1967 that included a visit to Acapulco, 260-264

Miami, Florida
    Site of the Submarine Chaser Training Center in World War II, 29-31, 33-34
    In 1945 Gravely was arrested by MPs in Miami for allegedly impersonating an officer, 39-40

Miles, Rear Admiral Milton E., USN (USNA, 1922)
    In the mid-1950s was Commandant, Third Naval District, 103

Monterey, California
    Site of a communications training course in the early 1950s, 56-57

Moran, Rear Admiral William J., USN
    In the late 1960s served as Director, Navy Space Program Division, OpNav, 286

Morman, Ensign Donald G., USNR
    During World War II served in the patrol craft PC-1264, 35-36

Nagler, Rear Admiral Gordon R., USN
    In the early 1960s commanded the picket destroyer escort Forrester (DER-334), 161-162
    In the mid-1970s commanded Cruiser-Destroyer Group Two, 342

Nash, Captain David, USN (USNA, 1935)
    In the late 1950s commanded Destroyer Squadron Five, 133-134

National Emergency Airborne Command Post
    Operation of in the mid-1960s by the Air Force, 203-205, 207-209

National Military Command Center
    Construction of in the Pentagon in the mid-1960s, 201-207

National Naval Officers Association
    Role in connection with minority officers of the sea services, 384-385, 387, 398
    In February 2000 held a tribute to Gravely in Coronado, California, 398, 407-408

National Security Agency
    Role in connection with the Defense Communications Agency in the late 1970s, 380-381

Naval Reserve, U.S.
    Ships assigned to the Third Naval District in the mid-1950s for training of reservists, 108-110
    Role in the 11th Naval District in Southern California in the mid-1970s, 348, 357

Naval War College, Newport, Rhode Island
  In 1963 Gravely and Lieutenant Commander George Thompson became the first two black officer students, 191, 398-399
  Course of study in the early 1960s, 192-198

Navigation
  On board the destroyer Theodore E. Chandler (DD-717) in the early 1960s, 139
  On board the picket destroyer escort Falgout (DER-324) in the early 1960s, 178-179

Nelson, Ensign Dennis Denmark II, USNR
  One of the first black naval officers commissioned in World War II, 30-31, 99, 103, 159, 354-357

Newcomb, Commander Zeanious L., USN
  Served as exec of the guided missile frigate Jouett (DLG-29) in the early 1970s, 296, 298, 310-311, 313-314

Newland, Captain John W., Jr., USN (USNA, 1943)
  Commanded an escort squadron in the early 1960s, 160-164, 173-176, 182

News Media
  Life magazine coverage in 1944 of the Golden Thirteen, 24
  Story in the Chicago Defender around 1950 about a segregated recruiting station, 52
  Publicity in 1962 when Gravely took command of the picket destroyer escort Falgout (DER-324), 163-164
  In 1966 Gravely accommodated a writer and photographer from Ebony magazine on board the destroyer Taussig (DD-746), 223-226, 241-242
  Coverage of Gravely's selection for flag rank in the spring of 1971, 312-314
  Ebony listed Gravely among the 100 most influential blacks in the nation, 324
  An aggressive reporter hit Gravely in the mid-1970s during coverage of the Hawaiian Island of Kahoolawe, 363-364

Nisewaner, Captain Terrell A., USN (USNA, 1932)
  In the late 1950s commanded Destroyer Squadron Five, 132-133

Norman, Lieutenant Commander William S., USN
  In the early 1970s was CNO's special assistant for equal opportunity, 327-328

Nuclear Weapons
  Testing of around Johnston and Christmas islands in 1962, 165-169, 172-173

O'Hare, USS (DD-889)
  Deployed to the Western Pacific in the mid-1960s, 249-251

Okinawa
  Difficult racial climate in the late 1950s, 120-121

PC-1264, USS
  Operated during World War II and shortly afterward with a mostly black crew, 34-42

Pay and Allowances
  For Gravely as an ensign in 1944, 4

Pearl Harbor, Hawaii
  In the early 1960s served as a base for DERs on radar picket duty, 160-161, 173-174
  In 1966 the destroyer Taussig (DD-746) visited Pearl en route to the Western Pacific, 225-226

Peet, Vice Admiral Raymond E., USN (USNA, 1943)
    In June 1971, as Commander First Fleet, frocked Gravely as a flag officer, 316

Pentagon, Arlington, Virginia
    Construction in the mid-1960s of the National Military Command Center, 201-207

Petersen, Lieutenant General Frank E., Jr., USMC
    In the early 1960s was stationed in Hawaii, 187

PIRAZ
    See: Positive Identification Radar Advisory Zone (PIRAZ)

Positive Identification Radar Advisory Zone (PIRAZ)
    Role of the guided missile frigate Jouett (DLG-29) off Vietnam in the early 1970s, 292-293

Post Office Department
    In the late 1940s Gravely had several postal jobs, 45-48

Promotion of Naval Officers
    Gravely's selection as the Navy's first black admiral in the spring of 1971, 310-316, 412-413
    Work of a board that selected officers for promotion to commander in the mid-1970s, 337

Propulsion Plants
    Diesel plant in the picket destroyer escort Falgout (DER-324) in the early 1960s, 164, 171, 178, 182
    In the mid-1960s the destroyer Taussig (DD-746) made a full-power run at 34 knots, 266-267
    Steam plant on board the guided missile frigate Jouett (DLG-29) in the early 1970s, 296-297

Prout, Commander Russell K., USN
    In the late 1950s commanded the destroyer Lofberg (DD-759), 131

Public Affairs
    In 1966 Gravely accommodated a writer and photographer from Ebony magazine on board the destroyer Taussig (DD-746), 223-226, 241-242
    Publicity in connection with Gravely's selection for flag rank in the spring of 1971, 312-313

Pueblo, USS (AGER-2)
    Her capture by North Korea in January 1968 led to a U.S. show of force in the Sea of Japan, 269-270

Purdon, Lieutenant Eric, USNR
    During World War II commanded the patrol craft PC-1264, 34-38, 40-41

Racial Issues
    Segregated society in Virginia prior to World War II, 8-9
    Segregated training for Navy enlisted personnel in World War II, 9-11, 27-29
    Segregation in berthing for enlisted personnel at San Diego in 1943, 14-16
    Segregated officer facilities at Great Lakes in 1945, 28-29
    In World War II the patrol craft PC-1264 operated with a mostly black crew, 34-42
    In 1945 Gravely was arrested by MPs in Miami for allegedly impersonating an officer, 39-40
    Gravely's problems finding housing in Norfolk shortly after World War II, 42-43
    In 1948 President Harry Truman issued an executive order that integrated the armed forces, 55
    In 1949-50 Gravely served in recruiting duty, presumably to enlist black sailors, 49-56
    Gravely's initial difficulties on board the battleship Iowa (BB-61) in the early 1950s, 59
    Incident involving bar girls in Japan in the early 1950s, 65
    Difficulties for the Gravely families in finding accommodations while traveling in the 1950s and 1960s, 85, 157-158, 356

In the mid-1950s someone threw a brick through Gravely's window, 102
Civil rights movement in the 1950s, 118-120
Difficult racial climate in Okinawa in the late 1950s, 120-121
Gravely's problems in finding housing in the Washington, D.C., area in the mid-1960s, 199-201, 321
The housing situation was better when Gravely returned to Washington in the late 1960s and early 1970s, 283, 321-322
Impact of Z-grams when Admiral Elmo Zumwalt was Chief of Naval Operations in the early 1970s, 297-300
Racial disturbances in the fleet in the early 1970s, 299, 327-328
CNO Elmo Zumwalt instituted measures designed to enhance racial awareness in the Navy, 328-330
Gravely's assessment of career opportunities for minorities in the Navy and society, 385-390, 409-410

Radar
On board the picket destroyer escort Falgout (DER-324) in the early 1960s, 166
Role in PIRAZ operations off the coast of Vietnam in the early 1970s, 292-293

Radio
Communications on board the battleship Iowa (BB-61) in the early 1950s, 59-60, 66-67-68, 71-72, 76-77
On board the heavy cruiser Toledo (CA-133) in the early 1950s, 87-91, 94-95
On board the picket destroyer escort Falgout (DER-324) in the early 1960s, 178-181
On board the destroyer Taussig (DD-746) in the mid-1960s, 248-249, 253-255
Development in the late 1960s-early 1970s of the Navy's satellite communication program, 283-288, 326-327

Reagan/ Ensign John Walter, USNR
One of the first black naval officers commissioned in World War II, 24-25, 377, 399

Recruit Training
At Great Lakes in World War II, 9-10, 27-29, 32

Recruiting
Efforts in 1949-50 to bring more black enlistees into the Navy, 49-56

Refueling
Replenishment at sea from oilers by the destroyer Taussig (DD-746) in the mid-1960s, 247-248, 258
Replenishment of the Taussig in 1967 by the carrier Yorktown (CVS-10), 265-266

Registered Publications
Control of classified publications on board the battleship Iowa (BB-61) during the Korean War, 72-74

Religion
During Gravely's growing-up years in Virginia in the 1920s-1930s, 4-5
Chapel services on board the picket destroyer escort Falgout (DER-324) in the early 1960s, 190-191
Source of solace to the Gravelys in the 1970s when their son Robby was killed, 370

Richards, Commodore John K., Jr., USN (Ret.) (USNA, 1912)
In World War II commanded the midshipman school at Columbia University, 23

Robinson, Ensign John Gregory, USN (USNA, 1970)
First shipboard duty was in the guided missile frigate Jouett (DLG-29) in the early 1970s, 301-302, 407-409
Career concerns, 317-318

Robinson, Rear Admiral Rembrandt C., USN
Joint Staff duty in the early 1970s, 317-319

Killed in a helicopter crash off Vietnam in 1972, 301
Son of, 301-302, 317-318, 407-408

Rock, Commander Herman K., USN (USNA, 1938)
Served as ops officer in the battleship Iowa (BB-61) during the Korean War, 63-64, 77

Rowan, Ensign Carl T., USNR
One of the early black naval officers commissioned in World War II, 31, 33-34

Rowan, USS (DD-782)
In 1966 deployed to the Western Pacific, 223, 227

Rumsfeld, Donald H.
As Secretary of Defense in 1976, interviewed Gravely about commanding the Third Fleet, 358-359

St. George, Vice Admiral William R., USN
As Commander Naval Surface Force Pacific Fleet, frocked Gravely with three stars in 1976, 361

San Diego, California
Activities of black enlisted personnel in World War II, 14-17
Role of the commandant of the 11th Naval District in the mid-1970s, 346-353

Satellites
Development in the late 1960s-early 1970s of the Navy's satellite communication program, 283-288, 326-327

Seal Beach, California, Naval Weapons Station
Provided ammunition for the destroyer Taussig (DD-746) in the mid-1960s, 219-221

Search and Rescue
Unsuccessful search in the spring of 1966 for men who were lost near Scarborough Shoal in the Pacific, 229-231

Seattle, Washington
Visited in the early 1950s by the heavy cruiser Toledo (CA-133), 94

Security
Control of registered publications on board the battleship Iowa (BB-61) during the Korean War, 72-74
Failed attempt to foil security at Alameda in the late 1950s, 126
Concerns for security during construction of the National Military Command Center in the mid-1960s, 203, 205-207

Selection Boards
Work of a board that selected officers for promotion to commander in the mid-1970s, 337

Seminole, USS (AKA-104)
Operations out of Southern California in the late 1950s, 112-118
Quality of the crew, 113
Communications, 114
Deployment to the Western Pacific in the late 1950s, 120-121, 126-127
Some officers held a drinking party on board the ship, 121-122
Intelligence publications on board, 122-124
Shipyard period in San Francisco in the late 1950s, 126-127

Seventh Fleet, U.S.
Korean War operations, 61-64, 66-74

Deployments in the mid-1950s by the heavy cruiser Toledo (CA-133), 91-95, 97-98
Deployment in the early 1960s by the destroyer Theodore E. Chandler (DD-717), 138

Shanker, Ensign Benjamin, USNR
During World War II served in the patrol craft PC-1264, 36-37

Shephard, Captain Tazewell T., Jr., USN (USNA, 1943)
In the early 1960s served as naval aide to President John F. Kennedy, 185-186

Ship Handling
On board the patrol craft PC-1264 in World War II, 38
On board the attack cargo ship Seminole (AKA-104) in the late 1950s, 116
On board the destroyer Theodore E. Chandler (DD-717) in the early 1960s, 136
On board the picket destroyer escort Falgout (DER-324) in the early 1960s, 161, 164-165
On board the destroyer Taussig (DD-746) in the mid-1960s, 219-221, 225-226
In the early 1970s on board the guided missile frigate Jouett (DLG-29), 290

Sixth Naval District, Charleston, South Carolina
Gravely's difficulties in getting desirable quarters assigned by the district commandant in the early 1970s, 334-336

Skubinna, Lieutenant Myron A., USN
In the early 1960s was operations officer of the destroyer Theodore E. Chandler (DD-717), 152

Smedberg, Vice Admiral William R. III, USN (USNA, 1926)
In 1951-52 commanded the battleship Iowa (BB-61), 58, 63-65, 72
In the early 1960s was Chief of Naval Personnel, 191

Somers, USS (DD-947)
In 1959 Gravely spent time on board while in training to be a destroyer executive officer, 132-134

Sonar
On board the picket destroyer escort Falgout (DER-324) in the early 1960s, 167
On board the destroyer Taussig (DD-746) in the mid-1960s, 218, 222, 266, 276-277
Use of the variable-depth sonar in the mid-1960s, 268, 344
Introduction of towed arrays in the 1970s, 343-344

Soviet Navy
Trawlers operated in the vicinity of U.S. nuclear weapons tests in the pacific in 1962, 166
The AGI Gidrofon operated near a U.S. carrier formation in the mid-1960s, 278-279, 400-401
Encounter between an AGI and the guided missile frigate Jouett (DLG-29) in the Western Pacific in the early 1970s, 307-308

Sperandio, Commander Joseph L., USN
In the early 1960s commanded the destroyer Theodore E. Chandler (DD-717), 155-156

Starbird, Major General Alfred Dodd, USA (USMA, 1933)
In the 1960s commanded Joint Task Force Eight and the Defense Communications Agency, 202

Submarine Chaser Training Center, Miami, Florida
Training role in World War II, 29-31, 33-34

Tachen Islands
Evacuation of in the mid-1950s, 93-94

Taussig, Captain Joseph K., Jr., USN (Ret.) (USNA, 1941)
    Contacted Gravely in the mid-1960s about the destroyer Taussig (DD-746), 242-243

Taussig, USS (DD-746)
    Operations out of San Diego in the mid-1960s, 215-223, 258-267
    Description of the ship, 216
    Yard period at Long Beach Naval Shipyard in 1966, 218-219, 222
    Handling of the ship, 219-221
    In 1966 Gravely accommodated a writer and photographer from Ebony magazine on board the ship, 223-226, 241-242
    Deployment to the Western Pacific via Hawaii in 1966, 223-239, 241-258, 276-279, 400-401
    Had a variety of roles in connection with the Vietnam War, 228, 232-239, 247-251
    Officers in the ship's crew in the mid-1960s, 228, 246-247, 275-276
    Served for a time as station ship in Hong Kong, 239
    The ship was sometimes confused with the destroyer escort Joseph K. Taussig (DE-1030), 243-244
    Contacts with families of crew members, 245-246
    Disciplinary problems were minor, 245
    Operation in early 1967 that included a visit to Mexico, 260-264
    Drug abuse problem among the crew, 261, 264-265
    Full-power run at 34 knots, 266-267
    Deployment in early 1968 to the Western Pacific as part of an ASW group, 268-273
    Maneuvers to move a Soviet AGI that was operating near U.S. warships in the mid-1960s, 277-279

Theodore E. Chandler, USS (DD-717)
    In the early 1960s procedures needed to be tightened to correct previous laxness, 135-138
    Deployment in 1960 to the Western Pacific, 138-140, 147
    Suffered damage from a large wave, 140, 147
    Role in plane-guarding for aircraft carriers, 138, 142-145
    Internal administration of the ship, 143-144, 152-153
    Role of the combat information center, 145-146
    Underwent FRAM I conversion in 1961 with Gravely as acting skipper, 146-156

Third Fleet, U.S.
    Concerns in the late 1970s about the use of the Hawaiian Island of Kahoolawe for Navy gunnery practice, 362-365
    Conducted both U.S. and multinational training exercises in the mid-Pacific in the late 1970s, 365-367, 373-375
    Role in defense of the United States, 372-373

Third Naval District
    Concerns in the mid-1950s in atomic, biological and chemical warfare, 101-105
    Rear Admiral Milton Miles as commandant, 103
    Inspections of commands in the district, 104, 108-110

Thomas, Rear Admiral Gerald E., USN
    In 1951 was commissioned through the NROTC program at Harvard, 54
    Service in the late 1960s as executive officer of the NROTC unit at Prairie View, 281

Thompson, Lieutenant Commander George I., USN
    In 1963 was one of the first two officer students at the Naval War College, 191, 196, 398-400

Thomson, Captain James W., USN (USNA, 1935)
    In the late 1950s commanded the attack cargo ship Seminole (AKA-104), 112-118, 126-127

Tiru, USS (SS-416)
    Submarine that ran aground near Australia in November 1966, 254-256

Toledo, USS (CA-133)
    In the early 1950s operated out of Long Beach, California, 85-90, 94
    Communications setup, 87-91, 94-95
    Enlisted crewmen in the early 1950s, 87-90
    Deployments in the mid-1950s to the Western Pacific, 91-95, 97-98
    Wardroom mess, 96-97

Training
    Boot camp at Great Lakes in World War II, 9-10, 27-29, 32
    Service school at Hampton, Virginia, in 1943, 10-12
    V-12 officer training program in World War II, 16-27
    Role of the Submarine Chaser Training Center in World War II, 29-31, 33-34
    Communications training course at Monterey, California, in the early 1950s, 56-57
    Courses in amphibious warfare at Coronado, California, in 1957, 112-113
    Underway training in 1966 for the destroyer Taussig (DD-746), 216-219
    In the summer of 1970 the guided missile frigate Jouett (DLG-29) did training exercises out of San Diego, 289-290
    Cruiser-Destroyer Group Two conducted a number of training exercises in the Atlantic in the early 1970s, 331-334, 337-344

Truman, President Harry S.
    In October 1945 reviewed the victorious U.S. fleet at New York, 42
    In 1948 issued an executive order that integrated the armed forces, 55

Turner, Vice Admiral Stansfield, USN (USNA, 1947)
    Served 1972-74 as president of the Naval War College, 196-197
    In 1974-75 commanded the U.S. Second Fleet, 333, 337-339, 344

Turner Joy, USS (DD-951)
    Vietnam War service in 1966, 237-238, 316-317

University of California at Los Angeles
    Site of Navy V-12 officer training in World War II, 17-21

V-12 Program
    World War II officer program that included both college education and naval training, 16-27

Vietnam War
    Various roles for the destroyer Taussig (DD-746) in the mid-1960s off the coast of Vietnam, 228-229, 232-239
    PIRAZ work by the guided missile frigate Jouett (DLG-29) in the early 1970s, 292-293

Virden, Rear Admiral Frank, USN (USNA, 1927)
    In the early 1960s served as Commander Cruiser-Destroyer Force, Pacific Fleet, 188-189

Virginia Union University, Richmond, Virginia
    Campus life in the late 1930s and mid-1940s, 5-6, 44-46

Visual Communications
    Use of in World War II, 30-31
    By the heavy cruiser Toledo (CA-133) in the mid-1950s, 90-91

Warner, John W.
Approach on racial issues while Secretary of the Navy in the early 1970s, 330

Washington, D.C.
Site of a Navy recruiting station in 1949-50, 49-56
In early 1963 President John F. Kennedy held a White House event to celebrate the 100th anniversary of the Emancipation Proclamation, 182-186

Weather
In 1960 the destroyer Theodore E. Chandler (DD-717) went through a typhoon in the Western Pacific, 140
Monitoring of weather in connection with U.S. nuclear weapons tests in the Pacific in 1962, 166
In 1966 the destroyer Taussig (DD-746) skirted a typhoon near the Philippines, 228-229

Wessman, Lieutenant Commander Robert L., USN
In the late 1960s was executive officer of the destroyer Taussig (DD-746), 275

Weymouth, Rear Admiral Ralph, USN (USNA, 1938)
In 1967-68 commanded ASW Group One with his flag on board the aircraft carrier Yorktown (CVS-10), 266, 273-274, 280-281

White House, Washington, D.C.
In early 1963 President John F. Kennedy held a White House event to celebrate the 100th anniversary of the Emancipation Proclamation, 182-186

Whittle, Vice Admiral Alfred J., Jr., USN (USNA, 1946)
In 1976 was slated to become Commander Third Fleet but was assigned another three-star job instead, 359-360

Wilson, Vice Admiral Ralph E., USN (USNA, 1924)
Commanded Cruiser Division Three in the mid-1950s, 95

Yarbrough, Lieutenant Herbert A., USN
In the early 1950s served in the battleship Iowa (BB-61), 59-61
In the early 1950s served in the heavy cruiser Toledo (CA-133), 83, 85-86

Yorktown, USS (CVS-10)
In the mid-1960s took part in ASW exercises off the West Coast, 265-26
Deployment in early 1968 to the Western Pacific as part of an ASW group, 268-274

Zumwalt, Admiral Elmo R., Jr., USN (USNA, 1943)
Impact of Z-grams when he was Chief of Naval Operations in the early 1970s, 297-300
Gravely was one of the newly selected flag officers who visited Zumwalt's quarters in 1971, 319-321
Measures designed to enhance racial awareness in the Navy, 328-330

Launched in 1969, the Naval Institute's oral history program is among the oldest in the country. Used in combination with documentary sources, oral histories offer a richer understanding of naval history. Often they contain candid recollections and explanations never entered into contemporaneous records. In addition, they can help depict the atmosphere of a particular event or era in a manner not available in official documents.

The Naval Institute gratefully accepts tax-deductible gifts to strengthen its oral history program. This support allows the Institute to preserve the hard-earned life lessons of today's service men and women so they may teach and inspire future generations.

For information about opportunities to underwrite Naval Institute oral history projects, please contact the Naval Institute Foundation at 291 Wood Road, Annapolis, Maryland 21402; by phone, (410) 295-1056; via e-mail, foundation@usni.org.

www.ingramcontent.com/pod-product-compliance
Lightning Source LLC
Chambersburg PA
CBHW080624170426
43209CB00007B/1506